HMH Tennessee Science

This Write-In Book belongs to

_____

Teacher/Room

_____

Houghton Mifflin Harcourt™

Consulting Authors

Michael A. DiSpezio

Global Educator
North Falmouth, Massachusetts

Michael DiSpezio has authored many HMH instructional programs for science and mathematics. He has also authored numerous trade books and multimedia programs on various topics and hosted dozens of studio and location broadcasts for various organizations in the U.S. and worldwide. Most recently, he has been working with educators to provide strategies for implementing science and engineering practices, including engineering design challenges. To all his projects, he brings his extensive background in science, his expertise in classroom teaching at the elementary, middle, and high school levels, and his deep experience in producing interactive and engaging instructional materials.

Marjorie Frank

Science Writer and Content-Area Reading Specialist
Brooklyn, New York

An educator and linguist by training, a writer and poet by nature, Marjorie Frank has authored and designed a generation of instructional materials in all subject areas, including past HMH Science programs. Her other credits include authoring science issues of an award-winning children's magazine, writing game-based digital assessments, developing blended learning materials for young children, and serving as instructional designer and co-author of pioneering school-to-work software. In addition, she has served on the adjunct faculty of Hunter, Manhattan, and Brooklyn Colleges, teaching courses in science methods, literacy, and writing.

Acknowledgments for Cover

Front cover: *iceberg* ©Hans Reinhard/Corbis.

Copyright © 2019 by Houghton Mifflin Harcourt Publishing Company

All rights reserved. No part of this work may be reproduced or transmitted in any form or by any means, electronic or mechanical, including photocopying or recording, or by any information storage or retrieval system, without the prior written permission of the copyright owner unless such copying is expressly permitted by federal copyright law. Requests for permission to make copies of any part of the work should be submitted through our Permissions website at https://customercare.hmhco.com/contactus/Permissions.html or mailed to Houghton Mifflin Harcourt Publishing Company, Attn: Intellectual Property Licensing, 9400 Southpark Center Loop, Orlando, Florida 32819-8647.

Tennessee Academic Standards courtesy of the Tennessee Department of Education.

Printed in the U.S.A.

ISBN 978-1-328-82860-6

6 7 8 9 10   0607   26 25 24 23 22 21

4500817331   B C D E F G

If you have received these materials as examination copies free of charge, Houghton Mifflin Harcourt Publishing Company retains title to the materials and they may not be resold. Resale of examination copies is strictly prohibited.

Possession of this publication in print format does not entitle users to convert this publication, or any portion of it, into electronic format.

© Houghton Mifflin Harcourt Publishing Company • Image Credits:

Michael R. Heithaus

Dean, College of Arts, Sciences & Education
Professor, Department of Biological Sciences
Florida International University
Miami, Florida

Mike Heithaus joined the FIU Biology Department in 2003, has served as Director of the Marine Sciences Program, and as Executive Director of the School of Environment, Arts, and Society, which brings together the natural and social sciences and humanities to develop solutions to today's environmental challenges. He now serves as Dean of the College of Arts, Sciences & Education. His research focuses on predator-prey interactions and the ecological importance of large marine species. He has helped to guide the development of Life Science content in this science program, with a focus on strategies for teaching challenging content as well as the science and engineering practices of analyzing data and using computational thinking.

Tennessee Reviewers

Emily C. Grayer
Richview Middle School
Clarksville, TN

Dale Land
Kenwood Middle School
Clarksville-Montgomery County
School System
Clarksville, TN

Patrece Morrow
Science, NBCT
Sherwood Middle School
Memphis, TN

Shari Myers
Academic Coach
Rossview Elementary School
Clarksville-Montgomery County
School System
Clarksville, TN

Sarah Becky Spain
Kenrose Elementary School
Brentwood, TN

Christy Walker, Ed.D., NBCT
Manley Elementary School
Morristown, TN

© Houghton Mifflin Harcourt Publishing Company

Content Reviewers

Paul D. Asimow, PhD
*Professor of Geology
and Geochemistry*
Division of Geological and Planetary Sciences
California Institute of Technology
Pasadena, CA

Laura K. Baumgartner, PhD
Postdoctoral Researcher
Molecular, Cellular, and Developmental
Biology
University of Colorado
Boulder, CO

Eileen Cashman, PhD
Professor
Department of Environmental Resources
Engineering
Humboldt State University
Arcata, CA

Hilary Clement Olson, PhD
Research Scientist Associate V
Institute for Geophysics, Jackson School of
Geosciences
The University of Texas at Austin
Austin, TX

Joe W. Crim, PhD
Professor Emeritus
Department of Cellular Biology
The University of Georgia
Athens, GA

Elizabeth A. De Stasio, PhD
*Raymond H. Herzog Professor
of Science*
Professor of Biology
Department of Biology
Lawrence University
Appleton, WI

Dan Franck, PhD
Botany Education Consultant
Chatham, NY

Julia R. Greer, PhD
*Assistant Professor of Materials Science and
Mechanics*
Division of Engineering and Applied Science
California Institute of Technology
Pasadena, CA

John E. Hoover, PhD
Professor
Department of Biology
Millersville University
Millersville, PA

William H. Ingham, PhD
Professor (Emeritus)
Department of Physics and Astronomy
James Madison University
Harrisonburg, VA

Charles W. Johnson, PhD
*Chairman, Division of Natural Sciences,
Mathematics, and Physical Education*
Associate Professor of Physics
South Georgia College
Douglas, GA

Tatiana A. Krivosheev, PhD
Associate Professor of Physics
Department of Natural Sciences
Clayton State University
Morrow, GA

Joseph A. McClure, PhD
Associate Professor Emeritus
Department of Physics
Georgetown University
Washington, DC

Mark Moldwin, PhD
Professor of Space Sciences
Atmospheric, Oceanic, and Space Sciences
University of Michigan
Ann Arbor, MI

Russell Patrick, PhD
Professor of Physics
Department of Biology, Chemistry, and Physics
Southern Polytechnic State University
Marietta, GA

Patricia M. Pauley, PhD
Meteorologist, Data Assimilation Group
Naval Research Laboratory
Monterey, CA

Stephen F. Pavkovic, PhD
Professor Emeritus
Department of Chemistry
Loyola University of Chicago
Chicago, IL

L. Jeanne Perry, PhD
Director (Retired)
Protein Expression Technology Center
Institute for Genomics and Proteomics
University of California,
Los Angeles
Los Angeles, CA

Kenneth H. Rubin, PhD
Professor
Department of Geology and Geophysics
University of Hawaii
Honolulu, HI

Brandon E. Schwab, PhD
Associate Professor
Department of Geology
Humboldt State University
Arcata, CA

Marllin L. Simon, PhD
Associate Professor
Department of Physics
Auburn University
Auburn, AL

Larry Stookey, PE
Upper Iowa University
Wausau, WI

Kim Withers, PhD
Associate Research Scientist
Center for Coastal Studies
Texas A&M University-Corpus Christi
Corpus Christi, TX

Matthew A. Wood, PhD
Professor
Department of Physics & Space Sciences
Florida Institute of Technology
Melbourne, FL

Adam D. Woods, PhD
Associate Professor
Department of Geological Sciences
California State University, Fullerton
Fullerton, CA

Natalie Zayas, MS, EdD
Lecturer
Division of Science and Environmental Policy
California State University, Monterey Bay
Seaside, CA

© Houghton Mifflin Harcourt Publishing Company

Contents in Brief

© Houghton Mifflin Harcourt Publishing Company

Tennessee Academic Standards for Science

Dear Students and Families,

   This book and this class are structured around the Tennessee Academic Standards for Science for Grade 6. As you read, experiment, and study, you will learn the concepts listed on these pages. You will also continue to build your science literacy, which will enrich your life both in and out of school.

Best wishes for a good school year,
The HMH Tennessee Science Team

PHYSICAL SCIENCES

6.PS3: Energy
1) Analyze the properties and compare sources of mechanical, electrical, chemical, radiant, and thermal energy.
2) Construct a scientific explanation of the transformations between potential and kinetic energy.
3) Analyze and interpret data to show the relationship between kinetic energy and the mass of an object in motion and its speed.
4) Conduct an investigation to demonstrate the way that heat (thermal energy) moves among objects through radiation, conduction, or convection.

LIFE SCIENCES

6.LS2: Ecosystems: Interactions, Energy, and Dynamics
1) Evaluate and communicate the impact of environmental variables on population size.
2) Determine the impact of competitive, symbiotic, and predatory interactions in an ecosystem.
3) Draw conclusions about the transfer of energy through a food web and energy pyramid in an ecosystem.
4) Using evidence from climate data, draw conclusions about the patterns of abiotic and biotic factors in different biomes, specifically the tundra, taiga, deciduous forest, desert, grasslands, rainforest, marine, and freshwater ecosystems.
5) Analyze existing evidence about the effect of a specific invasive species on native populations in Tennessee and design a solution to mitigate its impact.
6) Research the ways in which an ecosystem has changed over time in response to changes in physical conditions, population balances, human interactions, and natural catastrophes.
7) Compare and contrast auditory and visual methods of communication among organisms in relation to survival strategies of a population.

6.LS4: Biological Change: Unity and Diversity
1) Explain how changes in biodiversity would impact ecosystem stability and natural resources.
2) Design a possible solution for maintaining biodiversity of ecosystems while still providing necessary human resources without disrupting environmental equilibrium.

EARTH AND SPACE SCIENCES

6.ESS2: Earth's Systems

1) Gather evidence to justify that oceanic convection currents are caused by the sun's transfer of heat energy and differences in salt concentration leading to global water movement.
2) Diagram convection patterns that flow due to uneven heating of the earth.
3) Construct an explanation for how atmospheric flow, geographic features, and ocean currents affect the climate of a region through heat transfer.
4) Apply scientific principles to design a method to analyze and interpret the impact of humans and other organisms on the hydrologic cycle.
5) Analyze and interpret data from weather conditions, weather maps, satellites, and radar to predict probable local weather patterns and conditions.
6) Explain how relationships between the movement and interactions of air masses, high and low pressure systems, and frontal boundaries result in weather conditions and severe storms.

6.ESS3: Earth and Human Activity

1) Differentiate between renewable and nonrenewable resources by asking questions about their availability and sustainability.
2) Investigate and compare existing and developing technologies that utilize renewable and alternative energy resources.
3) Assess the impacts of human activities on the biosphere including conservation, habitat management, species endangerment, and extinction.

ENGINEERING, TECHNOLOGY, AND APPLICATIONS OF SCIENCE

6.ETS1: Engineering Design

1) Evaluate design constraints on solutions for maintaining ecosystems and biodiversity.
2) Design and test different solutions that impact energy transfer.

Contents

Polar bears "burn their blubber" (use their fat) to keep themselves warm. Some of the layers of fat can be 11 cm thick!

© Houghton Mifflin Harcourt Publishing Company • Image Credits: ©Andrew Watson/Fotolia LLC

Talons are very useful in snatching fish right out of the water. To prey, the sharp talons of an eagle are deadly weapons!

© Houghton Mifflin Harcourt Publishing Company • Image Credits: ©Pete Saloutos/Corbis

Contents *(continued)*

Although the coral animal is tiny, some corals help build reefs that support millions of organisms. The Great Barrier Reef is so large that it can be seen from space.

© Houghton Mifflin Harcourt Publishing Company • Image Credits: ©Stockbyte/Getty Images

Careful management
of renewable resources,
such as trees and fish,
will help maintain their
populations for the future.

© Houghton Mifflin Harcourt Publishing Company • Image Credits: ©David R. Frazier/Photo Researchers, Inc.; ©Jeff Rotman/The Image Bank/Getty Images; ©NASA Image by Marit Jentoft-Nilsen, based on data from NOAA GOES. Blue Marble imagery by NASA's Earth Observatory Team; ©artpartner-images/Photographer's Choice/Getty Images

Contents (continued)

Protecting our resources helps us and all of the other organisms that rely on the same resources.

Assignments:

_____

_____

_____

_____

_____

© Houghton Mifflin Harcourt Publishing Company • Image Credits: ©Tyrone Turner/National Geographic/Getty Images

These rafters are on a wild ride downriver! They are using the river currents that form as water flows from higher elevations to lower elevations.

Assignments:

_____

_____

_____

_____

_____

© Houghton Mifflin Harcourt Publishing Company • Image Credits: ©Fuse/Getty Images

Contents (continued)

Some green sea turtles migrate over 2,000 km on ocean currents in the Atlantic Ocean.

© Houghton Mifflin Harcourt Publishing Company • Image Credits: ©Frank Vetere/Alamy; (tr) © Gerald Nowak/Getty Images

Although humans don't have thick fur to keep warm, we have found other ways to live in extreme climates.

© Houghton Mifflin Harcourt Publishing Company • ©Wayne R Bilenduke/Photographer's Choice/Getty Images

Energy and Energy Transfer

© Houghton Mifflin Harcourt Publishing Company • Image Credits: (bkgd) ©Alfred Pasieka/Photo Researchers, Inc.; (br) ©David Hoffman Photo Library/Alamy

Big Idea

Energy exists in different forms and can change from one form to another, but energy is always conserved.

6.PS3.1, 6.PS3.2, 6.PS3.3, 6.PS3.4, 6.ESS.3.1, 6.ESS3.2, 6.ETS1.2

A thermogram is a special type of image that shows the relative temperatures of objects.

Sealing windows keeps the warmth inside.

What do you think?

See all the red areas in this thermogram? These areas show where energy (in the form of heat) is escaping through gaps around windows and doors. Why is it important to reduce this loss of energy from a home?

Unit 1
Energy and Energy Transfer

CITIZEN SCIENCE

Saving Energy

Humans use many sources of energy in our everyday lives. For example, we need electricity to see at night, fuel to keep our cars running, and food to nourish our bodies. But we need to be careful in our use of energy resources. And you can help!

① Ask a Question

How can individuals avoid wasting energy resources at home?

Make a list of all the sources of energy, such as electricity or natural gas, used in your home. Then, write down what those energy sources are used for, and estimate how much your family uses them each week. For example: "We use natural gas for cooking on our stove approximately three hours each week." Can your family reduce energy consumption in any areas? Work with your family to develop your ideas.

Using a programmable thermostat can help conserve energy.

© Houghton Mifflin Harcourt Publishing Company•Image Credits: (bkgd) ©SPL/PhotoStock/Photo Researchers, Inc.

② Think About It

A What is one source of energy used in your home?

_____

B Where is energy used most often in your school?

_____
_____
_____

C Where is energy used most often in your home?

_____
_____

D What are some possible areas in the home and at school where energy usage can be easily reduced?

_____
_____
_____
_____
_____

③ Apply Your Knowledge

A Choose some of the places you identified in your home. Develop strategies for reducing the amount of energy your family uses in those areas.

Area	Strategy

B Apply the strategies you listed above. Track how your energy usage changes as you conserve energy. Examine your utility bill if you have access to it.

_____
_____
_____
_____

Solar panels can convert energy from the sun into a form that can be used in a home.

Take It Home

As a class, create an energy conservation plan for your school. Implement it in your class and track how much energy you have saved. Share your results with your school. See *ScienceSaurus*® for more information about energy conservation.

© Houghton Mifflin Harcourt Publishing Company • Image Credits: (bkgd) ©GIPhotoStock/Photo Researchers, Inc.; (t) ©GIPhotoStock/Photo Researchers, Inc.

Introduction to Energy

ESSENTIAL QUESTION

What is energy?

By the end of this lesson, you should be able to describe how energy is conserved through transformation between different forms.

6.PS3.1, 6.PS3.2

The chemical energy contained in fireworks is transformed into sound, light, and energy as heat when the fireworks shells explode.

© Houghton Mifflin Harcourt Publishing Company • Image Credits: (bg) ©Thinkstock/Getty Images

Lesson Labs

Quick Labs
• Setting Objects in Motion
• Conservation of Energy
• Bungee Jumping

S.T.E.M. Lab
• Designing a Simple Device

Engage Your Brain

1 Predict Check T or F to show whether you think each statement is true or false.

T F

☐ ☐ Energy can change from one form to another.

☐ ☐ An object can have only one type of energy at a time.

☐ ☐ If an object has energy, it must be moving.

☐ ☐ All energy travels in waves.

2 Describe Write a caption for this picture that includes the concept of sound energy.

_____

_____

_____

Active Reading

3 Apply The phrase *conservation of energy* has an everyday meaning. We speak of trying to conserve, or save, energy for environmental reasons. It also refers to a law of nature. Use context clues to write your own definition for the meaning of the *law of conservation of energy*.

Example sentence
According to the <u>law of conservation of energy</u>, when a rolling ball slows, the energy of the ball does not disappear. Instead, it changes to energy as heat generated from moving across the ground.

law of conservation of energy:

_____

_____

_____

_____

Vocabulary Terms

• **energy**
• **kinetic energy**
• **potential energy**
• **energy transformation**
• **law of conservation of energy**

4 Apply As you learn the definition of each vocabulary term in this lesson, create your own definition or sketch to help you remember the meaning of the term.

© Houghton Mifflin Harcourt Publishing Company • Image Credits: (bg) ©Thinkstock/Getty Images; (tr) ©Jim West/Alamy

Get Energized!

![Active Reading]

5 Identify As you read this page and the next, underline the factors that affect an object's kinetic and potential energy.

What are two types of energy?

In science, **energy** is the ability to cause change. Energy takes many different forms and has many different effects. There are two general types of energy: kinetic energy and potential energy.

Kinetic Energy

Kinetic energy (kih•NET•ik EN•er•jee) is the energy of an object that is due to motion. All moving objects have kinetic energy. The amount of kinetic energy an object has depends on its mass and its speed. Kinetic energy increases as mass increases. Imagine that a bowling ball and a soccer ball roll across the floor at the same speed. The bowling ball has more kinetic energy than the soccer ball has because the bowling ball has a greater mass.

Kinetic energy also increases as speed increases. If two bowling balls with the same mass roll across the floor at different speeds, the faster ball will have the greater kinetic energy.

As the skater moves up the ramp, he gains height but loses speed. Some of his kinetic energy is converted back to potential energy. The rest of it is transferred as heat due to friction.

D

At the bottom of the ramp, the skater's kinetic energy is at its peak because he is going the fastest. His potential energy is at its lowest because he is closer to the ground than at any other point on the ramp.

C

© Houghton Mifflin Harcourt Publishing Company • Image Credits: ©Paul A. Souders/Corbis

Potential Energy

Potential energy (puh•TEN•shuhl EN•er•jee) is the energy that an object has due to its position, condition, or chemical composition. A ball held above the ground has potential energy because the force of gravity can pull it to the ground. Potential energy that is the result of an object's position is called gravitational potential energy. Gravitational potential energy increases as the object's height or mass increases.

A change in condition can also affect potential energy. For example, stretching a rubber band increases its potential energy.

Chemical potential energy depends on chemical composition. As bonds break and new bonds form between atoms during a chemical change, energy can be released.

Think Outside the Book Inquiry

6 Diagram Think of another situation that shows kinetic and potential energy. Draw a sketch of and write a description explaining the situation in terms of potential and kinetic energy.

Can objects have potential and kinetic energy at the same time?

An object can have both kinetic and potential energy. For example, the skater in the picture below has kinetic energy as he moves down the ramp. He has potential energy due to his position on the ramp. A flying bird has kinetic energy because of its speed and mass, and potential energy due to its height above the ground.

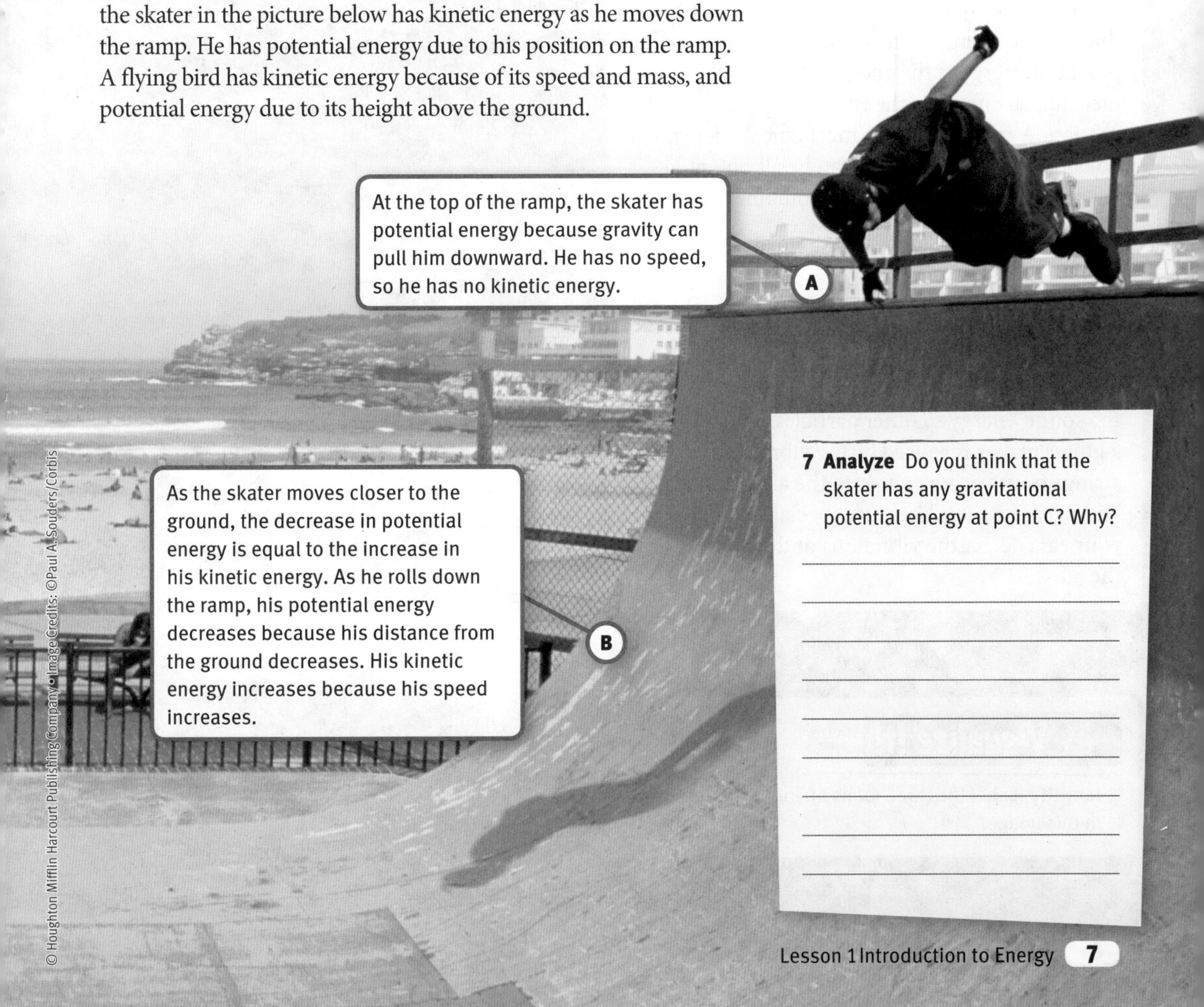

At the top of the ramp, the skater has potential energy because gravity can pull him downward. He has no speed, so he has no kinetic energy.

A

As the skater moves closer to the ground, the decrease in potential energy is equal to the increase in his kinetic energy. As he rolls down the ramp, his potential energy decreases because his distance from the ground decreases. His kinetic energy increases because his speed increases.

B

7 Analyze Do you think that the skater has any gravitational potential energy at point C? Why?

_____
_____
_____
_____
_____
_____
_____
_____
_____
_____

© Houghton Mifflin Harcourt Publishing Company • Image Credits: ©Paul A. Souders/Corbis

In Perfect Form

What forms can energy take?

Kinetic energy and potential energy are two types of energy that can come in many different forms. Some common forms of energy include mechanical, sound, radiant, electrical, chemical, thermal, and nuclear energy. Energy is expressed in joules (J) (JOOLZ).

Mechanical Energy

Mechanical energy is the sum of an object's kinetic energy and potential energy. Remember that kinetic energy is the energy of motion, and potential energy is the energy of position. So mechanical energy is the energy of position and motion. A moving car has mechanical energy. An object's mechanical energy can be all potential energy, all kinetic energy, or a combination of potential and kinetic energy.

Sound Energy

Sound energy is kinetic energy caused by the vibration of particles in a medium such as steel, water, or air. As the particles vibrate, they transfer the sound energy to other particles. The sound a guitar makes is caused by the vibrations of its strings transferring energy to the air around it. You hear the sound because special structures in your ears detect the vibrations of the particles in the air.

A _____

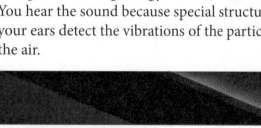 

8 Identify Label the three forms of energy represented in this image.

© Houghton Mifflin Harcourt Publishing Company

© Houghton Mifflin Harcourt Publishing Company

B _____

C _____

Radiant Energy

Radiant energy is the energy of electromagnetic waves. Electromagnetic waves are transmitted through space. These waves are caused by the vibration of electrically charged particles. Electromagnetic waves include visible light, x-rays, and microwaves. X-rays are high-energy waves used by doctors and dentists to look at your bones. Microwaves can be used to cook food or to transmit cellular telephone calls. The sun releases a large amount of electromagnetic energy, some of which reaches Earth as radiant energy. This radiant energy heats and lights Earth's surface, making life possible.

Electrical Energy

Electrical energy is the energy that results from the position or motion of charged particles. The electrical energy that powers the lights overhead is associated with negatively charged particles moving in a wire. The wire also has positively charged particles that do not move. The negatively charged particles move within the wire and create an electric current. Anything you plug in or use batteries to operate, from lamps to computers to flashlights, uses electrical energy.

9 **Compare** How does electrical energy differ from radiant energy? How does electrical energy differ from mechanical energy?

_____

_____

_____

10 **Infer** Would you expect to detect electrical energy if you played the pinball game shown in the picture? Explain your answer.

_____

_____

_____

_____

_____

11 Identify As you read, underline sources of chemical and thermal energy.

Chemical Energy

Chemical energy is a form of potential energy. The amount of chemical energy in a molecule depends on the kinds of atoms and their arrangement. During a chemical change, bonds between these atoms break, and new bonds form. The food you eat, batteries, and matches are sources of chemical energy.

Thermal Energy

The thermal energy of an object is the kinetic energy of its particles. Particles move faster at higher temperatures than at lower temperatures. The faster the molecules in an object move, the more thermal energy the object has. Also, the more particles an object has, the more thermal energy it has. Heat is the energy transferred from an object at a higher temperature to an object at a lower temperature.

Nuclear Energy

The nucleus of an atom is the source of nuclear energy. When an atom's nucleus breaks apart, or when the nuclei of two small atoms join together, energy is released. The energy given off by the sun comes from nuclear energy. In the sun, hydrogen nuclei join to make a helium nucleus. This reaction gives off a huge amount of energy. The sun's light and heat come from these reactions. Without nuclear energy from the sun, life would not exist on Earth.

12 Synthesize Why is the chemical energy of a battery potential energy and not kinetic energy?

_____

_____

_____

_____

_____

Solar flares are explosions of hot gases on the sun. They can release radiant energy that reaches all the way to Earth.

© Houghton Mifflin Harcourt Publishing Company • Image Credits: ©NASA

Space Weather and Technology

Every time you turn on a TV or use a cell phone, you may be affected by the "weather" in space. Space weather includes any activity happening in space that might affect Earth's environment, such as solar flares. A solar flare can release a million times more energy than the largest earthquake. It is an intense release of radiant energy as a burst of radiation.

Space Weather Can Affect Navigation
Space weather can also cause navigation errors by interrupting satellite signals to Global Positioning System (GPS) receivers.

Space Weather Can Damage Satellites
Many of the satellites orbiting Earth provide phone service. Damage from space weather can interrupt phone communications.

Space Weather Can Ground Planes
Auroras like the one shown here are caused by electrically charged particles of the solar wind hitting Earth's magnetic field. This activity can interrupt airplane communications, forcing the planes to land.

Extend

Inquiry

13 Identify What type of energy is monitored by scientists forecasting future space weather?

14 Infer Why is space weather a bigger concern now than it was in the past?

15 Research How do scientists forecast space weather? Why?

© Houghton Mifflin Harcourt Publishing Company • Image Credits: (bg) ©Robert Postma/All Canada Photos/Corbis; (t) ©Ryan McGinnis/Alamy Images

Transformers

What is an energy transformation?

An **energy transformation** (EN•er•jee trans•fohr•MAY•shuhn) takes place when energy changes from one form into another form. Any form of energy can change into any other form of energy. Often, one form of energy changes into more than one form. When you rub your hands together, you hear a sound, and your hands get warm. The mechanical energy of your moving hands was transformed into both sound energy and energy as heat.

Another example of an energy transformation is when chemical energy is converted in the body. Why is eating breakfast so important? Eating breakfast gives your body the energy needed to help you start your day. Chemical potential energy is stored in the food you eat. Your body breaks down the components of the food to access the energy stored in them. Some of this energy is then changed to the kinetic energy that allows you to move and play. Some of the chemical energy is converted into heat energy that keeps your body warm.

 **Visualize It!**

Some examples of energy transformation are illustrated in this flashlight. Follow the captions to learn how energy is transformed into the light energy that you rely on when you turn on a flashlight.

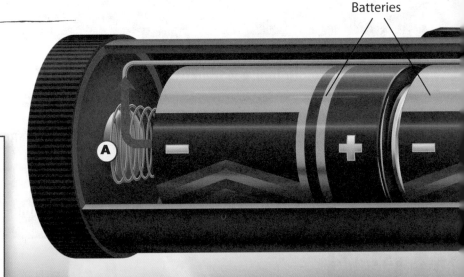

Batteries

A *The chemical energy from the batteries is transformed into electrical energy.*

16 Describe Give two examples of other devices in which the chemical energy in a battery is transformed into electrical energy.

_____

_____

_____

© Houghton Mifflin Harcourt Publishing Company • Image Credits: (bg) ©SuperStock RF/SuperStock

Is energy conserved?

A closed system is a group of objects that transfers energy only to one another. For example, a roller coaster can be considered a closed system if it includes everything involved, such as the track, the cars, and the air around them. Energy is conserved in all closed systems. The **law of conservation of energy** states that energy cannot be created or destroyed. It can only change forms. All of the different forms of energy in a closed system always add up to the same total amount of energy. It does not matter how many energy transformations take place.

For example, on a roller coaster some mechanical energy gets transformed into sound and heat energy as the roller coaster goes down a hill. The total of the coaster's mechanical energy at the bottom of the hill, the extra heat energy, and the sound energy is the same total amount of energy as the original amount of mechanical energy. In other words, total energy is conserved.

Active Reading **17 Relate** How are energy transformations related to the law of conservation of energy?

_____

_____

_____

_____

© Houghton Mifflin Harcourt Publishing Company • Image Credits: (bg) ©SuperStock RF/SuperStock

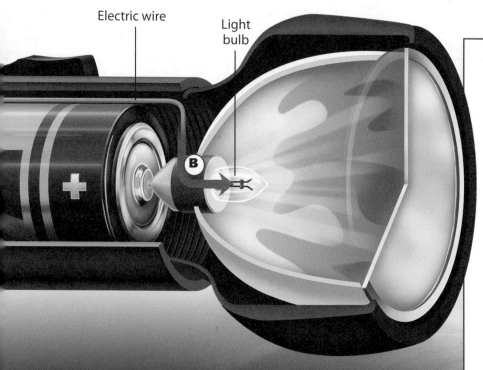

Electric wire

Light bulb

Think Outside the Book

18 Apply Have you ever thought about how cell phones work? What form of energy is used to power a cell phone? What form of energy do you use from a cell phone? Can you think of any other forms of energy that may be used inside of a cell phone?

B The electrical energy in the wire is transformed into light in the light bulb. Some of the electrical energy is also transformed into heat energy.

19 Describe Give another example of electrical energy being transformed into light.

_____

_____

_____

_____

_____

Visual Summary

To complete this summary, circle the correct word. Then use the key below to check your answers. You can use this page to review the main concepts of the lesson.

Introduction to Energy

Energy is the ability to cause change; it cannot be created or destroyed.

20 The total energy in a closed system remains the same / changes as energy changes forms.

Potential energy results from an object's position, composition, or condition, and kinetic energy results from an object's motion.

21 A basketball that is balanced on the rim of a basketball hoop has potential energy / kinetic energy.

22 A basketball that is rolling across a floor has potential energy / kinetic energy.

Energy transformation takes place when energy changes from one form to another.

23 When a candle is burned, some chemical energy is transformed into nuclear / heat energy.

Answers: 20 remains the same; 21 potential energy; 22 kinetic energy; 23 heat

24 Apply Identify and give examples of at least three types of energy you see being used as you look around your classroom.

© Houghton Mifflin Harcourt Publishing Company • Image Credits: (t) ©NASA; (tr) ©Paul A. Souders/Corbis; (bl) ©SuperStock RF/SuperStock

Lesson Review

Vocabulary

Draw a line to connect the following terms to their definitions.

1 kinetic energy   **A** energy of position

2 energy   **B** the ability to cause change

3 potential energy   **C** energy of motion

Key Concepts

4 Describe What happens to the kinetic energy of a snowball as it rolls across the lawn and gains mass?

_____

5 Relate How is the sun related to nuclear, radiant, and heat energy?

_____
_____
_____
_____
_____
_____

6 Apply When a person uses an iron to remove the wrinkles from a shirt, why does heat travel from the iron to the shirt?

_____
_____

7 Explain What determines the amount of chemical energy a substance has?

_____
_____
_____

Critical Thinking

Use the picture below to answer the following questions.

8 Identify Name at least three types of energy associated with the microwave.

_____
_____

9 Hypothesize How is radiant energy from the microwave transformed into heat energy?

_____
_____
_____
_____

10 Infer Explain the law of conservation of energy.

_____
_____
_____
_____
_____

© Houghton Mifflin Harcourt Publishing Company • Image Credits: ©Jupiterimages/FoodPix/Getty Images

My Notes

© Houghton Mifflin Harcourt Publishing Company

© Houghton Mifflin Harcourt Publishing Company

Lesson 2

Kinetic and Potential Energy

ESSENTIAL QUESTION

How can we calculate kinetic and potential energy?

By the end of this lesson, you should be able to calculate kinetic and potential energy and know how these two types of energy are related.

6.PS3.1, 6.PS3.2, 6.PS3.3

Climbing a hill requires a lot of energy but it makes the ride back down fun.

© Houghton Mifflin Harcourt Publishing Company • Image Credits: (bg) ©Juice Images/Alamy

Lesson Labs

Quick Labs
- Investigate Potential Energy
- Identify Potential and Kinetic Energy

Exploration Lab
- Mechanical Energy

Engage Your Brain

1 Predict Check T or F to show whether you think each statement is true or false.

T	F	
☐	☐	Objects that are sitting still have kinetic energy.
☐	☐	The kinetic energy of an object depends on how much space the object takes up.
☐	☐	The gravitational potential energy of an object depends on its height above a surface.

2 Analyze If the baseball and the plastic ball were moving at the same speed, which ball would hit a bat harder? Why?

_____

_____

_____

_____

_____

Active Reading

3 Synthesize Many English words have their roots in other languages. Use the Greek word below to make an educated guess about the meaning of the term *mechanical energy*.

Greek word	Meaning
kinetikos	machine

Example sentence:
We can calculate an object's <u>mechanical</u> energy.

mechanical energy:

_____

_____

_____

Vocabulary Terms

- mechanical energy

4 Identify As you read, create a reference card for each vocabulary term. On one side of the card, write the term and its meaning. On the other side, draw an image that illustrates or makes a connection to the term. The cards can be used as bookmarks in the text so that you can refer to them while studying.

© Houghton Mifflin Harcourt Publishing Company • Image Credits: (bg) ©Juice Images/Alamy; (l) PhotoDisc/ Getty Images; (t) ©HMH

On the Move

What is kinetic energy?

Energy is the ability to do work. There are different forms of energy. One form that you can find all around you is kinetic energy. Kinetic energy is the energy of motion. Every moving object has kinetic energy. For example, a hammer has kinetic energy as it moves toward a nail. When the hammer hits the nail, energy is transferred. Work is done when movement occurs in the direction of the force, and the nail is driven into a board.

The Energy of Motion

Active Reading **5 Identify** As you read, underline two factors that affect an object's kinetic energy.

What determines the amount of kinetic energy that an object has? The faster an object moves, the more kinetic energy it has. So kinetic energy depends, in part, on speed. Kinetic energy also depends on mass. If two objects move at the same speed, then the one that has more mass will have more kinetic energy. Imagine a bike and a car that are moving at the same speed. The car has more kinetic energy than the bike has because the car has more mass.

Visualize It!

6 Apply How does the rider's ability to stop the bike change as the bike moves down a steep hill?

_____

_____

_____

The bike at the top of the hill is not moving. It does not have kinetic energy. The bike that is going down the hill has kinetic energy. As the bike moves faster, its kinetic energy increases.

© Houghton Mifflin Harcourt Publishing Company • Image Credits: ©Wig Worland/Alamy

How is the kinetic energy of an object calculated?

An object's kinetic energy is related to its mass and speed. The speed of an object is the distance that it travels in a unit of time. The following equation shows how kinetic energy is calculated.

$$\text{kinetic energy} = \frac{1}{2}mv^2$$

The letter m is the object's mass, and the letter v is the object's speed. When the mass is expressed in kilograms and the speed in meters per second, kinetic energy is expressed in *joules* (J).

 **Do the Math**

Sample Problem

The foal has a mass of 100 kg and is moving at 8 m/s along the beach. What is the kinetic energy (KE) of the foal?

Identify

A. What do you know? The mass, m, is 100 kg.

The speed, v, is 8 m/s.

B. What do you want to find? kinetic energy

Plan

C. Write the formula: $KE = \frac{1}{2}mv^2$

D. Substitute into the formula: $KE = \frac{1}{2}(100 \text{ kg})(8 \text{ m/s})^2$

Solve

E. Multiply: $KE = \frac{1}{2}(100 \text{ kg})(64 \text{ m}^2/\text{s}^2) = 3{,}200 \text{ kg} \cdot \text{m}^2/\text{s}^2 = 3{,}200 \text{ J}$

Answer: 3,200 J

You Try It

7 Calculate Complete the table at the right to calculate the kinetic energy of the horses.

Horse	m	v	v²	KE
foal	100 kg	10 m/s		
mare	800 kg	10 m/s		
mare	800 kg	15 m/s		

© Houghton Mifflin Harcourt Publishing Company • Image Credits: ©John GiustinaPhotographer's Choice/Getty Images

It Could Change

What is potential energy?

Some energy is stored energy, or potential energy. Potential energy is the energy an object has because of its position, condition, or chemical composition. Like kinetic energy, potential energy is the ability to do work. For example, an object has *elastic potential energy* when it has been stretched or compressed. Elastic potential energy is stored in a stretched spring or rubber band. An object has *gravitational potential energy* due to its position above the ground. An object held above the ground has the potential to fall. The higher the object is above the ground, the greater its gravitational potential energy. Potential energy that depends on an object's position is referred to as *mechanical potential energy*. But there are other types of potential energy that do not depend on an object's position. For example, a substance stores *chemical potential energy* as a result of its chemical bonds. Some of that energy can be released during chemical reactions.

Think Outside the Book (Inquiry)

8 Classify With a partner, create a poster that shows examples of potential energy from everyday life. Label each example as gravitational, elastic, or chemical potential energy.

Visualize It!

9 Identify Fill in the type of potential energy that is illustrated in each image.

Fruit can provide energy to your body.

A _____

The boulder is high above the ground.

B _____

The archer pulls back on the string and bends the bow's limbs.

C _____

© Houghton Mifflin Harcourt Publishing Company • Image Credits: (l) ©Photodisc/Getty Images; (c) ©altrendo nature/Getty Images; (r) ©Pauline St. Denis/Corbis

How is the gravitational potential energy of an object calculated?

The following equation describes an object's gravitational potential energy.

$$\text{gravitational potential energy} = mgh$$

The letter m represents the object's mass expressed in kilograms. The letter g represents the acceleration due to Earth's gravity, which is 9.8 m/s². The letter h is the object's height from the ground in meters. The height is a measure of how far the object can fall. Like kinetic energy, potential energy is expressed in units of joules.

 **Do the Math**

Sample Problem

The cat has a mass of 4 kg and is 1.5 m above the ground. What is the gravitational potential energy of the cat?

Identify

A. What do you know? mass = 4 kg, height = 1.5 m, acceleration due to gravity = 9.8 m/s²

B. What do you want to find? gravitational potential energy

Plan

C. Write the formula: $GPE = mgh$

D. Substitute the given values into the formula:
$GPE = (4 \text{ kg})(9.8 \text{ m/s}^2)(1.5 \text{ m})$

Solve

E. Multiply: $PE = (4 \text{ kg})(9.8 \text{ m/s}^2)(1.5 \text{ m}) = 58.8 \text{ kg} \cdot \text{m}^2/\text{s}^2 = 58.8 \text{ J}$

Answer: 58.8 J

You Try It

10 Calculate Three books are on different shelves. Calculate the gravitational potential energy of each book based on its mass and its height above the floor.

Object	m	h	PE
picture book	0.2 kg	2 m	
picture book	0.2 kg	3 m	
textbook	1.5 kg	4 m	

© Houghton Mifflin Harcourt Publishing Company • Image Credits: ©C. Traer Scott/Flickr/Getty Images

It All Adds Up!

How is the mechanical energy of an object calculated?

Active Reading

11 Identify As you read, underline the two components of mechanical energy.

A moving object can have both kinetic and potential energy. **Mechanical energy** is the energy possessed by an object due to its motion and position. For example, a thrown baseball has kinetic energy. It also has potential energy because it is above the ground. The sum of the ball's kinetic energy and mechanical potential energy is its mechanical energy. You can use the following equation to find mechanical energy.

$$mechanical\ energy = KE + PE$$

If the object's only potential energy is gravitational potential energy, you can use the following equation to find mechanical energy.

$$ME = \frac{1}{2}mv^2 + mgh$$

Visualize It!

12 Compare Circle the position of the ball when its gravitational potential energy is greatest.

The mechanical energy of the ball is the sum of its kinetic energy and potential energy.

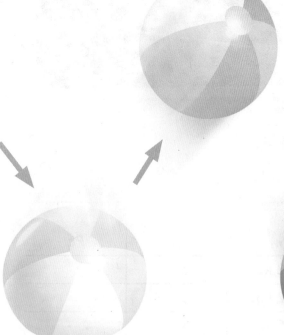

13 Analyze When does the ball have zero gravitational potential energy?

_____

_____

© Houghton Mifflin Harcourt Publishing Company

Do the Math You Try It

14 Calculate When the basketball is at its maximum height of 3 meters, it is not moving. The table below lists the KE and GPE for the basketball at heights of 3 m, 2 m, 1 m, and 0 m. Write the missing values for KE and GPE in the table. Then find the mechanical energy for each height.

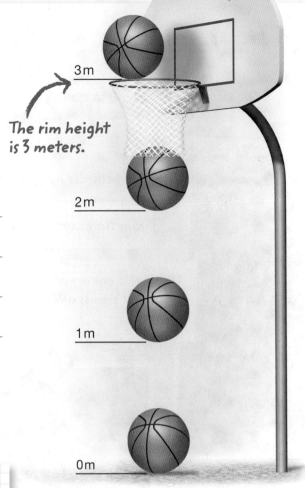

3 m

The rim height is 3 meters.

2 m

1 m

0 m

Height	KE	GPE	ME
3.0 m		18 J	
2.0 m	6 J	12 J	
1.0 m	12 J	6 J	
0 m	18 J		

15 Graph Use the data above to plot and label two lines representing the kinetic energy and the gravitational potential energy of the basketball.

Energy of the Basketball

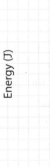

Energy (J)

Height above floor (m)

16 Analyze What is the relationship between the kinetic energy and the gravitational potential energy of the basketball?

_____

_____

_____

© Houghton Mifflin Harcourt Publishing Company • Image Credits: ©Jim Cummins/Taxi/Getty Images

Visual Summary

To complete this summary, fill in the blanks with the correct word. Then, use the key below to check your answers. You can use this page to review the main concepts of the lesson.

Kinetic and Potential Energy

All moving objects have kinetic energy.

$$\text{kinetic energy} = \frac{1}{2}mv^2$$

17 Kinetic energy depends on an object's mass and _____

Mechanical energy is kinetic energy plus potential energy due to position.

$$\text{mechanical energy} = KE + PE$$

Potential energy is stored energy.

$$\text{gravitational potential energy} = mgh$$

18 Potential energy can be gravitational, _____, or elastic.

19 The formula $ME = \frac{1}{2}mv^2 + mgh$ can be used to calculate mechanical energy if the only potential energy is _____ potential energy.

Answers: 17 speed; 18 chemical; 19 gravitational

20 Synthesize A skydiver jumps out of a plane. Describe how gravitational potential energy changes as the skydiver falls. Describe how the skydiver's kinetic energy changes when the parachute opens.

© Houghton Mifflin Harcourt Publishing Company • Image Credits: (l) ©Wig Worland/Alamy; (c) ©C. Traer Scott/Flickr/Getty Images; (r) ©Jim Cummins/Taxi/Getty Images

Lesson Review

Vocabulary

In your own words, define the following terms.

1 kinetic energy

_____

_____

2 potential energy

_____

_____

3 mechanical energy

_____

_____

Key Concepts

4 Relate Describe the relationship between a moving object's mass and its kinetic energy.

_____

_____

_____

_____

5 Identify What are two factors that determine an object's gravitational potential energy?

_____

_____

_____

6 Analyze A passenger plane is flying above the ground. Describe the two components of its mechanical energy.

_____

_____

_____

_____

_____

Critical Thinking

7 Evaluate Can an object's mechanical energy be equal to its gravitational potential energy? Explain.

_____

_____

_____

_____

Use this graph to answer the following questions.

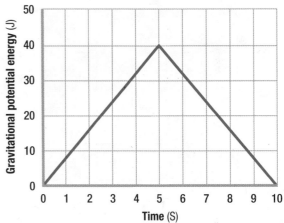

Gravitational Potential Energy over Time

8 Apply The graph shows the gravitational potential energy of a radio-controlled toy helicopter. Describe the motion of the toy.

_____

_____

_____

_____

9 Calculate At 2.5 seconds, the helicopter has a kinetic energy of 20 J. What is its mechanical energy at that time?

_____

_____

_____

_____

© Houghton Mifflin Harcourt Publishing Company

My Notes

© Houghton Mifflin Harcourt Publishing Company

© Houghton Mifflin Harcourt Publishing Company

Thermal Energy and Heat

ESSENTIAL QUESTION

What is the relationship between heat and temperature?

By the end of this lesson, you should be able to analyze the relationship between heat, temperature, and thermal energy.

6.PS3.1, 6.PS3.3, 6.PS3.4

The Afar Depression, in eastern Africa, is one of the hottest places on Earth. In the summer, temperatures average over 38 °C (100 °F)!

© Houghton Mifflin Harcourt Publishing Company • Image Credits: ©Carsten Peter/National Geographic/Getty Images

✋ **Lesson Labs**

Quick Labs
- Simple Heat Engine
- Observing the Transfer of Energy
- Exploring Thermal Conductivity

Field Lab
- Building a Solar Cooker

🧠 Engage Your Brain

1 Describe Fill in the blanks with the words that you think correctly complete the following sentences.

When you put your hands on a cold object, like a glass of ice water, your hands become

_____ The glass of water

becomes _____ if you

leave your hands on it for a long time. If you

leave the glass of ice water out in the sun, the

ice will start to _____

2 Describe Write your own caption for this photo.

_____

_____

_____

_____

✏️ Active Reading

3 Apply Many scientific words, such as *conductor*, also have everyday meanings. Use context clues to write your own definition for each meaning of the word *conductor*.

Example sentence
That school's band is very good because its <u>conductor</u> is a great teacher.

conductor:

_____

_____

Example sentence
That metal spoon is a good <u>conductor</u>, so it will get hot if you put it into boiling soup.

conductor:

_____

_____

Vocabulary Terms

- temperature
- thermal energy
- heat
- calorie
- conduction
- degrees
- conductor
- insulator
- convection
- radiation

4 Apply As you learn the definition of each vocabulary term in this lesson, create your own definition or sketch to help you remember the meaning of the term.

© Houghton Mifflin Harcourt Publishing Company • Image Credits: (bkgd) ©Carsten Peter/National Geographic/Getty Images; (t) ©Tim Pannell/Corbis

What is temperature?

Temperature is a measure of the average kinetic energy of all the particles in a substance. In the Celsius and Fahrenheit scales, temperature is measured in units called degrees. **Degrees** (°) are equally spaced units between two points. The space between degrees can vary from scale to scale. In the Kelvin scale, no degree sign is used. Instead, the unit is just called a kelvin. Temperature is measured using an instrument called a thermometer.

What is thermal energy?

Thermal energy is the total kinetic energy of all particles in a substance. In the SI system, thermal energy is measured in joules (J). If you have two identical glasses of water and one is at a higher temperature than the other, the particles in the hotter water have a higher average kinetic energy. The water at a higher temperature will have a higher amount of thermal energy.

What is the difference between thermal energy and temperature?

Temperature and thermal energy are different from each other. Temperature is related to the average kinetic energy of particles, while thermal energy is the total kinetic energy of all the particles. A glass of water can have the same temperature as Lake Superior, but the lake has much more thermal energy because the lake contains many more water molecules.

After you put ice cubes into a pitcher of lemonade, energy is transferred from the warmer lemonade to the colder ice. The lemonade's thermal energy decreases and the ice's thermal energy increases. Because the particles in the lemonade have transferred some of their energy to the particles in the ice, the average kinetic energy of the particles in the lemonade decreases. Thus, the temperature of the lemonade decreases.

There are more water molecules in this lake than in the glass of water on the right.

> **Active Reading** 5 **Explain** What are two factors that determine the thermal energy of a substance?
>
> _____
>
> _____

© Houghton Mifflin Harcourt Publishing Company • Image Credits: ©John Warden/SuperStock

Under Where?

There are fewer water molecules in this glass than in the lake.

6 Apply For each object pair in the table below, circle the object that has more thermal energy. Assume that both objects are at the same temperature.

bowl of soup	small balloon	tiger
pot of soup	large balloon	house cat

© Houghton Mifflin Harcourt Publishing Company • Image Credits: (bkgd) ©John Warden/SuperStock; (t) ©Tetra Images/Alamy

Heat It Up!

Energy in the form of heat flows from the warm drinks to the cold ice. The ice melts.

What is heat?

You might think of the word *heat* as having to do with things that feel hot. But heat also has to do with things that feel cold. Heat causes objects to feel hot or cold or to get hot or cold under the right conditions. You probably use the word *heat* every day to mean different things. However, in science, **heat** is the energy transferred from an object at a higher temperature to an object at a lower temperature.

When two objects at different temperatures come into contact, energy is always transferred from the object that has the higher temperature to the object that has the lower temperature. Energy in the form of heat always flows from hot to cold. For example, if you put an ice cube into a glass of water, energy is transferred from the warmer water to the colder ice cube.

7 Apply For each object pair in the table below, draw an arrow in the direction in which energy in the form of heat would flow.

Object 1	Direction of heat flow	Object 2
metal rod		fire
hat		snowman
ice cube		glass of warm water

© Houghton Mifflin Harcourt Publishing Company • Image Credits: (t) ©Darren Kemper/Corbis; (b) ©José Luis Peláez Inc/Blend Images/Age Fotostock

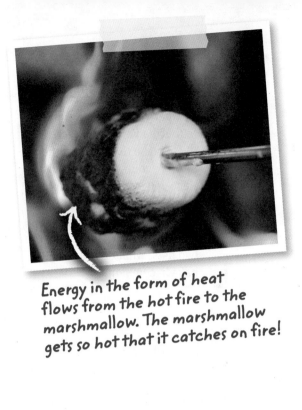

Energy in the form of heat flows from the hot fire to the marshmallow. The marshmallow gets so hot that it catches on fire!

Energy in the form of heat flows from the warm mugs to the girls' cold hands. Their hands get warmer.

Visualize It!

8 Apply What is another heat exchange happening in this picture?

_____

_____

_____

_____

How is heat measured?

Heat is measured in two ways. One way is the calorie (cal). One **calorie** is equal to the amount of energy needed to raise the temperature of 1 g of water by 1 °C. Heat can also be measured in joules (J) because heat is a form of energy. One calorie is equal to 4.18 J.

You probably think of calories in terms of food. However, in nutrition, one Calorie—written with a capital C—is actually one kilocalorie, or 1,000 calories. This means that one Calorie (Cal) contains enough energy to raise the temperature of 1 kg of water by 1 °C. Each Calorie in food contains 1,000 cal of energy.

To find out how many Calories are in an apple, the apple is burned inside an instrument called a calorimeter. A thermometer measures the increase in temperature, which is used to calculate how much energy is released. This amount is the number of Calories.

How is heat related to thermal energy?

Adding or removing heat from a substance will affect its temperature and thermal energy. Heat, however, is not the same as thermal energy and temperature. These are properties of a substance. Heat is the energy involved when these properties change.

Think of what happens when two objects at different temperatures come into contact. Energy as heat flows from the object at the higher temperature to the object at the lower temperature. When both objects come to the same temperature, no more energy as heat flows. Just because the temperature of the two objects is the same does not mean they have the same thermal energy. One object may be larger than the other and thus have more particles in motion.

Active Reading **9 Relate** What will happen if two objects at different temperatures come into contact?

_____

_____

_____

© Houghton Mifflin Harcourt Publishing Company • Image Credits: (t) ©Darren Kemper/Corbis; (tc) ©Getty Images/Jupiterimages; (b) ©Jose Luis Pelaez Inc/Blend Images/Age Fotostock

How can heat affect the state of an object?

The matter that makes up a frozen juice bar is the same whether the juice bar is frozen or has melted. The matter is just in a different form, or state. Remember that the kinetic theory of matter states that the particles that make up matter move around at different speeds. The state of a substance depends on the speed of its particles. Adding energy in the form of heat to a substance may result in a change of state. The added energy may cause the bonds between particles to break. This is what allows the state to change. Adding energy in the form of heat to a chunk of glacier may cause the ice to melt into water. Removing energy in the form of heat from a substance may also result in a change of state.

Active Reading 11 **Predict** What are two ways to change the state of a substance?

_____

_____

© Houghton Mifflin Harcourt Publishing Company • Image Credits: ©Andrew Watson/Fotolia LLC

Think Outside the Book Inquiry

10 **Compare** Have you ever needed to touch a very hot object? What did you use to touch it without burning yourself? Make a list. Have you ever needed to protect yourself from being cold? What sorts of things did you use? Make a list. Now, looking at the two lists, what do the things have in common?

Some of this ice is changing state. It is melting into water.

How do polar bears stay warm?

Keep Your Cool

What is conduction?

There are three main ways to transfer energy as heat: conduction, convection, and radiation. **Conduction** is the transfer of energy as heat from one substance to another through direct contact. It occurs any time that objects at different temperatures come into contact with each other. The average kinetic energy of particles in the warmer object is greater than the average kinetic energy of the particles in the cooler object. As the particles collide, some of the kinetic energy of the particles in the warmer object is transferred to the cooler object. As long as the objects are in contact, conduction continues until the temperatures of the objects are equal.

Conduction can also occur within a single object. In this case, energy in the form of heat is transferred from the warmer part of the object to the cooler part of the object. Imagine you put a metal spoon into a cup of hot cocoa. Energy will be conducted from the warm end of the spoon to the cool end until the temperature of the entire spoon is the same.

This is a photo of polar bear hair magnified about 350 times! Notice that it is hollow inside. The air inside is a good insulator.

Conductors

Some materials transfer the kinetic energy of particles better than others. A **conductor** is a material that transfers heat very well. Metals are typically good conductors. You know that when one end of a metal object gets hot, the other end quickly becomes hot as well. Consider pots or pans that have metal handles. A metal handle becomes too hot to touch soon after the pan is placed on a hot stove.

Insulators

An **insulator** (IN•suh•lay•ter) is a material that is a poor conductor of heat. Some examples of insulators are wood, paper, and plastic foam. Plastic foam is a good insulator because it contains many small spaces that are filled with air. A plastic foam cup will not easily transfer energy in the form of heat by conduction. That is why plastic foam is often used to keep hot drinks hot. Think about the metal pan handle mentioned above. It can be dangerous to have handles get hot so quickly. Instead, pot handles are often made of an insulator, such as wood or plastic. Although a plastic handle will also get hot when the pot is on the stove, it takes a much longer time for it to get hot than it would for a metal handle.

---

12 Classify Decide whether each object below is a conductor or an insulator. Then check the correct box.

Flannel shirt	☐ Conductor
	☐ Insulator
Iron skillet	☐ Conductor
	☐ Insulator
Copper pipe	☐ Conductor
	☐ Insulator
Oven mitt	☐ Conductor
	☐ Insulator

© Houghton Mifflin Harcourt Publishing Company • Image Credits: ©Andrew Syred/Photo Researchers, Inc.

What is convection?

Energy in the form of heat can also be transferred through the movement of gases or liquids. **Convection** (kuhn•VEK•shuhn) is the transfer of energy as heat by the movement of a liquid or gas. In most substances, as temperature increases, the density of the liquid or gas decreases. Convection occurs when a cooler, denser mass of a gas or liquid replaces a warmer, less dense mass of a gas or liquid by pushing it upward.

When you boil water in a pot, the water moves in roughly circular patterns because of convection. The water at the bottom of the pot gets hot because there is a source of heat at the bottom. As the water heats, it becomes less dense. The warmer water rises through the denser, cooler water above it. At the surface, the warm water begins to cool. The particles move closer together, making the water denser. The cooler water then sinks back to the bottom, is heated again, and the cycle repeats. This cycle causes a circular motion of liquids or gases. The motion is due to density differences that result from temperature differences. The motion is called a *convection current.*

What is radiation?

Radiation is another way in which heat can be transferred. **Radiation** is the transfer of energy by electromagnetic waves. Some examples of electromagnetic waves include visible light, microwaves, and infrared light. The sun is the most significant source of radiation that you experience on a daily basis. However, all objects—even you—emit radiation and release energy.

When radiation is emitted from one object and then absorbed by another, the result is often a transfer of heat. Like conduction and convection, radiation can transfer heat from warmer to cooler objects. However, radiation differs from conduction and convection in a very significant way. Radiation can travel through empty space, as it does when it moves from the sun to Earth.

Active Reading

13 Identify As you read, underline examples of heat transfer.

This pot of boiling water shows how convection currents move.

14 Classify Fill in the blanks in the chart below.

Example	Conduction, Convection, or Radiation
When you put some food in the microwave, it gets hot.	
	Conduction
A heater on the first floor of the school makes the air on the second floor warm.	

© Houghton Mifflin Harcourt Publishing Company

Practical Uses of Radiation

SOCIETY AND TECHNOLOGY

Do you think that you could cook your food using the energy from the sun? Using a device called a solar cooker, you could! A solar cooker works by concentrating the radiation from the sun into a small area using mirrors. Solar cookers aren't just fun to use—they also help some people eat clean food!

In a refugee camp
This woman, who lives in a refugee camp in Sudan, is making tea with water that she boiled in a solar cooker. For many people living far from electricity or a source of clean water, a solar cooker provides a cheap and portable way to sterilize their water. This helps to prevent disease.

As a hobby
This woman demonstrates how her solar cooker works. Many people like to use solar cookers because they do not require any fuel. They also do not release any emissions that are harmful to the planet.

Extend

Inquiry

15 Identify Two examples of radiation are shown in the photos above. What is the source of the radiation in the examples?

16 Relate Research other places throughout the world where solar cookers are being used.

17 Produce Explain how solar cookers are useful to society by doing one of the following:
- Make a solar cooker and demonstrate how it works.
- Write a story about a family who uses a solar cooker to stay healthy and safe.

© Houghton Mifflin Harcourt Publishing Company • Image Credits: (bkgd) ©NASA; (l) ©Orjan F. Ellingvag/Dagens Naringsliv/Corbis; (r) ©Howard Davies/Alamy

Visual Summary

To complete this summary, circle the correct word or phrase. Then use the key below to check your answers. You can use this page to review the main concepts of the lesson.

Thermal energy is the total kinetic energy of all particles in a substance.

18 If two objects are at the same temperature, the one with more / fewer / the same amount of particles will have a higher thermal energy.

Heat is the energy transferred from an object at a higher temperature to an object at a lower temperature.

19 Heat always flows from cold to hot / hot to cold / left to right.

Heat can change the state of a substance.

20 Adding heat to an object causes bonds between particles to form / break / combine. This is what allows the state change.

Heat

There are three main ways to transfer energy as heat: conduction, convection, and radiation.

conduction

convection

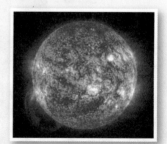
radiation

21 Conduction is the transfer of energy from a warmer object to a cooler object through a gas / empty space / direct contact.

22 Energy from the sun travels to Earth through conduction / convection / radiation.

Answers: 18 more; 19 hot to cold; 20 break; 21 direct contact; 22 radiation

23 Conclude Suppose you are outside on a hot day and you move into the shade of a tree. Which form of energy transfer are you avoiding? Explain.

© Houghton Mifflin Harcourt Publishing Company • Image Credits: (t) ©Tetra Images/Alamy; (tr) ©Getty Images/Jupiterimages; (b) ©Andrew Syred/Photo Researchers, Inc.; (br) ©NASA

Lesson Review

Vocabulary

In your own words, define the following terms.

1 heat

_____

_____

_____

2 thermal energy

_____

_____

_____

3 conduction

_____

_____

_____

4 convection

_____

_____

_____

5 radiation

_____

_____

_____

Key Concepts

6 Compare What is the difference between heat and temperature?

_____

_____

_____

_____

7 Predict If two objects at different temperatures are in contact with each other, what happens to their temperatures?

_____

_____

_____

_____

_____

Use this photo to answer the following questions.

8 Classify Which type of energy transfer is occurring at each lettered area?

A _____

B _____

C _____

Critical Thinking

9 Synthesize Describe the relationships among temperature, heat, and thermal energy.

_____

_____

_____

_____

10 Synthesize Do you think that solids can undergo convection? Explain.

_____

_____

_____

_____

_____

© Houghton Mifflin Harcourt Publishing Company • Image Credits: ©Jupiterimages/Thinkstock/Getty Images

My Notes

© Houghton Mifflin Harcourt Publishing Company

© Houghton Mifflin Harcourt Publishing Company

Planning an Investigation

Scientists ask many questions and develop hypotheses about the natural world. They conduct investigations to help answer these questions. A scientist must plan an investigation carefully. The investigation should gather information that might support or disprove the hypothesis.

Tutorial

Use the following steps to help plan an investigation.

(1) Write a hypothesis.
The hypothesis should offer an explanation for the question that you are asking. The hypothesis must also be testable. If it is not testable, rewrite the hypothesis.

(2) Identify and list the possible variables in your experiment.
Select the independent variable and the dependent variable. In your investigation, you will change the independent variable to see any effect it may have on the dependent variable.

(3) List the materials that you will need to perform the experiment.
This list should also include equipment that you need for safety.

(4) Determine the method you will use to test your hypothesis.
Clearly describe the steps you will follow. If you change any part of the procedure while you are conducting the investigation, record the change. Another scientist should be able to follow your procedure to repeat your investigation.

(5) Analyze the results.
Your data and observations from all of your experiments should be recorded carefully and clearly to maintain credibility. Record how you analyze your results so others can review your work and spot any problems or errors in your analysis.

(6) Draw conclusions.
Describe what the results of the investigation show. Tell whether the results support your hypothesis.

© Houghton Mifflin Harcourt Publishing Company

You Try It!

You are a member of a research team that is trying to design and test a roof system that can maintain a comfortable temperature inside a building during hot days. The system you design and test will be a scale model To begin, you need to find an answer to the following question: **What material will minimize the rate of heat transfer inside a building?**

1 Forming a Hypothesis Write down your hypothesis. How does your hypothesis explain or answer your question? Is your hypothesis testable?

_____

_____

_____

_____

2 Identifying Variables List the possible variables in this experiment. Identify dependent variables and independent variables.

_____

_____

_____

_____

3 Selecting Materials What equipment and tools will you need to test this variable? What might happen if you select inappropriate tools?

_____

_____

_____

_____

4 Testing Your Hypothesis What will your system look like? Will it support your testing? You may sketch the system on a separate page.

_____

_____

_____

_____

5 Maintaining Accurate Records What steps will you need to follow in order to test your hypothesis? What kinds of measurements will you collect? What kind of graphic organizer will you use to record your information?

_____

_____

_____

_____

6 Drawing Conclusions What conclusions can you draw from your data? Was your hypothesis useful?

_____

_____

_____

Take It Home

Look closely at objects and materials in your home. Write a list of things that help to prevent the transfer of energy as heat. Design an investigation using one or more of these items to learn more about the job they do. Record your observations. Evaluate your results to see if they might point to a further investigation or an improvement to a product. Present your results in a pamphlet.

© Houghton Mifflin Harcourt Publishing Company • Image Credits: (tr) ©Jupiterimages/Getty Images

Engineering Design Process

Skills
Conduct research
✔ Brainstorm solutions
✔ Select a solution
✔ Design a solution
✔ Test and evaluate
✔ Redesign to improve
✔ Communicate results

Objectives
• Demonstrate how heat moves among objects.

Engineering Solutions

Engineers solve problems by designing experiments. Experiments allow them test possible solutions to a problem. To design an experiment, engineers follow a process with several steps. First, they research the problem to learn as much as they can about it. Next, they brainstorm possible solutions to the problem. Then, they select one possible solution to develop further. After designing the possible solution, they test and evaluate the solution. Finally, they redesign and improve the solution and communicate their results.

Engineers often start by stating the problem as a question. In this activity, you will address the question *How does heat move among specific objects?* You will use what you know about heat transfer to design and test a solution for this problem, following the process described above.

1 Brainstorm Name some ways that heat moves among the objects in the photo.

_____

_____

_____

_____

© Houghton Mifflin Harcourt Publishing Company • Image Credits: (bg) ©Design Pics/Richard Wear/Getty Images

Heat from a hot beverage is transferred first to the mug, then to the hands. What type(s) of energy transfer does this involve?

Transfers of Energy

Heat moves from objects of a higher temperature to objects at a lower temperature. Heat is transferred among objects in three main ways: conduction, convection, and radiation. With conduction, the heat is transferred through direct contact between the objects. With convection, the energy is transferred as heat by the movement of a liquid or gas. Radiation is the transfer of energy by electromagnetic waves and not direct contact with objects. To test the movement of heat from a hot mug of liquid to your hands, you are testing conduction.

🖐 You Try It! ⟶

Now it's your turn to design an experiment to demonstrate how heat moves among specific objects.

© Houghton Mifflin Harcourt Publishing Company • Image Credits: (tg) ©Design Pics/Richard Wear/Getty Images; (t) ©Brand X Pictures/Alamy Images

 # You Try It!

Now it's your turn to design an experiment to demonstrate how heat moves among specific objects.

You Will Need

✓ Long, large, shallow pan or tray

✓ Several thermometers

✓ Source of tap water

✓ Plastic liter bottles

✓ Other objects of your choice

① Brainstorm Solutions

Brainstorm ideas for demonstrating the way that heat moves among objects.

A Which objects would you like to test? What is your plan?

_____

_____

_____

B What are the advantages of testing how heat moves in a liquid?

_____

_____

_____

C What tool will be the most helpful for testing your ideas?

_____

_____

② Select a Solution

Which of your ideas seems to offer the best promise of success?

_____

③ Design a Solution

In the space below, write your plan. Then try it out.

© Houghton Mifflin Harcourt Publishing Company

④ Test and Evaluate

Based on your test, how does heat move through objects? Use the chart to record your results. Then write a sentence or two evaluating your results.

_____

_____

_____

⑤ Redesign to Improve

A What about your plan did not go as expected? How can you fix the problem?

_____

_____

_____

B How can you redesign the test to show how heat moves in other ways?

_____

_____

_____

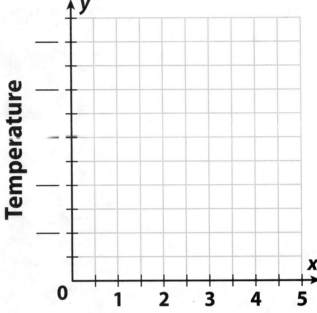

⑥ Communicate Results

Based on your original and redesigned tests, how can you describe how heat moves among objects?

_____

_____

_____

_____

_____

_____

_____

_____

_____

_____

© Houghton Mifflin Harcourt Publishing Company

Effects of Energy Transfer

ESSENTIAL QUESTION

How does the use of energy resources affect the environment?

By the end of this lesson, you should be able to recognize how the production and use of different types of energy resources can have environmental consequences.

🖚 **6.ESS3.1, 6.ESS3.2, 6.ETS1.2**

This power generation plant transforms the heat released from burning coal into electrical energy. Unfiltered smoke from the plant causes air pollution.

© Houghton Mifflin Harcourt Publishing Company • Image Credits: ©Mark Green/Taxi/Getty Images

Lesson Labs

Quick Labs
• Modeling Renewable Energy
• Designing a Vehicle Using Alternative Energy
Exploration Lab
• Sustainable Resource Management

Engage Your Brain

1 Identify In the space below, list as many sources of energy as you can think of. Circle the sources you use most often during a typical day.

_____
_____
_____
_____
_____
_____
_____
_____

2 Describe Write your own caption for this photo of a polluted city.

_____
_____
_____

Active Reading

3 Synthesize You can often define an unknown word if you know the meaning of its word parts. Use the word parts and sentence below to make an educated guess about the meaning of *renewable*.

Word part	Meaning
re-	again, back
new	having been recently made
-able	capable of

Example sentence
Sunlight is classified as a <u>renewable</u> resource because it is constantly replaced.

renewable:

_____
_____

Vocabulary Terms
• renewable resource
• nonrenewable resource
• fossil fuel

4 Apply As you learn the definition of each vocabulary term in this lesson, create your own definition or sketch to help you remember the meaning of the term.

Check the Source!

Active Reading

5 Identify As you read, underline ways in which humans use energy.

Solar panels can help people harness the energy from the sun to use at home!

How do people use energy?

Recall that energy is the capacity to do work. Any work that you do or that you observe around you requires energy. Humans use energy to heat and cool their homes and provide light. Factories use energy to produce everything from toothpicks to airplanes. Energy is required to produce and prepare the food that you eat and beverages that you drink. Vehicles that move you from one place to another require energy. Where does all the energy you use come from?

What are sources of energy?

The sun is Earth's main source of energy. When it reaches Earth, the sun's energy can be stored in various ways, such as in green plants. Useful chemical energy is sometimes stored in minerals. Earth's internal heat, or geothermal energy, is another energy source. An *energy source* is an available source of stored energy that humans can use.

Visualize It!

6 Identify List all of the examples of objects that use energy in this room.

_____

_____

_____

_____

© Houghton Mifflin Harcourt Publishing Company • Image Credits: (t) ©GIPhotoStock/Photo Researchers, Inc.; (b) ©Inc Greer & Associates/SuperStock/Photolibrary

Renewable Energy Sources

A **renewable resource** is an energy source that can be easily reproduced or replaced by nature. Renewable resources are replaced at a rate equal to or greater than the rate that they are used. For example, sunlight and wind are continually available. Humans can use these resources to produce energy without using them up. Other renewable resources, such as trees or crops, are destroyed as they are used. They are renewable because they grow back in a relatively short time.

Trees are a renewable resource as long as we do not use them faster than they can reproduce.

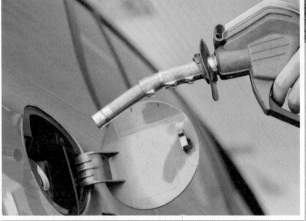

Gasoline is nonrenewable. Its chemical energy comes from organisms that died millions of years ago.

Nonrenewable Energy Sources

A **nonrenewable resource** is an energy source that cannot be produced, grown, or restored as fast as it is used. For example, energy-rich minerals, such as uranium, are nonrenewable because they do not form on Earth. Coal, petroleum, and natural gas are found deep below Earth's surface. They formed over millions of years, so there is a fixed amount of these resources currently available. Humans are using them much more quickly than they can form, so they will eventually run out if we continue to use them at the same rate.

7 Compare Fill in the Venn diagram to compare and contrast characteristics of renewable and nonrenewable energy sources.

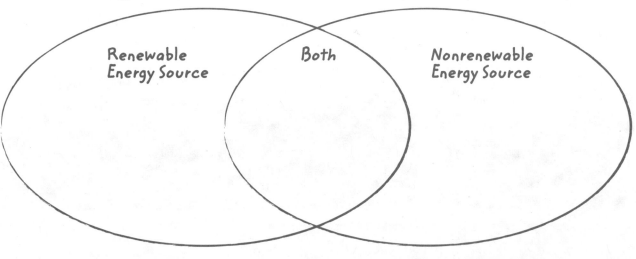

Renewable Energy Source   Both   Nonrenewable Energy Source

© Houghton Mifflin Harcourt Publishing Company • Image Credits: (tr) ©H. Mark Weidman Photography/Alamy; (bl) ©Polka Dot Images/Jupiterimages Corporation

To Burn or Not?

What are some fossil fuels?

Fossil fuels are energy resources made from carbon-rich plant and animal remains. Fossil fuels form through chemical interactions between these remains of ancient living things. Heat and pressure from layers of sediment converted the remains to coal, petroleum, or natural gas. Fossil fuels are nonrenewable because they take millions of years to form. Burning fossil fuels produces carbon dioxide, a greenhouse gas, as well as harmful acids and other forms of pollution.

📰 **Active Reading**

8 Synthesize What environmental impact is shared by all fossil fuels?

_____

_____

Coal

Coal is a sedimentary rock formed from the remains of dead plants at the bottom of ancient swamps. Coal mining can involve removing soil and rocks or creating deep mines. These processes can destroy landscapes and pollute water supplies.

Natural Gas

Some fossil fuels are gases that became trapped in rock formations. Methane (CH_4) is the main component of natural gas. About half of the homes in the United States use natural gas for heating. Natural gas burns more cleanly than other fossil fuels. However, it still produces carbon dioxide.

Petroleum

Petroleum means "rock oil." It formed from the remains of single-celled aquatic organisms that lived long ago. Petroleum is mined on land or under the ocean. It is then separated into fuels such as gasoline, diesel, and jet fuel. Pollutants produced by burning petroleum can react with sunlight to produce smog, a foglike layer of air pollution.

👁 **Visualize It!**

9 Analyze Use the diagrams below to describe how plant and animal remains can become buried and form natural gas or petroleum (oil) after millions of years of heat and pressure.

_____

_____

_____

_____

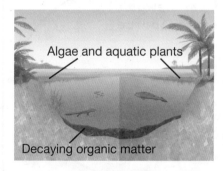

Algae and aquatic plants

Decaying organic matter

Mud

Decaying organic matter

Rock

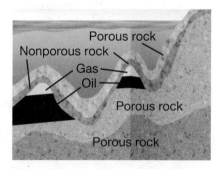

Porous rock

Nonporous rock

Gas

Oil

Porous rock

Porous rock

© Houghton Mifflin Harcourt Publishing Company

What transformations do fossil fuels undergo?

First, raw fossil fuels are obtained by drilling or mining. Then, the fossil fuels are transported, converted into useful forms, stored, and eventually burned for energy. Each transformation can potentially affect the environment in negative ways.

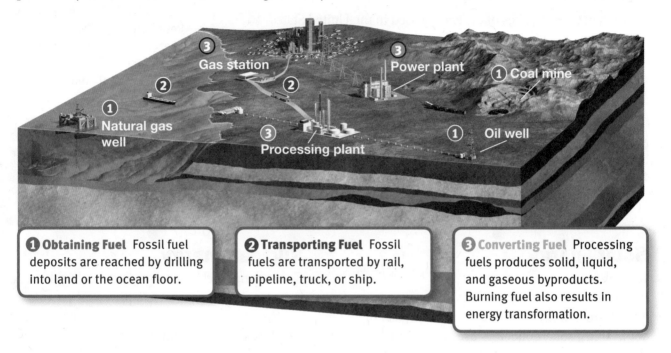

① Obtaining Fuel Fossil fuel deposits are reached by drilling into land or the ocean floor.

② Transporting Fuel Fossil fuels are transported by rail, pipeline, truck, or ship.

③ Converting Fuel Processing fuels produces solid, liquid, and gaseous byproducts. Burning fuel also results in energy transformation.

Visualize It!

10 Apply Fossil fuels have some advantages. But they may also have environmental consequences, as shown in the photographs. Study them and write captions for the second and third ones.

Mining fossil fuels from the ocean floor can disrupt marine habitats.

Ⓐ _____
_____
_____
_____

Ⓑ _____
_____
_____
_____

© Houghton Mifflin Harcourt Publishing Company • Image Credits: (bl) ©Paul Andrew Lawrence/Alamy; (bc) ©Photodisc/Getty Images; (br) ©AP Photo/Jack Smith, File

Nature's Storehouse

What are some alternative sources of energy?

More than three-fourths of the energy used in the United States comes from fossil fuels. These fuels will eventually run out if we keep using them. An alternative energy source is a resource that can be used in place of fossil fuels. Most of these sources are renewable. Using these sources can *conserve*, or save, fossil fuels. Using alternative energy can have less of an impact on the environment.

Think Outside the Book

12 **Research** Choose one of these alternative energy sources. Research ways in which the energy from your source is distributed to users. Prepare a brochure explaining your energy source.

Active Reading

11 **Identify** As you read the cards on this page and the next two pages, underline whether each source is renewable or nonrenewable.

Solar Energy

Renewable energy from the sun can be converted into electrical energy. Solar panels absorb the energy from the sun for our use. In some areas, solar collectors use energy from the sun to produce steam. The steam runs generators to produce electrical energy.

Solar energy is free and clean, but the technologies to transform it into electrical energy aren't widely used. Also, sunlight does not fall evenly over Earth.

These portable solar panels can charge batteries on the go!

Nuclear Energy

Converting nuclear energy into electrical energy is a complex process with a powerful payoff. Splitting the nuclei of a kilogram of uranium atoms releases thousands of times more energy than burning the same mass of coal.

Nuclear energy is nonrenewable because minerals in Earth's crust cannot be replaced. Nuclear power plants do not produce carbon dioxide, but they do produce harmful radioactive wastes that must be safely stored.

Nuclear power plants must be carefully designed to prevent harmful radiation from leaking into the environment.

© Houghton Mifflin Harcourt Publishing Company • Image Credits: (bkgd) ©Getty Images; (b) ©David Burton/Alamy; (b) ©Mark Burnett/Photo Researchers, Inc.

Hydroelectric Energy

Energy from water is one of the most widely used alternative energy sources. Water in fast-moving rivers or flowing downhill through dams turns generators that generate electrical energy.

Hydroelectric energy is powered by the water cycle, so it is a renewable resource. However, it can only be produced by large volumes of falling water. Flooding land to produce reservoirs can destroy habitats. Dams can also disrupt the migratory paths of fish and create erosion problems.

Water flowing through a failed dam could threaten thousands of people living downstream.

To capture more wind, turbines may be 20 stories tall with blades 60 meters (200 ft) in length.

Wind Energy

Blowing wind causes the blades of wind turbines to turn. The blades are connected to a shaft that turns a generator, converting wind energy into electrical energy.

Wind energy is renewable and it doesn't cause any pollution. However, it depends on steady, strong winds that are found only in certain places. Wind farms can also create noise pollution and threaten birds and bats that fly too close to the giant turning blades.

13 Summarize Use the table to list advantages and disadvantages of each alternative energy source.

Energy source	Advantages	Disadvantages
Solar		
Nuclear		
Hydroelectric		
Wind		

© Houghton Mifflin Harcourt Publishing Company • Image Credits: (bkgd) ©Getty Images; (inset) ©Corbis

Geothermal Energy

Geothermal energy is extracted from heat stored within Earth. This energy source is available near hot springs, geysers, or active volcanoes. Water or steam heated by geothermal energy can be used to heat buildings directly or to generate electrical energy.

Geothermal energy is renewable, but it is found only in specific areas on Earth. Some of these areas are protected within national parks.

Energy from Burning Biomass

Biomass includes living or recently dead organic material that can be used as fuel. Examples include trees, crops, or decaying organic matter. Some types of biomass are directly burned for fuel. Others, such as corn, are first converted into fuels such as methane or alcohol.

Energy from biomass is renewable. Using organic waste as an energy source is useful. However, burning biomass or its fuels releases carbon dioxide into the environment.

A nearby processing plant captures the geothermal energy from its natural source, an underground hot zone in Iceland.

Gasoline burns cleaner when it is mixed with ethanol made from corn. Growing corn absorbs carbon dioxide from the air.

14 Summarize Use the table to list advantages and disadvantages of geothermal and biomass energy sources.

Energy source	Advantages	Disadvantages
Geothermal		
Biomass		

15 Justify Which of the alternative energy sources do you think would have the least impact on the environment? Explain.

_____
_____
_____
_____
_____

© Houghton Mifflin Harcourt Publishing Company • Image Credits: (bkgd) ©Neale Clark/Robert Harding World Imagery/Getty Images; (inset) ©Photodisc/Getty Images

Acid Rain

Burning some fossil fuels produces the gases sulfur dioxide and nitrogen oxides. Acid rain forms when these gases combine with water in the air and then fall to Earth as rain. The acids have harmful effects on plants, aquatic animals, and human-made objects, such as buildings.

Effect on Aquatic Organisms

Acid rain falling into rivers and lakes changes the acidity of the water. Fish and other aquatic life forms can become deformed or die.

Effect on Materials

The acids in acid rain react with metals and with substances in marble and stone. The surface becomes weakened and wears away, as shown on this statue.

Effect on Trees

Acid rain damages leaves and causes substances toxic to trees to be released from the soil in which the trees live.

Extend

Inquiry

16 Predict Develop a prediction about where the effects of acid rain would be the most pronounced.

17 Assemble Gather more information about acid rain and organize this information in a poster or illustrated report. Present your poster to your class.

18 Research Identify an area somewhere in the world that has been affected by acid rain. What effects are clearly visible? How might those effects be reduced?

© Houghton Mifflin Harcourt Publishing Company • Image Credits: (bkgd) ©Photoshot Holdings Ltd/Alamy; (c) ©Bettmann/Corbis; (cr) ©Mark Leach/Alamy

Visual Summary

To complete this summary, fill in the blank for each statement. Then, use the key below to check your answers. You can use this page to review the main concepts of the lesson.

Energy sources may be renewable or nonrenewable.

19 _____ resources are those that are easily replaced in nature.

Obtaining, transporting, and burning fossil fuels has many environmental consequences.

20 Spills that endanger animals sometimes occur while transporting _____

Energy and the Environment

Alternative energy sources have the potential to replace fossil fuels.

21 Sources of renewable alternative energy include wind, solar, hydroelectric,

_____ , and

_____

Answers: 19 renewable; 20 oil; 21 biomass, geothermal

22 Debate What are some arguments for and against the use of alternative energy sources rather than fossil fuels?

© Houghton Mifflin Harcourt Publishing Company • Image Credits: (tl) ©H. Mark Weidman Photography/Alamy; (tr) ©AP Photo/Jack Smith, File; (b) ©Getty Images

Lesson Review

Vocabulary

Circle the terms that best complete the following sentences.

1 An example of a renewable energy resource is *uranium/wind/natural gas*.

2 An example of a nonrenewable energy resource is *the sun/biomass/coal*.

3 Fossil fuels include petroleum, coal, and *natural gas/biomass/geothermal*.

Key Concepts

4 Explain How might a renewable energy source become nonrenewable?

_____

_____

_____

_____

_____

5 Differentiate Compare the environmental consequences related to obtaining the three major types of fossil fuels.

_____

_____

_____

_____

_____

_____

6 Summarize Why are wind, hydroelectric, and geothermal energy resources not suitable for providing energy worldwide?

_____

_____

_____

_____

_____

_____

_____

Critical Thinking

Use this table to answer the following questions.

The Role of Renewable Energy Resources in the Nation's Energy Supply

U.S. Energy Supply		Renewable Energy	
petroleum	37%	biomass	50%
natural gas	25%	hydropower	35%
coal	21%	wind	9%
nuclear electric power	9%	geothermal	5%
renewable energy	8%	solar	1%

Source: U.S. Energy Information Administration

7 Analyze What percentage of the total energy supply was provided by fossil fuels?

_____

8 Analyze Which renewable resource had the highest percentage of use?

_____

9 Recommend Which alternative energy source do you think should be developed in the future? Explain.

_____

_____

_____

_____

10 Evaluate What factors will be important in deciding the future use of energy resources?

_____

_____

_____

_____

_____

_____

© Houghton Mifflin Harcourt Publishing Company

My Notes

© Houghton Mifflin Harcourt Publishing Company

© Houghton Mifflin Harcourt Publishing Company

Big Idea Energy exists in different forms and can change from one form to another, but energy is always conserved.

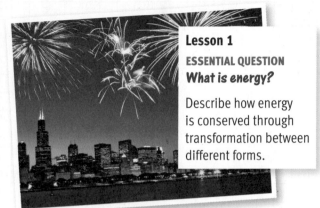

Lesson 1
ESSENTIAL QUESTION
What is energy?

Describe how energy is conserved through transformation between different forms.

Lesson 3
ESSENTIAL QUESTION
What is the relationship between heat and temperature?

Analyze the relationship between heat, temperature, and thermal energy.

Lesson 2
ESSENTIAL QUESTION
How can we calculate kinetic and potential energy?

Calculate kinetic and potential energy and know how these two types of energy are related.

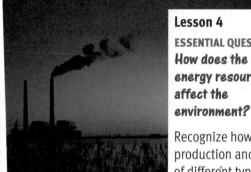

Lesson 4
ESSENTIAL QUESTION
How does the use of energy resources affect the environment?

Recognize how the production and use of different types of energy resources can have environmental consequences.

Connect **ESSENTIAL QUESTIONS**
Lessons 1 and 3

1 **Synthesize** Give an example of an energy transformation that results in a temperature change.

_____
_____
_____
_____
_____
_____
_____

Think Outside the Book

2 **Synthesize** Choose one of these activities to help synthesize what you have learned in this unit.

☐ Using what you learned in lessons 1, 2, and 3, explain the movement of particles in a cold glass as energy is transferred to it from warm hands by making a poster presentation. Include captions and labels.

☐ Using what you learned in lessons 1 and 4, describe the energy conversions related to the use of renewable and nonrenewable energy resources by creating a brochure.

© Houghton Mifflin Harcourt Publishing Company • Image Credits: (tl) ©Thinkstock/Getty Images; (tr) ©Carsten Peter/National Geographic/Getty Images; (bl) ©Steve Allen/Photo Researchers, Inc.; (br) ©Mark Green/Taxi/Getty Images

Unit 1 Review

Name _____

Vocabulary

Check the box to show whether each statement is true or false.

T	F	
☐	☐	**1** A <u>fossil fuel</u> is a renewable resource formed from the remains of ancient organisms.
☐	☐	**2** <u>Mechanical energy</u> is the sum of an object's kinetic and potential energy.
☐	☐	**3** A <u>renewable resource</u> forms at a rate that is much slower than the rate in which the resource is used.
☐	☐	**4** The amount of <u>kinetic energy</u> and <u>potential energy</u> in a system can be calculated.
☐	☐	**5** <u>Heat</u> is the energy transferred from an object at a higher temperature to an object at a lower temperature.

Key Concepts

Read each question below, and circle the best answer.

6 How could two objects have the same temperature but different thermal energies?

A One object could have more heat.

B One object could have more calories.

C One object could have more particles and lesser total kinetic energy.

D One object could have more particles and greater total kinetic energy.

7 What is any energy resource that can be used in place of fossil fuels called?

A alternative energy

C nuclear energy

B solar energy

D biomass energy

8 Energy exists in different forms. Which of the following forms of energy best describes the energy stored in food?

A radiant energy

C sound energy

B mechanical energy

D chemical energy

© Houghton Mifflin Harcourt Publishing Company

9 A mass hanging from a spring moves up and down. The mass stops moving temporarily each time the spring is extended to its fullest at Position 2 and each time it returns to its tight coil at Position 4.

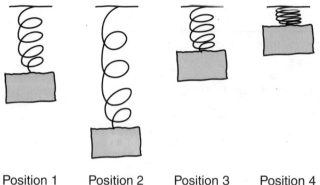

| Position 1 | Position 2 | Position 3 | Position 4 |

Which answer choice best describes the type of energy the spring has at Position 1?

A potential energy

B kinetic energy

C both potential energy and kinetic energy

D neither potential energy or kinetic energy

10 Which of the following is the transfer of energy as heat by the movement of a liquid or gas?

A conduction

B convection

C emission

D radiation

11 Which of the following terms means the amount of energy needed to raise the temperature of 1 gram of water by 1 degree Celsius?

A heat

B temperature

C thermal energy

D calorie

© Houghton Mifflin Harcourt Publishing Company

12 A student collects and records the following data throughout the day.

Time	Temperature (°C)
9 a.m.	12
11 a.m.	14
3 p.m.	16
5 p.m.	13

What instrument did the student use to collect these data?

A barometer

B scale

C thermometer

D balance

13 What is the difference between a conductor and an insulator?

A Wood is a good conductor but not a good insulator.

B Metal is a good insulator but not a good conductor.

C A conductor transmits energy very well while an insulator does not.

D An insulator transmits energy very well while a conductor does not.

Critical Thinking

Answer the following questions in the space provided.

14 Describe the law of conservation of energy.

_____

_____

_____

Give two examples of energy being transformed from one type to another.

_____

_____

_____

_____

_____

© Houghton Mifflin Harcourt Publishing Company

15 Three thermometers are lined up side by side.

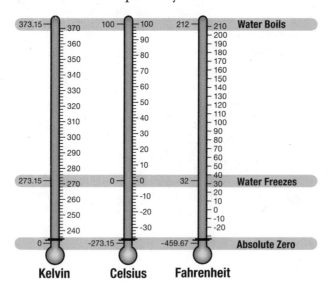

If the temperature outside is 60°F, what is the approximate temperature on the Celsius scale? _____ What is the approximate temperature on the Kelvin scale? _____

If the air temperature drops to 30°F during the night, how has the kinetic energy of the air particles changed?

_____

Connect ESSENTIAL QUESTIONS
Lessons 1, 2 and 3

Answer the following question in the space provided.

16 Describe the energy transformations involved in the creation and burning of fossil fuels to produce electricity.

_____

_____

_____

Does all of the energy in burned fossil fuel become electricity? Explain.

_____

_____

Does the law of conservation of energy apply to burning fossil fuels? Explain.

_____

_____

© Houghton Mifflin Harcourt Publishing Company

Interactions of Living Things

© Houghton Mifflin Harcourt Publishing Company • Image Credits: (bkgd) ©Comstock/age fotostock; (br) ©Millard H. Sharp/Photo Researchers, Inc.

Big Idea

Organisms interact with each other and with the nonliving parts of their environment.

6.LS2.1, 6.LS2.2, 6.LS2.3, 6.LS2.4, 6.LS2.7, 6.ESS3.3

Fish and sponges in a coral reef.

What do you think?

Ecosystems consist of living things that depend on each other to survive. How might these fish depend on a coral reef? How might this bird depend on a dragonfly population?

Eastern bluebirds feed on insects.

Interactions of Living Things

CITIZEN SCIENCE

Sharing Spaces

Wetlands provide living space for many kinds of birds. Ospreys are large birds of prey that eat mostly fish. They often nest on telephone poles and other man-made structures. Yellow-rumped warblers are small birds that live in trees and eat insects and berries.

① Ask A Question

How can organisms affect each other and a whole ecosystem?

An ecosystem is made up of all the living and nonliving things in an environment. Ospreys and yellow-rumped warblers are part of the same ecosystem. With your teacher and your classmates, brainstorm ways in which ospreys and yellow-rumped warblers might affect each other.

Yellow-rumped Warbler

© Houghton Mifflin Harcourt Publishing Company • Image Credits: (bkgd) ©Terry J Alcorn/iStockPhoto.com; (br) ©blickwinkel/Alamy

② Think About It

A Look at the photos of the ospreys in their environment. List at least two resources they need to survive and explain how the ospreys get them.

_____

_____

_____

B What are two ways nonliving things could affect yellow-rumped warblers?

_____

_____

_____

Osprey nest

③ Apply Your Knowledge

A List the ways in which yellow-rumped warblers and ospreys share resources.

_____

_____

_____

B Yellow-rumped warblers have a diet that consists mainly of insects and berries. Make a list of other organisms you know that might compete with the warblers for these same food resources.

_____

_____

_____

_____

C Describe a situation that could negatively affect both the osprey population and the yellow-rumped warbler population.

_____

_____

_____

Take It Home

Are ecologists looking for people to report observations in your community? Contact a university near your community to see if you can help gather information about plants, flowers, birds, or invasive species. Then, share your results with your class. See _ScienceSaurus_® for more information about ecosystems.

© Houghton Mifflin Harcourt Publishing Company • Image Credits: (bkgd) ©Terry Alcorn/iStockPhoto.com; (tl) ©INTERFOTO/Alamy

Introduction to Ecology

ESSENTIAL QUESTION

How are different parts of the environment connected?

By the end of this lesson, you should be able to analyze the parts of an environment.

6.LS2.1, 6.LS2.4

This rain forest is an ecosystem. Hornbills are organisms in the ecosystem that use the trees for shelter.

© Houghton Mifflin Harcourt Publishing Company • Image Credits: ©Timothy Laman/National Geographic/Getty Images

 Lesson Labs

Quick Labs
- Which Abiotic and Biotic Factors Are Found in an Ecosystem?
- Which Biome?

Field Lab
- What's in an Ecosystem?

 **Engage Your Brain**

1 Describe In your own words, write a list of living or nonliving things that are in your neighborhood.

_____

_____

_____

_____

_____

_____

_____

_____

2 Relate Write a photo caption that compares the ecosystem shown below and the ecosystem shown on the previous page.

_____

_____

_____

_____

_____

 Active Reading

3 Synthesize You can often define an unknown word or term if you know the meaning of its word parts. Use the word parts and sentence below to make an educated guess about the meaning of the term *abiotic factor*.

Word part	Meaning
a-	without
bio-	life

Example sentence

In an ecosystem, rocks are an example of an <u>abiotic factor</u> since they are not a living part of the environment.

abiotic factor:

_____

_____

Vocabulary Terms

- ecology
- biotic factor
- abiotic factor
- population
- species
- community
- ecosystem
- biome
- habitat
- niche

4 Apply As you learn the definition of each vocabulary term in this lesson, create your own definition or sketch to help you remember the meaning of the term.

© Houghton Mifflin Harcourt Publishing Company • Image Credits: ©Agus Photo/Alamy

The Web of Life

How are all living things connected?

Organisms need energy and matter to live. Interactions between organisms cause an exchange of energy and matter. This exchange creates a web of life in which all organisms are connected to each other and to their environment. **Ecology** is the study of how organisms interact with one another and with the environment.

Through the Living Environment

Each individual organism has a role to play in the flow of energy and matter. In this way, organisms are connected to all other organisms. Relationships among organisms affect each one's growth and survival. A **biotic factor** is an interaction between organisms in an area. Competition is one way that organisms interact. For example, different kinds of plants might compete for water in the desert.

This desert includes all of the organisms that live there, and all of the living and nonliving things that they need to survive.

This horse is a part of the living environment.

© Houghton Mifflin Harcourt Publishing Company • Image Credits: ©peter foley/Moment Open/Getty Images

Through the Nonliving Environment

All organisms rely on the nonliving environment for survival. An **abiotic factor** is a nonliving part of an environment, such as water, nutrients, soil, sunlight, rainfall, or temperature. Some of these are resources that organisms need to grow and survive. For example, plants use sunlight, water, and soil nutrients to make food. Similarly, some organisms rely on soil or rocks for shelter.

Abiotic factors influence where organisms can survive. In a terrestrial environment, temperature and rainfall are important abiotic factors. In aquatic environments, the water's temperature, salt, and oxygen content are important abiotic factors. Changes in these basic abiotic factors affect where organisms can live and how many individuals are able to survive in the environment.

Active Reading **5 Infer** How does the environment determine where an organism can survive? Explain your answer.

_____

_____

_____

_____

_____

_____

The rocks and air are parts of the nonliving environment.

Visualize It!

6 Categorize List the abiotic factors that are present in the photo.

_____   _____

_____   _____

7 Relate Choose one abiotic factor that you listed above and explain how the horse interacts with it.

_____

_____

_____

© Houghton Mifflin Harcourt Publishing Company • Image Credits: ©peter foley/Moment Open/Getty Images

Stay Organized!

What are the levels of organization in the environment?

The environment can be organized into different levels. These levels range from a single organism to all of the organisms and their surroundings in an area. The levels of organization get more complex as more of the environment is considered.

Active Reading **8 Identify** As you read, underline the characteristics of each of the following levels of organization.

Populations

A **population** is a group of individuals of the same species that live in the same place at the same time. A **species** includes organisms that are closely related and can mate to produce fertile offspring. The alligators that live in the Everglades form a population. Individuals within a population often compete with each other for resources.

Population

Individual

© Houghton Mifflin Harcourt Publishing Company

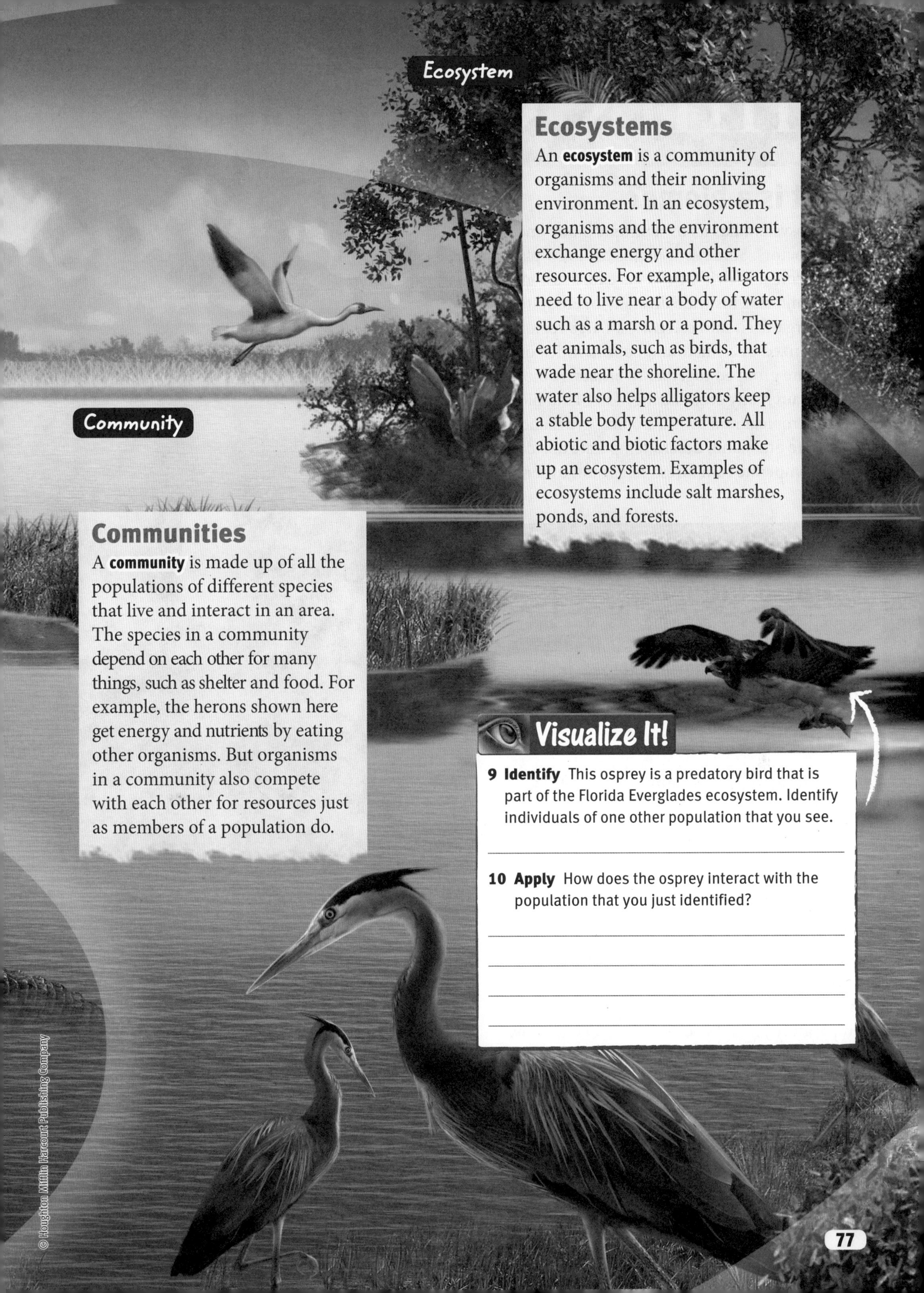

Ecosystems

An **ecosystem** is a community of organisms and their nonliving environment. In an ecosystem, organisms and the environment exchange energy and other resources. For example, alligators need to live near a body of water such as a marsh or a pond. They eat animals, such as birds, that wade near the shoreline. The water also helps alligators keep a stable body temperature. All abiotic and biotic factors make up an ecosystem. Examples of ecosystems include salt marshes, ponds, and forests.

Community

Communities

A **community** is made up of all the populations of different species that live and interact in an area. The species in a community depend on each other for many things, such as shelter and food. For example, the herons shown here get energy and nutrients by eating other organisms. But organisms in a community also compete with each other for resources just as members of a population do.

👁 Visualize It!

9 Identify This osprey is a predatory bird that is part of the Florida Everglades ecosystem. Identify individuals of one other population that you see.

_____

10 Apply How does the osprey interact with the population that you just identified?

_____

_____

_____

_____

© Houghton Mifflin Harcourt Publishing Company

Think Globally!

This temperate rain forest gets a lot of rainfall. The organisms here have adapted to the wet climate.

What is a biome?

Each ecosystem has its own unique biotic and abiotic factors. Some ecosystems have few plants and are cold and dry. Others have forests and are hot and moist. This wide diversity of ecosystems can be organized into categories. Large regions characterized by climate and communities of species are grouped together as **biomes**. A biome can contain many ecosystems. Major land biomes include tropical rain forest, tropical grassland, temperate grassland, desert, temperate deciduous forest, temperate rain forest, taiga, and tundra.

What characteristics define a biome?

All of the ecosystems in a biome share some traits. They share climate conditions, such as temperature and rainfall, and have similar communities.

Climate Conditions

Active Reading **11 Identify** As you read, underline the climate factors that characterize biomes.

Temperature is an important climate factor that characterizes biomes. For example, some biomes have a constant temperature. The taiga and tundra have cold temperatures all year. Tropical biomes are warm all year. In other biomes, the temperature changes over the course of a year. Temperate biomes have warm summers and colder winters. In some biomes, major temperature changes occur within a single day. For example, some deserts are hot during the day but cold at night.

Biomes also differ in the amount of precipitation they receive. For example, tropical biomes receive a lot of rainfall, while deserts receive little precipitation. The taiga and tundra have moist summers and dry winters.

Think Outside the Book Inquiry

12 Apply What biome do you live in? Describe your climate and make a list of the living things that are found in natural undeveloped areas nearby. Research which biome has these features. Then look at a biome map to see if your observations match the biome that is mapped for your location.

© Houghton Mifflin Harcourt Publishing Company • Image Credits: ©Andrew Brown/Photo Researchers, Inc.

Communities of Living Things

Biomes contain communities of living things that have adapted to the climate of the region. Thus, ecosystems within the same biome tend to have similar species across the globe. Monkeys, vines, and colorful birds live in hot and humid tropical rain forests. Grasses, large mammals, and predatory birds inhabit tropical grasslands on several continents.

Only certain types of plants and animals can live in extreme climate conditions. For example, caribou, polar bears, and small plants live in the tundra, but trees cannot grow there. Similarly, the plant and animal species that live in the desert are also unique. Cacti and certain animal species have adaptations that let them tolerate the dry desert climate.

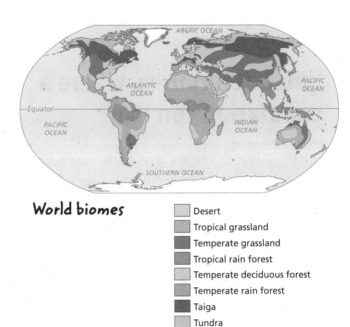

World biomes

☐ Desert
☐ Tropical grassland
☐ Temperate grassland
☐ Tropical rain forest
☐ Temperate deciduous forest
☐ Temperate rain forest
☐ Taiga
☐ Tundra

 **Visualize It!**

13 Compare The photos below show two different biomes. Use what you learned about the characteristics of biomes to compare these environments, and then explain why they are categorized as different biomes. Write your answers in the space provided.

Compare: _____
_____
_____
_____
_____
_____
_____

Explain: _____
_____
_____
_____
_____
_____
_____
_____
_____

© Houghton Mifflin Harcourt Publishing Company • Image Credits: (t) ©Paul A. Souders/Corbis; (b) ©Staffan Widstrand/Corbis

Home Sweet Home

What determines where a population can live?

Ecologists study the specific needs of different kinds of organisms and the role each species plays in the environment. Organisms that live in the same area have different ways of getting the resources they need.

Niche

Each population in an ecosystem plays a specific role. A population's **niche** (NICH) is the abiotic conditions under which individuals can survive and the role they play in the ecosystem. For example, one part of a shark population's niche is eating fish.

A **habitat** is the place where an organism usually lives and is part of an organism's niche. The habitat must provide all of the resources that an organism needs to grow and survive. Abiotic factors, such as temperature, often influence whether a species can live in a certain place. Biotic factors, such as the interactions with other organisms that live in the area, also play a role. For example, the habitat of a shark must include populations of fish it can eat.

Two populations cannot occupy exactly the same niche. Even small differences in habitats, roles, and adaptations can allow similar species to live together in the same ecosystem. For example, green and brown anoles sometimes live on the same trees, but they avoid competition by living in different parts of the trees.

14 Relate How is a habitat like a person's address? How is a niche like a person's job?

_____

_____

_____

_____

_____

_____

_____

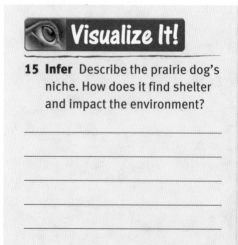

Visualize It!

15 Infer Describe the prairie dog's niche. How does it find shelter and impact the environment?

_____

_____

_____

_____

_____

Prairie dogs dig burrows in grassy plains. They eat plants and are hunted by predators such as owls and foxes.

© Houghton Mifflin Harcourt Publishing Company • Image Credits: ©Raymond K. Gehman/National Geographic/Getty Images

Lizard Invasion

Green anole lizards (*Anolis carolinensis*) have been part of the South Florida ecosystem for a long time. Recently, a closely related lizard, the nonnative brown anole (*Anolis sagrei*), invaded the green anoles' habitat. How do they avoid competing with each other for resources?

Home Base

Green anoles live on perches throughout a tree. Brown anoles live mainly on branches that are close to the ground. If they have to share a tree, green anoles will move away from perches close to the ground. In this way, both kinds of anoles can live in the same tree while avoiding competition with each other.

Intrusive Neighbors

Although brown and green anoles can coexist by sharing their habitats, they do not live together peacefully. For example, brown anoles affect green anoles by eating their young.

© Houghton Mifflin Harcourt Publishing Company • Image Credits: (bkgd) ©Wirepec/iStockphoto.com/Getty Images; (l) ©Tim Laman/Getty Images; (t) ©Trevor Hunt/Getty Images

Extend

Inquiry

16 Describe How do green and brown anoles avoid competition? Draw a picture of a tree showing both green and brown anoles living in it.

17 Research What are other examples of two species dividing up the parts of a habitat?

18 Relate Infer what would happen if the habitats of two species overlapped. Present your findings in a format such as a short story, a music video, or a play.

81

Visual Summary

To complete this summary, circle the correct word. Then use the key below to check your answers. You can use this page to review the main concepts of the lesson.

Ecology and Ecosystems

Ecology is the study of the biotic and abiotic factors in an ecosystem, and the relationships between them.

19 In a desert ecosystem, the sand is a(n) biotic / abiotic factor, and a lizard eating an insect is a(n) biotic / abiotic factor.

Every organism has a habitat and a niche.

20 Horses that live in the desert feed on other organisms that live there, such as low, dry shrubs. In this example, the desert is a habitat / niche and the horses' feeding behavior is part of a habitat / niche.

The environment can be organized into different levels, including populations, communities, and ecosystems.

21 Populations of cacti, together with sand and rocks, are included in a desert community / ecosystem.

Biomes are characterized by climate conditions and the communities of living things found within them.

22 Biomes are large / small regions that make up / contain ecosystems.

Answers: 19 abiotic, biotic; 20 habitat, niche; 21 ecosystem; 22 large, contain

23 **Predict** In the desert ecosystem shown above, name a biotic factor, and describe the effect on the horses if it were removed from the ecosystem.

© Houghton Mifflin Harcourt Publishing Company • Image Credits: © Pete Foley/Moment Open/Getty Images

Lesson Review

Vocabulary

1 Explain how the meanings of the terms *biotic factor* and *abiotic factor* differ.

_____

_____

_____

2 In your own words, write a definition for *ecology*.

_____

_____

_____

3 Explain how the meanings of the terms *habitat* and *niche* differ.

_____

_____

_____

Key Concepts

4 Compare What is the relationship between ecosystems and biomes?

_____

_____

_____

_____

5 Explain Within each biome, how can the environment be organized into levels from complex to simple?

_____

_____

_____

_____

6 Infer How do the populations in a community depend on each other?

_____

_____

_____

7 Identify What factors determine where a population can live?

_____

_____

_____

_____

Critical Thinking

8 Evaluate How might populations be affected in a tropical rain forest biome if the area received very little rain for an extended period of time?

_____

_____

_____

_____

9 Infer Owls and hawks both eat rodents. They are also found in the same habitats. Since no two populations can occupy exactly the same niche, how can owls and hawks coexist?

_____

_____

_____

_____

_____

Use this graph to answer the following question.

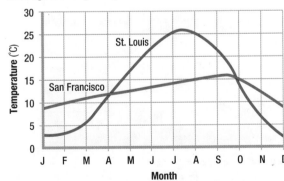

Average Monthly Temperatures

10 Interpret What is the difference in average temperature between the two cities in July?

© Houghton Mifflin Harcourt Publishing Company

My Notes

© Houghton Mifflin Harcourt Publishing Company

© Houghton Mifflin Harcourt Publishing Company

Kenneth Krysko
ECOLOGIST

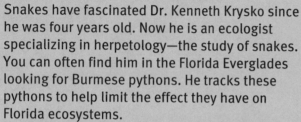

Snakes have fascinated Dr. Kenneth Krysko since he was four years old. Now he is an ecologist specializing in herpetology—the study of snakes. You can often find him in the Florida Everglades looking for Burmese pythons. He tracks these pythons to help limit the effect they have on Florida ecosystems.

Burmese pythons can grow to be 6 meters long. They are native to southeast Asia and were illegally brought to Florida as pets. Many owners released them into the wild when the snakes grew too large. The snakes breed well in Florida's subtropical climate. And they eat just about any animal they can swallow, including many native species. Dr. Krysko tracks down these invasive pythons. Through wildlife management, molecular genetics, and other areas of study, he works with other scientists to search for ways to reduce the python population.

Dr. Krysko studies many other invasive species, that is, nonnative species that can do harm in Florida ecosystems. He shares what he learns, including ways to identify and deal with invasive species with other ecologists. Along with invasion ecology, he has done research in reproduction and conservation biology. Dr. Krysko also works as a collections manager in the herpetology division at the Florida Museum of Natural History.

Dr. Krysko works to get a handle on what to do about the invasive pythons.

© Houghton Mifflin Harcourt Publishing Company • Image Credits: (bkgd) ©Willard Clay/Taxi/Getty Images; (tr) ©Dorling Kindersley/Getty Images; (bl) ©Dr. Kenneth Krysko

JOB BOARD

Park Naturalist

What You'll Do: Teach visitors at state and national parks about the park's ecology, geology, and landscape. Lead field trips, prepare and deliver lectures with slides, and create educational programs for park visitors. You may participate in research projects and track organisms in the park.

Where You Might Work: State and national parks

Education: An advanced degree in science and teacher certification

Other Job Requirements: You need to be good at communicating and teaching. Having photography and writing skills helps you prepare interesting educational materials.

Conservation Warden

What You'll Do: Patrol an area to enforce rules, and work with communities and groups to help educate the public about conservation and ecology.

Where You Might Work: Indoors and outdoors in state and national parks and ecologically sensitive areas

Education: A two-year associate's degree or at least 60 fully accredited college-level credits

Other Job Requirements: To work in the wild, good wilderness skills, map-reading, hiking, and excellent hearing are useful.

PEOPLE IN SCIENCE NEWS

Phil McCRORY

Saved by a Hair!

Phil McCrory, a hairdresser in Huntsville, Alabama, asked a brilliant question when he saw an otter whose fur was drenched with oil from the Exxon Valdez oil spill. If the otter's fur soaked up oil, why wouldn't human hair do the same? McCrory gathered hair from the floor of his salon and performed his own experiments. He stuffed hair into a pair of pantyhose and tied the ankles together. McCrory floated this bundle in his son's wading pool and poured used motor oil into the center of the ring. When he pulled the ring closed, not a drop of oil remained in the water! McCrory's discovery was tested as an alternative method for cleaning up oil spills. Many people donated their hair to be used for cleanup efforts. Although the method worked well, the engineers conducting the research concluded that hair is not as useful as other oil-absorbing materials for cleaning up large-scale spills.

© Houghton Mifflin Harcourt Publishing Company • Image Credits: (bkgd) ©Willard Clay/Taxi/Getty Images; (br) ©Terry Fincher.Photo Int/Alamy

Roles in Energy Transfer

ESSENTIAL QUESTION

How does energy flow through an ecosystem?

By the end of this lesson, you should be able to relate the roles of organisms to the transfer of energy in food chains, food webs, and food pyramids.

6.LS2.3, 6.ESS3.3

Energy is transferred from the sun to producers, such as kelp. It flows through the rest of the ecosystem.

This fish also needs energy to live. How do you think it gets this energy? From the sun like kelp do?

© Houghton Mifflin Harcourt Publishing Company • Image Credits: © Steven Trainoff Ph.D./Flickr/Getty Images

Lesson Labs

Quick Labs
- Making Compost
- Energy Role Game

Field Lab
- Food Webs

Engage Your Brain

1 Describe Most organisms on Earth get energy from the sun. How is energy flowing through the ecosystem pictured on the opposite page?

_____
_____
_____
_____
_____

2 Predict List two of your favorite foods. Then, explain how the sun's energy helped make those foods available to you.

_____
_____
_____
_____
_____

Active Reading

3 Synthesize You can often define an unknown word if you know the meaning of its word parts. Use the word parts and sentences below to make an educated guess about the meaning of the words *herbivore* and *carnivore*.

Word part	Meaning
-vore	to eat
herbi-	plant
carni-	meat

Example sentence
A koala bear is an <u>herbivore</u> that eats eucalyptus leaves.

herbivore:

_____
_____
_____

Example sentence
A great white shark is a <u>carnivore</u> that eats fish and other marine animals.

carnivore:

_____
_____
_____

Vocabulary Terms

- producer
- decomposer
- consumer
- herbivore
- carnivore
- omnivore
- food chain
- food web
- energy pyramid

4 Apply As you learn the definition of each vocabulary term in this lesson, create your own definition or sketch to help you remember the meaning of the term.

© Houghton Mifflin Harcourt Publishing Company • Image Credits: ©Steven Trainoff Ph.D./Flickr/Getty Images

Get Energized!

How do organisms get energy?

Energy is all around you. Chemical energy is stored in the bonds of molecules and holds molecules together. The energy from food is chemical energy in the bonds of food molecules. All living things need a source of chemical energy to survive.

Active Reading **6 Identify** As you read, underline examples of producers, decomposers, and consumers.

Think Outside the Book

5 Apply Record what you eat at your next meal. Where do you think these items come from, before they reach the market?

Producers Convert Energy Into Food

A **producer**, also called an autotroph, uses energy to make food. Most producers use sunlight to make food in a process called photosynthesis. The sun powers most life on Earth. In photosynthesis, producers use light energy to make food from water, carbon dioxide, and nutrients found in water and soil. The food contains chemical energy and can be used immediately or stored for later use. All green plants, such as grasses and trees, are producers. Algae and some bacteria are also producers. The food that these producers make supplies the energy for other living things in an ecosystem.

Decomposers Break Down Matter

An organism that gets energy and nutrients by breaking down the remains of other organisms is a **decomposer**. Fungi, such as the mushrooms on this log, and some bacteria are decomposers. Decomposers are nature's recyclers. By converting dead organisms and animal and plant waste into materials such as water and nutrients, decomposers help move matter through ecosystems. Decomposers make these simple materials available to other organisms.

These mushrooms are decomposers. They break down the remains of plants and animals.

This plant is a producer. Producers make food using light energy from the sun.

© Houghton Mifflin Harcourt Publishing Company • Image Credits: (l) ©Jason Edwards/National Geographic/Getty Images; (r) ©Jaileybug/Alamy

Consumers Eat Other Organisms

A **consumer** is an organism that eats other organisms. Consumers use the energy and nutrients stored in other living organisms because they cannot make their own food. A consumer that eats only plants, such as a grasshopper or bison, is called an **herbivore**. A **carnivore**, such as a badger or this wolf, eats other animals. An **omnivore** eats both plants and animals. A *scavenger* is a specialized consumer that feeds on dead organisms. Scavengers, such as the turkey vulture, eat the leftovers of the meals of other animals or eat dead animals.

This wolf is a consumer. It eats other organisms to get energy.

Consumers

Visualize It!

7 List Beside each image, place a check mark next to the word that matches the type of consumer the animal is.

Name: Hedgehog
What I eat: leaves, earthworms, insects

What am I?
- ☐ herbivore
- ☐ omnivore
- ☐ carnivore

Name: Moose
What I eat: grasses, fruits

What am I?
- ☐ herbivore
- ☐ omnivore
- ☐ carnivore

Name: Komodo dragon
What I eat: insects, birds, mammals

What am I?
- ☐ herbivore
- ☐ omnivore
- ☐ carnivore

8 Infer Explain how carnivores might be affected if the main plant species in a community were to disappear.

_____

_____

_____

© Houghton Mifflin Harcourt Publishing Company • Image Credits: (l) ©DLILLC/Corbis; (tr) ©Hans Reinhard/Corbis; (cr) ©Arco Images GmbH/Alamy; (br) ©Danita Delimont/Alamy

Energy Transfer

How is energy transferred among organisms?

Organisms change energy from the environment or from their food into other types of energy. Some of this energy is used for the organism's activities, such as breathing or moving. Some of the energy is saved within the organism to use later. If an organism is eaten or decomposes, the consumer or decomposer takes in the energy stored in the original organism. Only chemical energy that an organism has stored in its tissues is available to consumers. In this way, energy is transferred from organism to organism.

Active Reading **9 Infer** When a grasshopper eats grass, only some of the energy from the grass is stored in the grasshopper's body. How does the grasshopper use the rest of the energy?

_____

_____

This tree gets its energy from the sun.

10 Identify By what process does this tree get its energy?

_____

_____

This ant eats plants like the mesquite tree, and other insects.

11 Apply What type of energy is this ant consuming?

_____

_____

© Houghton Mifflin Harcourt Publishing Company • Image Credits: (bkgd) ©Creative Travel Projects/Shutterstock; (t) ©Jamie Pham/Alamy; (l) ©Perennou Nuridsany/Photo Researchers, Inc.

Energy Flows Through a Food Chain

A **food chain** is the path of energy transfer from producers to consumers. Energy moves from one organism to the next in one direction. The arrows in a food chain represent the transfer of energy, as one organism is eaten by another. Arrows represent the flow of energy from the body of the consumed organism to the body of the consumer of that organism.

Producers form the base of food chains. Producers transfer energy to the first, or primary, consumer in the food chain. The next, or secondary, consumer in the food chain consumes the primary consumer. A tertiary consumer eats the secondary consumer. Finally, decomposers recycle matter back to the soil.

 **Visualize It!**

The photographs below show a typical desert food chain. Answer the following four questions from left to right based on your understanding of how energy flows in a food chain.

This hawk eats the lizard. It is at the top of the food chain.

13 Predict If nothing ever eats this hawk, what might eventually happen to the energy that is stored in its body?

_____

_____

This lizard eats mostly insects.

12 Apply What does the arrow between the ant and the lizard represent?

_____

_____

© Houghton Mifflin Harcourt Publishing Company • Image Credits: (bkgd) ©Jamie Pham/Alamy; (l) ©Trubacha/iStock/Getty Images Plus/Getty Images; (r) ©James McLaughlin/Alamy

World Wide Webs

How do food webs show energy connections?

Active Reading

14 Identify Underline the type of organism that typically forms the base of the food web.

Few organisms eat just one kind of food. So, the energy and nutrient connections in nature are more complicated than a simple food chain. A **food web** is the feeding relationships among organisms in an ecosystem. Food webs are made up of many food chains.

The next page shows a coastal food web. Most of the organisms in this food web live in the water. The web also includes some birds that live on land and eat fish. Tiny algae called phytoplankton form the base of this food web. Like plants on land, phytoplankton are producers. Tiny consumers called zooplankton eat phytoplankton. Larger animals, such as fish and squid, eat zooplankton. At the top of each chain are top predators, animals that eat other animals but are rarely eaten. In this food web, the killer whale is a top predator. Notice how many different energy paths lead from phytoplankton to the killer whale.

Visualize It!

15 Apply Complete the statements to the right with the correct organism names from the food web.

ENERGY

Energy flows up the food web when

_____ eat puffins.

Puffins are connected to many organisms in the food web.

ENERGY

Puffins get energy by eating

_____ ,

_____ ,

and _____ .

© Houghton Mifflin Harcourt Publishing Company • Image Credits: ©Randy Rimland/Shutterstock

Food Web

The top predator is shown at the top of the food web. What is the top predator in this food web?

Killer whale

Gull

Seal

Puffin

Cod

Squid

Sand lance

Herring

Consumers can eat producers and other consumers.

Zooplankton

Phytoplankton

Producers, such as these phytoplankton, form the base of the food web.

© Houghton Mifflin Harcourt Publishing Company • Image Credits: (tl) ©Stockbyte/Getty Images; (tc) ©ImageState/Alamy; (tr) ©WILDLIFE GmbH/Alamy; (cl) ©Randy Rimland/Shutterstock; (cc) ©Jeff Rotman/Photo Researchers, Inc.; (cr) ©blickwinkel/Alamy; (bl) ©blickwinkel/Alamy; (bc) ©CLICK_HERE/Alamy; (br) ©PicturesScotland/Alamy; (inset top) ©Natural Visions/Alamy; (inset bottom) ©Science Photo Library/Alamy

How does energy move through an ecosystem?

Another way to visualize the transfer of energy between organisms is with an **energy pyramid**. The shape of a pyramid represents the decreasing amount of energy at each level of an ecosystem's food chain. The base of the pyramid represents the producer level of an ecosystem—organisms that utilize energy most efficiently. The second level represents primary consumers, and the third level represents secondary consumers. More levels can be added to represent tertiary consumers. At each level, energy is lost to the environment.

There is a direct relationship between the energy available to organisms at each level of a pyramid and population size. Secondary and tertiary consumers have smaller populations because there is less energy available to them.

> **Visualize It!**
>
> **16 Analyze** Describe how energy flows in the ecosystem represented by this food pyramid. How would you translate the pyramid into words?
>
> _____
> _____
> _____
> _____
> _____
> _____

Tertiary consumers

The amount of energy available and population size decrease as you go up the energy pyramid.

Secondary consumers

Primary consumers

Producers

© Houghton Mifflin Harcourt Publishing Company

How many levels can an energy pyramid have?

Ecosystems are more like pyramids than skyscrapers. There are limits to the number of levels they can have. Most ecosystems can only sustain tertiary consumers, not fourth- or fifth-level consumers. There is only so much energy in an ecosystem, and organisms lose energy at each level.

Organisms do not retain all of the energy they consume. Every action—even the act of consuming—requires energy. Organisms lose about 90% of all energy they consume in the form of heat. This heat is released into the environment. This phenomenon is known as the "10% rule." At each level of an ecosystem, only about 10% of energy is passed along.

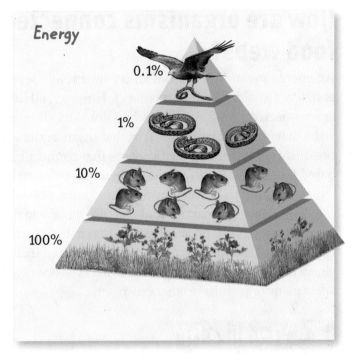

The 10% rule says that at each level of the energy pyramid, consumers only retain about 10% of the energy they consume.

Think Outside the Book Inquiry

17 Apply With a classmate, think of a local ecosystem and fill in the energy pyramid with producers and consumers. Label the percentages of energy retained at each level. Circle the organism with the highest population and explain your choice.

© Houghton Mifflin Harcourt Publishing Company

How are organisms connected by food webs?

An energy pyramid simplifies an ecosystem into levels to make it easier to visualize the flow of energy. However, all living organisms are connected by global food webs. Global food webs include webs that begin on land and webs that begin in the water. Many organisms have feeding relationships that connect land- and water-based food webs. For example, algae might be eaten by a fish, which might then be eaten by a bird.

Food webs that start on land may also move into the water. Many insects that eat plants on land lay their eggs in the water. Some fish eat these eggs and the insect larvae that hatch from them. Because the global food webs are connected, removing even one organism can affect many organisms in other ecosystems.

20 Infer Gulls don't eat herring but they are still connected by the food web. How might gull populations be affected?

_____
_____
_____
_____

Visualize It!

Imagine how these organisms would be affected if herring disappeared from the food web. Answer the questions starting at the bottom of the page.

■ Puffin

■ Gull

■ Cod

■ Squid

Herring

18 Identify Put a check mark next to the organisms that eat herring.

19 Predict With no herring to eat, how might the eating habits of cod change?

_____
_____
_____
_____
_____
_____
_____
_____

© Houghton Mifflin Harcourt Publishing Company • Image Credits: (tr) ©Stockbyte/Getty Images; (cl) ©Randy Rimland/Shutterstock; (cc) ©Jeff Rotman/Photo Researchers, Inc.; (cr) ©blickwinkel/Alamy; (bl) ©blickwinkel/Alamy

Dangerous Competition

Sometimes species are introduced into a new area. These invasive species often compete with native species for energy resources, such as sunlight and food.

Full Coverage

The kudzu plant was introduced to stop soil erosion, but in the process it outgrew all the native plants, preventing them from getting sunlight. Sometimes it completely covers houses or cars!

Destructive Zebras

The zebra mussel is one of the most destructive invasive species in the United States. They eat by filtering tiny organisms out of the water, often leaving nothing for the native mussel species.

Across the Grass

The walking catfish can actually move across land to get from one pond to another! As a result, sometimes the catfish competes with native species for food.

Extend

Inquiry

21 Relate Describe how the competition between invasive and native species might affect a food web.

22 Describe Give an example of competition for a food resource that may occur in an ecosystem near you.

23 Illustrate Provide an illustration of your example of competition in a sketch or a short story. Be sure to include the important aspects of food webs that you learned in the lesson.

© Houghton Mifflin Harcourt Publishing Company • Image Credits: (bkgd) ©Valerie Giles/Photo Researchers, Inc.; (tl) ©Melissa Farlow/National Geographic/Getty Images; (l) ©Tom Myers/Photo Researchers, Inc.; (bl) ©Peter Yates/Photo Researchers, Inc.

Visual Summary

To complete this summary, circle the correct word. Then use the key below to check your answers. You can use this page to review the main concepts of the lesson.

Energy Transfer in Ecosystems

Organisms get energy in different ways.

- Producers make their own food.
- Consumers eat other living organisms.
- Decomposers break down dead organisms.

24 Herbivores, carnivores, and omnivores are three types of producers / consumers / decomposers.

Food chains, food webs, and energy pyramids describe the flow of energy in an ecosystem.

25 All food chains start with producers / consumers / decomposers.

Answers: 24 consumers; 25 producers

26 Predict Describe the effects on global food webs if the sun's energy could no longer reach Earth.

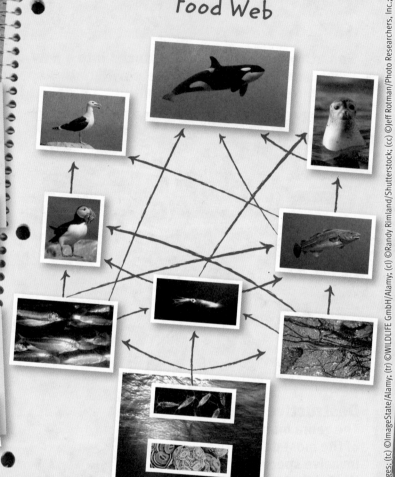

Food Web

© Houghton Mifflin Harcourt Publishing Company • Image Credits: (tl) ©Stockbyte/Getty Images; (tc) ©ImageState/Alamy; (tr) ©WILDLIFE GmbH/Alamy; (cl) ©Randy Rimland/Shutterstock; (cc) ©Jeff Rotman/Photo Researchers, Inc.; (cr) ©blickwinkel/Alamy; (bl) ©blickwinkel/Alamy; (bc) ©CLICK_HERE/Alamy; (br) ©PictureScotland/Alamy; (inset:top) ©Science Photo Library/Alamy; (inset:bottom) ©Natural Visions/Alamy

Lesson Review

Vocabulary

Fill in the blanks with the term that best completes the following sentences.

1 _____ is the primary source of energy for most ecosystems.

2 A _____ eats mostly dead matter.

3 A _____ contains many food chains.

4 _____ is the process by which light energy from the sun is converted to food.

Key Concepts

5 Describe What are the roles of producers, consumers, and decomposers in an ecosystem?

_____

_____

_____

_____

_____

6 Apply What types of organisms typically make up the base, middle, and top of a food web?

_____

_____

_____

_____

_____

_____

7 Describe Identify the two types of global food webs and describe how they are connected.

_____

_____

_____

_____

_____

Use the figure to answer the following questions.

8 Apply Describe the flow of energy in this food chain. Be sure to use the names of the organisms and what role they serve in the food chain (producer, consumer, or decomposer). If an organism is a consumer, identify whether it is an herbivore, carnivore, or omnivore.

_____

_____

_____

_____

9 Apply If the above illustration were converted to an energy pyramid, which organism would be placed at each level?

_____

_____

_____

Critical Thinking

10 Predict Give an example of a decomposer, and explain what would happen if decomposers were absent from a forest ecosystem.

_____

_____

_____

_____

11 Predict How would a food web be affected if a species disappeared from an ecosystem?

_____

_____

_____

_____

_____

© Houghton Mifflin Harcourt Publishing Company

My Notes

© Houghton Mifflin Harcourt Publishing Company

© Houghton Mifflin Harcourt Publishing Company

Population Dynamics

ESSENTIAL QUESTION

What determines a population's size?

By the end of this lesson, you should be able to explain how population size changes in response to environmental factors and interactions between organisms.

By looking like a snake, this caterpillar may scare off predators. However, the effectiveness of this defense depends on population size. If there are few real snakes, predators won't be fooled for long.

6.LS2.1, 6.LS2.2, 6.LS2.4, 6.ESS3.3

© Houghton Mifflin Harcourt Publishing Company • Image Credits: (p) ©Photoshot Holdings Ltd/Alamy

Lesson Labs

Quick Labs
• What Factors Influence a Population Change?
• Investigate an Abiotic Limiting Factor

Exploration Lab
• How Do Populations Interact?

Engage Your Brain

1 Predict Check T or F to show whether you think each statement is true or false.

T	F	
☐	☐	Plants compete for resources.
☐	☐	Populations of organisms never stop growing.
☐	☐	Animals never help other animals survive.
☐	☐	Living things need the nonliving parts of an environment to survive.

2 Explain When a chameleon eats a butterfly, what happens to the number of butterflies in the population? How could a sudden decrease in butterflies affect chameleons?

_____

_____

_____

Active Reading

3 Synthesize You can often define an unknown word if you know the meaning of its word parts. Use the word parts and sentences below to make an educated guess about the meaning of the words *immigrate* and *emigrate*.

Word part	Meaning
im-	into
e-	out
-migrate	move

Example sentence
Many deer will <u>immigrate</u> to the new park.

immigrate:

_____

Example sentence
Birds will <u>emigrate</u> from the crowded island.

emigrate:

_____

Vocabulary Terms

• carrying capacity   • competition
• limiting factor   • cooperation

4 Identify This list contains the vocabulary terms you'll learn in this lesson. As you read, circle the definition of each term.

© Houghton Mifflin Harcourt Publishing Company • Image Credits: (bg) ©Photoshot Holdings Ltd/Alamy; (tr) ©Heinrich van den Berg/Gallo Images/Getty Images

Movin' Out

How can a population grow or get smaller?

Active Reading **5 Identify** As you read, underline the processes that can cause a population to grow or to get smaller.

A population is a group of organisms of one species that lives in the same area at the same time. If new individuals are added to the population, it grows. The population gets smaller if individuals are removed from it. The population stays at about the same size if the number of individuals that are added is close to the number of individuals that are removed.

By Immigration and Emigration

Populations change in size when individuals move to new locations. *Immigration* occurs when individuals join a population. For example, fruit flies may travel on fruit to a new island. The population of fruit flies on the new island grows as fruit flies immigrate. *Emigration* occurs when individuals leave a population. The population of fruit flies on the original island decreases when fruit flies emigrate.

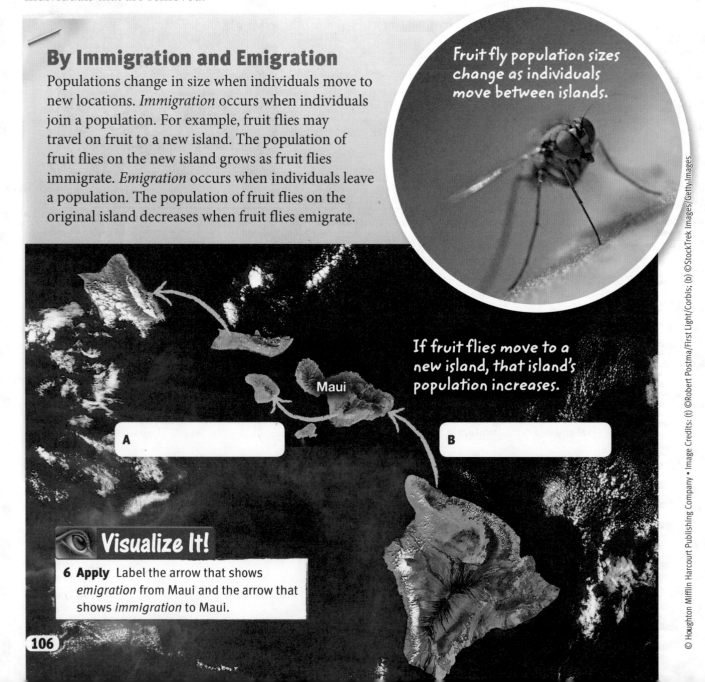

Fruit fly population sizes change as individuals move between islands.

Maui

A

B

If fruit flies move to a new island, that island's population increases.

Visualize It!

6 Apply Label the arrow that shows *emigration* from Maui and the arrow that shows *immigration* to Maui.

© Houghton Mifflin Harcourt Publishing Company • Image Credits: (t) ©Robert Postma/First Light/Corbis; (b) ©StockTrek Images/GettyImages

By Birth and Death

Populations increase as individuals are born. For example, consider a population of 100 deer in a forest. The population will increase if 20 fawns are born that year. But what if 12 deer are killed by predators or disease that year? Populations decrease as individuals die. If 20 deer are added and 12 are lost, the population will have an overall increase. At the end of the year, there will be 108 deer. The number of births compared to the number of deaths helps to determine if a population is increasing or decreasing.

Visualize It!

7 Apply Use the terms *birth*, *death*, and *immigration* to label each way that this population is changing.

An individual being carried off by a predator

A

A wandering male joins the population

B

A mother with nursing babies

C

© Houghton Mifflin Harcourt Publishing Company

Know Your Limits

What environmental factors influence population size?

A tropical rain forest can support large populations of trees. A desert, however, will probably support few or no trees. Each environment has different amounts of the resources that living things need, such as food, water, and space.

Resource Availability

The amount of resources in an area influences the size of a population. If important resources are lost from the environment, a population may shrink. The population may grow if the amount of resources in the environment is increased. But if the population continues to grow, the individuals would eventually run out of resources. The **carrying capacity** is the maximum number of individuals of one species that the environment can support. For example, the carrying capacity, or the number of owls that a forest can support, depends on how many mice are available to eat and how many trees are available for the owls to live in.

Deforestation causes a sudden change in resource availability.

© Houghton Mifflin Harcourt Publishing Company • Image Credits: (bg) ©DLILLC/Corbis; (inset) ©SuperStudio/Iconica/Getty Images

Animals use plants as food and shelter. Plants depend on sunlight and water as resources.

Visualize It!

8 Identify Make a list of each population in the image that would be affected by drought.

_____

_____

_____

_____

Changes in the Environment

The carrying capacity can change when the environment changes. For example, after a rainy season, plants may produce a large crop of leaves and seeds. This large amount of food may allow an herbivore population to grow. But what if important resources are destroyed? A population crash occurs when the carrying capacity of the environment suddenly drops. Natural disasters, such as forest fires, and harsh weather, such as droughts, can cause population crashes. The carrying capacity can also be reduced when new competitors enter an area and outcompete existing populations for resources. This would cause existing populations to become smaller or crash.

Active Reading **9 Describe** What are two ways in which the environment can influence population size?

_____

_____

_____

Drought slowly reduces the amount of water available as a resource to different populations.

Think Outside the Book

10 Apply With a classmate, discuss how the immigration of new herbivores might affect the carrying capacity of the local zebra population.

© Houghton Mifflin Harcourt Publishing Company • Image Credits: (bg) ©DLILLC/Corbis

Maximum Capacity

What factors can limit population size?

A part of the environment that keeps a population's size at a level below its full potential is called a **limiting factor**. Limiting factors can be living or nonliving things in an environment.

Abiotic Factors

The nonliving parts of an environment are called *abiotic factors*. Abiotic factors include water, nutrients, soil, sunlight, temperature, and living space. Organisms need these resources to survive. For example, plants use sunlight, water, and carbon dioxide to make food. If there are few rocks in a desert, lizard populations that use rocks for shelter will not become very large.

Biotic Factors

Relationships among organisms affect each one's growth and survival. A *biotic factor* is an interaction between living things. For example, zebras interact with many organisms. Zebras eat grass, and they compete with antelope for this food. Lions prey on zebras. Each of these interactions is a biotic factor that affects the population of zebras.

11 Apply Think about how people limit the populations of pests such as insects and mice. List one abiotic factor and one biotic factor that humans use to limit these pest populations.

Abiotic _____

Biotic _____

© Houghton Mifflin Harcourt Publishing Company • Image Credits: (t) ©Nigel Cattlin/Photo Researchers, Inc.; (c) ©William Manning Photography/ Alamy Royalty Free; (b) ©CW Images/Alamy Images

Visualize It!

12 Identify Label each of the following factors that limit plant population growth as abiotic or biotic.

This plant has a disease.

A

This plant grows between the rocks.

B

Herbivores are eating this leaf.

C

A Fungus Among Us!

In many parts of the world, frog populations are shrinking. We now know that many of these frogs have died because of a fungal infection.

Meet the fungus

Chytrid fungi [KY•trid FUHN•jy] live in water. They are important decomposers. One of them, called Bd, infects frogs.

Deadly Disease

Frogs take in oxygen and water through their skin. Bd interferes with this process. The fungus also affects an infected frog's nervous system.

Stop the Spread

Bd is found in wet mud. If you go hiking in muddy places, washing and drying your boots can help stop Bd from spreading.

Extend

Inquiry

13 Describe How does Bd fungus harm frogs?

14 Recommend Imagine that an endangered frog lives near an area where Bd was just found. How could you help protect that frog species?

15 Apply Design an experiment to test whether using soap or using bleach is the better way to clean boots to prevent Bd contamination. What are the independent and dependent variables? Remember to include a control in designing your experiment.

© Houghton Mifflin Harcourt Publishing Company • Image Credits: (bg) © Biology Pics/Photo Researchers, Inc.; (cl) ©Danny Lehman/Corbis; (br) ©HMH

111

Teamwork

Animals compete for access to water.

What interactions between organisms can influence population size?

As living things try to gather the resources they need, they often interact with each other. Sometimes interactions help one individual and harm another. At other times, all of the organisms benefit by working together.

Competition

When two or more individuals or populations try to use the same limited resource, such as food, water, shelter, space, or sunlight, it is called **competition**. Competition can happen among individuals within a population. The elk in a forest compete with each other for the same food plants. This competition increases in winter when many plants die. Competition also happens among populations. For example, different species of trees in a forest compete with each other for sunlight and space.

© Houghton Mifflin Harcourt Publishing Company • Image Credits: ©Natphotos/Digital Vision/Getty Images

Visualize It!

16 Predict The image above shows individuals from two populations competing for access to water.

What would happen to the size of the lion population if elephants usually won this competition?

_____

_____

_____

What would happen to each population if lions usually won this competition?

_____

_____

_____

© Houghton Mifflin Harcourt Publishing Company • Image Credits: ©Ted Kinsman/Photo Researchers, Inc.

17 Identify As you read, underline how cooperation can influence population dynamics.

Cooperation

Cooperation occurs when individuals work together. Some animals, such as killer whales, hunt in groups. Emperor penguins in Antarctica stay close together to stay warm. Some populations have a structured social order that determines how the individuals work with each other. For example, ants live in colonies in which the members have different jobs. Some ants find food, others defend the colony, and others take care of the young. Cooperation helps individuals get resources, which can make populations grow.

18 Compare Make an analogy between an ant colony and a sports team. How does each group work together to achieve a goal?

_____

_____

_____

_____

_____

_____

These ants cooperate to protect aphids that produce a substance that ants eat.

Visual Summary

To complete this summary, fill in the blanks with the correct word or phrase. Then use the key below to check your answers. You can use this page to review the main concepts of the lesson.

Population Dynamics

Populations grow due to birth and immigration and get smaller due to death and emigration.

19 If more individuals are born in a population than die or emigrate, the population will _____

Both populations and individuals can compete or cooperate.

21 Some birds warn other birds when predators are close. This type of interaction is called

_____

The carrying capacity is the maximum number of individuals of one species an environment can support.

20 If the amount of resources in an environment decreases, the carrying capacity for a population will probably

_____

Answers: 19 grow; 20 decrease; 21 cooperation

22 Synthesize Describe how a change in the environment could lead to increased immigration or emigration.

© Houghton Mifflin Harcourt Publishing Company • Image Credits: (t) ©Robert Postma/First Light/Corbis; (tr) ©Natphotos/Digital Vision/Getty Images; (b) ©DLILLC/Corbis

Lesson Review

Vocabulary

Circle the term that best completes the following sentences.

1 Individuals joining a population is an example of *emigration / immigration*.

2 A part of the environment that prevents a population from growing too large is a(n) *abiotic / limiting / biotic* factor.

3 Individuals *cooperate / compete* when they work together to obtain resources.

Key Concepts

4 Identify What is a limiting factor?

_____

_____

_____

_____

5 Describe How do limiting factors affect the carrying capacity of an environment?

_____

_____

_____

_____

_____

_____

6 Explain Give one example of how cooperation can help organisms survive.

_____

_____

_____

7 Provide Name two factors that increase population size and two factors that decrease population size.

_____

_____

_____

_____

Critical Thinking

Use the illustration to answer the following questions.

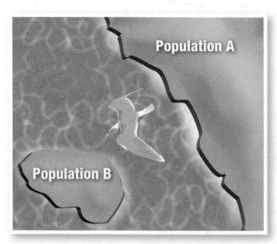

8 Infer What might cause birds in Population A to immigrate to the island?

_____

_____

_____

9 Predict How will the level of competition among birds in Population B change if many birds from Population A join Population B?

_____

_____

_____

10 Conclude Explain how a change in the environment could cause a population crash.

_____

_____

_____

_____

_____

11 Relate How does population size relate to resource availability in an environment?

_____

_____

_____

_____

© Houghton Mifflin Harcourt Publishing Company

My Notes

© Houghton Mifflin Harcourt Publishing Company

© Houghton Mifflin Harcourt Publishing Company

Interactions in Communities

ESSENTIAL QUESTION

How do organisms interact?

By the end of this lesson, you should be able to predict the effects of different interactions in communities.

➥ **6.LS2.1, 6.LS2.2, 6.LS2.7**

These birds, called tickbirds, eat ticks and flies on a rhinoceros. This behavior helps the rhino. The ticks are also parasites that sometimes drink the rhino's blood!

© Houghton Mifflin Harcourt Publishing Company • Image Credits: ©Dale C. Spartas/Corbis

✋ **Lesson Labs**

Quick Labs
• Prey Coloration
• Identifying Predators and Prey
Exploration Lab
• Modeling the Predator-Prey Cycle

 Engage Your Brain

1 Predict Check T or F to show whether you think each statement is true or false.

T   F

☐ ☐ Different animals can compete for the same food.

☐ ☐ Parasites help the organisms that they feed on.

☐ ☐ Some organisms rely on each other for necessities such as food or shelter.

☐ ☐ Organisms can defend themselves against predators that try to eat them.

2 Explain Draw an interaction between two living things that you might observe while on a picnic. Write a caption to go with your sketch.

 Active Reading

3 Synthesize You can often define an unknown word if you know the meaning of its word parts. Use the word parts and sentence below to make an educated guess about the meaning of the word *symbiosis*.

Word part	Meaning
bio-	life
sym-	together

Example sentence
The relationship between a sunflower and the insect that pollinates it is an example of symbiosis.

symbiosis:

_____

_____

_____

Vocabulary Terms

• **predator**
• **prey**
• **symbiosis**
• **mutualism**
• **commensalism**
• **parasitism**
• **competition**

4 Apply As you learn the meaning of each vocabulary term in this lesson, create your own definition or sketch to help you remember the meaning of the term.

© Houghton Mifflin Harcourt Publishing Company • Image Credits: © Dale C. Spartas/Corbis

Feeding Frenzy!

How do predator and prey interact?

Every organism lives with and affects other organisms. Many organisms must feed on other organisms in order to get the energy and nutrients they need to survive. These feeding relationships establish structure in a community.

Predators Eat Prey

In a predator–prey relationship, an animal eats another animal for energy and nutrients. The **predator** eats another animal. The **prey** is an animal that is eaten by a predator. An animal can be both predator and prey. For example, if a warthog eats a lizard, and is, in turn, eaten by a lion, the warthog is both predator and prey.

Predators and prey have adaptations that help them survive. Some predators have talons, claws, or sharp teeth, which provide them with deadly weapons. Spiders, which are small predators, use their webs to trap unsuspecting prey. Camouflage (CAM•ah•flaj) can also help a predator or prey to blend in with its environment. A tiger's stripes help it to blend in with tall grasses so that it can ambush its prey, and the wings of some moths look just like tree bark, which makes them difficult for predators to see. Some animals defend themselves with chemicals. For example, skunks and bombardier beetles spray predators with irritating chemicals.

Active Reading

5 Identify As you read, underline examples of predator–prey adaptations.

This lion is a predator. The warthog is its prey.

Adaptations of Predators and Prey

Most organisms wouldn't last a day without their adaptations. This bald eagle's vision and sharp talons allow it to find and catch prey.

sharp talons

© Houghton Mifflin Harcourt Publishing Company • Image Credits: (l) ©Kevin Schafer/Corbis; (r) ©Pete Saloutos/Corbis

Predators and Prey Populations Are Connected

Predators rely on prey for food, so the sizes of predator and prey populations are linked together very closely. If one population grows or shrinks, the other population is affected. For example, when there are a lot of warthogs to eat, the lion population may grow because the food supply is plentiful. As the lion population grows, it requires more and more food, so more and more warthogs are hunted by the lions. The increased predation may cause the warthog population to shrink. If the warthog population shrinks enough, the lion population may shrink due to a shortage in food supply. If the lion population shrinks, the warthog population may grow due to a lack of predators.

This lion is hunting down the antelope. If most of the antelope are killed, the lions will have less food to eat.

6 Compare Fill in the Venn diagram to compare and contrast predators and prey.

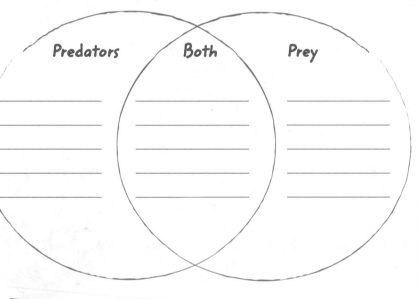

Predators   Both   Prey

Think Outside the Book

7 Apply Choose a predator and think about what it eats and how it hunts. Then do one of the following:
- Write a nomination for the predator to be "Predator of the Year."
- Draw the predator and label the adaptations that help it hunt.

Don't be surprised if this "leaf" walks away—it's actually an insect.

Visualize It!

8 Analyze How might this insect's appearance help keep it from getting eaten?

_____

_____

_____

_____

_____

© Houghton Mifflin Harcourt Publishing Company • Image Credits: (t) ©Gallo Images/Corbis; (b) ©Hemera Technologies/Photos.com/Getty Images

Living Together

What are the types of symbiotic relationships?

A close long-term relationship between different species in a community is called **symbiosis** (sim•bee•OH•sis). In symbiosis, the organisms in the relationship can benefit from, be unaffected by, or be harmed by the relationship. Often, one organism lives in or on the other organism. Symbiotic relationships are classified as mutualism, commensalism, or parasitism.

Active Reading **9 Identify** As you read, underline examples of symbiotic relationships.

Mutualism

A symbiotic relationship in which both organisms benefit is called **mutualism**. For example, when the bee in the photo drinks nectar from a flower, it gets pollen on its hind legs. When the bee visits another flower, it transfers pollen from the first flower to the second flower. In this interaction, the bee is fed and the second flower is pollinated for reproduction. So, both organisms benefit from the relationship. In this example, the mutualism benefits the bee and the two parent plants that are reproducing.

Commensalism

A symbiotic relationship in which one organism benefits while the other is unaffected is called **commensalism.** For example, orchids and other plants that often live in the branches of trees gain better access to sunlight without affecting the trees. In addition, the tree trunk shown here provides a living space for lichens, which do not affect the tree in any way. Some examples of commensalism involve protection. For example, certain shrimp live among the spines of the fire urchin. The fire urchin's spines are poisonous but not to the shrimp. By living among the urchin's spines, the shrimp are protected from predators. In this relationship, the shrimp benefits and the fire urchin is unaffected.

Lichens can live on tree bark.

10 Compare How does commensalism differ from mutualism?

_____

_____

_____

_____

Bees pollinate flowers. This is an example of mutualism.

© Houghton Mifflin Harcourt Publishing Company • Image Credits: (l) ©Jason Hosking/Getty Images; (r) ©Kathy Wright/Alamy

© Houghton Mifflin Harcourt Publishing Company • Image Credits: (bkgd) ©Randy M. Ury/Corbis; (inset) ©Stefan Sollfors/Alamy

parasite

host

12 Predict Observe and take notes about how the organisms in your area interact with one another. Imagine what would happen if one of these organisms disappeared. Write down three effects that you can think of.

Parasitism

A symbiotic relationship in which one organism benefits and another is harmed is called **parasitism** (PAR•uh•sih•tiz•uhm). The organism that benefits is the *parasite*. The organism that is harmed is the *host*. The parasite gets food from its host, which weakens the host. Some parasites, such as ticks, live on the host's surface and feed on its blood. These parasites can cause diseases such as Lyme disease. Other parasites, such as tapeworms, live within the host's body. They can weaken their host so much that the host dies.

11 Summarize Using the key, complete the table to show how organisms are affected by symbiotic relationships.

Symbiosis	Species 1	Species 2
Mutualism	+	
	+	0
Parasitism		

Key + organism benefits
0 organism not affected
– organism harmed

Nature's Cues

How do organisms communicate with each other?

For many reasons, organisms must be able to communicate with other organisms. This includes members of their own species as well as other organisms. The ability to communicate is often critical to an organism's survival. For example, many organisms use communication to find food, locate a mate, alert each other to danger, and teach their young how to survive.

Visual Communication

One way that organisms communicate is through visual cues. The way an organism looks or behaves can provide meaningful signals to other organisms. Many animals have adaptations that provide visual cues to other animals. For example, the antlers of a male white-tailed deer signal its strength to other deer. During mating season, the males with the largest antlers seek each other out and fight for the right to mate with females.

Some organisms use their bright colors to signal danger to others. For example, poison dart frogs are often bright red or blue. This makes them stand out in their environment. But predators know not to eat these frogs because they are very poisonous. The frogs' color is a warning signal that helps it—and the predator—survive.

This strawberry poison dart frog uses its bright colors to scare off predators.

13 Analyze Describe how visual communication can help an animal survive.

_____

_____

_____

_____

_____

_____

This buck's antlers are an important visual cue for other deer.

© Houghton Mifflin Harcourt • Image Credits: ©Dirk Ercken/Alamy Images ©Jim Cumming/Shutterstock

Auditory Communication

Auditory communication is communication through sound. Many of the sounds you might hear in a forest at night are organisms communicating with each other. Chirps, howls, barks, and hoots are forms of auditory communication that help animals survive.

A coyote's howl can be heard many miles away. This powerful sound is not without meaning. It conveys messages to other organisms in the vicinity. For example, it helps the coyote mark its territory. Other coyotes hear the howl and can tell where the howling coyote is.

Sometimes auditory communication can help an organism "see." Dolphins determine the location of other objects by making high-pitched sounds. The sound waves bounce off the objects and travel back to the dolphin. This behavior is called echolocation. It helps dolphins locate food and communicate with other dolphins nearby.

© Houghton Mifflin Harcourt • Image Credits: (t) ©Warren Metcalf/Shutterstock; (b) ©wildestanimal/Moment Open/Getty Images

Let the Games Begin!

Why does competition occur in communities?

In a team game, two groups compete against each other with the same goal in mind—to win the game. In a biological community, organisms compete for resources. **Competition** occurs when organisms fight for the same limited resource. Organisms compete for resources such as food, water, sunlight, shelter, and mates. If an organism doesn't get all the resources it needs, it could die.

Sometimes competition happens among individuals of the same species. For example, different groups of lions compete with each other for living space. Males within these groups also compete with each other for mates.

Competition can also happen among individuals of different species. Lions mainly eat large animals, such as zebras. They compete for zebras with leopards and cheetahs. When zebras are scarce, competition increases among animals that eat zebras. As a result, lions may steal food or compete with other predators for smaller animals.

Active Reading

14 Identify Underline each example of competition.

Think Outside the Book

16 Apply With a classmate, discuss how competition might affect the organisms in this photo.

15 Predict In the table below, fill in the missing cause and effect of two examples of competition in a community.

Cause	Effect
A population of lions grows too large to share their current territory.	
	Several male hyenas compete to mate with the females present in their area.

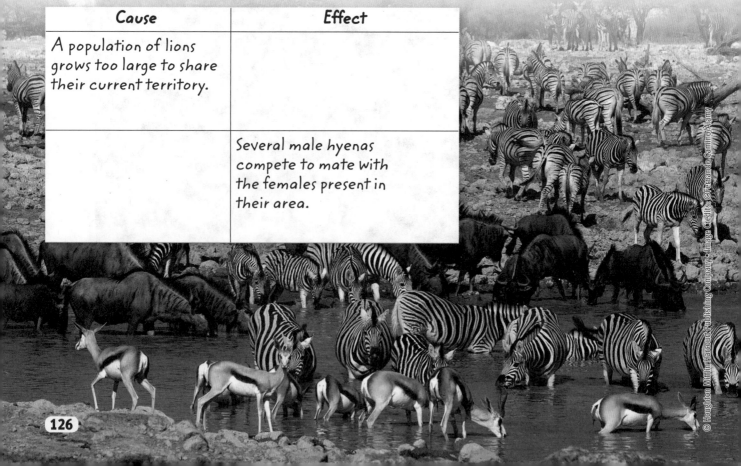

Many organisms rely on the same water source.

© Houghton Mifflin Harcourt Publishing Company • Image Credits: ©Fernando Camino/Alamy

Strange Relationships

WEIRD SCIENCE

Glow worms? Blind salamanders? Even creepy crawlers in this extreme cave community interact in ways that help them meet their needs. How do these interactions differ from ones in your own community?

Guano Buffet

Cave swiftlets venture out of the cave daily to feed. The food they eat is recycled as bird dung, or guano, which piles up beneath the nests. The guano feeds many cave dwellers, such as insects. As a result, these insects never have to leave the cave!

A Blind Hunter

Caves are very dark and, over generations, these salamanders have lost the use of their eyes for seeing. Instead of looking for food, they track prey by following water movements.

Sticky Traps

Bioluminescent glow worms make lines of sticky beads to attract prey. Once a prey is stuck, the worm pulls in the line to feast.

© Houghton Mifflin Harcourt Publishing Company • Image Credits: (bkgd) ©Rich Reid/Getty Images; (t) ©Eric and David Hosking/Corbis; (b) ©Dante Fenolio/Photo Researchers, Inc.; (br) ©ANT Photo Library/Photo Researchers, Inc.

Extend

Inquiry

17 Identify Name the type of relationship illustrated in two of the examples shown above.

18 Research Name some organisms in your community and the interactions they have.

19 Create Illustrate two of the interactions you just described by doing one of the following:
- make a poster
- write a song
- write a play
- draw a graphic novel

Visual Summary

To complete this summary, fill in the blanks with the correct word or phrase. Then, use the key below to check your answers. You can use this page to review the main concepts of the lesson.

Organisms interact in feeding relationships.

20 Predators eat

_____

Organisms interact in symbiosis—very close relationships between two species.

Mutualism:

Commensalism:

Parasitism:

21 A parasite gets nourishment from its

_____

Interactions
in Communities

Organisms interact in competition.

22 Organisms compete for resources such as

_____
_____
_____
_____

Competition can occur between:

Members of the same species

Members of different species

Answers: 20 prey; 21 host; 22 food, mates, shelter, and water.

23 **Synthesize** Explain how interactions can be both beneficial and harmful to the organisms in a community.

128 Unit 2 Interactions of Living Things

© Houghton Mifflin Harcourt Publishing Company • Image Credits: (tl) ©Infocusphotos.com/Alamy; (tr) ©Kevin Schafer/Corbis; (zebra) ©AfriPics.com/Alamy

Lesson Review

Vocabulary

Fill in the blank with the term that best completes the following sentences.

1 A _____ is an animal that kills and eats another animal, known as prey.

2 A long-term relationship between two different species within a community is called _____

3 _____ occurs when organisms fight for limited resources.

Key Concepts

Fill in the table below.

Example	Type of symbiosis
4 Identify Tiny organisms called mites live in human eyelashes and feed on dead skin, without harming humans.	
5 Identify Certain bacteria live in human intestines, where they get food and also help humans break down their food.	

6 Describe Think of an animal, and list two resources that it might compete for in its community. Then describe what adaptations the animal has to compete for these resources.

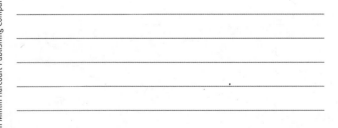

7 Explain What is the relationship between the size of a predator population and the size of a prey population?

_____

_____

_____

Critical Thinking

Use this graph to answer the following question.

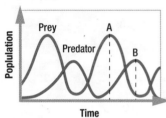

Predator and Prey Populations Over Time

8 Analyze At which point (A or B) on this graph would you expect competition within the predator population to be the highest?

_____

9 Infer Think of a resource, and predict what happens to the resource when competition for it increases.

_____

_____

_____

10 Apply Identify a community near where you live, such as a forest, a pond, or your own backyard. Think about the interactions of the organisms in this community. Describe an interaction and identify it as predation, mutualism, commensalism, parasitism, or competition.

_____

_____

_____

© Houghton Mifflin Harcourt Publishing Company

My Notes

© Houghton Mifflin Harcourt Publishing Company

© Houghton Mifflin Harcourt Publishing Company

Unit 2 Big Idea ◀ Organisms interact with each other and with the nonliving parts of their environment.

Lesson 1

ESSENTIAL QUESTION

How are different parts of the environment connected?

Analyze the parts of an environment.

Lesson 3

ESSENTIAL QUESTION

What determines a population's size?

Explain how population size changes in response to environmental factors and interactions between organisms.

Lesson 2

ESSENTIAL QUESTION

How does energy flow through an ecosystem?

Relate the roles of organisms to the transfer of energy in food chains and food webs.

Lesson 4

ESSENTIAL QUESTION

How do organisms interact?

Predict the effects of different interactions in communities.

Connect ESSENTIAL QUESTIONS
Lessons 1 and 3

1 Explain Do organisms compete for abiotic resources? Explain your answer.

_____

_____

_____

_____

Think Outside the Book

2 Synthesize Choose one of these activities to help synthesize what you have learned in this unit.

☐ Using what you learned in lessons 2 and 3, write a short story that describes what might happen in a food web when a new species is introduced to an ecosystem.

☐ Using what you learned in lessons 1 through 4, choose an ecosystem and explain three interactions that might occur within it. In your poster presentation, use the terms *cooperation, competition, predator*, and *prey*.

© Houghton Mifflin Harcourt Publishing Company • Image Credits: (tl) ©Timothy Laman/National Geographic/Getty Images; (tr) ©Photoshot Holdings Ltd/Alamy; (bl) ©Steven Trainoff Ph.D./Flickr/Getty Images; (br) ©Dale C. Spartas/Corbis

Name _____

Vocabulary

Check the box to show whether each statement is true or false.

T	F	
☐	☐	**1** <u>Competition</u> occurs when organisms try to use the same limited resource.
☐	☐	**2** <u>Biomes</u> are characterized by temperature, precipitation, and the plant and animal communities that live there.
☐	☐	**3** A <u>habitat</u> is the role of a population in its community, including its environment and its relationship with other species.
☐	☐	**4** A <u>food chain</u> is the feeding relationships among all of the organisms in an ecosystem.
☐	☐	**5** A <u>limiting factor</u> is an environmental factor that increases the growth of a population.

Key Concepts

Read each question below, and circle the best answer.

6 A small fish called a cleaner wrasse darts in and out of a larger fish's mouth, removing and eating parasites and dead tissue. Which term best describes the relationship between the cleaner wrasse and the large fish?

A mutualism

B commensalism

C parasitism

D competition

7 Bees have a society in which different members have different responsibilities. The interaction among bees is an example of what type of behavior?

A cooperation

B competition

C consumerism

D commensalism

8 After a mild winter with plenty of food, a deer population grew rapidly. What most likely happened to the wolf population in that same ecosystem?

A It was unaffected.

B It grew.

C It shrank.

D It became extinct.

© Houghton Mifflin Harcourt Publishing Company

9 The diagram below shows an aquatic ecosystem.

What is one abiotic factor shown in this diagram?

A the snails

C the crab

B the water

D the tree roots

10 Which of the following is an example of a biotic limiting factor for a population?

A water availability

C disease

B climate

D natural disasters

11 Which of the following is the most likely reason that a population might crash?

A The competition for the same resource suddenly drops.

B The number of prey suddenly increases.

C The number of predators suddenly decreases.

D The carrying capacity of the environment suddenly drops.

12 Grizzly bears are classified in the order Carnivora. Their diet consists of roots, tubers, berries, nuts, fungi, insects, rodents, and fish. What ecological role best describes grizzly bears?

A carnivores

C herbivores

B omnivores

D producers

© Houghton Mifflin Harcourt Publishing Company

13 The graph below shows the size of a squirrel population over 20 years.

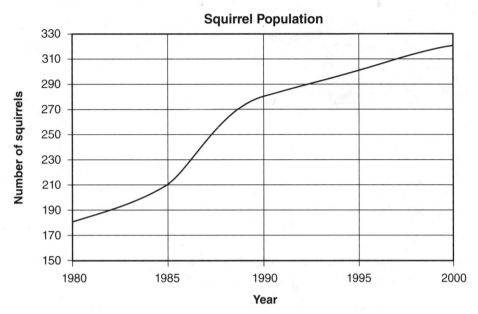

Squirrel Population

The trend displayed on the graph could be a result of what factor?

A emigration

C increased death rate

B immigration

D scarce resources

Critical Thinking

Answer the following questions in the space provided.

14 The diagram below shows how a manatee gets its energy.

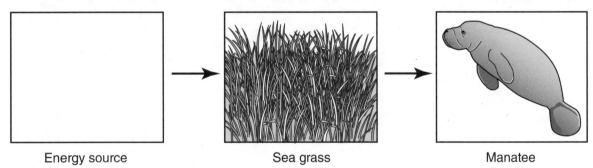

Energy source   Sea grass   Manatee

What provides the energy for the sea grass, the manatee, and most life on Earth? _____.

What role does the sea grass play in this food chain? _____

According to this diagram, what type of consumer is the manatee? _____

© Houghton Mifflin Harcourt Publishing Company

15 Use the diagram to help you answer the following question.

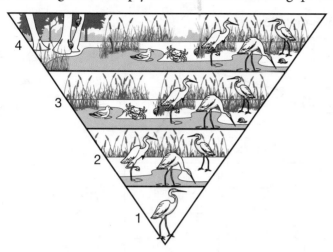

If there is a decrease in food availability for the wading birds, how will the different levels of organization shown in the diagram be affected?

_____

_____

_____

_____

Connect ESSENTIAL QUESTIONS
Lessons 2 and 4

Answer the following question in the space provided.

16 The diagram below shows an example of a food web.

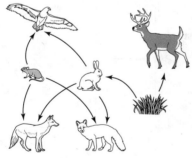

What traits do the prey animals shown here have in common that help them survive?

_____

What important ecological group is missing from this food web? _____

What might happen if the rabbit population suddenly shrank due to disease?

_____

_____

© Houghton Mifflin Harcourt Publishing Company

UNIT 3

Earth's Biomes and Ecosystems

Great Smoky Mountains

© Houghton Mifflin Harcourt Publishing Company • Image Credits: (bkgd) ©seladot/iStock/Getty Images; (br) ©Getty Images

Big Idea

Biomes and ecosystems change due to natural processes and human activity.

➤ 6.LS2.1, 6.LS2.4, 6.LS2.5, 6.LS2.6, 6.LS4.1, 6.LS4.2, 6.ESS2.4, 6.ESS3.3

American Black Bear

What do you think?

About 1,500 American Black Bears live in Great Smoky Mountains National Park. What characteristics of the ecosystem make it a good home for the mammal?

Unit 3
Earth's Biomes and Ecosystems

CITIZEN SCIENCE
It's Alive!

This garden is home to many vegetables and other plants.

1 Think About It

What role do plants play in your life?

_____

_____

_____

_____

_____

_____

_____

© Houghton Mifflin Harcourt Publishing Company • Image Credits: (bkgd) ©Alan Buckingham/Dorling Kindersley/Getty Images; (br) ©Alan Buckingham/Dorling Kindersley/Getty Images; (inset) ©YoungveME/Getty Images

② Ask A Question

How do plants use their environment?

As a class, design a plan for a garden plot or window box garden in which the class can grow a variety of plants. Remember that plants have different growing periods and requirements.

Sketch It!

Draw your plan to show where each plant will be placed.

③ Apply Your Knowledge

A What do your plants need in order to grow?

_____

_____

_____

B Where do your plants get what they need to grow?

_____

_____

_____

_____

C Create and care for your classroom garden and observe the plant growth.

Take It Home

Describe an area in your community that is used for growing food. If there is no such area, initiate a plan to plant in an area that you think could be used. See *ScienceSaurus*® for more information about plants.

© Houghton Mifflin Harcourt Publishing Company • Image Credits: (bkgd) ©youngvet/E+/Getty Images; (b) ©Hero Images/Getty Images

Land Biomes

ESSENTIAL QUESTION

What are land biomes?

By the end of this lesson, you should be able to describe the characteristics of different biomes that exist on land.

6.LS2.4, 6.ESS3.3

The North American prairie is an example of a grassland biome. It is home to grazing animals such as the bison.

Herds of thousands of bison used to roam the prairies. Bison became rare as people hunted them and developed the prairie into farmland.

© Houghton Mifflin Harcourt Publishing Company • Image Credits: (bg) ©Jake Rajs/Stone/Getty Images

✋ **Lesson Labs**

Quick Labs
• Climate Determines Plant Life
• Identify Your Land Biome

Field Lab
• Survey of a Biome's Biotic and Abiotic Factors

🧠 Engage Your Brain

1 Compare How are the two biomes in the pictures at right different from each other?

_____
_____
_____
_____
_____
_____

Ⓐ

2 Infer Which of these biomes gets more rain? Explain your answer.

_____
_____
_____
_____
_____
_____

Ⓑ

📖 Active Reading

3 Word Parts Parts of words that you know can help you find the meanings of words you don't know. The suffix *-ous* means "possessing" or "full of." Use the meanings of the root word and suffix to write the meaning of the term *coniferous tree*.

Root Word	Meaning
conifer	tree or shrub that produces cones

coniferous tree:

_____
_____
_____

Vocabulary Terms

• biome
• tundra
• taiga
• coniferous tree
• desert
• grassland
• deciduous tree

4 Apply As you learn the definition of each vocabulary term in this lesson, create your own definition or sketch to help you remember the meaning of the term.

© Houghton Mifflin Harcourt Publishing Company • Image Credits: (bg) ©Jake Rajs/Stone/Getty Images; (t) ©Publiphoto/ Paul G. Adam/Photo Researchers, Inc.; (b) ©Terry W. Eggers/Corbis

Home Sweet Biome

The taiga is a northern latitude biome that has low average temperatures, nutrient-poor soil, and coniferous trees.

What is a biome?

If you could travel Earth from pole to pole, you would pass through many different biomes. A **biome** is a region of Earth where the climate determines the types of plants that live there. The types of plants in a biome are biotic, or living, factors that determine the types of animals that live there. Deserts, grasslands, tundra, taiga, temperate forests, and tropical forests are all types of biomes.

What makes one biome different from another?

Each biome has a unique community of plants and animals. The types of organisms that can live in a biome depend on the biome's climate and other abiotic, or nonliving, factors.

Climate

Climate is the main abiotic factor that characterizes a biome. Climate describes the long-term patterns of temperature and precipitation in a region. The position of a biome on Earth affects its climate. Biomes that are closer to the poles receive less annual solar energy and have colder climates. Biomes that are near the equator receive more annual solar energy and have warmer climates. Biomes that are close to oceans often have wet climates. Scientists collect data over a long period of time to find climate patterns in ecosystems.

Earth's Major Land Biomes

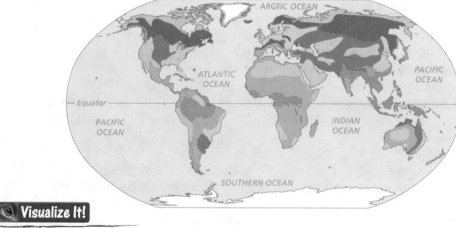

- Desert
- Tropical grassland
- Temperate grassland
- Tropical rain forest
- Temperate deciduous forest
- Temperate rain forest
- Taiga
- Tundra

Visualize It!

5 Predict Find the locations of the major land biomes on the map. Underline the names of two biomes that would have some of the coldest temperatures. Place a check mark next to the names of two biomes that would have some of the warmest temperatures.

© Houghton Mifflin Harcourt Publishing Company • Image Credits: ©Radius Images/Corbis

Other Abiotic Factors

Other abiotic factors that characterize a biome include soil type, amount of sunlight, and amount of water that is available. Abiotic factors affect which organisms can live in a biome.

Plant and Animal Communities

Adaptations are features that allow organisms to survive and reproduce. Plants and animals that live in a biome have adaptations to its unique conditions. For example, animals that live in biomes that are cold all year often grow thick fur coats. Plants that live in biomes with seasonal temperature changes lose their leaves and become inactive in winter. Plants that live in warm, rainy biomes stay green and grow all year long.

Active Reading

6 Identify As you read, underline the abiotic factors besides climate that characterize a biome.

Visualize It!

7 Infer Place a check mark in each box to predict the average temperature range for each of the biomes shown.

- ☐ Warm All Year
- ☐ Cool All Year
- ☐ Seasonal Temperatures

- ☐ Warm All Year
- ☐ Cool All Year
- ☐ Seasonal Temperatures

- ☐ Warm All Year
- ☐ Cool All Year
- ☐ Seasonal Temperatures

© Houghton Mifflin Harcourt Publishing Company • Image Credits: (tr) ©Ian Carroll/Alamy; (bl) ©Mike Grandmaison/First Light/Alamy; (br) ©Grambo/First Light/Corbis

Life in a Biome

How are ecosystems related to biomes?

Most biomes stretch across huge areas of land. Within each biome are smaller areas called ecosystems. Each *ecosystem* includes a specific community of organisms and their physical environment. A temperate forest biome can contain pond or river ecosystems. Each of these ecosystems has floating plants, fish, and other organisms that are adapted to living in or near water. A grassland biome can contain areas of small shrubs and trees. These ecosystems have woody plants, insects, and nesting birds.

Visualize It!

Three different ecosystems are shown in this temperate rain forest biome. Different organisms live in each of these ecosystems.

8 Identify List three organisms that you see in the picture that are part of each ecosystem within the biome.

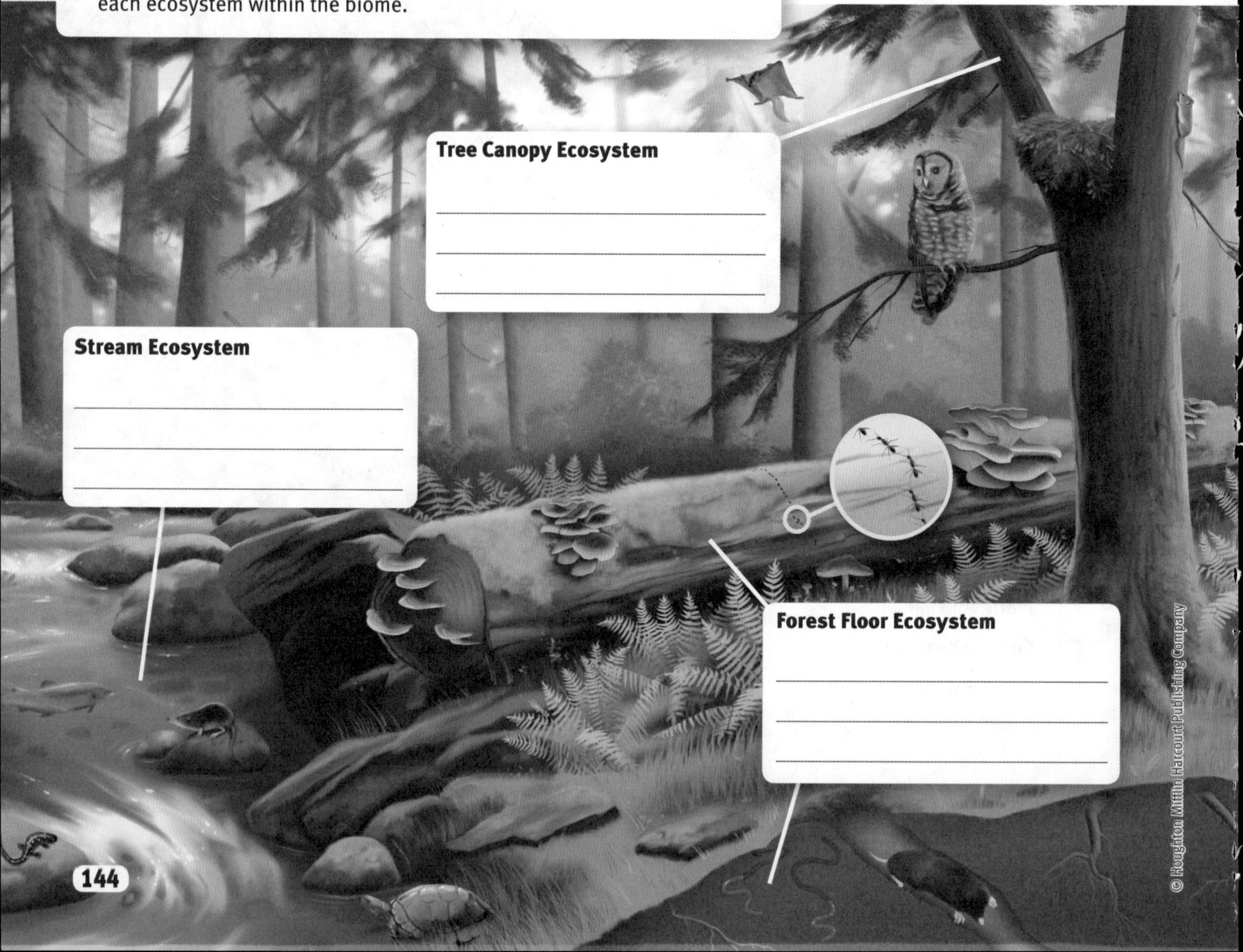

Tree Canopy Ecosystem

_____

_____

_____

Stream Ecosystem

_____

_____

_____

Forest Floor Ecosystem

_____

_____

_____

© Houghton Mifflin Harcourt Publishing Company

What are the major land biomes?

There are six major land biomes. These include tundra, taiga, desert, grassland, temperate forest, and tropical forest.

 **Active Reading** **9 Identify** Underline the abiotic features that characterize tundra and taiga biomes.

Tundra

Tundra has low average temperatures and very little precipitation. The ground contains permafrost, a thick layer of permanently frozen soil beneath the surface. Tundra is found in the Arctic and in high mountain regions. Tundra plants include mosses and woody shrubs. These plants have shallow roots, since they cannot grow into the permafrost. Tundra winters are dark, cold, and windy. Animals such as musk oxen have thick fur and fat deposits that protect them from the cold. Some animals, such as caribou, migrate to warmer areas before winter. Ground squirrels hibernate, or become dormant, underground.

Taiga

Taiga is also called the boreal forest. **Taiga** has low average temperatures like those in the tundra biome, but more precipitation. The soil layer in taiga is thin, acidic, and nutrient-poor. Taiga biomes are found in Canada and northern Europe and Asia. Taiga plants include **coniferous trees**, which are trees that have evergreen, needlelike leaves. These thin leaves let trees conserve water and produce food all year long. Migratory birds live in taiga in summer. Wolves, owls, and elk live in taiga year-round. Some animals, such as snowshoe hares, experience a change in fur color as the seasons change. Hares that match their surroundings are not seen by predators as easily.

Visualize It!

10 Describe Below each picture, describe how organisms that you see are adapted to the biome in which they live.

Tundra

_____
_____
_____
_____

Taiga

_____
_____
_____
_____

© Houghton Mifflin Harcourt Publishing Company • Image Credits: (l) ©John E Marriott/All Canada Photos/Corbis; (r) ©Frank van Egmond/Alamy Images

Desert

Desert biomes are very dry. Some deserts receive less than 8 centimeters (3 inches) of precipitation each year. Desert soil is rocky or sandy. Many deserts are hot during the day and cold at night, although some have milder temperatures. Plants and animals in this biome have adaptations that let them conserve water and survive extreme temperatures. Members of the cactus family have needlelike leaves that conserve water. They also contain structures that store water. Many desert animals are active only at night. Some animals burrow underground or move into shade to stay cool during the day.

Active Reading

11 Identify As you read, underline the characteristics of deserts.

Visualize It!

12 Describe List the ways that each plant or animal in the picture is adapted to the desert biome.

Saguaro Cactus
_____
_____
_____
_____
_____

Desert Tortoise

A tortoise can crawl into shade or retreat into its shell to avoid the heat. A tortoise has thick skin that prevents water loss.

Kangaroo Rat
_____
_____
_____
_____
_____

© Houghton Mifflin Harcourt Publishing Company

Tropical Grassland

Temperate Grassland

Tropical Grassland

A **grassland** is a biome that has grasses and few trees. Tropical grasslands, such as the African savanna, have high average temperatures throughout the year. They also have wet and dry seasons. Thin soils support grasses and some trees in this biome. Grazing animals, such as antelope and zebras, feed on grasses. Predators such as lions hunt grazing animals. Animals in tropical grasslands migrate to find water during dry seasons. Plants in tropical grasslands are adapted to survive periodic fires.

Temperate Grassland

Temperate grasslands, such as the North American prairie, have moderate precipitation, hot summers, and cold winters. These grasslands have deep soils that are rich in nutrients. Grasses are the dominant plants in this biome. Bison, antelope, prairie dogs, and coyotes are common animals. Periodic fires sweep through temperate grasslands. These fires burn dead plant material and kill trees and shrubs. Grasses and other nonwoody plants are adapted to fire. Some of these plants regrow from their roots after a fire. Others grow from seeds that survived the fire.

Visualize It!

13 Describe Write captions to explain how fire shapes a temperate grassland biome.

Between fires, small trees begin to grow in a temperate grassland.

_____

_____

_____

_____

_____

_____

_____

_____

_____

© Houghton Mifflin Harcourt Publishing Company • Image Credits: (tl) ©Charles V. Angelo/Photo Researchers, Inc.; (tr) ©Andrew Woodley/Alamy

Temperate Deciduous Forest

Temperate deciduous forests have moderate precipitation, hot summers, and cold winters. These forests are located in the northeastern United States, East Asia, and much of Europe. This biome has **deciduous trees**, which are broadleaf trees that drop their leaves as winter approaches. Fallen leaves decay and add organic matter to the soil, making it nutrient-rich. Songbirds nest in these forests during summer, but many migrate to warmer areas before winter. Animals such as chipmunks and black bears hibernate during winter. Deer and bobcats are active year-round.

Temperate Rain Forest

Temperate rain forests have a long, cool wet season and a relatively dry summer. Temperate rain forests exist in the Pacific Northwest and on the western coast of South America. This biome is home to many coniferous trees, including Douglas fir and cedar. The forest floor is covered with mosses and ferns and contains nutrient-rich soil. Plants grow throughout the year in the temperate rain forest. Animals in this biome include spotted owls, shrews, elk, and cougars.

Visualize It!

14 Summarize Fill in the missing information on the cards to describe each of these temperate forest biomes.

Temperate Rain Forest

A. Climate: _____

_____

B. Soil: _____

_____

C. Plants: _____

_____

D. Animals: _____

_____

Temperate Deciduous Forest

A. Climate: _____

_____

B. Soil: _____

_____

C. Plants: _____

_____

D. Animals: _____

_____

Think Outside the Book (Inquiry)

15 Apply With a classmate, compare the adaptations of animals that migrate, hibernate, or stay active year-round in a temperate deciduous forest.

© Houghton Mifflin Harcourt Publishing Company • Image Credits: (l) ©Alan Majchrowicz/Alamy (r) ©Richard and Ellen Thane/Photo Researchers, Inc.

Tropical Rain Forest

Tropical rain forests are located near Earth's equator. This biome is warm throughout the year. It also receives more rain than any other biome on Earth. The soil in tropical rain forests is acidic and low in nutrients. Even with poor soil, tropical rain forests have some of the highest biological diversity on Earth. Dense layers of plants develop in a tropical rain forest. These layers block sunlight from reaching the forest floor. Some plants such as orchids grow on tree branches instead of on the dark forest floor. Birds, monkeys, and sloths live in the upper layers of the rain forest. Leaf-cutter ants, jaguars, snakes, and anteaters live in the lower layers.

16 Display Color in the band labeled *Light Level* next to the picture of the tropical rain forest. Make the band darkest at the level where the forest would receive the least light. Make the band lightest at the level where the forest would receive the most light.

Light Level

© Houghton Mifflin Harcourt Publishing Company

Visual Summary

To complete this summary, fill in the answers to the questions. Then, use the key below to check your answers. You can use this page to review the main concepts of the lesson.

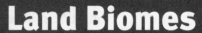

Land Biomes

A biome is a region of Earth characterized by a specific climate and specific plants and animals.

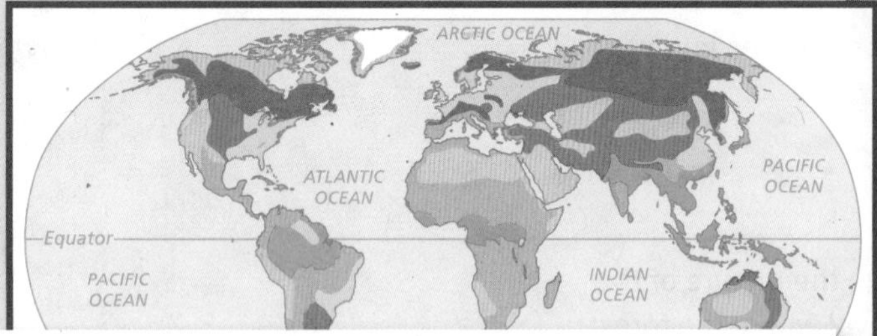

17 *What are the major land biomes?*

____

____

____

Each biome can contain many ecosystems.

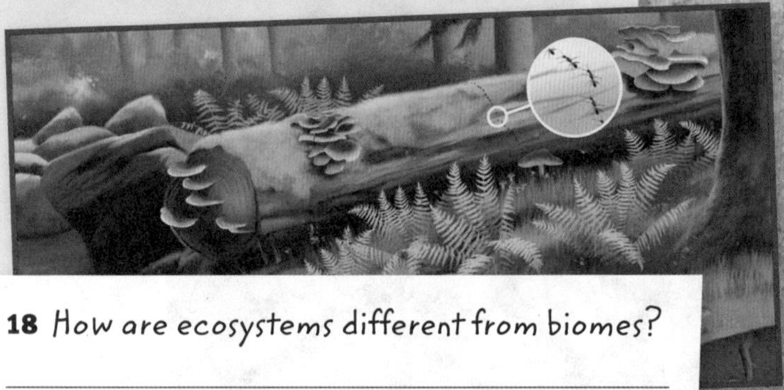

18 *How are ecosystems different from biomes?*

____

____

____

Plants and animals are adapted to the conditions in their biome.

19 *The plant below is adapted to what conditions?*

____

____

____

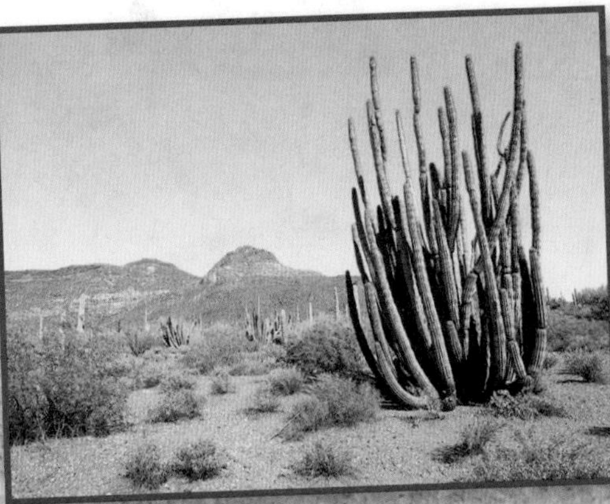

Sample answers: 17 tundra, taiga, desert, grassland, temperate forest, tropical forest; 18 Ecosystems are smaller areas within biomes that include communities of organisms and their nonliving environment.; 19 dry conditions

20 Predict Describe what might happen to the organisms in a desert if the climate changed and rainfall increased.

© Houghton Mifflin Harcourt Publishing Company • Image Credits: ©Publiphoto/ Paul G. Adam/Photo Researchers, Inc.

Lesson Review

Vocabulary

Define Draw a line to connect the following terms to their definitions.

1 a region that has a specific climate and a specific community of plants and animals

A taiga

2 a region with low average temperatures and little precipitation

B climate

3 long-term temperature and precipitation patterns in a region

C biome

Key Concepts

4 **Identify** What are the abiotic factors that help to characterize a biome?

_____

_____

_____

_____

5 **Describe** Describe a tropical grassland biome.

_____

_____

_____

_____

6 **Draw Conclusions** An ecosystem has high average temperatures and long summers. What can you conclude about the plants and animals that live there?

_____

_____

_____

_____

7 **Summarize** Why can many ecosystems exist in one biome?

_____

_____

_____

_____

Critical Thinking

Use the Venn diagram to answer the following questions.

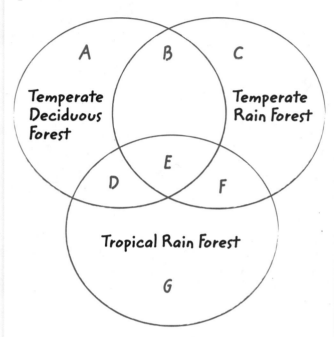

8 **Infer** In which space on the Venn diagram would you write *coniferous trees*?

_____

9 **Analyze** What is common among all three types of forests in the diagram?

_____

_____

_____

10 **Relate** What biome do you think you live in? Explain your answer.

_____

_____

_____

_____

_____

_____

© Houghton Mifflin Harcourt Publishing Company

My Notes

© Houghton Mifflin Harcourt Publishing Company

© Houghton Mifflin Harcourt Publishing Company

Lesson 2

Aquatic Ecosystems

ESSENTIAL QUESTION

What are aquatic ecosystems?

By the end of this lesson, you should be able to describe the characteristics of marine, freshwater, and other aquatic ecosystems.

6.LS2.1, 6.LS2.4

Coral reefs are coastal ocean ecosystems that are located in many tropical areas. Coral reefs have some of the highest biological diversity on Earth.

© Houghton Mifflin Harcourt Publishing Company • Image Credits: (bg) ©Jeffrey Rotman/Corbis

154

Engage Your Brain

1 Predict Check T or F to show whether you think each statement is true or false.

T	F	
☐	☐	Wetlands can protect areas close to shorelines from flooding.
☐	☐	Most ponds contain both salt water and fresh water.
☐	☐	Plants and animals cannot live in fast-moving waters.
☐	☐	The deep ocean is colder and darker than other marine ecosystems.

2 Predict How do you think organisms like this squid are adapted to life in the deep ocean?

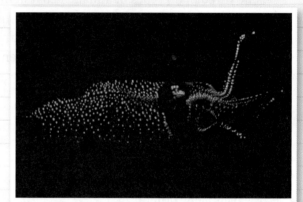

_____

_____

_____

Active Reading

3 Synthesize You can often define an unknown word if you know the meaning of its word parts. Use the word parts and sentence below to make an educated guess about the meaning of the word *wetland*.

Word part	Meaning
wet-	having water or liquid on the surface
-land	solid part of Earth's surface

Example sentence:
Many species of birds and mammals rely on <u>wetlands</u> for food, water, and shelter.

wetland: _____

_____

_____

Vocabulary Terms
- wetland
- estuary

4 Identify As you read, place a question mark next to any words that you don't understand. When you finish reading the lesson, go back and review the text you marked. Work with a classmate to define the words that are still unclear.

© Houghton Mifflin Harcourt Publishing Company • Image Credits: (bg) ©Jeffrey Rotman/Corbis; (tr) ©Dante Fenolio/Photo Researchers, Inc.

Splish Splash

What are the major types of aquatic ecosystems?

Have you ever gone swimming in the ocean, or fishing on a lake? Oceans and lakes support many of the aquatic ecosystems on Earth. An *aquatic ecosystem* includes any water environment and the community of organisms that live there.

The three main types of aquatic ecosystems are freshwater ecosystems, estuaries, and marine ecosystems. Freshwater ecosystems can be found in rivers, lakes, and wetlands. Marine ecosystems are found in oceans. Rivers and oceans form estuaries where they meet at a coastline.

What abiotic factors affect aquatic ecosystems?

Abiotic factors are the nonliving things in an environment. The major abiotic factors that affect aquatic ecosystems include water temperature, water depth, amount of light, oxygen level, water pH, salinity (salt level), and the rate of water flow. An aquatic ecosystem may be influenced by some of these factors but not others. For example, a river would be influenced by rate of water flow but not typically by salinity.

Visualize It!

5 Identify Fill in the major types of aquatic ecosystems in the picture.

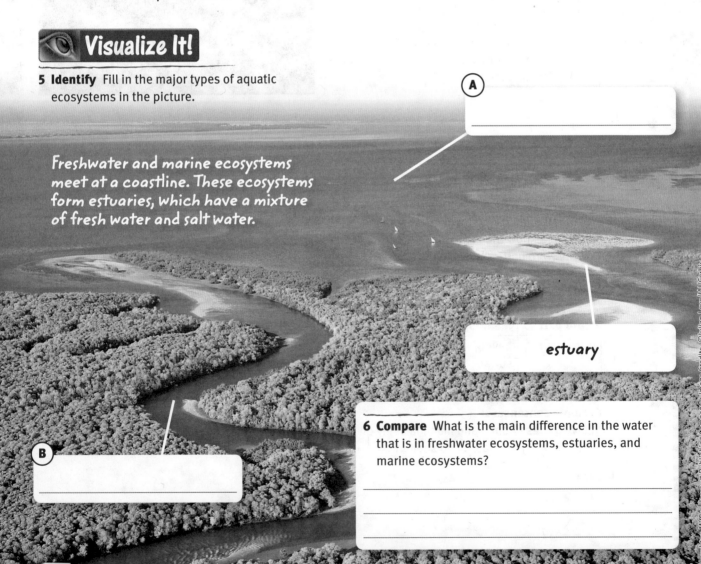

Freshwater and marine ecosystems meet at a coastline. These ecosystems form estuaries, which have a mixture of fresh water and salt water.

A _____

estuary

B _____

6 Compare What is the main difference in the water that is in freshwater ecosystems, estuaries, and marine ecosystems?

_____

_____

_____

© Houghton Mifflin Harcourt Publishing Company • Image Credits: ©Julian Love/AV/Corbis

Where are examples of freshwater ecosystems found?

Freshwater ecosystems contain water that has very little salt in it. Freshwater ecosystems are found in lakes, ponds, wetlands, rivers, and streams. Although freshwater ecosystems seem common, they actually contain less than one percent of all the water on Earth.

In Lakes and Ponds

Lakes and ponds are bodies of water surrounded by land. Lakes are larger than ponds. Some plants grow at the edges of these water bodies. Others live underwater or grow leaves that float on the surface. Protists such as algae and amoebas float in the water. Frogs and some insects lay eggs in the water, and their young develop there. Clams, bacteria, and worms live on the bottom of lakes and ponds and break down dead materials for food. Frogs, turtles, fish, and ducks have adaptations that let them swim in water.

Active Reading

7 Identify As you read, underline the names of organisms that live in or near lakes and ponds.

8 Describe Pick a plant and animal in the picture. Describe how each is adapted to a pond.

Plant

_____

_____

_____

_____

Animal

_____

_____

_____

_____

© Houghton Mifflin Harcourt Publishing Company

In Wetlands

A **wetland** is an area of land that is saturated, or soaked, with water for at least part of the year. Bogs, marshes, and swamps are types of wetlands. Bogs contain living and decomposing mosses. Many grasslike plants grow in marshes. Swamps have trees and vines. Plants that live in wetlands are adapted to living in wet soil.

Wetlands have high species diversity. Common wetland plants include cattails, duckweed, sphagnum moss, sedges, orchids, willows, tamarack, and black ash trees. Animals found in wetlands include ducks, frogs, shrews, herons, and alligators. Water collects and slowly filters through a wetland. In this way, some pollutants are removed from the water. Since wetlands can hold water, they also protect nearby land and shore from floods and erosion.

Think Outside the Book Inquiry

9 Apply Use library and Internet resources to put together an identification guide to common wetland plants.

Visualize It!

Wetland

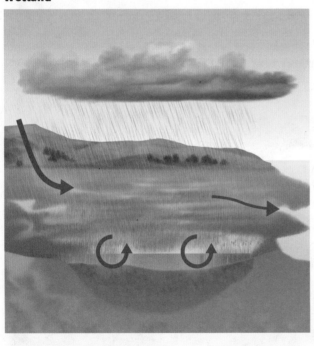

Development That Replaced Wetland

10 Describe What can happen when a wetland is replaced by a development in an area?

_____

_____

_____

_____

© Houghton Mifflin Harcourt Publishing Company

In Rivers and Streams

Water moves in one direction in a stream. As water moves, it interacts with air and oxygen is added to the water. A large stream is called a river. Rivers and streams are home to many organisms, including fish, aquatic insects, and mosses. Freshwater ecosystems in streams can have areas of fast-moving and slow-moving water. Some organisms that live in fast-moving water have adaptations that let them resist being washed away. Immature black flies can attach themselves to rocks in a fast-moving stream. Rootlike rhizoids let mosses stick to rocks. In slow-moving waters of a stream, water striders are adapted to live on the water's surface.

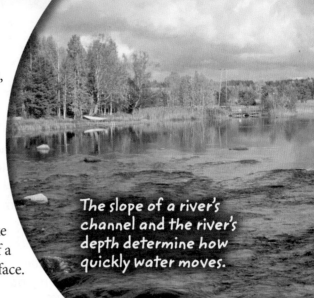

The slope of a river's channel and the river's depth determine how quickly water moves.

11 Match Match the correct captions to the pictures showing areas of fast-moving and slow-moving water.

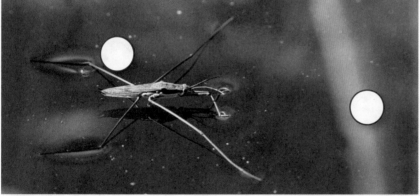

A Water striders move across the surface of a pool of water in a river.

B Rocks form small waterfalls in areas of some streams.

C Aquatic plants can live below the surface of a river.

D Mosses can grow on the surface of rocks even in fast-moving water.

12 Infer Why might stream water have more oxygen in it than pond water does?

_____

_____

_____

_____

© Houghton Mifflin Harcourt Publishing Company • Image Credits: (t) ©Reino Hanninen/Alamy; (c) ©Willard Clay/Photographers Choice RF/Getty Images; (b) ©Andrew Darrington/Alamy Images

Where River Meets Sea

What is an estuary?

An **estuary** is a partially enclosed body of water formed where a river flows into an ocean. Because estuaries have a mixture of fresh water and salt water, they support ecosystems that have a unique and diverse community of organisms. Seagrasses, marsh grasses, mangrove trees, fish, oysters, mussels, and water birds all live in estuaries. Fish and shrimp lay eggs in the calm waters of an estuary. Their young mature here before moving out into the ocean. Many birds feed on the young shrimp and fish in an estuary.

Organisms in estuaries must be able to survive in constantly changing salt levels due to the rise and fall of tides. Some estuary grasses, such as smooth cordgrass, have special structures in their roots and leaves that let them get rid of excess salt.

Visualize It!

13 Describe Fill in the rest of the name tags for each estuary organism. List at least one way the organism uses an estuary to survive.

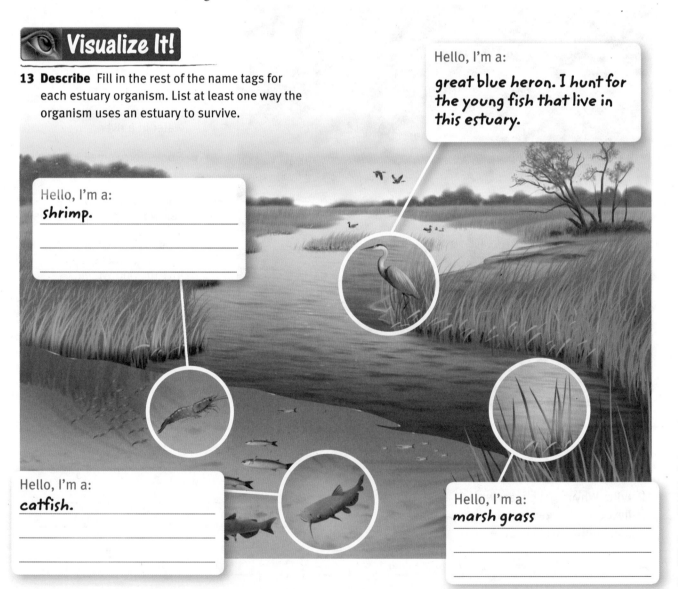

Hello, I'm a:
great blue heron. I hunt for the young fish that live in this estuary.

Hello, I'm a:
shrimp.

Hello, I'm a:
catfish.

Hello, I'm a:
marsh grass

© Houghton Mifflin Harcourt Publishing Company

EYE ON THE ENVIRONMENT

Protecting Estuaries

Why are estuaries important? The mixture of salt water and nutrient-rich fresh water in an estuary supports breeding grounds for birds, commercial fish, and shellfish such as crabs and shrimp. The grasses in estuaries also protect coastal areas from erosion and flooding.

Oil Spill!

In 2010, a major oil spill occurred in the Gulf of Mexico. Oil flowed into the ocean for almost three months.

Coastal Damage

Estuaries along the northern Gulf Coast were affected. Oil killed birds and other animals. It soaked seagrasses and damaged fish and shellfish nurseries.

Cleaning Up

A large cleanup effort began after the spill. Continuing work will be important to restore ecosystems and protect fishing and tourism jobs in the area.

Extend

Inquiry

14 Explain What are the economic benefits from estuaries?

15 Research Find out about another damaged estuary ecosystem. How has the estuary been restored?

16 Hypothesize Form a hypothesis about how the loss of estuaries can increase erosion along shorelines.

© Houghton Mifflin Harcourt Publishing Company • Image Credits: (bg) ©NASA Image by Jeff Schmaltz, MODIS Rapid Response Team; (t) ©Julie Dermansky/Corbis; (b) ©Tannen Maury/epa/Corbis

The open ocean is vast and contains a variety of life forms. The ocean's largest, fastest, and deepest-diving organisms are found here.

Where are examples of marine ecosystems found?

Marine ecosystems are saltwater ecosystems. They cover more than 70 percent of Earth's surface. Marine ecosystems are found in the coastal ocean, the open ocean, and the deep ocean. Different abiotic, or nonliving, factors affect each marine ecosystem.

In and Along Coastal Oceans

Marine ecosystems in and along coastal oceans include the intertidal zone and the neritic zone. The intertidal zone is the land between high and low tides that includes beaches and rocky shores. Organisms that live in this zone are often adapted to changing water depth, wave action, exposure to air, and changing salinity. Crabs and seagrasses live on beaches. Barnacles and anemones live in tidal pools on rocky shores.

The neritic zone is the underwater zone from the shore to the edge of the continental shelf. Light reaches the bottom of the neritic zone, allowing algae and many plants to live there. Coral reefs, seagrass meadows, and kelp forests are found in the neritic zone. Coral reefs are located mainly in warm tropical areas. They support many species of colorful fish, anemones, and coral. Kelp forests are found in cold, nutrient-rich waters. Kelp forests support brown and red algae, shrimp, fish, brittle stars, and sea otters.

Visualize It!

17 List Below each photo, list abiotic factors that affect the coastal ocean ecosystem that is shown.

Sandy Beach	Rocky Shore	Coral Reef	Kelp Forest

A	B	C	D

_____ _____ _____ _____

_____ _____ _____ _____

_____ _____ _____ _____

© Houghton Mifflin Harcourt Publishing Company • Image Credits: (bg) ©James Forte/National Geographic/Getty Images; (b) ©Kenneth Murray/Photo Researchers, Inc.; (bd) ©Peter Scoones/Photo Researchers, Inc.; (bc) ©Digital Vision/Getty Images; (br) ©Mark Conlin/Alamy

In Open Oceans

The open ocean includes all surface waters down to a depth of about 2,000 meters (6,562 feet). Ecosystems at the surface are often dominated by tiny floating organisms called plankton. Organisms that are adapted to dark and cold conditions live at greater depths. Because the open ocean is so large, the majority of sea life is found there. Animals found in open ocean ecosystems include sharks, whales, dolphins, fish, and sea turtles. Ecosystems in the bathyal zone, which extends from the edge of the continental shelf to its base, are also considered open ocean ecosystems.

In Deep Oceans

The deep ocean has the coldest and darkest conditions. Deep ocean ecosystems include those in the abyssal zone, which is the part of the ocean below 2,000 meters (6,562 feet). Some species that live in the deep ocean have bioluminescence, which lets them produce a glowing light to attract mates or prey. Female anglerfish attract prey using bioluminescent structures that act as bait.

No light can reach the deep ocean, so no photosynthesis can happen there. Organisms in the deep ocean must get energy in other ways. Some feed on the organic material that is constantly falling from shallower ocean depths. Microorganisms living near hydrothermal vents use chemicals in the water as an energy source.

 **Active Reading**

18 Infer How do organisms in the deep ocean get energy to live?

_____

_____

Hydrothermal vents release super-hot, acidic water in the deep ocean. Microorganisms called archaea convert chemicals from the vents into food using chemosynthesis. Archaea, tube worms, crabs, clams, and shrimp are part of hydrothermal vent communities.

© Houghton Mifflin Harcourt Publishing Company • Image Credits: (bg) ©James Forte/National Geographic/Getty Images; (b) ©Ralph White/Corbis

Visual Summary

To complete this summary, fill in the answer to each question. Then, use the key below to check your answers. You can use this page to review the main concepts of the lesson.

Aquatic Ecosystems

Freshwater ecosystems contain still or moving fresh water.

19 Where are freshwater ecosystems found?

_____

_____

An estuary is an ecosystem that forms where a river empties into an ocean.

21 Which abiotic factor would likely have the greatest effect on an estuary?

_____

_____

Marine ecosystems are located in or near oceans.

20 Where are ecosystems found in the ocean?

_____

_____

Sample answers: 19 In lakes, ponds, wetlands, rivers, and streams; 20 In the coastal ocean, open ocean, and deep ocean; 21 changing salinity

22 Compare How are estuaries and coral reefs similar?

© Houghton Mifflin Harcourt Publishing Company • Image Credits: (t) ©Reino Hanninen/Alamy; (b) ©Julian Love/AI/Corbis; (br) ©Digital Vision/Getty Images

Lesson Review

Vocabulary

Fill in the blank with the term that best completes the following sentences.

1 A(n) _____ is a partially enclosed body of water formed where a river flows into an ocean.

2 A(n) _____ is an area of land that is covered or saturated with water for at least part of the year.

Key Concepts

3 Identify What kinds of organisms live in estuaries?

_____

_____

_____

_____

_____

4 Describe What types of adaptations would be needed by organisms that live in a river?

_____

_____

_____

_____

_____

5 Describe Describe the characteristics of the four zones found in the ocean.

_____

_____

_____

_____

_____

_____

_____

_____

Critical Thinking

Use the photo to answer the following question.

6 Predict Organisms in the aquatic ecosystem in the picture must be adapted to which abiotic factors?

_____

_____

_____

_____

7 Draw Draw an organism that is adapted to the abyssal zone of the ocean, and label its adaptations.

8 Analyze Salt water is denser than fresh water. What ecosystem would be most affected by this fact? Explain your answer.

_____

_____

_____

_____

_____

_____

_____

© Houghton Mifflin Harcourt Publishing Company • Image Credits: ©Jim Zipp/Photo Researchers, Inc.

My Notes

© Houghton Mifflin Harcourt Publishing Company

© Houghton Mifflin Harcourt Publishing Company

Interpreting Circle Graphs

Scientists display data in tables and graphs in order to organize it and show relationships. A *circle graph*, also called a *pie graph*, is used to show and compare the pieces of a whole.

Tutorial

In a circle graph, the entire circle represents the whole, and each piece is called a *sector*. Follow the instructions below to learn how to interpret a circle graph.

1 Evaluating Data Data on circle graphs may be given in one of two ways: as values (such as dollars, days, or numbers of items) or as percentages of the whole.

2 Changing Percentage to Value The word *percent* means "per hundred," so 25% means 25 per 100, or 25/100. To find the total volume represented by a sector, such as the volume of fresh water in surface water, multiply the whole value by the percent of the sector, and then divide by 100.

$$35,030,000 \text{ km}^3 \times \frac{0.3}{100} = 105,090 \text{ km}^3 \text{ of Earth's fresh water is in surface water.}$$

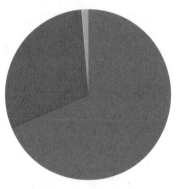

Distribution of Fresh Water (in values)

- ■ Icecaps and Glaciers 24,065,610 km³
- ■ Groundwater 10,544,030 km³
- ■ Surface Water 105,090 km³
- ■ Other 315,270 km³

Source: Gleick, P. H., 1996: Water resources. In Encyclopedia of Climate and Weather, ed. by S. H. Schneider, Oxford University Press, New York, vol. 2, pp.817-823

3 Changing Value to Ratio The sum of the sectors, 35,030,000 km³, is the whole, or total value. Divide the value of a sector, such as the icecaps and glaciers sector, by the value of the whole. Simplify this fraction to express it as a ratio.

$$\frac{24,065,610 \text{ km}^3}{35,030,000 \text{ km}^3} \approx \frac{25}{35} = \frac{5}{7}$$

About $\frac{5}{7}$ of Earth's fresh water is in icecaps and glaciers.

This ratio can be expressed as $\frac{5}{7}$, 5:7, or 5 to 7.

4 Changing Value to Percentage The whole circle graph is 100%. To find the percentage of a sector, such as the world's fresh water that is found as groundwater, divide the value of the sector by the value of the whole, and then multiply by 100%.

$$\frac{10,544,030 \text{ km}^3}{35,030,000 \text{ km}^3} \times 100\% = 30.1\% \text{ of Earth's fresh water is groundwater.}$$

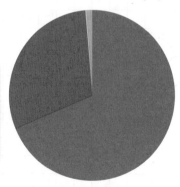

Distribution of Fresh Water (in percentages)

- ■ Icecaps and Glaciers 68.7%
- ■ Groundwater 30.1%
- ■ Surface Water 0.3%
- ■ Other 0.9%

Source: Gleick, P. H., 1996: Water resources. In Encyclopedia of Climate and Weather, ed. by S. H. Schneider, Oxford University Press, New York, vol. 2, pp.817-823

© Houghton Mifflin Harcourt Publishing Company

You Try It!

Use the circle graphs below to answer the following questions.

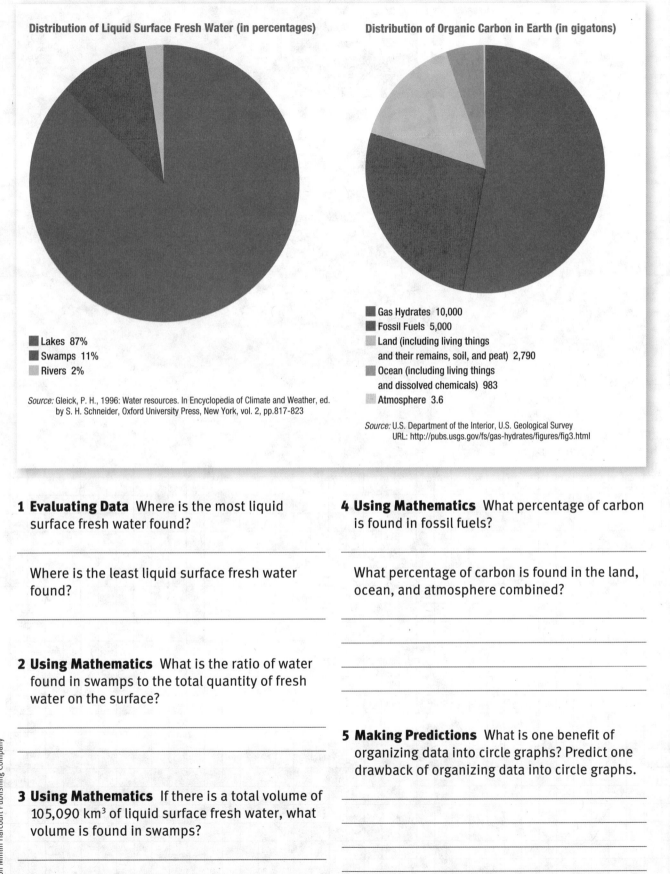

Distribution of Liquid Surface Fresh Water (in percentages)

- ■ Lakes 87%
- ■ Swamps 11%
- ■ Rivers 2%

Source: Gleick, P. H., 1996: Water resources. In Encyclopedia of Climate and Weather, ed. by S. H. Schneider, Oxford University Press, New York, vol. 2, pp.817-823

Distribution of Organic Carbon in Earth (in gigatons)

- ■ Gas Hydrates 10,000
- ■ Fossil Fuels 5,000
- ■ Land (including living things and their remains, soil, and peat) 2,790
- ■ Ocean (including living things and dissolved chemicals) 983
- ■ Atmosphere 3.6

Source: U.S. Department of the Interior, U.S. Geological Survey URL: http://pubs.usgs.gov/fs/gas-hydrates/figures/fig3.html

1 Evaluating Data Where is the most liquid surface fresh water found?

_____

Where is the least liquid surface fresh water found?

_____

2 Using Mathematics What is the ratio of water found in swamps to the total quantity of fresh water on the surface?

_____

_____

3 Using Mathematics If there is a total volume of 105,090 km³ of liquid surface fresh water, what volume is found in swamps?

_____

_____

4 Using Mathematics What percentage of carbon is found in fossil fuels?

_____

What percentage of carbon is found in the land, ocean, and atmosphere combined?

_____

_____

_____

_____

5 Making Predictions What is one benefit of organizing data into circle graphs? Predict one drawback of organizing data into circle graphs.

_____

_____

_____

_____

© Houghton Mifflin Harcourt Publishing Company

Changes in Ecosystems

ESSENTIAL QUESTION

How do ecosystems change?

By the end of this lesson, you should be able to describe how natural processes change ecosystems and help them develop after a natural disturbance.

6.LS2.1, 6.LS2.6, 6.LS4.1, 6.ESS3.3

Ecosystems are always changing. Many changes in ecosystems are due to natural disturbances. This forest fire in Yellowstone National Park was caused by lightning.

© Houghton Mifflin Harcourt Publishing Company • Image Credits: (bg) ©David R. Frazier Photolibrary, Inc./Photo Researchers, Inc.

Lesson Labs

Quick Labs
• Measuring Species Diversity
• Investigate Evidence of Succession

Field Lab
• Predicting How Succession Follows a Human Disturbance

Engage Your Brain

1 Predict Check T or F to show whether you think each statement is true or false.

T   F

☐ ☐ Some damaged ecosystems can recover after a disturbance.

☐ ☐ Ecosystems only change slowly after natural disturbances.

☐ ☐ Changes in ecosystems proceed in a fairly predictable way after a disturbance occurs.

☐ ☐ Ecosystems eventually stop changing.

2 Describe Use the picture below to describe how beavers change their environment.

_____

_____

_____

Active Reading

3 Synthesize A compound term is a term made from two or more words. The term *pioneer species* is a compound term. Use the definitions and sentence below to make an educated guess about the meaning of the compound term *pioneer species*.

Word	Meaning
pioneer	the first ones to do something
species	a group of very similar organisms

Example sentence
Lichens and other <u>pioneer species</u> break down rock and leave organic matter that mix together to make soil.

pioneer species:

_____

_____

Vocabulary Terms

• eutrophication   • pioneer species
• succession   • biodiversity

4 Identify As you read, create a reference card for each vocabulary term. On one side of the card, write the term and its meaning. On the other side, draw a picture that illustrates or makes a connection to the term. These cards can be used as bookmarks in the text. You can also refer to the cards while studying.

© Houghton Mifflin Harcourt Publishing Company • Image Credits: (bg) ©David R. Frazier Photolibrary, Inc./Photo Researchers, Inc.; (tr) ©William Smithey Jr./Photographer's Choice/Getty Images

Nothing Stays the Same

How quickly do ecosystems change?

Ecosystems and organisms are constantly changing and responding to daily, seasonal, and long-term changes in the environment. Most ecosystem changes are gradual. Some are sudden and irregular.

 **Active Reading** **5 Describe** As you read, underline one example of a slow change and one example of a sudden change in an ecosystem.

Ecosystems May Change Slowly

Some changes happen slowly. Over time, a pond can develop into a meadow. **Eutrophication** (yoo•trohf•ih•KAY• shuhn) is the process in which organic matter and nutrients slowly build up in a body of water. The nutrients increase the growth of plants and microorganisms. When these organisms die, decaying matter sinks to the bottom of the pond. This organic matter can eventually fill the pond and become soil that grasses and other meadow plants can grow in.

Ecosystem changes can also be caused by seasonal or long-term changes in climate.

Ecosystems May Change Suddenly

Ecosystems can suddenly change due to catastrophic natural disturbances. A hurricane's strong winds can blow down trees and destroy vegetation in a few hours. Lightning can start a forest fire that rapidly clears away plants and alters animal habitats. A volcano, such as Washington's Mount St. Helens, can erupt and cause massive destruction to an ecosystem. But destruction is not the end of the story. Recovery brings new changes to an ecosystem and the populations that live in it.

Visualize It! (Inquiry)

6 Hypothesize What natural ecological change might happen to the meadow that forms where the pond was?

_____

_____

The organic matter growing in a pond dies and falls to the bottom. The pond gets shallower as the matter piles up.

Eventually, the pond fills in, and land plants grow there. The pond becomes a level meadow.

© Houghton Mifflin Harcourt Publishing Company

Ruin and Recovery

Ecosystems can change very fast. The volcanic eruption of Mount St. Helens in southern Washington devastated the mountain on May 18, 1980, killing 57 people. The hot gas and debris also killed native plant and animal species and damaged 596 square kilometers (230 square miles) of forest.

1979

Today

A Changed Landscape

The eruption changed the ecosystem dramatically. Trees fell and forests burned. Much of the ice and snow melted. The water mixed with ash and dirt that covered the ground. Thick mud formed and slid down the mountain. Flowing mud removed more trees and changed the shape of the landscape.

Road to Recovery

How did the ecosystem recover? Snow patches and ice protected some species. Some small mammals were sheltered in burrows. With the trees gone, more sunlight reached the ground. Seeds sprouted, and the recovery began.

Extend

Inquiry

7 Explain How do sudden catastrophes such as the eruption of Mount St. Helens change the landscape of ecosystems?

8 Research Find out about how natural catastrophic events, such as volcanic eruptions, can affect the climate on Earth.

9 Hypothesize Form a hypothesis based on your research in question 8 about how changes in climate can lead to changes in ecosystems.

© Houghton Mifflin Harcourt Publishing Company • Image Credits: (bg) ©Science Source/Photo Researchers, Inc.; (t) ©Science Source/Photo Researchers, Inc.; (b) ©EdBookPhoto/Alamy

What are the two types of ecological succession?

Ecosystems can develop from bare rock or cleared land. This development is the result of slow and constructive gradual changes. The slow development or replacement of an ecological community by another ecological community over time is called **succession**.

Primary Succession

A community may start to grow in an area that has no soil. This process is called primary succession. The first organisms to live in an uninhabited area are called **pioneer species**. Pioneer species, such as lichens, grow on rock and help to form soil in which plants can grow.

Visualize It!

10 Label Write a title for each step of primary succession.

A _____

A slowly retreating glacier exposes bare rock where nothing lives, and primary succession begins.

B _____

Acids from lichens break down the rock into particles. These particles mix with the remains of dead lichens to make soil.

C _____

After many years, there is enough soil for mosses to grow. The mosses replace the lichens. Insects and other small organisms begin to live there, enriching the soil.

D _____

As the soil deepens, mosses are replaced by ferns. The ferns may slowly be replaced by grasses and wildflowers. If there is enough soil, shrubs and small trees may grow.

E _____

After hundreds or even thousands of years, the soil may be deep and fertile enough to support a forest.

© Houghton Mifflin Harcourt Publishing Company • Image Credits: (tr) ©Fernando Camino/Contributor/Cover/Getty Images

Secondary Succession

Succession also happens to areas that have been disturbed but that still have soil. Sometimes an existing ecosystem is damaged by a natural disaster, such as a fire or a flood. Sometimes farmland is cleared but is left unmanaged. In either case, if soil is left intact, the original community may regrow through a series of stages called secondary succession.

11 Identify Underline one or two distinctive features of each stage of secondary succession.

Think Outside the Book

12 Describe Find an example of secondary succession in your community, and make a poster that describes each stage.

A

The first year after a farmer stops growing crops or the first year after some other major disturbance, wild plants start to grow. In farmland, crabgrass often grows first.

B

By the second year, new wild plants appear. Their seeds may have been blown into the field by the wind, or they may have been carried by insects or birds. Horseweed is common during the second year.

C

In 5 to 15 years, small conifer trees may start growing among the weeds. The trees continue to grow, and after about 100 years, a forest may form.

D

As older conifers die, they may be replaced by hardwoods, such as oak or maple trees, if the climate can support them.

© Houghton Mifflin Harcourt Publishing Company • Image Credits: (bg) ©Emil Enchev/Alamy

It's a Balancing Act

What are two signs of a mature ecosystem?

In the early stages of succession, only a few species live and grow in an area. As the ecosystem matures, more species become established.

Climax Species

Succession can happen over decades or over hundreds of years. A community of producers forms first. These organisms are followed by decomposers and consumers. Over time, a stable, balanced ecosystem develops.

As a community matures, it may become dominated by well-adapted *climax species*. The redwoods in a temperate rain forest are a climax species. An ecosystem dominated by climax species is stable until the ecosystem is disturbed.

Biodiversity

As succession moves along, richer soil, nutrients, and other resources become available. This increase in resource availability lets more species become established. By the time climax species are established, the resources in the area support many different kinds of organisms. The number and variety of species that are present in an area is referred to as **biodiversity**.

A diverse forest is more stable and less likely to be destroyed by sudden changes, such as an insect invasion. Most plant-damaging insects attack only one kind of plant. The presence of a variety of plants can reduce the impact of the insects. Even if an entire plant species dies off, other similar plant species may survive.

Active Reading **13 Summarize** How is biodiversity beneficial to an ecosystem?

_____

_____

_____

Rain forests are not just found at the equator. Temperate rain forests along the Pacific Northwest host a diversity of life. Temperate rain forests are often dominated by conifers. Rain forests can receive 350 cm or more of rain annually.

Ferns and other small plants live on the wet, shady forest floor.

© Houghton Mifflin Harcourt Publishing Company • Image Credits: (bg) ©Larry Lee Photography/Corbis

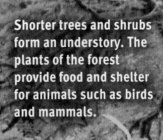

Shorter trees and shrubs form an understory. The plants of the forest provide food and shelter for animals such as birds and mammals.

A desert is very different from a rain forest, but it can also be an example of a mature ecosystem. Deserts receive as little as 8 cm of rain per year. But a desert has climax species well-adapted to its dry climate. These species form a balanced ecosystem.

Large cactuses are climax species in deserts.

Desert plants are adapted to live in hot, dry conditions and provide food and shelter for animals.

14 Compare Use the Venn diagram to compare and contrast deserts and rain forests.

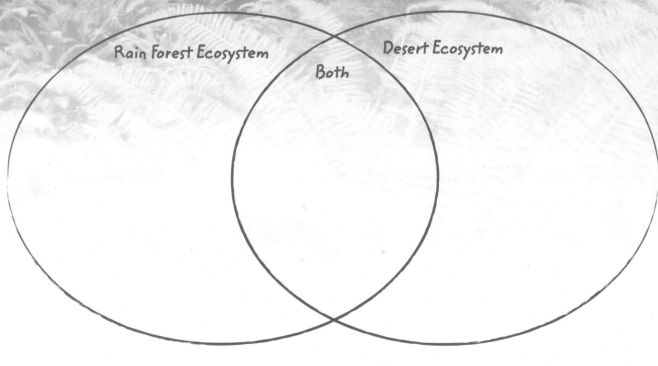

Rain Forest Ecosystem

Both

Desert Ecosystem

© Houghton Mifflin Harcourt Publishing Company • Image Credits: (bg) ©Larry Lee Photography/Corbis; (t) ©George H.H. Huey/Corbis

Visual Summary

To complete this summary, fill in the blanks with the correct word or phrase. Then use the key below to check your answers. You can use this page to review the main concepts of the lesson.

Changes in Ecosystems

Ecosystems are always changing.

Ecosystems can change rapidly or slowly.

15 A pond fills in with organic matter during _____

Secondary succession occurs in damaged ecosystems that still have soil.

17 Soil in damaged ecosystems enables _____ to grow right away.

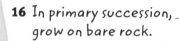

Primary succession begins with bare rock.

16 In primary succession, _____ grow on bare rock.

Mature ecosystems include many kinds of diverse organisms living in balance.

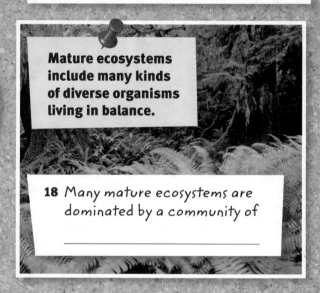

18 Many mature ecosystems are dominated by a community of _____

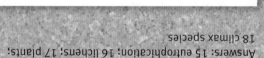

Answers: 15 eutrophication; 16 lichens; 17 plants; 18 climax species

19 Relate How is diversity related to changes in ecosystems?

© Houghton Mifflin Harcourt Publishing Company • Image Credits: ©Larry Lee Photography/Corbis

Lesson Review

Vocabulary

Fill in the blank with the term that best completes the following sentences.

1 _____ are the first organisms to live in an uninhabited area.

2 _____ is the number and variety of species that are present in an area.

3 The gradual development or replacement of one ecological community by another is called

_____

Key Concepts

4 Describe Explain how eutrophication can change an aquatic ecosystem into a land ecosystem.

_____
_____
_____
_____
_____
_____

5 Compare What is the major difference between primary and secondary succession?

_____
_____
_____
_____

6 Summarize Explain the important role a pioneer species plays in succession.

_____
_____
_____
_____
_____

Critical Thinking

Use the diagram to answer the following questions.

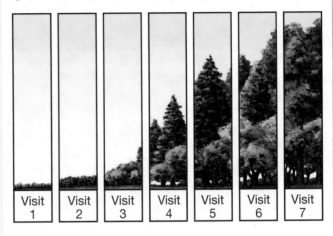

| Visit 1 | Visit 2 | Visit 3 | Visit 4 | Visit 5 | Visit 6 | Visit 7 |

7 Analyze Between visits 1 and 7, what kind of ecological succession is shown? Explain your answer.

_____
_____
_____

8 Predict If a fire occurs at visit 5, what kind of ecological succession is more likely to occur thereafter?

_____
_____
_____

9 Synthesize How might biodiversity help an ecosystem recover from a volcanic eruption?

_____
_____
_____
_____
_____
_____

© Houghton Mifflin Harcourt Publishing Company

My Notes

© Houghton Mifflin Harcourt Publishing Company

© Houghton Mifflin Harcourt Publishing Company

Engineering Design Process

Skills

Identify a need

✓ Conduct research

Brainstorm solutions

✓ Select a solution

✓ Build a prototype

✓ Test and evaluate

✓ Redesign to improve

✓ Communicate results

Objectives

- Design and build a closed ecosystem.
- Evaluate design constraints that affect the biodiversity of the ecosystem.

Design an Ecosystem

An ecosystem is a community of organisms that interact with each other and with the nonliving environment in a specific area. Factors, such as temperature, the amount of sunlight, water, and minerals, determine which species can live in an ecosystem. Populations of organisms in an ecosystem can be classified by their function. Some producers, such as algae and green plants, make their own food by using sunlight through a process called photosynthesis. Consumers can be carnivores, herbivores, or omnivores. Decomposers, such as fungi and some bacteria, are consumers that break down dead plants and animals and recycle them as nutrients that other organisms can use.

1 Identify List signs of biodiversity in the illustration.

© Houghton Mifflin Harcourt Publishing Company

Biodiversity

The biodiversity of an ecosystem is the number and variety of species it contains. This includes plants, animals, and other organisms. The more variety there is in an ecosystem, the healthier that ecosystem will be.

Changing conditions can threaten the biodiversity of an ecosystem. For example, a hurricane might cause flooding, damage plant life, and destroy animal habitats. A drought might dry up a pond, killing its fish.

Aquariums are artificial aquatic ecosystems. Maintaining an aquarium is one way to study the effects of changes on an ecosystem's biodiversity.

2 Apply An aquarium is an artificial aquatic environment. What characteristics of an aquarium help preserve biodiversity?

_____

_____

_____

✋ **You Try It!** ⟶

Now it's your turn to design a self-contained aquatic ecosystem.

© Houghton Mifflin Harcourt Publishing Company Image Credits: (t) ©S-F/Shutterstock

 You Try It!

Now it's your turn to design and analyze a self-contained aquatic ecosystem. Make a plan to show how biodiversity affects an ecosystem.

① Conduct Research

Brainstorm plants and animals to put in your aquarium. Do research to find out what these organisms need to survive. Brainstorm ways to test changes to the biodiversity of the ecosystem.

_____

_____

_____

_____

_____

You Will Need

✔ one-gallon glass jar with tight-fitting lid or sealable clear plastic container

✔ fresh water; can use tap water, but water from natural source is preferable

✔ gravel

✔ aquatic plants and animals to be selected by students

✔ light source if needed

✔ decorative aquarium items (optional)

② Select a Solution

Based on your research, choose the plants and animals that you will include. Put them in your aquarium. Write down how you will test elements that affect the ecosystem's biodiversity. Explain your reasoning.

_____

_____

_____

_____

③ Build a Prototype

Follow these steps to build a prototype of your system.

- Clean your container, and put enough gravel in to cover the bottom.
- Fill the container with water, and add decorative items.
- Let the water and decorative items settle for at least 24 hours to allow the chemicals in the water to evaporate and the water to come to room temperature.
- Add your plants, and wait 24 hours.

- Before releasing the animals into the tank, float the containers holding the animals in the water in the tank for a few hours. This allows the animals to adjust to the temperature of the water in the tank.
- Close the lid tightly to prevent evaporation.
- Store your ecosystem where it will receive indirect sunlight.

© Houghton Mifflin Harcourt Publishing Company

(4) Test and Evaluate

Change something about the nonliving elements in the ecosystem. Keep a journal in which you record daily observations of your ecosystem for several weeks. Record how the biodiversity of the ecosystem changes during that time.

_____
_____
_____
_____
_____

(5) Redesign to Improve

After observing your system and keeping a journal for several weeks, what would you change about your system? Is there a better way to analyze how nonliving factors in the ecosystem affect its biodiversity?

_____
_____
_____
_____
_____
_____

(6) Communicate Results

Summarize the observations you made in your journal. Consider these questions: What things do you think made your ecosystem successful or unsuccessful in studying biodiversity? What things, if any, would you change to improve your ecosystem even more? Finally, make a report of your findings to present to the class.

_____
_____
_____
_____
_____
_____

© Houghton Mifflin Harcourt Publishing Company

Human Activity and Ecosystems

ESSENTIAL QUESTION

How do human activities affect ecosystems?

By the end of this lesson, you should be able to describe the effects of human activities on ecosystems, and explain the role of conservation in protecting natural resources.

6.LS2.5, 6.LS2.6, 6.LS4.1, 6.LS4.2, 6.ESS2.4, 6.ESS3.3

Human activities can disturb habitats and wildlife. Coastal developments may prevent species such as leatherback sea turtles from reproducing.

© Houghton Mifflin Harcourt Publishing Company • Image Credits: (bg) ©Jim Richardson/National Geographic/Getty Images

✋ Lesson Labs

Quick Labs
- Biodiversity All Around Us
- Investigate Acidity of Water

Field Lab
- Field Investigation of Plant Quantity and Diversity

Engage Your Brain

1 Explain Think about what you see as you go to and from school. What is one example of human activity that you would change if you could?

_____

Why and how would you make this change?

_____
_____
_____
_____
_____

2 Describe Write your own caption to this photo.

_____
_____
_____

Active Reading

3 Synthesize Many English words have their roots in other languages. Use the Latin words below to make an educated guess about the meaning of the words *urbanization* and *biodiversity*.

Latin word	Meaning
urbanus	city
divertus	diverse
bio	life

Example sentence
The population of Los Angeles increased during the 20th century because of <u>urbanization</u>.

urbanization:

_____
_____

Example sentence
The <u>biodiversity</u> of our food crops has decreased over the last several decades.

biodiversity:

_____
_____

Vocabulary Terms

- **urbanization**
- **biodiversity**
- **eutrophication**
- **stewardship**
- **conservation**

4 Identify As you read, place a question mark next to any words that you don't understand. After you finish reading the lesson, go back and review the text that you marked. If the information is still confusing, consult a classmate or your teacher.

© Houghton Mifflin Harcourt Publishing Company • Image Credits: (bg) ©Jim Richardson/National Geographic/Getty Images; (t) ©Photoshot Holdings Ltd/Alamy

Growing Pains

How do humans negatively affect ecosystems?

Human activities can change and even harm ecosystems. An *ecosystem* is all of the living and nonliving things within a given area. Changing one thing in an ecosystem can affect many other things, because everything in an ecosystem is connected.

Humans can affect ecosystems through pollution. *Pollution* is caused by any material or condition that harms the environment. For example, factories and automobiles burn fossil fuels. This releases harmful chemicals into the environment. Farms that produce our food may also burn fossil fuels and release chemicals, such as pesticides or fertilizers, into the environment.

Even simple actions can harm ecosystems. For example, the trash we throw out may end up in a landfill. Landfills take up space and may contain harmful materials like batteries. Toxic metals in batteries can leak into soil or groundwater, with drastic consequences for organisms and ecosystems.

5 Relate Identify a form of pollution that you observe in your community.

_____

_____

Tons of garbage are put into landfills every day.

As cities and suburbs expand closer to natural areas, wildlife may wander into our backyards and onto our streets.

© Houghton Mifflin Harcourt Publishing Company • Image Credits: (t) ©Gerhard Egger/Corbis; (b) ©Lucas Payne/Alamy

By Depleting Resources

The number of people on Earth has increased from 1 billion to more than 7 billion people in the last 200 years. The growing human population has created a greater need for natural resources. This need has created problems for ecosystems. When we cut down trees, we remove a resource that many organisms need for food and shelter. The loss of many trees in an area can affect shade and local temperatures. These changes can disturb ecosystems.

The overuse of resources causes them to be depleted, or used up. *Resource depletion* occurs when a large fraction of a resource has been used up. Fresh water was once a renewable resource. But in some areas, humans use fresh water faster than it can be replenished by the water cycle.

By Destroying Habitats

Human population growth in and around cities is called **urbanization** (er•buh•nih•ZAY•shuhn). Urban growth within ecosystems often destroys natural habitats. Roads can divide habitats and prevent animals from safely roaming their territory. If animals cannot interact with each other and their surroundings, the ecosystem will not thrive.

An ecosystem may be converted into housing and shopping areas that further shrink habitats. This can bring humans and wildlife into contact. Deer, raccoons, and even coyotes have become common sights in some suburban areas.

Every habitat has its own number and variety of organisms, or **biodiversity**. If a habitat is damaged or destroyed, biodiversity is lost. Because living things are connected with each other and with their environment, loss of biodiversity affects the entire ecosystem. Organisms that are already endangered may become extinct, meaning that there are no organisms left of that kind.

Active Reading **6 Provide** Give one example of how urbanization affects natural ecosystems.

_____

_____

_____

An open-pit mine like this one is one way that humans remove minerals from the ground. Minerals are nonrenewable resources.

Cutting down forests destroys habitats and affects the physical features of the ecosystem.

Think Outside the Book Inquiry

7 Apply Do research to find out what the environment around your school looked like 100 years ago.

© Houghton Mifflin Harcourt Publishing Company • Image Credits: (bg) ©Arno Massee/Photo Researchers, Inc.; (t) ©Rex Ziak/Stone/Getty Images

Water, Water Everywhere?

How do humans impact oceans?

Active Reading

8 Identify As you read, underline the sources of ocean pollution.

Oceans support a variety of ecosystems that together contain nearly half of Earth's species. Pollution from human activities damages ocean ecosystems and threatens marine biodiversity.

Point-source pollution comes from one source. Oil spills, such as the one shown above, are an example of this. Spilled oil pollutes open waters and coastal habitats. *Nonpoint-source pollution* comes from many sources. For example, chemicals such as fertilizers and pesticides may be washed into oceans, where they harm many marine organisms.

Raw sewage and trash are frequently dumped into marine habitats. Plastic bags and packaging are dangerous to marine animals. Some animals mistake bags for food or become tangled in packaging. Dumping trash in the ocean is illegal. Many people and agencies work hard to enforce laws that protect the oceans.

Visualize It!

9 Predict Compare these pictures. What is one problem that could arise if a sea turtle sees the plastic bag underwater?

_____

_____

Jellyfish have translucent, sac-like bodies. Sea turtles and dolphins eat jellyfish.

Underwater, plastic bags look like jellyfish.

© Houghton Mifflin Harcourt Publishing Company • Image Credits: (t) ©Andy Levin/Photo Researchers, Inc.; (bl) ©Irma thea marren/Shutterstock (br) ©F.Bettex-Mysterra.org/Alamy

Through Fishing and Overfishing

A greater demand for seafood from the growing human population has led to *overfishing* of some ocean species. Many fish species cannot reproduce fast enough to replace individuals that are harvested for food. When large numbers of a single fish population are caught, the remaining population may be too small to successfully reproduce. If the population cannot replace itself, it can become locally extinct. As local extinction occurs, overfishing may begin in new locations and endanger new local populations. The local loss of a species can disturb ocean food webs and threaten ecosystem stability.

Through Coastal Development

The growing human population also has led to increased coastal development. Homes and business are built on and near beaches and wetlands. Sadly, this can destroy the very coastlines we want to be near. Roads and shopping centers divide habitats. Increased human activity increases pollution both on shore and in coastal waters.

In some places, development has almost completely replaced natural coastlines. For example, construction of new homes and businesses is rapidly destroying mangrove forests. Mangroves are unique trees found only in certain coastal regions. Mangrove forests play a key role in maintaining coastlines. The thick roots stabilize the sandy soil and prevent erosion. The trees are home to a wide range of species.

Human activity has also damaged coral reefs, but people and scientists are working to correct this damage. Coral reefs are vital ecosystems because so many species live in or around them. To replace this lost habitat, scientists have created artificial reefs. First, different fish species will find safety in the structures. Next, algae and soft corals begin to grow. Over time, hard corals grow and other sea life can be seen. Artificial reefs preserve the reef food web and stabilize the ecosystem.

Overfishing means that the rate at which fish are caught exceeds the rate at which the species can reproduce. This can lead to the endangerment or extinction of a population.

10 List What are three ways that human activities impact ocean ecosystems?

_____

_____

_____

Artificial reefs, such as sunken ships or other human-made objects, are being used to make up for the loss of natural coral reefs.

© Houghton Mifflin Harcourt Publishing Company • Image Credits: (t) ©Aurora Photos/Alamy; (b) ©Alexis Rosenfeld/Photo Researchers, Inc.

How do humans affect freshwater ecosystems?

Active Reading

11 Identify As you read, number the steps involved in the formation of acid rain.

Human activities have decreased the amount of water, or *water quantity*, in many river ecosystems. Dams and river channelization are two examples of this. Dams block the flow of river water. That means there is less water downstream of the dam. Channelization is used to straighten rivers to improve travel and other activities. However, changing the natural course of a river also changes the amount of water in it. Differences in water levels can change water temperature and chemistry. These changes can affect the reproduction and survival of many river species.

Human activities can also decrease *water quality*, or change how clean or polluted the water is, in ecosystems. Pollution disturbs water quality. Animal waste and fertilizer from farms contain nutrients that can enter ponds and lakes as runoff. An increase in the amount of nutrients, such as nitrates, in an aquatic ecosystem is called **eutrophication** (yoo•trohf•ih•KAY•shuhn). The extra nutrients cause overgrowth of algae. The excess algae die and decompose, using up the pond's dissolved oxygen. As dissolved oxygen levels decrease, fish begin to die. If eutrophication continues, the pond ecosystem will not recover.

Water quality is also affected by air pollution. For example, some freshwater ecosystems are affected by acid rain. Burning fossil fuels releases chemicals into the air. Some of these combine with rain to form acids. Small amounts of acid in rain cause its pH to fall below its normal value of 5.6. Acid rain can damage both aquatic and land ecosystems.

Eutrophication causes overgrowth of algae and can disrupt pond ecosystems.

© Houghton Mifflin Harcourt Publishing Company • Image Credits: ©James Leighton/Corbis

Invasive Species

An *invasive species* is nonnative organism that can do harm in an ecosystem. Invasive species often thrive in new places because they are free from the predators found in their native homes. Tennessee has invasive plant and animal species that threaten ecosystems and their biodiversity.

The bighead carp is one of the largest fish in the Tennessee rivers, making it a big competitor for food and space.

The Asian carp (or bighead carp) is an invasive species that has been in Tennessee's rivers for decades. The fish is native to Asia, but it was brought to the United States in the 1970s to help improve water quality in some ponds in Arkansas. The carp were kept at special facilities, but some escaped over the years.

The fish spread throughout the Mississippi River and into southern states, including Tennessee. Bighead carp grow to larger than 23 kg (50 lbs), and they outcompete native fish for food in the local ecosystems. They also feed on the eggs of other species of fish. As populations of bighead carp spread, the biodiversity of Tennessee's river systems is affected.

Extend

Inquiry

12 Explain How do bighead carp contribute to a reduction in biodiversity in Tennessee's river systems?

13 Hypothesize Form a hypothesis about a method that might be effective in controlling populations of bighead carp in Tennessee.

14 Research Identify another invasive species that has been introduced to the United States. Explain how the species was introduced and spread. Then design a possible solution that might have prevented this species from disrupting the biodiversity of the ecosystem.

© Houghton Mifflin Harcourt Publishing Company • Image Credits: (t) ©Kaloosha/Shutterstock; (b) ©pancha/Getty Images

Save It!

![Active Reading icon] **Active Reading**

15 Identify As you read, underline the definition of stewardship.

How do humans protect ecosystems?

There are many ways that humans can protect ecosystems. One way is by using Earth's resources in a careful manner. The careful and responsible management of a resource is called **stewardship**. The resources of an ecosystem include all of its living and nonliving parts.

By Maintaining Biodiversity

The organisms in an ecosystem depend on each other and interact with each other in a vast interconnected food web. Each species has a place in this web and a role to play. The loss of a species or introduction of an exotic species creates gaps in the web. This can disrupt species interactions. Protecting habitats and helping species survive protects the biodiversity in an ecosystem. The greater the biodiversity, the healthier the ecosystem.

16 State What are two ways that humans can help maintain biodiversity in ecosystems?

_____

_____

_____

You can reduce pollution by participating in a local cleanup project.

You can protect habitats by staying on marked trails when visiting national parks and forests.

© Houghton Mifflin Harcourt Publishing Company • Image Credits: (l) ©Mike Greenslade/Alamy; (r) ©Raymond Gehman/Corbis

By Conserving Natural Resources

Humans can protect ecosystems through conservation. **Conservation** is the protection and wise use of natural resources. Practicing conservation means using fewer natural resources and reducing waste. It also helps prevent habitat destruction.

The "three Rs" are three ways to conserve resources.

- *Reduce* what you buy and use—this is the first goal of conservation.
- *Reuse* what you already have. For example, carry water in a reusable bottle and lunch in a reusable lunch bag.
- *Recycle* by recovering materials from waste and by always choosing to use recycling bins.

You can practice conservation every day by making wise choices. Even small changes make a difference!

17 Synthesize Suppose you wanted to stop eating fast food to cut down on excess fat and sodium. How might this benefit the environment as well?

_____

_____

_____

_____

You can help prevent water shortages by turning off the water as you brush your teeth.

You can reduce pesticide use by supporting responsible agriculture.

You can reduce the use of fossil fuels by turning off lights and supporting alternative energy sources.

© Houghton Mifflin Harcourt Publishing Company • Image Credits: (t) ©ImageShop/Corbis; (c) ©Sarah Hadley/Sarah Hadley Photography; (b) ©Mike Kipling Photography/Alamy

Visual Summary

To complete this summary, fill in the blanks with the correct word. Then use the key below to check your answers. You can use this page to review the main concepts of the lesson.

Human demand for resources and land can destroy habitats and disturb ecosystems.

Human Activity and Ecosystems

18 Habitat destruction can lead to a loss of _____

Dumping trash and chemicals into waterways can damage aquatic ecosystems.

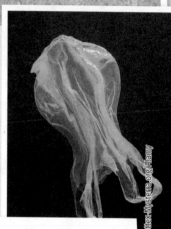

Conservation and stewardship help protect ecosystems.

19 Materials that cause unwanted changes in the environment cause
_____

20 The protection and wise use of natural resources is called _____

Answers: 18 biodiversity; 19 pollution; 20 conservation

21 **Predict** Imagine that everyone in the United States chose to ride bicycles rather than drive cars. What effect would this have on your local ecosystem?

_____

_____

_____

© Houghton Mifflin Harcourt Publishing Company • Image Credits: (t) ©Arno Massee/Photo Researchers, Inc.; (b) ©ImageShop/Corbis; (b) ©F.Bettex-Mystera.org/Alamy

Lesson Review

Vocabulary

In your own words, define the following terms.

1 eutrophication

_____

_____

2 stewardship

_____

_____

3 urbanization

_____

_____

Key Concepts

4 Illustrate Name two ways that humans affect land ecosystems.

_____

_____

5 Describe Explain the difference between an *exotic species* and an *invasive exotic species*.

_____

_____

_____

_____

6 Summarize What is pollution?

_____

_____

_____

_____

_____

7 Identify What are two ways to practice conservation?

_____

_____

_____

Critical Thinking

Use this table to answer the following questions.

Human Population Growth

Human population	Year
1 billion	1804
2 billion	1927
3 billion	1960
4 billion	1974
5 billion	1987
6 billion	1999
7 billion	2011
Projected	
8 billion	2026

8 Calculate How many years did it take for the population to double from 1 billion to 2 billion?

_____

_____

9 Calculate How many years did it take for the population to double from 3 billion to 6 billion?

_____

_____

10 Hypothesize If Earth's population continues to increase without limit, how might this affect natural ecosystems? Be specific in your answer.

_____

_____

_____

_____

_____

11 Synthesize Some detergents contain phosphates, chemicals that act like fertilizers. If wastewater from washing machines enters a local lake, will the fish population increase or decrease? Explain your answer.

_____

_____

_____

_____

© Houghton Mifflin Harcourt Publishing Company

My Notes

© Houghton Mifflin Harcourt Publishing Company

© Houghton Mifflin Harcourt Publishing Company

Combating an Invasive Species

Skills
Conduct research
✔ Brainstorm solutions
✔ Select a solution
✔ Design a solution
✔ Test and evaluate
✔ Redesign to improve
✔ Communicate results

Objectives
• Design a solution to reduce the impact of an invasive species.

Bush Honeysuckles

The bush honeysuckle is a plant that is native to Asia. Seeds of the plant were first brought to North America in the 1700s. They became a popular choice for decorating private landscapes throughout the South, including Tennessee. But over time, the bush honeysuckle began to compete with native plants for space, water, and sunlight. When bush honeysuckle crowds out native plants, it can affect animals that rely on those plants for food or habitat.

1 Brainstorm What are some ways that humans can help reduce the impact of an invasive species like the bush honeysuckle?

_____

_____

_____

_____

Native plants   Bush honeysuckle

© Houghton Mifflin Harcourt Publishing Company • Image Credits: (bg) ©Linda Freshwaters Arndt/Alamy

Weeding Out an Invader

Removing bush honeysuckle is not easy. Like most plants, the bush can be dug up by hand or using machinery. But even after it is removed, bush honeysuckle may grow back. Some herbicides (chemicals that are used to kill plants) may be effective. However, many herbicides pose a danger to the environment. In addition to eliminating invasive species, they may kill native plants too. Also, herbicides can wash into streams and rivers, where they can harm plants and animals.

2 Infer This person is spraying invasive weeds with an herbicide. Why is he wearing protective clothing? What effect will the herbicide have on the weeds and other living things?

_____

_____

_____

_____

_____

🖐 **You Try It!** ⟶

Now it's your turn to design a solution for reducing the impact of an invasive species.

© Houghton Mifflin Harcourt Publishing Company • Image Credits: (bg) ©Linda Freshwaters Arndt/Alamy; (t) ©FLPA/Alamy

 # You Try It!

Now it's your turn to come up with a way to control invasive species. Remember that plants need air, water, sunlight, and space to grow. How can you design a solution that keeps an invasive species from growing but allows other plants to survive?

(1) Brainstorm Solutions

Brainstorm ideas for a solution that can keep an invasive species from becoming a problem in an ecosystem. What kinds of solutions might work for controlling an invasive plant species?

_____

_____

_____

_____

_____

(2) Select a Solution

Which of your ideas seems to offer the best promise of success? Explain your reasoning.

_____

_____

_____

_____

(3) Design a Solution

In the space below, write down your plan. Will you need to develop new technology for your solution? Or can you use technology that already exists?

_____

_____

_____

_____

_____

© Houghton Mifflin Harcourt Publishing Company

④ Test and Evaluate

In the space below, make a diagram to show how you would test your solution.

⑤ Redesign to Improve

Based on your drawing, what details might you have forgotten? How can you improve the design? Write your ideas.

_____

_____

_____

_____

⑥ Communicate Results

Explain the potential of your design for reducing the impact of invasive species on an ecosystem. How will you know if your solution is effective?

_____

_____

_____

_____

© Houghton Mifflin Harcourt Publishing Company

Lesson 1

ESSENTIAL QUESTION
What are land biomes?

Describe the characteristics of different biomes that exist on land.

Lesson 3

ESSENTIAL QUESTION
How do ecosystems change?

Describe how natural processes change ecosystems and help them develop after a natural disturbance.

Lesson 2

ESSENTIAL QUESTION
What are aquatic ecosystems?

Describe the characteristics of marine, freshwater, and other aquatic ecosystems.

Lesson 4

ESSENTIAL QUESTION
How do human activities affect ecosystems?

Describe the effect of human activities on ecosystems, and explain the role of conservation in protecting natural resources.

Connect ESSENTIAL QUESTIONS
Lessons 3 and 4

1 Explain How might human activity cause secondary succession? In your answer, identify each stage of secondary succession.

_____
_____
_____
_____
_____
_____
_____
_____
_____
_____
_____
_____
_____

Think Outside the Book

2 Synthesize Choose one of these activities to help synthesize what you have learned in this unit.

☐ Using what you learned in lessons 1 and 2, create a brochure that describes the characteristics of the biome in which you live. In your brochure list what aquatic systems, if any, can also be found where you live.

☐ Using what you learned in lessons 1, 2, and 3, choose two land biomes and two aquatic ecosystems. Research seasonal climate data such as temperature for each location. Make a graph of the data and draw a conclusion about which biome is most suitable for human life and activity.

© Houghton Mifflin Harcourt Publishing Company • Image Credits: (tl) ©Jake Rajs/Stone/Getty Images; (tr) ©David R. Frazier Photolibrary, Inc./Photo Researchers, Inc.; (bl) ©Jeffrey Rotman/Corbis; (br) ©Jim Richardson/National Geographic/Getty Images

Unit 3 Review

Name _____

Vocabulary

Fill in each blank with the term that best completes the following sentences.

1 A _____ is a community of organisms at a major regional or global level.

2 A _____ tree has leaves that drop in the winter as an adaptation to cold temperatures.

3 _____ is an increase in the ratio or density of people living in urban areas rather than rural areas.

4 A _____ is one of the first species of organisms to live in an area.

Key Concepts

Read each question below, and circle the best answer.

5 What are the ocean zones of a marine ecosystem, from most shallow to deepest?

 A intertidal, neritic, bathyal, abyssal

 B abyssal, neritic, intertidal, bathyal

 C neritic, intertidal, bathyal, abyssal

 D bathyal, abyssal, intertidal, neritic

6 Resource depletion, pollution, and habitat loss are all environmental problems caused by what factor?

 A acid rain

 B eutrophication

 C introduced species

 D human activities

© Houghton Mifflin Harcourt Publishing Company

7 The chart below shows the average monthly temperatures in a certain desert ecosystem in the northern hemisphere over a 20-year period.

Month	Average Temperature (°C)
January	12.1
February	13.8
March	14.9
April	16.7
May	17.9
June	19.2
July	20.0
August	19.8
September	18.4
October	15.0
November	12.6
December	11.9

Based on the data table, what conclusion can be drawn about the climate in the desert?

A The general climate patterns match those of many forest ecosystems.

B The general climate patterns are the opposite of those of many forest ecosystems.

C There is no recognizable pattern that can be compared to other ecosystems.

D Deserts have no significant seasonal temperature changes.

8 The climate of a certain rain forest has changed over the last decade. Average temperatures have increased by about 1 °C. The biodiversity in the area has decreased over the same time period. What conclusion can be drawn about the rain forest ecosystem?

A The ecosystem will likely continue in the same pattern for another decade.

B The ecosystem experienced a natural or human-made environmental change.

C The ecosystem must have been affected by human activity.

D The ecosystem will return to its original climate patterns in the next decade.

© Houghton Mifflin Harcourt Publishing Company

9 What is an adaptation that allows some animals to survive in the tundra?

   A living underground   **C** being active at night only

   B having thick layers of fur   **D** living within the upper branches of trees

10 Some grass species need fire in order for their seeds to germinate. Why might this adaptation be useful for grasses?

   A Fire allows trees to grow and provide shade for the grasses.

   B The hot temperature of the fire helps the grasses grow faster.

   C Seeds can germinate in an area that has been cleared by a fire.

   D Fire discourages grazing by large animals so grass can grow higher.

Critical Thinking

Answer the following questions in the space provided.

11 Draw a diagram of ecological succession in an ecosystem and label it with the terms given below.

In the space provided, identify what each term means.

Pioneer species: _____

Primary succession: _____

Secondary succession: _____

Climax species: _____

© Houghton Mifflin Harcourt Publishing Company

12 The picture below shows a land ecosystem that experiences annual flooding.

Is this ecosystem more likely a result of primary succession or secondary succession? _____

Predict what would happen if a fast growing non-native species of plant was introduced to this ecosystem.

_____

_____

Connect **ESSENTIAL QUESTIONS**
Lessons 2 and 3

Answer the following question in the space provided.

13 Below is an example of an aquatic food web common in mangrove forests.

Mangrove Food Web

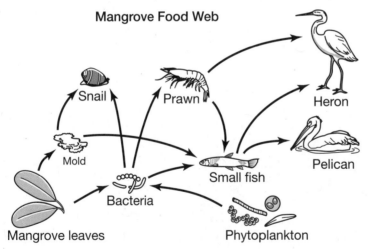

Mangroves commonly grow in estuaries. What are the characteristics of an estuary? _____

What might happen if the prawns and fish shown in the diagram were fished to near extinction? _____

_____

© Houghton Mifflin Harcourt Publishing Company

Earth's Resources

Common building materials such as lumber, bricks, and glass are all made from natural resources.

Big Idea

Humans depend on natural resources for materials and for energy.

6.ESS2.4, 6.ESS3.1, 6.ESS3.2, 6.ESS3.3, 6.ETS1.2, 6.PS3.1, 6.PS3.4

Wood for buildings comes from forests that have to be managed wisely.

What do you think?

The resources that humans need to live are found on Earth or come from the sun. What would happen if one or more of these resources were used up?

© Houghton Mifflin Harcourt Publishing Company • Image Credits: (bg) ©Philip Quirk/Alamy Images; (inset) ©Calvin Larsen/Photo Researchers, Inc.

Unit 4
Earth's Resources

The type of lighting as well as the quality of doors and windows can make a difference in a building's energy costs and efficiency.

Energy Sources

The world is filled with valuable resources. How we use, reuse, or use up those resources is important to this and future generations.

① Think About It

Every time you walk into school on a normal school day, the lights are on, the rooms are comfortable, and there are material resources available for teacher and student use. Where does your school get its energy? Is it from a renewable or nonrenewable resource? Could the energy be used more efficiently?

_____
_____
_____
_____

© Houghton Mifflin Harcourt Publishing Company • Image Credits: (bg) ©David Wall/Alamy Images; (b) ©SwellMedia/UpperCut Images/Alamy

② Ask a Question

What is the energy source for your school's heating and cooling system?

With a partner or as a class, learn more about the source of energy for your school's heating and cooling system and the energy efficiency of your school building. As you talk about it, consider the items below.

Things to Consider

☐ Does your school have more than one energy source?

☐ Is your school building energy efficient?

Many older schools have been modified with new windows, doors, and insulation. These changes were made to save on heating and cooling costs and to provide a more comfortable learning environment.

③ Make a Plan

Once you have learned about your school building's energy efficiency, develop a proposal for your principal. Propose an alternative energy source for the heating and cooling system and ways to improve the building's energy efficiency.

A Describe the current energy source for your school's heating and cooling system.

_____

_____

B Describe one alternative energy source your school could use.

_____

_____

C List any noted energy inefficiencies and suggestions for improvements.

_____

_____

Ideas for saving resources can help schools save money.

Take It Home

What energy sources supply your home? With an adult, talk about possible ways to improve energy efficiency where you live. See *ScienceSaurus*® for more information about energy conservation.

© Houghton Mifflin Harcourt Publishing Company • Image Credits: (bg) ©David Wei/Alamy Images; (b) ©HMH

Earth's Support of Life

Earth's land, water, and atmosphere help to support life on the planet's surface and in its oceans.

ESSENTIAL QUESTION

How can Earth support life?

By the end of this lesson, you should be able to explain how the unique properties of Earth make it possible for life to exist.

6.PS3.4

© Houghton Mifflin Harcourt Publishing Company • Image Credits: (bg) ©NASA/K. Horgan/Stone/Getty Images

Lesson Labs

Quick Labs
- How Water Forms on Earth's Surface
- Temperature Variations on Earth

Exploration Lab
- Modeling the Greenhouse Effect

 ## Engage Your Brain

1 Describe What kind of life is found on Earth?

_____

_____

_____

2 Compare Look at the differences between the pictures of Earth and Mars. Why do you think that Mars does not support the kind of life found on Earth?

_____

_____

_____

_____

_____

Mars

 ## Active Reading

3 Synthesize You can often define an unknown word if you know the meaning of its word parts. Use the word parts and sentence below to make an educated guess about the meaning of the word *atmosphere*.

Word part	Meaning
atmo-	vapor, steam
-sphere	globe, ball

Example sentence
Earth's <u>atmosphere</u> is made of different layers of gases.

atmosphere:

_____

_____

_____

Vocabulary Terms
- **photosynthesis**
- **atmosphere**
- **ultraviolet radiation**
- **ozone**

4 Identify As you read, place a question mark next to any words that you don't understand. When you finish reading the lesson, go back and review the text that you marked. If the information is still confusing, consult a classmate or teacher.

© Houghton Mifflin Harcourt Publishing Company • Image Credits: (b) ©NASA/K. Horgan/Stone/Getty Images; (t) ©StockTrek/Photodisc/Getty Images

Living it Up

This poison dart frog lives in a bromeliad in the rain forest canopy.

What do living things need to survive?

Earth is covered in living things. Plants, animals, and other organisms live in oceans, rivers, forests, and any other place that you can think of. What do these organisms need to survive? Animals like the poison dart frog in the picture need to breathe air, drink water, and eat food. They need a place to live where they have protection from things that can harm them and where they can dispose of wastes. What do plants need to stay alive? Plants like the bromeliad in the picture need many of the same basic things that animals do. The basic necessities of life are air, water, a source of energy, and a habitat to live in.

How do Earth and the sun interact to support life on Earth?

The sun is a star, so it radiates energy out into space. Some of this energy reaches Earth's surface. Plants on Earth use the sun's energy to make food through the process of photosynthesis. During **photosynthesis**, plants convert carbon dioxide and water to oxygen and glucose. Glucose is a sugar that can be stored in cells. When plants need energy, they break down and use the glucose they have stored. Plant life on Earth forms the foundation of many food chains. Some animals eat plants to gain energy. Other animals eat these animals. In this way, energy from the sun is passed from plants to other organisms.

Visualize It!

5 List What necessities of life does the frog get from the bromeliad?

_____
_____
_____
_____

Plants use energy from sunlight to perform photosynthesis.

---

6 Identify Underline the food that is produced during photosynthesis.

$$\text{carbon dioxide} + \text{water} \xrightarrow{\text{solar energy}} \text{oxygen} + \text{glucose}$$

© Houghton Mifflin Harcourt Publishing Company • Image Credits: (bg) ©D. Sim/Taxi/Getty Images; (t) ©Kris Mercer/Alamy

Earth's Rotation Distributes Solar Energy

Earth rotates continuously on its axis, spinning around completely every 24 hours. Earth's rotation allows most regions of Earth to receive sunlight regularly. Regular sunlight allows plants to grow in almost all places on Earth. Earth's rotation also protects areas on Earth from temperature extremes. Imagine how hot it would be if your town always faced the sun. And imagine how cold it would be if your town never faced the sun!

Earth Has a Unique Temperature Range

Earth's distance from the sun also protects it from temperature extremes. If Earth were closer to the sun, it might be like Venus. Venus has extremely high temperatures because it is closer to the sun, and because it has a very thick atmosphere. These factors make it is too hot to support life. If Earth were farther away from the sun, it might be like Mars. Mars has extremely low temperatures, so it is too cold to support life as we know it. Earth has an average temperature of 15° C (59° F). Regions of Earth range from freezing temperatures below 0° C (32° F) to hot temperatures above 38° C (100° F). This temperature range allows life to survive in even the coldest and hottest places on Earth.

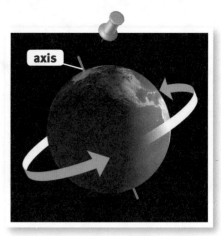

Earth's rotation allows all parts of Earth to receive energy from the sun.

Think Outside the Book Inquiry

7 Apply Write a news story about what would happen to life on Earth if Earth stopped rotating.

 **Visualize It!**

8 Identify Write whether each planet in the drawing is too hot, too cold, or just right to support life.

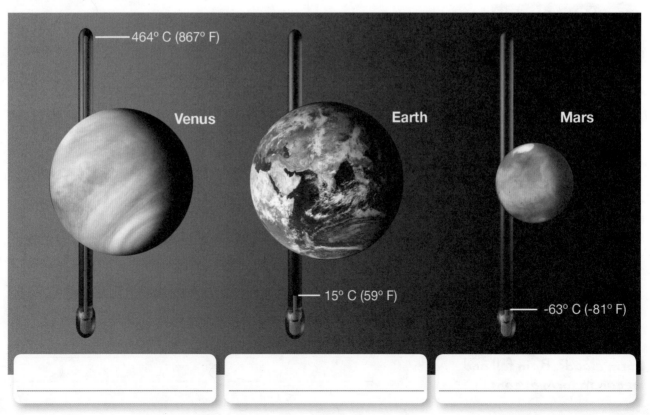

© Houghton Mifflin Harcourt Publishing Company

Water, Water Everywhere

What is unique about Earth's water?

When you look at a picture of Earth, you see lots and lots of water. How did Earth get so much water? Early Earth formed from molten materials, such as iron, nickel, and silica. These materials separated into layers and began to cool. As Earth cooled, it released steam and other gases into the air around its surface. The steam formed clouds, and water fell to Earth as rain. This was the beginning of Earth's oceans. Some of Earth's water also came from space. Icy comets and meteors impacted Earth and added water to Earth's oceans.

Only Earth Has Liquid Water to Support Life

Earth is unique in the solar system because it contains water in three states: solid, liquid, and gas. Most of Earth's water is in liquid form. In fact, Earth is the only known planet with a large supply of liquid water on its surface. About 71% of Earth's surface is now covered with water. Liquid water is essential to life because cells need liquid water in order to perform life processes. Water remains a liquid on Earth because surface temperatures generally stay above the freezing point of water. Temperatures also stay far below water's boiling point.

Active Reading

9 Infer As you read, underline the reason that liquid water is essential to life.

Visualize It!

10 Summarize The pictures below show how Earth's oceans formed. Write a caption for the last two pictures in your own words.

Earth's Formation

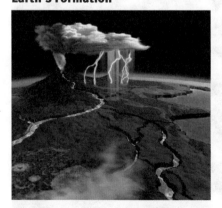

As Earth cooled, it released steam. The steam cooled to form clouds. Rain fell and began to form oceans.

Objects from Space

_____

_____

_____

_____

Modern Earth

_____

_____

_____

_____

© Houghton Mifflin Harcourt Publishing Company

Extremophiles

Extremophiles are organisms that live in extreme environments. Most extremophiles are unicellular, but some are multicellular. Extremophiles live in some of the coldest, hottest, driest, and saltiest places on Earth.

Living in the Cold

The Antarctic is home to ice-covered lakes and cold, dry valleys. Surprisingly, life can still be found in these harsh conditions.

Extreme Adaptations

A type of worm called a nematode survives in the cold by producing antifreeze in its cells. The nematode can also dry itself out when groundwater is not available. The nematode can then become active when water flows again underground.

Life on Other Planets?

The cold, dry Antarctic has some similarities to the cold, dry surface of Mars. The presence of organisms in extreme environments on Earth makes it seem more possible that some kind of life could exist in the extreme conditions on other planets.

Extend

Inquiry

11 Explain What is an extremophile?

12 Describe What are some adaptations that an extremophile might have in order to survive in a very salty environment?

13 Extend How could a greater knowledge of extremophiles help scientists to search for life on other planets?

© Houghton Mifflin Harcourt Publishing Company • Image Credits: (bg) ©MyLoupe/Universal Images Group/Getty Images; (t) ©Biophoto Associates/Photo Researchers, Inc.

Security Blanket

How does Earth's atmosphere support life?

Take a deep breath. The air you are breathing is part of Earth's atmosphere. An **atmosphere** is a mixture of gases that surround a planet, moon, or other space object.

Some space objects have atmospheres, and some do not. It often depends on the object's gravity. Earth and Venus have atmospheres because their gravity is strong enough to hold gases in place. Mercury and the moon each have weaker gravity, so they do not have atmospheres.

Gases Fuel Life Processes

Earth's atmosphere is composed mainly of nitrogen and oxygen. It also has traces of other gases like carbon dioxide. Carbon dioxide and oxygen support most forms of life. Plants and some single-celled organisms use carbon dioxide for photosynthesis. Plants, animals, and most other organisms use oxygen to perform cell processes. Anaerobic bacteria are some forms of life that do not need oxygen to survive.

Earth's atmosphere has not always contained nitrogen, oxygen, and carbon dioxide. It was originally just hydrogen and helium. These gases were too light for Earth's gravity to hold, so they escaped into space. Volcanoes released water vapor, carbon dioxide, and ammonia into Earth's early atmosphere. Solar energy broke ammonia apart, adding nitrogen and hydrogen to the atmosphere. Hydrogen escaped into space, but the nitrogen stayed in the atmosphere. Bacteria used carbon dioxide to perform photosynthesis, which released oxygen into the atmosphere.

Planet	% Gravity Compared to Earth
Mercury	38%
Venus	91%
Earth	100%

14 Infer Why doesn't Mercury have an atmosphere?

_____

_____

_____

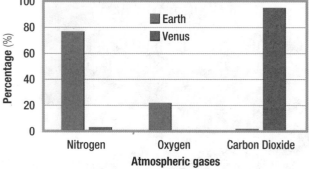

Major Atmospheric Gases on Earth and Venus

15 Infer If Venus has an atmosphere, why doesn't it support the kind of life that is now found on Earth?

_____

_____

_____

© Houghton Mifflin Harcourt Publishing Company

Gases Insulate Earth

The gases in Earth's atmosphere support life in other ways. As radiation from the sun reaches Earth's atmosphere, some of it is reflected back into space. Some is absorbed by water vapor, carbon dioxide, and other gases in the atmosphere. Some solar radiation passes through the atmosphere and is absorbed by Earth's surface. Radiation from Earth's surface then moves into the atmosphere. This energy is absorbed and re-radiated by atmospheric gases, through a process called the greenhouse effect. The greenhouse effect keeps Earth warmer than it would be if Earth had no atmosphere.

The Ozone Layer Protects Earth

One type of solar radiation that can harm life is **ultraviolet radiation**. Ultraviolet radiation is harmful because it can damage the genetic material in organisms. Earth has a protective ozone layer that blocks most ultraviolet radiation before it reaches Earth's surface. The ozone layer contains ozone gas in addition to the other atmospheric gases. **Ozone** is a molecule that is made up of three oxygen atoms. Some human-made chemicals have damaged the ozone layer by breaking apart ozone molecules. International laws have banned the use of these ozone-destroying chemicals.

Solar Radiation

Visible Light and Infrared Radiation

Ultraviolet Radiation

Earth's ozone layer blocks most ultraviolet radiation.

Atmospheric gases absorb and re-radiate energy through a process called the greenhouse effect.

Ozone Layer

Infrared Radiation

Visualize It!

16 Explain How does the ozone layer protect life on Earth?

_____

_____

_____

© Houghton Mifflin Harcourt Publishing Company

Visual Summary

To complete this summary, answer each question in the space provided. Then use the key below to check your answers. You can use this page to review the main concepts of the lesson.

Earth's Support of Life

Organisms need certain things to survive.

17 What do animals need to survive?

_____
_____

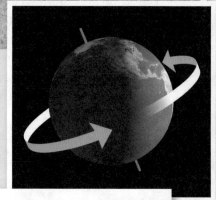

Earth's rotation and distance from the sun allow it to support life.

19 How does the sun support life on Earth?

_____
_____

Liquid water supports life on Earth.

18 Why is liquid water important to life?

_____
_____

Earth's atmosphere protects life on Earth.

20 What is an atmosphere?

_____
_____

Sample answers: **17** air, water, food, and a place to live; **18** Cells need liquid water to perform life processes; **19** It provides energy that warms Earth and allows plants to make food; **20** a blanket of gases around a space object

21 Describe How does Earth's position in space affect water on Earth?

© Houghton Mifflin Harcourt Publishing Company • Image Credits: (t) ©kris Mercer/Alamy; (b) ©NASA/K. Horgan/Stone/Getty Images

Lesson Review

Vocabulary

Fill in the blank with the term that best completes the following sentences.

1 Plants produce glucose and oxygen during the process of _____

2 Earth's _____ absorbs solar radiation and re-radiates it to Earth's surface.

Key Concepts

3 Describe How does Earth's rotation affect life on Earth?

_____

_____

_____

_____

4 List What are three ways that Earth is different from other planets?

_____

_____

_____

_____

5 Describe How did Earth's oceans form?

_____

_____

_____

_____

_____

_____

6 Explain How does the carbon dioxide in Earth's atmosphere allow Earth to support life?

_____

_____

_____

_____

Critical Thinking

Use the image to answer the following questions.

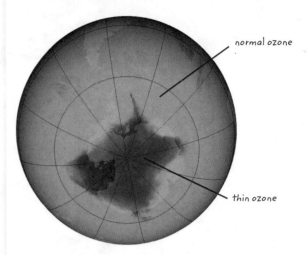

normal ozone

thin ozone

7 Describe The image shows the ozone layer. Why do you think it looks this way?

_____

_____

_____

_____

8 Explain Why is it important to protect the ozone layer?

_____

_____

_____

_____

_____

9 Apply What conditions would you look for if you were looking for life on moons or other planets besides Earth?

_____

_____

_____

_____

© Houghton Mifflin Harcourt Publishing Company • Image Credits: ©NASA

My Notes

© Houghton Mifflin Harcourt Publishing Company

© Houghton Mifflin Harcourt Publishing Company

Natural Resources

ESSENTIAL QUESTION

What are Earth's natural resources?

By the end of this lesson, you should be able to understand the types and uses of Earth's natural resources.

6.ESS3.1, 6.ESS3.3

Light produced from electrical energy helps people see at night. Natural resources are needed to produce electrical energy.

© Houghton Mifflin Harcourt Publishing Company ∘ Image Credits: (bg) ©World Perspectives/Photographer's Choice/Getty Images

✋ **Lesson Labs**

Quick Labs
Renewable or Not?
Production Impacts

Field Labs
Natural Resources Used at Lunch

Engage Your Brain

1 Predict Check T or F to show whether you think each statement is true or false.

T F

☐ ☐ Energy from the sun can be used to make electrical energy.

☐ ☐ All of Earth's resources will last forever.

☐ ☐ Food, cloth, rope, lumber, paper, and rubber come from plants.

☐ ☐ Human activity can negatively affect Earth's resources.

2 Describe Name one item that you use every day. Describe how you think that item is made.

_____

_____

_____

_____

_____

_____

_____

_____

_____

Active Reading

3 Apply Many scientific words, such as *natural* and *resource,* also have everyday meanings. Use context clues to write your own definition for each underlined word.

Oranges are a <u>natural</u> source of vitamin C.

natural:

_____

_____

His curly hair is <u>natural</u>.

natural:

_____

_____

A dictionary is a useful <u>resource</u> for learning words.

resource:

_____

_____

In the desert, water is a limited <u>resource</u>.

resource:

_____

_____

Vocabulary Terms

- natural resource
- renewable resource
- nonrenewable resource
- fossil fuel
- material resource
- energy resource

4 Identify This list contains the key terms you'll learn in this lesson. As you read, circle the definition of each term.

© Houghton Mifflin Harcourt Publishing Company • Image Credits: (b) ©World Perspectives/Photographer's Choice/Getty Images

It's Only Natural

What are natural resources?

What do the water you drink, the paper you write on, the gasoline used in cars, and the air you breathe all have in common? They all come from Earth's natural resources. A **natural resource** is any natural material that is used by humans. Natural resources include air, soil, minerals, water, oil, plants, and animals.

Earth's natural resources provide everything needed for life. The atmosphere contains the air we breathe and produces rain as part of the water cycle. Rainfall from the atmosphere renews the water in oceans, rivers, lakes, streams, and underground. In turn, these water sources provide water for drinking, cleaning, and other uses. Earth's soil provides nutrients and a place for plants to grow. Plants provide food for some animals and humans. Animals provide food as well. Many of Earth's resources, such as oil and wind, provide energy for human use. The energy in these resources comes from the sun's energy. Earth's resources are also used to make products that make people's lives more convenient.

© Houghton Mifflin Harcourt Publishing Company • Image Credits: (inset) © George Whiteley/Photo Researchers, Inc.

Active Reading

5 Identify List four examples of natural resources.

_____

_____

_____

Bauxite is a rock that is used to make aluminum.

Visualize It!

6 Illustrate Draw or label the missing natural resources.

A

How can we categorize natural resources?

There are many different types of natural resources. Some can be replaced more quickly than others. A natural resource may be categorized as a renewable resource or a nonrenewable resource.

Think Outside the Book Inquiry

7 Debate Research why water or soil can be a renewable or nonrenewable resource. Discuss your points with a classmate.

Renewable Resources

Some natural resources can be replaced in a relatively short time. A natural resource that can be replaced at the same rate at which it is consumed is a **renewable resource**. Solar energy, water, and air are all renewable resources. Some renewable resources are considered to be *inexhaustible resources* [in•ig•ZAW•stuh•buhl REE•sohrs•iz] because the resources can never be used up. Solar energy and wind energy, which is powered by the sun, are examples of inexhaustible resources. Other renewable resources are not inexhaustible. Trees and crops that are used for food must be replanted and regrown. Water must be managed so that it does not become scarce.

Nonrenewable Resources

A resource that forms much more slowly than it is consumed is a **nonrenewable resource**. Some natural resources, such as minerals, form very slowly. Iron ore and copper are important minerals. A **fossil fuel** is a nonrenewable resource formed from the buried remains of plants and animals that lived long ago. Coal, oil, and natural gas are examples of fossil fuels. Coal and oil take millions of years to form. Once these resources are used up, humans will have to find other resources to use instead. Some renewable resources, such as water and wood, may become nonrenewable if they are not used wisely.

8 Compare List some examples of renewable and nonrenewable resources.

Renewable resources	Nonrenewable resources

Natural fibers from cotton plants are processed to make fabric.

B

© Houghton Mifflin Harcourt Publishing Company • Image Credits: (inset) ©Waldo4/Fotolia

A Material World

How do we use material resources?

Look around your classroom. The walls, windows, desks, pencils, books, and even the clothing you see are made of material resources. Natural resources that are used to make objects, food, or drink are called **material resources**. Material resources can be either renewable or nonrenewable. The cotton used in T-shirts is an example of a renewable resource. The metal used in your desk is an example of a nonrenewable resource.

To Make Food or Drink

Material resources come from Earth's atmosphere, crust, and waters. They also come from organisms that live on Earth. Think about what you eat and drink every day. All foods and beverages are made from material resources. Some foods come from plants, such as the wheat in bread or the corn in tortillas. These resources are renewable, since farmers can grow more. Other foods, such as milk, cheese, eggs, and meat, come from animals. Juices, sodas, and sport drinks contain water, which is a renewable resource.

© Houghton Mifflin Harcourt Publishing Company • Image Credits: (l) ©Nic Miller/Alamy; (tr) ©The Irish Image Collection/Design Pics/Corbis; (br) ©Frank Krahmer/Corbis

Active Reading

9 Identify As you read, underline examples of material resources.

Visualize It!

10 List List two types of food or drink that are made from the material resources in each picture.

B _____

A _____

C _____

To Make Objects

Any object you see is made from material resources. For example, cars are made of steel, plastic, rubber, glass, and leather. Steel comes from iron, which is mined from rock. Plastic is made from oil, which must be drilled from areas underground. Natural rubber comes from tropical trees. Glass is made from minerals found in sand. Leather comes from the hides of animals.

Iron, oil, and sand are nonrenewable. If these materials are used too quickly, they can run out. Rubber, leather, and wood are renewable resources. The plants and animals that produce these resources can be managed so that these resources do not run out.

Visualize It!

11 Label Write the name of each material resource that is used to make objects in this house.

A house is made from many material resources.

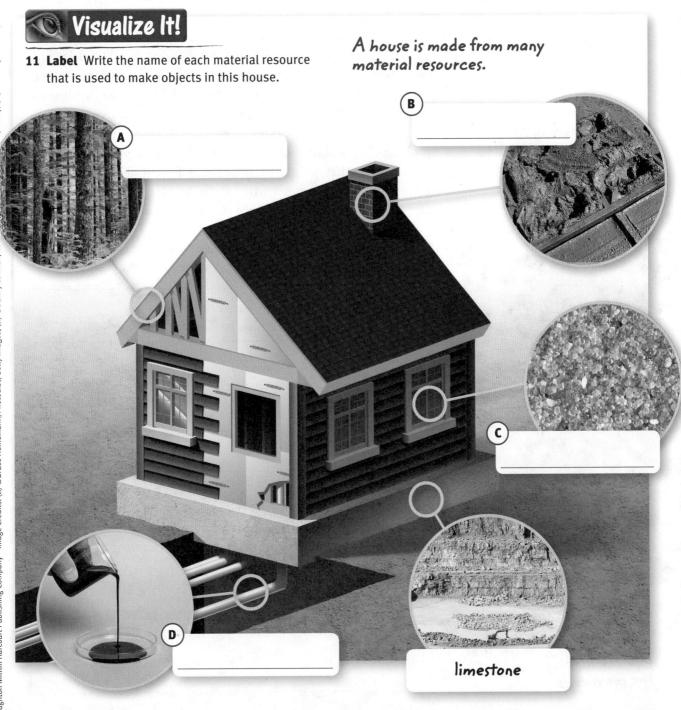

A

B

C

D

limestone

© Houghton Mifflin Harcourt Publishing Company • Image Credits: (tl) ©Bruce Heinemann/Photodisc/Getty Images; (tr) ©Danny Lehman/Corbis; (cr) ©Anthony Buckingham/Alamy; (br) ©Antony Edwards/The Image Bank/Getty Images

Change It Up!

12 Identify As you read, underline the different forms of energy.

How do we use energy resources?

Many objects need energy in order to be useful. For example, a bus needs energy so that it can move people around. Natural resources used to generate energy are called **energy resources**.

Energy is often stored in objects or substances. Stored energy is called *potential energy*. Food and products made from oil have potential energy that is stored in their chemical bonds. For this energy to be useful, it must be converted to *kinetic energy*, which is the energy of movement. Body cells perform chemical reactions that convert the potential energy in food to the kinetic energy that moves your body. Gasoline engines break the bonds in gasoline to convert potential energy to the kinetic energy that moves a car.

An object can have potential energy because of its position. An object that is high above the ground has more potential energy than an object that is close to the ground. Potential energy is converted to kinetic energy when the object falls, such as when water falls over a dam to produce electricity in a power plant.

13 List Look at the examples in the table. Write down three more situations in which potential energy changes to kinetic energy.

The gasoline being pumped into this car has potential energy in its chemical bonds.

This car's engine burns gasoline, converting the potential energy in the fuel into the kinetic energy of the moving car.

When Does Potential Energy Change to Kinetic Energy?
when coal burns to produce electrical energy in a power plant
when your body digests food to give you energy to move

© Houghton Mifflin Harcourt Publishing Company • Image Credits: (t) ©Steve Krongard/Photographer's Choice/Getty Images; (b) ©Wes Allison/Transtock/Corbis

How do everyday objects convert energy?

Energy cannot be created or destroyed, and energy must be converted to be useful. Energy conversions happen around us every day. Think about the appliances in your home. An electric oven warms food by converting electrical energy to energy as heat. A television converts electrical energy to light energy and sound energy, which is a type of kinetic energy. A fan moves by converting electrical energy to kinetic energy. Your body converts the chemical energy in food to kinetic energy as well as thermal energy. When you talk on the phone, the sound energy from your voice is converted to electrical energy. The phone on the other end of the conversation changes the electrical energy back to sound.

Visualize It!

14 Identify Which energy conversion allows you to feel warm?

_____

_____

15 Identify Which energy conversion allows this lamp to light up a room?

_____

_____

16 Identify Which energy conversion lets you hear the music?

_____

_____

© Houghton Mifflin Harcourt Publishing Company • Image Credits: ©Andrew Brookes/Corbis

Power Trip

How is electrical energy produced?

Active Reading

17 Identify As you read, underline the resources that can provide energy for a power plant.

Computers and appliances need electrical energy to work. Electrical energy is available from outlets, but how does this energy get to the outlets?

In most electrical power plants, an energy source converts potential energy to kinetic energy, causing wheels in a turbine to spin. The spinning wheels cause coils of wire to spin inside a magnet in a generator. The generator converts kinetic energy to electrical energy, which travels through wires to your school. Different energy resources can provide the energy for a power plant. Moving wind or water can turn wheels in a turbine. Burning coal or biofuels made from crop plants can warm water, producing steam that moves the turbine.

Fuel cells and batteries are other sources of electrical energy. A battery has chemicals inside that convert chemical energy to electrical energy. Fuel cells convert chemical energy from hydrogen to produce electrical energy.

Visualize It!

18 Describe After looking at the diagram, describe how energy is converted in a power plant to produce electrical energy.

Electrical energy is generated when coils of wire are turned inside a large magnet. This magnet might look different from bar magnets you have seen, but it still has north and south poles.

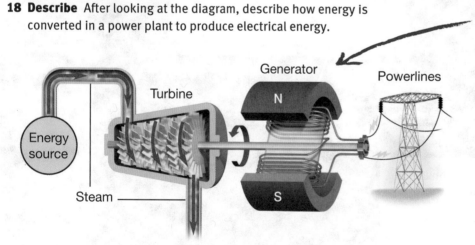

Energy source

Turbine

Steam

Generator

N

S

Powerlines

_____

_____

_____

_____

_____

_____

© Houghton Mifflin Harcourt Publishing Company

Clean Machines

Many car companies are introducing vehicles with hydrogen fuel cells. Hydrogen fuel cells use chemical reactions to produce electrical energy. These reactions produce no pollutants. If hydrogen fuel is made using renewable energy sources, these cars could truly be clean machines.

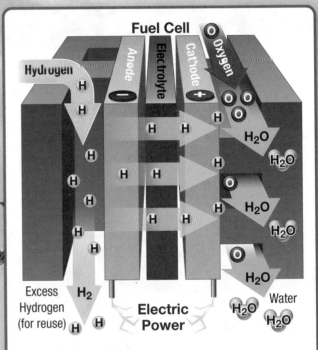

Fuel Cell

Hydrogen · Anode · Electrolyte · Cathode · Oxygen

H₂O

Excess Hydrogen (for reuse) · H₂ · **Electric Power** · Water · H₂O

Small Packages
The hydrogen fuel cell in a car is about the size of a microwave oven.

HYDROGEN FUEL CELL ELECTRIC

Cell Technology
The fuel cell removes electrons from hydrogen atoms. Electron movement generates electrical energy. Hydrogen then combines with oxygen to form water. Water and excess hydrogen are the products of this reaction. No carbon dioxide or other pollutants are produced.

© Houghton Mifflin Harcourt Publishing Company • Image Credits: (bg) ©Dieter Wanke/Alamy; (bl) ©Car Culture/Collection Mix: Subjects/Getty Images

Extend

Inquiry

19 Explain What kind of energy conversion happens in a hydrogen fuel cell?

20 Compare How is the process of energy conversion different between a fuel-cell vehicle and a gasoline vehicle?

21 Infer Hydrogen fuel must be produced by splitting water into hydrogen and oxygen. This process requires energy. Does it matter if nonrenewable energy is used to produce hydrogen fuel? Support your answer.

Visual Summary

To complete this summary, answer the questions using the lines provided. Then, use the key below to check your answers. You can use this page to review the main concepts of the lesson.

Natural resources can be renewable or nonrenewable.

22 What makes a resource renewable?

_____

_____

Material resources are used to make objects, food, and drink.

23 What are two material resources in this picture?

_____

_____

Natural Resources

Energy can be converted from one form to another. Potential energy in energy resources can be converted to kinetic energy.

24 What are all the energy conversions that happen when wood burns?

_____

_____

_____

Answers: 22 Renewable resources are used more slowly than they are replaced; 23 cattle for food, trees for wood; 24 Chemical energy in the wood is converted to light energy, energy as heat, and sound energy

25 Illustrate Think of a natural resource that can be used as both a material resource and as an energy resource. Draw two pictures to illustrate each use of the resource.

© Houghton Mifflin Harcourt Publishing Company • Image Credits: (tl) ©Waldo4/Fotolia; (tr) ©The Irish Image Collection/Design Pics/Corbis; (b) ©Andrew Brookes/Corbis

Lesson Review

Vocabulary

Draw a line to connect the following terms to their definitions.

1 fossil fuel

2 material resource

3 natural resource

A resource used to make objects, food, or drink

B any natural material used by people

C a nonrenewable resource formed by buried remains of plants and animals

Key Concepts

4 List Name two material resources and give an example of how each is used.

_____

_____

_____

_____

5 Describe What makes a resource nonrenewable?

_____

_____

_____

_____

6 Explain How can the conversion from potential energy to kinetic energy provide energy that is useful to people.

_____

_____

_____

_____

_____

Critical Thinking

7 Apply What could people do in order to make nonrenewable resources last longer?

_____

_____

_____

_____

Use the drawing to answer the following questions.

8 Analyze What energy conversions are occurring in the illustration?

_____

_____

_____

9 Infer What form of energy that is not useful is being released from the flashlight when it is on?

_____

_____

10 Relate Assume that the batteries in the flashlight are rechargeable. What energy conversion would have to take place in order to recharge the batteries?

_____

_____

_____

© Houghton Mifflin Harcourt Publishing Company

My Notes

© Houghton Mifflin Harcourt Publishing Company

© Houghton Mifflin Harcourt Publishing Company

Analyzing Technology

Skills
Identify risks
✓ Identify benefits
✓ Evaluate cost of technology
✓ Evaluate environmental impact
✓ Propose improvements
Propose risk reduction
Plan for technology failures
Compare technology
✓ Communicate results

Objectives
• Describe the effects of making paper cups on Earth's resources.
• Estimate the carbon dioxide saved by recycling paper cups.
• Propose improvements for the life cycle of a paper cup.

Analyzing the Life Cycle of a Paper Cup

A product's life cycle includes all of the phases in its "life," from getting raw materials to disposing of it once it has served its purpose. Most steps in the life cycle of a paper product affects the environment in some way.

Impact of a Paper Cup

A life cycle analysis of a paper cup shows that making it requires trees, water, ink, and plastic for a waterproof lining. The process also uses several different kinds of fuel, such as natural gas and diesel truck fuel for energy to make and transport the cups. The whole process releases about 110 grams (about ¼ pound) of carbon dioxide (KAR•buhn dy•AHK•syd) per cup into the atmosphere. This amount is 3 to 4 times the weight of a cup itself. And because of the plastic lining, paper cups are difficult to recycle.

Newspapers awaiting recycling

These paper cups probably will not be recycled.

1 Estimate Assume that a recycled paper cup is made up of only paper, and that paper could be recycled 5 times. About how much carbon dioxide would this prevent from being released into the atmosphere?

_____

_____

_____

_____

Corbis; (t) ©Alex Segre/Alamy Images; (b) ©Joeysworld.com/Alamy Images

© Houghton Mifflin Harcourt Publishing Company • Image Credits: (bg) ©Jana Renee Cruder/

Recycling Paper Products

Many paper products are more easily recycled than paper cups are. Over 70% of newspaper is recycled to make various products such as cereal boxes, egg cartons, and tissue paper. Many paper products can be recycled 5 to 7 times, after which the paper fibers are too short and no longer stick together well enough to make paper. Recycling paper products not only saves trees but also saves a lot of water, electricity, and gas and reduces air pollution.

The life of a paper product starts with trees. Loggers cut the tree, and a paper mill grinds it into pulp.

Most newspapers are recycled, saving trees and energy used in logging.

The mill mixes the pulp with water and other chemicals to make paper, which is used to make paper products such as paper cups.

Most paper cups end up in a landfill.

These products are used by all of us and then either recycled, incinerated, or buried in a landfill.

2 Infer Most newspaper is recycled. Most paper cups are not. What is one difference in environmental impact between burial and incineration for used paper products?

Incineration makes smoke and causes polution while burial dresnt.

✋ You Try It!

Now it's your turn to analyze the life cycle of a paper cup.

©Houghton Mifflin Harcourt Publishing Company • Image Credits: (bg) ©Jana Renee Cruder/Corbis; (t) ©Martin Shields/Alamy Images; (cl) ©Radius/Jupiter/Alamy Images; (cr) ©Eyewire/Getty Images; (bl) ©Mettafoto/Alamy Images; (b) ©Paul Bradbury/Alamy Images

 You Try It!

Now it's your turn to analyze the life cycle of a paper cup. You'll consider things such as the benefits of paper cups and their cost in both money and environmental impact. Then you can suggest some ways to improve the cycle.

① Identify Benefits

With your class, research the benefits of making and using paper cups. List those benefits below.

Benefits

You recycle/newspapers

② Evaluate Cost of Technology

A A paper mill uses about 16,000 gallons of water and about 400 kWh of electricity to produce one ton of paper cups. Using the information shown here, what is the cost of the water and electricity that are used to make one ton of paper cups?

40 #

B A modern paper mill costs around $1 billion to build. How many cups would a company need to sell to pay for the cost of the plant, the water, and the electricity?

- Water costs about $0.0007 per gallon.

- Electricity costs about $0.072/kWh.

- 33,000 cups weighs about a ton.

- One ton of cups sells for $2,000.

© Houghton Mifflin Harcourt Publishing Company

(3) Evaluate Environmental Impact

With a partner, discuss possible impacts of the life cycle of a paper cup on the environment. Consider things such as the harvesting of trees, the use of chlorine-based chemicals to bleach the pulp, the energy required by the paper mill, problems associated with disposal of paper cups after their use, etc.

_____

_____

_____

_____

_____

_____

_____

(4) Propose Improvements

With a partner, propose some improvements to the process of making or disposing of paper cups that might help make the life cycle of paper cups more environmentally friendly.

_____

_____

_____

_____

_____

_____

_____

(5) Communicate Results

With your partner, tell the class the most important thing you have learned about the life cycle of a paper cup, and explain why you think it is important.

_____

_____

_____

_____

_____

_____

_____

_____

© Houghton Mifflin Harcourt Publishing Company

Lesson 3

Nonrenewable Energy Resources

ESSENTIAL QUESTION

How do we use nonrenewable energy resources?

By the end of this lesson, you should be able to describe how humans use energy resources and the role of nonrenewable energy resources in society.

6.ESS3.1, 6.ESS3.2, 6.ESS3.3

The energy that lights up this city and powers the vehicles comes from energy resources. Most of our energy resources are being used up faster than natural processes can replace them.

© Houghton Mifflin Harcourt Publishing Company • Image Credits: (bg) ©Chad Ehlers/Alamy

Engage Your Brain

1 Identify Unscramble the letters below to find substances that are nonrenewable resources.

ALCO _____

AUNTRLA SGA _____

NUUIMAR _____

MLPEOUTRE _____

2 Describe Write your own caption for this photo.

_____

_____

_____

Active Reading

3 Synthesize Many English words have their roots in other languages. Use the Latin word below to make an educated guess about the meaning of the word *fission*.

Latin word	Meaning
fissus	to split

Example sentence
An atomic nucleus can undergo <u>fission</u>.

fission:

_____

_____

Vocabulary Terms

- energy resource
- fossil fuel
- nuclear energy
- fission

4 Identify This list contains the vocabulary terms you'll learn in this lesson. As you read, circle the definition of each term.

© Houghton Mifflin Harcourt Publishing Company • Image Credits: (bg) ©Chand Ehlers/Alamy; (t) ©Justin Sullivan/Getty Images

Be Resourceful!

What are the two main types of nonrenewable energy resources?

An **energy resource** is a natural resource that humans use to generate energy and can be renewable or nonrenewable. *Renewable resources* are replaced by natural processes at least as quickly as they are used. *Nonrenewable resources* are used up faster than they can be replaced. Most of the energy used in the United States comes from nonrenewable resources.

Fossil Fuels

A **fossil fuel** is a nonrenewable energy resource that forms from the remains of organisms that lived long ago. Fossil fuels release energy when they are burned. This energy can be converted to electricity or used to power engines. Fossil fuels are the most commonly used energy resource because they are relatively inexpensive to locate and process.

Nuclear Fuel

The energy released when the nuclei of atoms are split or combined is called **nuclear energy**. This energy can be obtained by two kinds of nuclear reactions—fusion and fission. Today's nuclear power plants use fission, because the technology for fusion power plants does not currently exist. The most common nuclear fuel is uranium. Uranium is obtained by mining and processing uranium ore, which is a nonrenewable resource.

Do the Math

You Try It

Nonrenewable Energy Resources Consumed in the U.S. in 2009

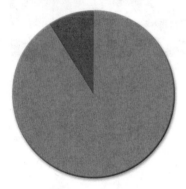

- Fossil Fuels 90.37%
- Nuclear Fuel 9.63%

5 Calculate In 2009, 86.8 quadrillion BTUs of the energy used in the United States was produced from nonrenewable energy resources. Using the graph above, calculate how much of this energy was produced from nuclear fuel.

6 Compare Fill in the Venn diagram to compare and contrast fossil fuels and nuclear fuel.

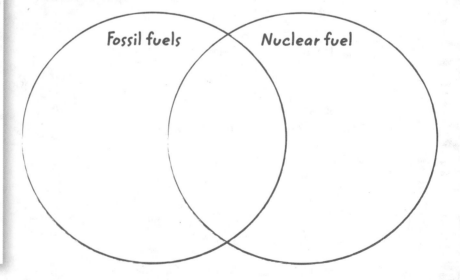

Fossil fuels   Nuclear fuel

© Houghton Mifflin Harcourt Publishing Company

What are the three main types of fossil fuels?

All living things contain the element carbon. Fossil fuels form from the remains of living things, so they also contain carbon. Most of this carbon is in the form of hydrocarbons, which are compounds made of hydrogen and carbon. Fossil fuels can be liquids, gases, or solids. Fossil fuels include petroleum, natural gas, and coal.

Active Reading **7 Identify** As you read, underline the state of matter for each fossil fuel.

Petroleum

Petroleum, or *crude oil*, is a liquid mixture of complex hydrocarbon compounds. Crude oil is extracted from the ground by drilling then processed for use. This process, called *refining*, separates the crude oil into different products such as gasoline, kerosene, and diesel fuel. More than 35 percent of the world's energy comes from crude oil products. Crude oil is also used to make products such as ink, bubble gum, and plastics.

This crude oil will be refined into gasoline, diesel fuel, heating oil, kerosene, and other products.

Natural Gas

Natural gas is a mixture of gaseous hydrocarbons. Most natural gas is used for heating and cooking, but some is used to generate electricity. Also, some vehicles use natural gas as fuel.

Methane is the main component of natural gas. Butane and propane can also be separated from natural gas. Butane and propane are used as fuel for camp stoves and outdoor grills. Some rural homes also use propane as a heating fuel.

Natural gas is a popular fuel for cooking because it is inexpensive.

Coal

The fossil fuel most widely used for generating electrical power is a solid called coal. Coal was once used to heat homes and for transportation. In fact, many trains in the 1800s and early 1900s were pulled by coal-burning steam locomotives. Now, most people use gasoline for transportation fuel. But more than half of our nation's electricity comes from coal-burning power plants.

Coal is a fossil fuel often used to generate electricity.

© Houghton Mifflin Harcourt Publishing Company • Image Credits: (t) ©Pablo Paul/Alamy; (c) ©IFMC/Alamy; (b) ©Dmitriy Sechin/Alamy Images

How do fossil fuels form?

How might a sunny day 200 million years ago relate to your life today? If you traveled to school by bus or car, you likely used energy from sunlight that warmed Earth that long ago.

Fossil fuels form over millions of years from the buried remains of ancient organisms. Fossil fuels differ in the kinds of organisms from which they form and in how they form. This process is continuing, too. The fossil fuels forming today will be available for use in a few million years!

Petroleum and Natural Gas Form from Marine Organisms

Petroleum and natural gas form mainly from the remains of microscopic sea organisms. When these organisms die, their remains sink and settle on the ocean floor. There, the dead organisms are gradually buried by sediment. The sediment is compacted by more layers of dead organisms and sediment. Over time the sediment layers become layers of rock.

Over millions of years, heat and pressure turn the remains of the organisms into petroleum and natural gas. The petroleum and natural gas, along with groundwater, flow into pores in the rock. A rock with pores is a *permeable rock*. Permeable rocks become reservoirs where the petroleum and natural gas are trapped and concentrated over time. Humans can extract the fuels from these reservoirs.

Think Outside the Book Inquiry

8 Apply With a classmate, discuss how the process of petroleum formation might affect oil availability in the future.

Petroleum and Natural Gas Formation

1 Microscopic marine organisms die and settle to the bottom of the sea.

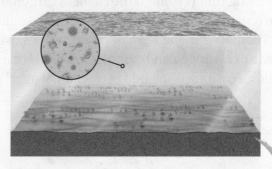

2 Layers of sediment slowly bury the dead marine organisms.

3 Heat and pressure on these layers slowly turn the remains of these organisms into petroleum and natural gas.

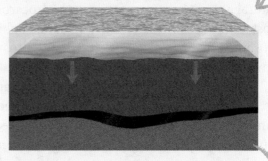

4 Petroleum and natural gas flow through permeable rocks, where they are trapped and become concentrated into reservoirs.

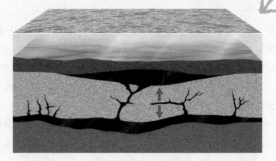

© Houghton Mifflin Harcourt Publishing Company

Coal Formation

1 Peat Partially decayed swamp plants sink and change into peat.

2 Lignite As sediment buries the peat, increases in temperature and pressure change peat to lignite.

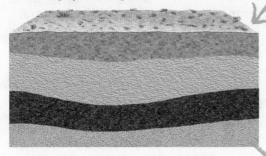

3 Bituminous Coal As sediment builds, increased temperature and pressure change lignite to bituminous coal.

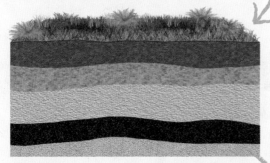

4 Anthracite As sediments accumulate and temperature and pressure rise, bituminous coal changes to anthracite.

Coal Forms from Plant Remains

Active Reading **9 Identify** As you read, underline the factors that convert the buried plants into coal.

Coal is formed over millions of years from the remains of swamp plants. When the plants die, they sink to the swamp floor. Low oxygen levels in the water keep many plants from decaying and allow the process of coal formation to begin. Today's swamp plants may eventually turn into coal millions of years from now.

The first step of coal formation is plant matter changing into peat. Peat is made mostly of plant material and water. Peat is not coal. In some parts of the world, peat is dried and burned for warmth or used as fuel. Peat that is buried by layers of sediment can turn into coal after millions of years.

Over time, pressure and high temperature force water and gases out of the peat. The peat gradually becomes harder, and its carbon content increases. The amount of heat and pressure determines the type of coal that forms. Lignite forms first, followed by bituminous coal and, finally, anthracite. Anthracite is highly valued because it has the highest carbon content and gives off the most energy as heat when burned.

Today, all three types of coal are mined around the world. When burned, coal releases energy as heat and pollutes the air. The greater the carbon content of the coal, the fewer pollutants are released and the cleaner the coal burns.

Visualize It!

10 Compare What is similar about the way petroleum and coal form? What is different?

_____

_____

_____

_____

_____

_____

© Houghton Mifflin Harcourt Publishing Company

Power Trip

How are fossil fuels used as energy sources?

Active Reading

11 Identify As you read, underline the uses of fossil fuels.

In the United States, petroleum fuels are mainly used for transportation and heating. Airplanes, trains, boats, and cars all use petroleum for energy. Some people also use petroleum as a heating fuel. There are some oil-fired power plants in the United States, but most are found in other parts of the world.

Natural gas can be used as transportation fuel but is mainly used for heating and cooking. The use of natural gas as a source of electrical power is increasing. The U.S. Department of Energy projects that most power plants in the near future will use natural gas. Today, coal is mainly used in the U.S. to generate electricity, which we use for lighting and to power appliances and technology.

Visualize It!

Burning coal heats water to produce steam. The steam turns the turbines to generate electricity. Scrubbers and filters in the smokestack help reduce air pollution.

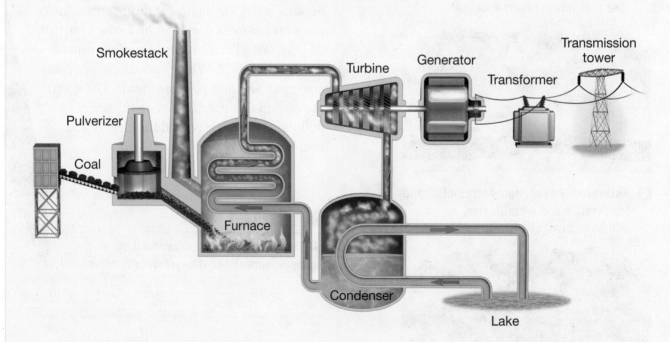

Coal-Fired Power Plant

© Houghton Mifflin Harcourt Publishing Company

How is energy produced from nuclear fuels?

During **fission**, the nuclei of radioactive atoms are split into two or more fragments. A small particle called a neutron hits and splits an atom. This process releases large amounts of energy as heat and radiation. Fission also releases more neutrons that bombard other atoms. The process repeats as a chain reaction. Fission takes place inside a reactor core. Fuel rods containing uranium, shown in green below, provide the material for the chain reaction. Control rods that absorb neutrons are used to regulate the chain reaction. The energy is released, which is used to generate electrical power. A closed reactor system contains the radioactivity. Nuclear wastes are contained separately for disposal.

During nuclear reactions, energy in the form of heat is released, which turns water into steam. Steam turns the turbines to generate electricity.

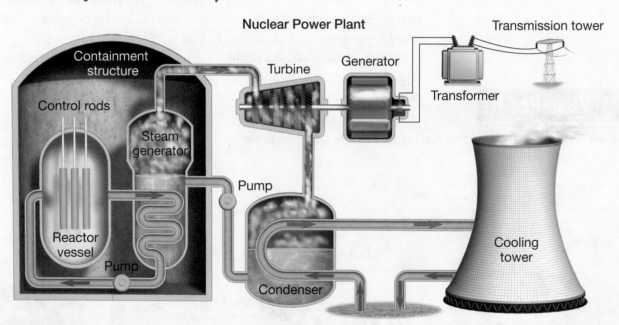

Nuclear Power Plant

12 Compare How are the two types of power plants similar? How are they different?

Similar	Different
_____	_____
_____	_____
_____	_____
_____	_____

© Houghton Mifflin Harcourt Publishing Company

The Pros and Cons

How can we evaluate nonrenewable energy resources?

There are advantages and disadvantages to using nonrenewable energy resources. Nonrenewable resources provide much of the energy that humans need to power transportation, warm homes, and produce electricity relatively cheaply. But the methods of obtaining and using these resources can have negative effects on the environment.

The Pros and Cons of Nuclear Fuel

Nuclear fission produces a large amount of energy and does not cause air pollution because no fuel is burned. Mining uranium also does not usually result in massive strip mines or large loss of habitats.

However, nuclear power does have drawbacks. Nuclear power plants produce dangerous wastes that remain radioactive for thousands of years. So the waste must be specially stored to prevent harm to anyone. Harmful radiation may also be released into the environment accidentally. Hot water released from the power plant can also be a problem. This heated water can disrupt aquatic ecosystems. So the hot water must be cooled before it is released into local bodies of water.

Active Reading

13 Identify As you read, underline the effects that nuclear power plants have on their surroundings.

Visualize It!

14 Infer Why do you think nuclear fuel rods are usually transported by train instead of by trucks?

_____

_____

Used nuclear fuel rods must be transported in specially built steel containers.

© Houghton Mifflin Harcourt Publishing Company • Image Credits: ©Martin Bond/Photo Researchers, Inc.

The Pros and Cons of Fossil Fuels

Fossil fuels are relatively inexpensive to obtain and use. However, there are problems associated with their use. Burning coal can release sulfur dioxide, which combines with moisture in the air to form acid rain. Acid rain causes damage to structures and the environment. Coal mining also disturbs habitats, lowers water tables, and pollutes water.

Environmental problems are also associated with using oil. In 2010, a blown oil well spilled an estimated 126 million gallons of crude oil in the Gulf of Mexico for 87 days. The environmental costs may continue for years.

Burning fossil fuels can cause smog, especially in cities with millions of vehicles. Smog is a brownish haze that can cause respiratory problems and contribute to acid rain. Burning fossil fuels also releases carbon dioxide into the atmosphere. Increases in atmospheric carbon dioxide can lead to global warming.

Some coal is mined by removing the tops of mountains to expose the coal. This damages habitats and can cause water pollution as well.

15 Evaluate In the chart below, list the advantages and disadvantages of using nuclear fuel and fossil fuels.

Type of fuel	Pros	Cons
nuclear fuel		
fossil fuels		

© Houghton Mifflin Harcourt Publishing Company • Image Credits: ©Mandel Ngan/AFP/Getty Images

Visual Summary

To complete this summary, check the box that indicates true or false. Then use the key below to check your answers. You can use this page to review the main concepts of the lesson.

Nuclear fuel is an energy resource that undergoes the process of fission to release energy for human use.

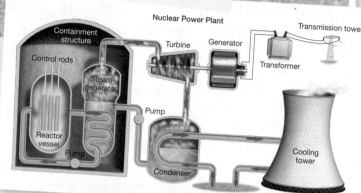

Nuclear Power Plant

Containment structure

Control rods

Reactor vessel

Steam generator

Pump

Turbine

Generator

Transformer

Transmission tower

Pump

Condenser

Cooling tower

	T	F	
16	☐	☐	Uranium is often used as fuel in nuclear fission.
17	☐	☐	One disadvantage of nuclear fission is that it produces only a small amount of energy.

Nonrenewable Energy Resources

Most of the energy used today comes from fossil fuels, which include petroleum, natural gas, and coal.

	T	F	
18	☐	☐	Natural gas forms from microscopic marine organisms.
19	☐	☐	Most transportation fuels are products of coal.
20	☐	☐	Burning fossil fuels decreases the amount of carbon dioxide in the atmosphere.

Answers: 16 True; 17 False; 18 True; 19 False; 20 False

21 **Summarize** Identify the advantages and disadvantages for both fossil fuels and nuclear fuels.

© Houghton Mifflin Harcourt Publishing Company • Image Credits: ©Dmitriy Sechin/Alamy Images

Lesson Review

Vocabulary

Fill in the blank with the term that best completes the following sentences.

1 _____ is energy in an atom's nucleus.

2 Crude oil is a liquid kind of _____

3 _____ can be renewable or nonrenewable.

4 During the process of _____, the nuclei of radioactive atoms are split into two or more smaller nuclei.

Key Concepts

5 Describe Describe how fossil fuels are converted into usable energy?

_____

_____

_____

_____

_____

6 Sequence Which of the following sequences of processes best describes how electricity is generated in a nuclear power plant?

A fission reaction, produce steam, turn turbine, generate electricity, cool water

B produce steam, fission reaction, turn turbine, generate electricity, cool water

C cool water, fission reaction, produce steam, turn turbine, generate electricity

D produce steam, turn turbine, cool water, fission reaction, generate electricity

7 Identify Which is an example of how people use nonrenewable energy resources?

A eating a banana

B sailing a boat

C walking to school

D driving a car

Critical Thinking

8 Hypothesize Why do some places in the United States have deposits of coal but others have deposits of petroleum and natural gas?

_____

_____

_____

_____

_____

Use the graph to answer the following questions.

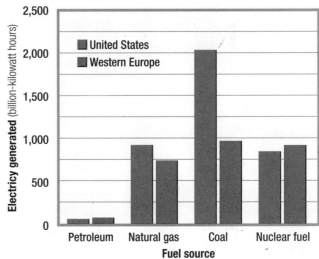

Electricity Produced from Nonrenewable Energy Resources in 2007

9 Calculate About how much more coal than petroleum is used to generate electricity in the United States and Western Europe?

_____

_____

_____

10 Analyze What patterns of energy resource use do you see in the graph?

_____

_____

_____

_____

© Houghton Mifflin Harcourt Publishing Company

My Notes

© Houghton Mifflin Harcourt Publishing Company

© Houghton Mifflin Harcourt Publishing Company

Renewable Energy Resources

ESSENTIAL QUESTION

How do humans use renewable energy resources?

By the end of this lesson, you should be able to describe how humans use energy resources and the role of renewable energy resources in society.

6.ESS3.1, 6.ESS3.2, 6.ESS3.3, 6.ETS1.2, 6.PS3.1, 6.PS3.4

Panels such as these can turn an unused city roof into a miniature solar energy plant.

© Houghton Mifflin Harcourt Publishing Company • Image Credits: (bg) ©ssuaphotos/Shutterstock

 **Lesson Labs**

Quick Labs
• Design a Turbine
• Understanding Solar Panels

S.T.E.M. Lab
• Modeling Geothermal Power

Engage Your Brain

1 Predict Check T or F to show whether you think each statement is true or false.

T	F	
☐	☐	Renewable energy resources can never run out.
☐	☐	Renewable energy resources do not cause any type of pollution.
☐	☐	Solar energy is the most widely used renewable energy resource in the United States.
☐	☐	Renewable energy resources include solar energy, wind energy, and geothermal energy.

2 Describe Write a caption to explain how the sun's energy is being used in this photo.

_____

_____

_____

_____

Active Reading

3 Synthesize You can often define an unknown word if you know the meaning of its word parts. Use the word parts and sentence below to make an educated guess about the meaning of the word *geothermal*.

Word part	Meaning
geo-	Earth
therm-	heat

Example sentence
A geothermal power plant uses steam produced deep in the ground to generate electricity.

geothermal:

_____

_____

_____

Vocabulary Terms

• energy resource
• wind energy
• hydroelectric energy
• solar energy
• biomass
• geothermal energy

4 Apply As you learn the definition of each vocabulary term in this lesson, create your own definition or sketch to help you remember the meaning of the term.

© Houghton Mifflin Harcourt Publishing Company • Image Credits: (b) ©ssuaphotos/Shutterstock; (t) ©apply pictures/Alamy Images

Energy *Déjà Vu*

What are the two main sources of renewable energy?

An **energy resource** is a natural resource used to generate electricity and other forms of energy. Most of the energy used by humans comes from *nonrenewable resources*. These resources are used more quickly than they can be replaced. But *renewable resources* can be replaced almost as quickly as they are used. Most renewable energy resources come from the sun and some from Earth itself.

The Sun

The sun's energy is a result of nuclear fusion. Fusion is the process by which two or more nuclei fuse together to form a larger nucleus. Fusion produces a large amount of energy, which is released into space as light and heat.

Solar energy warms Earth, causing the movement of air masses. Moving air masses form winds and some ocean currents. Solar energy also fuels plant growth. Animals get energy by eating plants. Humans can harness energy from wind, moving water, plant and animal materials, and directly from the light and heat that comes from the sun.

Earth

Energy from within Earth comes from two sources. One source is the decay of radioactive elements in Earth's mantle and crust, caused by nuclear fission. Fission is the splitting of the nuclei of radioactive atoms. The second source of energy within Earth is energy stored during Earth's formation. The heat produced from these sources radiates outward toward Earth's surface. Humans can harness this heat to use as an energy source.

5 Contrast Explain how energy production in the sun differs from energy production in Earth's interior.

_____
_____
_____
_____
_____
_____

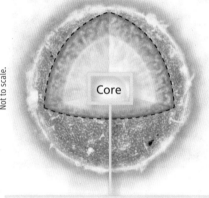

Not to scale.

Core

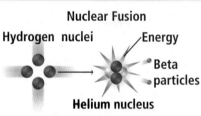

Nuclear Fusion

Hydrogen nuclei → Energy

Beta particles

Helium nucleus

When atomic nuclei fuse, energy is released.

Not to scale.

Core

Earth's internal energy comes from the process of nuclear fission and the events that formed Earth.

© Houghton Mifflin Harcourt Publishing Company

How might a renewable energy resource become nonrenewable?

All of the energy resources you will learn about in this lesson are renewable. That doesn't mean that they can't become nonrenewable resources. Trees, for example, are a renewable resource. Some people burn wood from trees to heat their homes and cook food. However, some forests are being cut down but are not being replanted in a timely manner. Others are being cut down and replaced with buildings. If this process continues, eventually these forests will no longer be considered renewable resources.

6 Apply Read the caption below, then describe what might happen if the community uses too much of the water in the reservoir.

_____

_____

_____

_____

_____

7 Distinguish What is the difference between nonrenewable and renewable energy resources?

_____

_____

_____

_____

_____

Think Outside the Book

8 Apply Write an interview with a renewable resource that is afraid it might become nonrenewable. Be sure to include questions and answers.

A community uses this reservoir for water. The dam at the end of the reservoir uses moving water to produce electricity for the community.

© Houghton Mifflin Harcourt Publishing Company • Image Credits: © Edward M. Wylonis Jr./Alamy Images

Turn, Turn, Turn

How do humans use wind energy?

Wind is created by the sun's uneven heating of air masses in Earth's atmosphere. **Wind energy** uses the force of moving air to drive an electric generator or do other work. Wind energy is renewable because the wind will blow as long as the sun warms Earth. Wind energy is harnessed by machines called wind turbines. Electricity is generated when moving air turns turbine blades that drive an electric generator. Clusters of wind turbines, called wind farms, generate large amounts of electricity.

Although wind energy is a renewable energy resource, it has several disadvantages. Wind farms can be placed only in areas that receive large amounts of wind. The equipment required to collect and convert wind energy is also expensive to produce and maintain. And the production and maintenance of this equipment produces a small amount of pollution. The turbine blades can also be hazardous to birds.

Windmills such as these have been used for centuries to grind grain and pump surface water for irrigation.

A wind-powered water pump can pull water from deep underground when electricity is not available.

9 Infer What is the main benefit of placing these turbines in open water?

_____

_____

_____

_____

_____

Wind farms are a form of clean energy, because they do not generate air pollution as they generate electricity.

© Houghton Mifflin Harcourt Publishing Company • Image Credits: (bg) ©Ingo Wagner/dpa/Corbis; (t) ©Chris Cheadle/All Canada Photos/Corbis; (b) ©David Muenker/Alamy Images

How do humans get energy from moving water?

Like wind, moving water has kinetic energy. People have harnessed the energy of falling or flowing water to power machines since ancient times. Some grain and saw mills still use water to power their equipment. Electrical energy produced by moving water is called **hydroelectric energy**. Hydroelectric energy is renewable because the water cycle is driven by the sun. Water that evaporates from oceans and lakes falls on higher elevations and flows downhill in streams, rivers, and waterfalls. The energy in flowing water is converted to electrical energy when it spins turbines connected to electric generators inside the dam.

Hydroelectric energy is a good source of energy only in locations where there are large, reliable amounts of flowing water. Another disadvantage of hydroelectric energy is that hydroelectric dams and their technology are expensive to build. The dams also can block the movement of fish between the sea and their spawning grounds. Special fish ladders must be built to allow fish to swim around the dam.

Active Reading

10 Identify Underline the kind of energy that is found in moving water.

Visualize It!

11 Explain What is the purpose of the lake that is located behind the dam of a hydroelectric plant?

_____

_____

_____

_____

_____

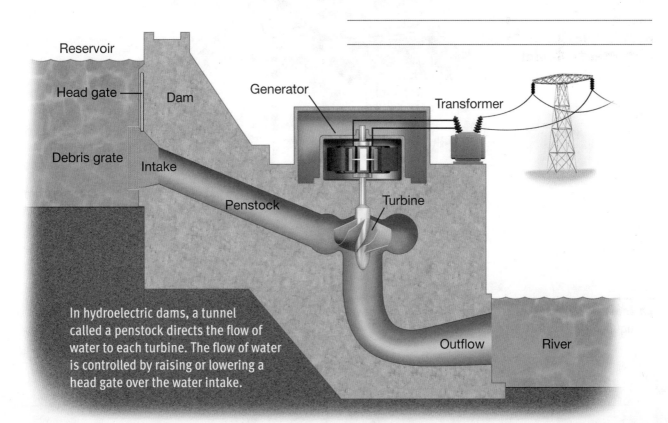

In hydroelectric dams, a tunnel called a penstock directs the flow of water to each turbine. The flow of water is controlled by raising or lowering a head gate over the water intake.

© Houghton Mifflin Harcourt Publishing Company

Let the Sunshine In

How do humans use solar energy?

Most forms of energy come from the sun—even fossil fuels begin with the sun as an energy resource. **Solar energy** is the energy received by Earth from the sun in the form of radiation. Solar energy can be used to warm buildings directly. Solar energy can also be converted into electricity by solar cells.

To Provide Energy as Heat

We can use liquids warmed by the sun to warm water and buildings. Some liquids, such as water, have a high capacity for absorbing and holding heat. When the heat is absorbed by the liquid in a solar collector, it can be transferred to water that circulates through a building. The hot water can be used for bathing or other household uses, or to warm the building. The only pollution generated by solar heating systems comes from the manufacture and maintenance of their equipment. Solar heating systems work best in areas with large amounts of sunlight.

Solar collectors absorb energy from the sun in the form of heat. The heat is transferred to water that circulates through the house.

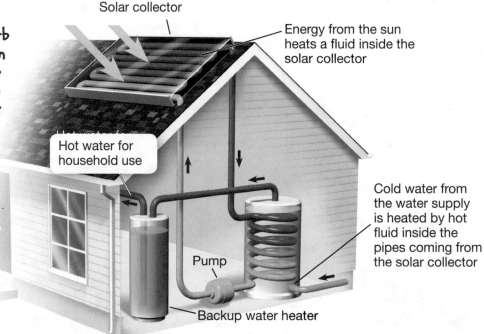

Solar collector

Energy from the sun heats a fluid inside the solar collector

Hot water for household use

Cold water from the water supply is heated by hot fluid inside the pipes coming from the solar collector

Pump

Backup water heater

12 Infer Not all solar collectors use water to absorb energy from the sun. Why might a solar heating system use a liquid other than water?

_____

_____

_____

© Houghton Mifflin Harcourt Publishing Company • Image Credits: ©amana images inc./Alamy Images

Active Reading **13 Identify** As you read, underline the characteristics of a photovoltaic cell.

To Produce Electricity

Solar collectors can also be used to generate electricity. First, heated fluid is used to produce steam. Then, the steam turns a turbine connected to an electric generator.

Electricity can also be generated when sunlight is absorbed by a photovoltaic cell. A single photovoltaic cell produces a small amount of electricity. The electricity from joined photovoltaic cells can power anything from calculators to entire communities. Many cells must be joined together to form each solar panel, as shown in the solar power plant below. Solar power plants must be built in places with adequate space and abundant sunshine year-round. These requirements increase the costs of solar power.

This calculator is powered by solar cells instead of a battery.

Visualize It! (Inquiry)

14 Infer Based on this image and your reading, what might be a disadvantage to using solar energy to supply electricity to a large community?

_____

_____

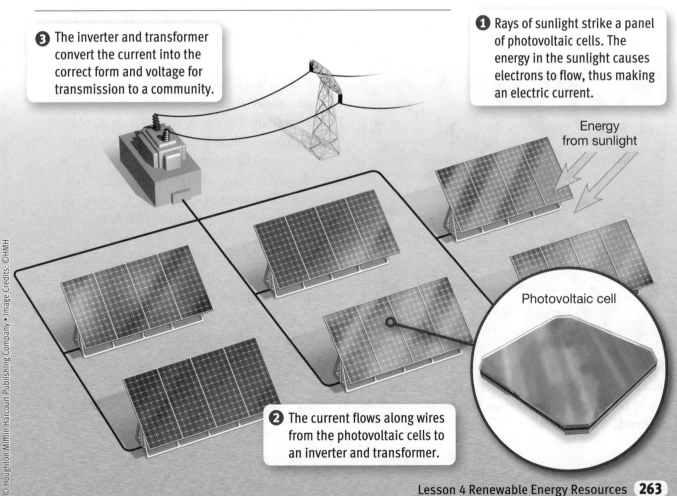

❸ The inverter and transformer convert the current into the correct form and voltage for transmission to a community.

❶ Rays of sunlight strike a panel of photovoltaic cells. The energy in the sunlight causes electrons to flow, thus making an electric current.

Energy from sunlight

Photovoltaic cell

❷ The current flows along wires from the photovoltaic cells to an inverter and transformer.

© Houghton Mifflin Harcourt Publishing Company • Image Credits: ©HMH

How do humans get energy from living things?

Plants absorb light energy from the sun and convert it to chemical energy through *photosynthesis*. This energy is stored in leaves, stems, and roots. Chemical energy is also present in the dung of animals. These sources of energy make up biomass.

By Burning Biomass

Biomass is organic matter from plants and from animal waste that contains chemical energy. Biomass can be burned to release energy. This energy can be used to cook food, provide warmth, or power an engine. Biomass sources include trees, crops, animal waste, and peat.

Biomass is inexpensive and can usually be replaced relatively quickly, so it is considered to be a renewable resource. Some types of biomass renew more slowly than others. Peat renews so slowly in areas where it is used heavily that it is treated as a nonrenewable resource. Like fossil fuels, biomass produces pollutants when it burns.

These peat pellets will be used to generate steam in the power plant in the background. The steam will generate electricity by turning turbines.

These wagons are loaded with sugar cane wastes from sugar production. The cellulose from these plant materials will be processed to produce ethanol.

Active Reading **15 Identify** As you read, number the steps that occur during the production of ethanol.

By Burning Alcohol

Biomass material can be used to produce a liquid fuel called ethanol, which is an alcohol. The sugars or cellulose in the plants are eaten by microbes. The microbes then give off carbon dioxide and ethanol. Over 1,000 L of ethanol can be made from 1 acre of corn. The ethanol is collected and burned as a fuel. Ethanol can also be mixed with gasoline to make a fuel called gasohol. The ethanol produced from about 40% of one corn harvest in the United States would provide only 10% of the fuel used in our cars!

16 List What are three examples of how biomass can be used for energy?

_____

_____

_____

_____

© Houghton Mifflin Harcourt Publishing Company • Image Credits: (t) ©Hank Morgan/Photo Researchers, Inc.; (b) ©Christian Tragni/Aurora Photos/Alamy Images

How do humans use geothermal energy?

The water in the geyser at right is heated by geothermal energy. **Geothermal energy** is energy produced by heat from Earth's interior. Geothermal energy heats rock formations deep within the ground. Groundwater absorbs this heat and forms hot springs and geysers where the water reaches Earth's surface. Geothermal energy is used to produce energy as heat and electricity.

To Provide Energy as Heat

Geothermal energy can be used to warm and cool buildings. A closed loop system of pipes runs from underground into the heating system of a home or building. Water pumped through these pipes absorbs heat from the ground and is used to warm the building. Hot groundwater can also be pumped in and used in a similar way. In warmer months, the ground is cooler than the air, so this system can also be used for cooling.

To Produce Electricity

Geothermal energy is also used to produce electricity. Wells are drilled into areas of superheated groundwater, allowing steam and hot water to escape. Geothermal power plants pump the steam or hot water from underground to spin turbines that generate electricity, as shown at right. A disadvantage of geothermal energy is pollution that occurs during production of the technology needed to capture it. The technology is also expensive to make and maintain.

Because Earth's core will be very hot for billions of years, geothermal energy will be available for a long time.

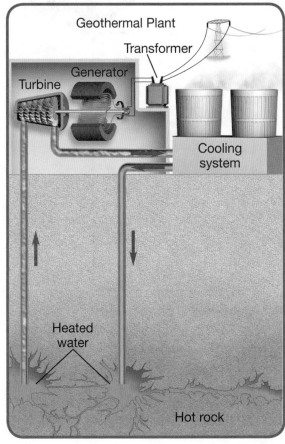

Geothermal Plant

Transformer

Generator

Turbine

Cooling system

Heated water

Hot rock

17 List What are some advantages and disadvantages to using geothermal energy?

Advantages	Disadvantages

© Houghton Mifflin Harcourt Publishing Company • Image Credits: ©Arco Images GmbH/Alamy Images

Visual Summary

To complete this summary, fill in the blanks with the correct word or phrase. Then, use the key below to check your answers. You can use this page to review the main concepts of the lesson.

The source of geothermal energy is energy from within Earth.

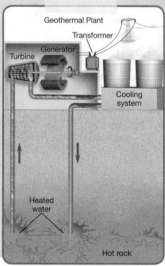

Renewable Energy Resources

Most of the renewable energy resources that people use come from the sun.

18 In geothermal power plants, hot water or _____ is pumped from within Earth's crust to produce electricity.

19 Renewable resources that come from the sun include _____ _____ _____

Answers: 18 steam; 19 biomass, solar energy, wind energy, and hydroelectric energy

20 **Synthesize** Which type of renewable energy resource would be best to use to provide electricity for your town? Explain your answer.

© Houghton Mifflin Harcourt Publishing Company • Image Credits: ©David Muenker/Alamy Images

Lesson Review

Vocabulary

Fill in the blanks with the term that best completes the following sentences.

1 Organic matter that contains stored energy is called _____

2 A resource that humans can use to produce energy is a(n) _____

3 _____ is an energy resource harnessed from flowing water.

Key Concepts

4 Describe Identify a major advantage and a major disadvantage of using renewable energy resources to produce electricity.

_____

_____

_____

_____

_____

_____

5 Explain If renewable energy resources can be replaced, why do we need to conserve them? Use an example to support your answer.

_____

_____

_____

_____

_____

_____

6 Describe What is the source of energy that powers wind and flowing water?

_____

_____

_____

_____

_____

Critical Thinking

Use this graph to answer the following questions.

Total Renewable Energy Resources Consumed in 2014 in the United States

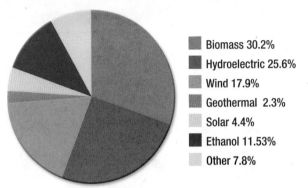

- Biomass 30.2%
- Hydroelectric 25.6%
- Wind 17.9%
- Geothermal 2.3%
- Solar 4.4%
- Ethanol 11.53%
- Other 7.8%

Source: EIA Short-Term Energy Outlook 2014

7 Evaluate Which is the most used renewable energy resource in the United States? Why do you think this is the case?

_____

_____

_____

_____

8 Evaluate Which is the least used renewable energy resource in the United States? Why do you think this is the case?

_____

_____

_____

_____

_____

_____

9 Relate How are biomass and alcohol production related to energy from the sun?

_____

_____

_____

_____

© Houghton Mifflin Harcourt Publishing Company

My Notes

© Houghton Mifflin Harcourt Publishing Company

© Houghton Mifflin Harcourt Publishing Company

Analyzing Technology

Skills

Identify risks

✓ Identify benefits

✓ Evaluate cost of technology

Propose risk reduction

Plan for technology failures

✓ Compare technology

✓ Propose improvements

✓ Communicate results

Objectives

- Investigate and compare current and new alternative energy technologies.
- Build an argument for the best form of alternative energy.

Alternative Thinking: Different Forms of Energy

Alternative energy is a field that is growing quickly. Many forms of alternative energy rely on renewable resources. Water, geothermal, wind, and solar power are renewable. Unlike fossil fuels, these alternative energy sources do not produce greenhouse gases. Alternative energy can also reduce the need to mine for fossil fuels. Mining can often damage ecosystems, so many scientists believe that alternative energies are better for the environment.

Making the Switch

Switching to alternative energy sources is not always easy. Sunshine, wind, and flowing water are not plentiful everywhere. Also, switching to alternative energy sources may cost a lot of money up front. Building a dam, erecting wind turbines, or installing solar panels can be very expensive.

1 Brainstorm What local factors might affect a community's alternative energy choices?

_____

_____

_____

The Hoover Dam generates enough hydroelectric power each year to serve 1.3 million people in Nevada, Arizona, and California. It relies on the steady flow of the Colorado River into Lake Mead. This artificial lake was created by building the dam.

© Houghton Mifflin Harcourt Publishing Company • Image Credits: (bg) ©Rafa Irusta/Fotolia; (b) ©Andrew Zarivny/Shutterstock

Solar panels need direct access to sunlight to produce power.

One way engineers can make wind turbines more reliable is to build them taller. At higher altitudes, wind speeds are greater, and winds are not blocked by buildings and trees.

Challenges

Most alternative energy systems have some drawbacks. Solar panels produce lots of power during the long, sunny days of summer. But on cloudy days, they make much less power. During the winter, there are fewer hours of daylight. Then solar panels make relatively small amounts of power.

Wind turbines make power only when the wind blows. Hydroelectric turbines make power as long as water is flowing, but a drought will decrease water levels and reduce power output. Geothermal energy provides a more reliable source of energy, but it requires drilling into Earth. This can be costly and impractical, especially in densely populated cities and towns.

2 Infer Solar panels are more effective on long, sunny days. What areas of the United States do you think would benefit most from solar power?

_____

_____

_____

 You Try It! ⟶

Now it's your turn to analyze and compare different forms of renewable energy.

© Houghton Mifflin Harcourt Publishing Company • Image Credits: (bg) ©Rafa Irusta/Fotolia; (t) ©dvoevnore/Fotolia; (b) ©Alex Emanuel Koch/Shutterstock

 You Try It!

Now it's your turn to analyze and compare different forms of renewable energy. You'll consider the benefits of different sources, come up with arguments, and create an energy plan.

(1) Identify Benefits

Choose one of the following types of renewable energy: hydroelectric, solar, geothermal, or wind power. List the benefits below.

_____

_____

_____

_____

_____

(2) Evaluate Cost of Technology

A Look at the list of cons for renewable energy. How would you address this point in your energy plan?

_____

_____

_____

_____

_____

B What would be the costs involved in your energy plan? Explain how your plan might save costs over the long run?

> **Cons of Renewable Energy Systems**
>
> - Clouds can reduce electricity from solar power plants.
>
> - Days with low winds can reduce electricity from wind farms.
>
> - Periods of drought reduce the energy a hydroelectric plant can produce.
>
> - Geothermal energy still needs electricity to operate heat pumps.

_____

_____

_____

_____

© Houghton Mifflin Harcourt Publishing Company

③ Compare Technology

Pair with a partner who has chosen a different source of renewable energy for his or her plan. Together, fill in the pros and cons of each energy source in the chart below.

Energy Source #1		Energy Source #2	
Pros	Cons	Pros	Cons

④ Propose Improvements

With your partner, list some improvements that could help address the cons of the energy sources you have chosen.

_____

_____

_____

_____

_____

⑤ Communicate Results

With your partner, share your top proposed improvement with the class. Give reasons why it would work.

_____

_____

_____

_____

_____

_____

_____

_____

© Houghton Mifflin Harcourt Publishing Company

Managing Resources

Bauxite is a mineral that is mined to make aluminum. The company that removed the bauxite replanted the mined area with trees. Replanting restores habitat and helps to prevent erosion.

ESSENTIAL QUESTION

Why should natural resources be managed?

By the end of this lesson, you should be able to explain the consequences of society's use of natural resources and the importance of managing these resources wisely.

▬ 6.ESS2.4, 6.ESS3.1, 6.ESS3.2, 6.ESS3.

© Houghton Mifflin Harcourt Publishing Company • Image Credits: (bg) ©Eco Images/Universal Images Group/Collection Mix:Subjects/Getty Images

🧠 Engage Your Brain

1 Predict Check T or F to show whether you think each statement is true or false.

T F

☐ ☐ Renewable resources cannot be replaced at the same rate that they are used.

☐ ☐ Resource use always results in the pollution of natural areas.

☐ ☐ Placing limits on the amount of fish that can be caught can cause fish populations to increase.

☐ ☐ Recycling nonrenewable resources can cause them to be used up more quickly.

2 Describe What natural resources could be obtained from the areas in the picture?

_____

_____

_____

_____

✏️ Active Reading

3 Apply Some words have similar meanings. Use context clues to write your own definitions for the words *conservation* and *stewardship*.

Example sentence

Hotels practice water <u>conservation</u> by installing water-saving showerheads.

conservation:

_____

_____

Example sentence

Fertilizers can run off into lakes and cause algae to bloom. People who live near lakes can practice good <u>stewardship</u> of the lake by not using lawn fertilizers.

stewardship:

_____

_____

Vocabulary Terms

• natural resource
• renewable resource
• nonrenewable resource
• stewardship
• conservation

4 Identify This list shows vocabulary terms you'll learn in this lesson. As you read, underline the definition of each term.

© Houghton Mifflin Harcourt Publishing Company • Image Credits: (bg) ©Eco Images/Universal Images Group/Collection Mix:Subjects/Getty Images; (t) ©Taylor S. Kennedy/National Geographic/Getty Images

Useful Stuff

What are the two main types of resources?

Any natural material that is used by people is a **natural resource**. Water, trees, minerals, air, and oil are just a few examples of Earth's resources. Resources can be divided into renewable and nonrenewable resources.

Renewable Resources

A natural resource that can be replaced as quickly as the resource is used is a **renewable resource**. Water, trees, and fish are examples of renewable resources. Renewable resources can become nonrenewable resources if they are used too quickly. For example, trees in a forest can become nonrenewable if they are cut down faster than new trees can grow to replace them.

Nonrenewable Resources

A natural resource that is used much faster than it can be replaced is a **nonrenewable resource**. Coal is an example of a nonrenewable resource. It takes millions of years for coal to form. Once coal is used up, it is no longer available. Minerals, oil, and natural gas are other examples of nonrenewable resources.

5 Compare How is a renewable resource different from a nonrenewable resource?

_____

_____

_____

_____

_____

_____

_____

6 Identify Label each picture as a renewable resource or nonrenewable resource.

salt mine

_____   _____   _____

© Houghton Mifflin Harcourt Publishing Company • Image Credits: (l) ©Jeff Rotman/The Image Bank/Getty Images; (c) ©Paul A. Souders/Corbis; (r) ©David R. Frazier/Photo Researchers, Inc.

What can happen when we use resources?

Natural resources can make people's lives easier. Natural resources allow us to heat and cool buildings, produce and use electricity, transport people and goods, and make products.

While natural resources are helpful, the way they are used can cause harm. Mining and oil spills can damage ecosystems. Oil spills can also harm local fishing or tourism industries. Burning coal or other fossil fuels can cause air and water pollution. Used products can fill landfills or litter beaches and other natural areas. Overuse of resources can make them hard to find. When resources are hard to find, they become more expensive.

© Houghton Mifflin Harcourt Publishing Company • Image Credits: (t) ©Ryan McVay/Photodisc/Getty Images; (c) ©Win McNamee/Photodisc/Getty Images News/Getty Images; (b) ©Charles Bowman/Axiom Photographic Agency/Getty Images

Active Reading

7 Identify As you read, underline the possible effects of resource use by people.

Visualize It!

8 List What are three ways that natural resources are making life easier for this family?

_____
_____
_____
_____
_____
_____

9 Explain How can the extraction of natural resources damage the environment?

_____
_____
_____
_____
_____
_____

10 Describe How can human use of natural resources pollute the environment?

_____
_____
_____
_____
_____
_____

Best Practices

What are some effective ways to manage resources?

As human populations continue to grow, we will need more and more resources in order to survive. People can make sure that resources continue to be available by practicing stewardship and conservation. **Stewardship** is the careful and responsible management of resources. **Conservation** is the protection and wise use of natural resources.

Conserving Renewable Resources

Stewardship of renewable resources involves a variety of conservation practices. Limits on fishing or logging can increase fish populations and protect forest ecosystems. Fish can be restocked in lakes and rivers. Logged areas can be replanted with trees. Water conservation can reduce the amount of water used in an area, so that rain can renew the water supply. Reducing the use of chemicals and energy resources can reduce the amount of pollution in air and water, and on land.

Active Reading

11 Identify As you read, underline the ways that resources can be managed effectively.

Visualize It!

12 Identify Describe the ways that each activity in the picture shows stewardship of natural resources.

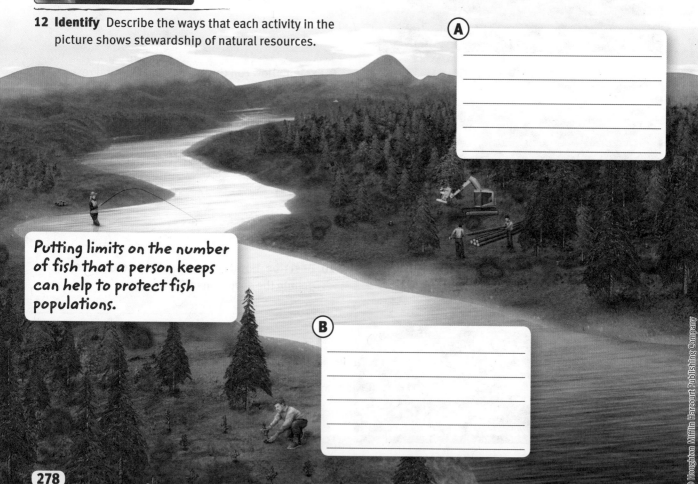

Ⓐ

Ⓑ

Putting limits on the number of fish that a person keeps can help to protect fish populations.

© Houghton Mifflin Harcourt Publishing Company

Reducing the Use of Nonrenewable Resources

Nonrenewable resources last longer if they are used efficiently. For example, compact fluorescent light bulbs, or CFLs, use much less energy to produce the same amount of light as incandescent light bulbs do. By using less electrical energy, fewer resources like coal are needed to produce electricity. Reducing, reusing, and recycling also reduce the amount of natural resources that must be obtained from Earth. Although recycling materials requires energy, it takes much less energy to recycle an aluminum can than it does to make a new one!

You can reuse a plastic water bottle instead of buying bottled water. Reusing conserves water and oil.

13 Apply How can you reduce the use of nonrenewable resources? Write your ideas in the table below.

Resource	Is used to...	Ways to reduce
oil	Make plastic objects. Provide energy.	Use reusable containers. Recycle plastics. Drive less.
coal		
metal		

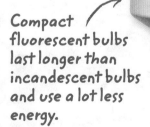

Compact fluorescent bulbs last longer than incandescent bulbs and use a lot less energy.

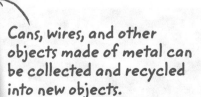

Cans, wires, and other objects made of metal can be collected and recycled into new objects.

© Houghton Mifflin Harcourt Publishing Company • Image Credits: (t) ©Ingram Publishing/Alamy; (c) ©Adrianna Williams/Corbis; (b) ©Erik Isakson/Getty Images

Pluses and Minuses

What are the disadvantages and advantages of managing resources?

Managing resources has disadvantages. Developing new technologies that use fewer resources is expensive. Changing how people use resources can be difficult, because some people have a hard time breaking old habits. Recycling resources can sometimes be expensive and inconvenient.

Managing resources also has many advantages. Management can reduce the loss of a valuable resource. It can also reduce waste. Less waste means less space is needed for landfills. Many resources produce pollution as they are gathered or used, so resource management can lead to less pollution.

Active Reading

14 Identify As you read, underline the advantages of managing resources.

Visualize It!

15 Place a (–) next to each property of the hybrid electric car that is a disadvantage. Place a (+) next to each property of the car that is an advantage.

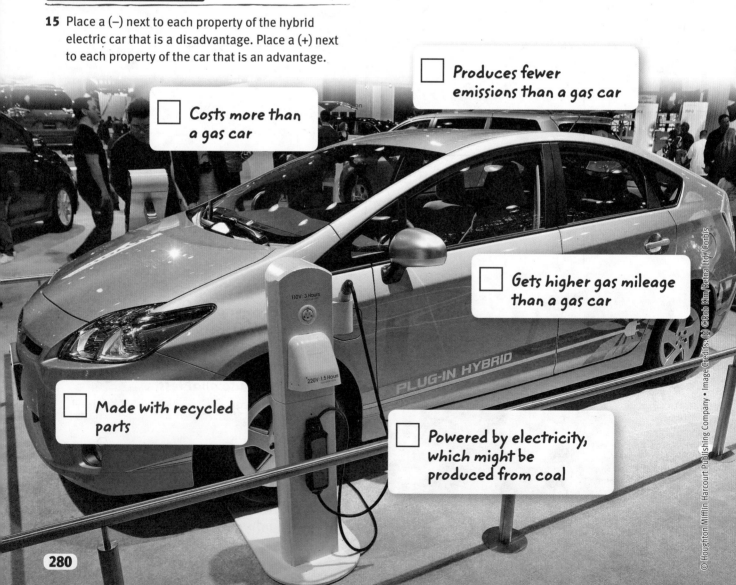

☐ Produces fewer emissions than a gas car

☐ Costs more than a gas car

☐ Gets higher gas mileage than a gas car

☐ Made with recycled parts

☐ Powered by electricity, which might be produced from coal

© Houghton Mifflin Harcourt Publishing Company • Image Credits: (b) ©Rob Kim/Retna Ltd./Corbis

What kinds of changes can we make to manage resources?

Managing natural resources takes place on global, national, state, local, and individual levels. On the global level, countries make agreements to help manage international resources. For example, countries agreed to stop using chemicals called CFCs after scientists discovered that CFCs were causing damage to the ozone layer. The ozone layer is a resource that protects Earth from harmful radiation. Eliminating the use of CFCs has slowed the breakdown of the ozone layer.

Change Laws

On the national level, countries pass laws to manage resources. Many nations have laws that determine where, when, and how many trees can be harvested for timber. Laws also govern how materials must be disposed of to prevent and reduce harm to land and water. Governments spend money to promote recycling programs. In addition, government funding allows scientists to develop technologies for using resources more efficiently.

Change Habits

Think about all the things you do every day. Changing some of your habits can help to conserve resources. You can conserve water by taking shorter showers and turning off the faucet while brushing your teeth. You can use reusable lunch containers and water bottles. You can recycle disposable materials, such as plastic bottles or newspaper, instead of throwing them away. You can bike or walk instead of riding in a car. You can save energy by turning off lights or TV sets when they are not being used. Families can buy energy-efficient appliances to save even more energy.

Think Outside the Book Inquiry

16 Apply With a partner, suggest laws that could be enacted in your community to protect resources.

Visualize It!

17 List What are some of the ways these students are conserving resources in their school lunchroom?

_____
_____
_____
_____
_____
_____
_____

You can conserve resources in your school lunchroom.

ALUMINUM   MILK CARTONS   PLASTIC

© Houghton Mifflin Harcourt Publishing Company • Image Credits: ©HMH

Visual Summary

To complete this summary, write the answer to each question. Then use the key below to check your answers. You can use this page to review the main concepts of the lesson.

Managing Resources

Humans use natural resources to carry out daily activities.

18 What is a negative impact of resource use?

_____

_____

_____

Managing resources has advantages and disadvantages.

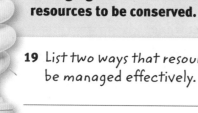

Managing resources can allow resources to be conserved.

19 List two ways that resources can be managed effectively.

_____

_____

_____

20 What is one advantage of developing energy-efficient technologies?

_____

_____

_____

Answers: **18** Using resources can cause pollution and damage to ecosystems; **19** Sample answers: practicing water conservation; limiting logging to protect forests; **20** a reduction in pollution

21 Apply What would a scientist need to consider when developing biofuels from plants like sugar cane and corn to use instead of fossil fuels?

© Houghton Mifflin Harcourt Publishing Company • Image Credits: (t) ©Ryan McVay/Photodisc/Getty Images; (c) ©Rob Kim/Retna Ltd/Corbis; (bl) ©Adrianna Williams/Corbis

Lesson Review

Vocabulary

Circle the term that best completes the following sentence.

1 *Conservation/Stewardship* is the protection and wise use of resources.

2 Anything that can be used to take care of a need is a *renewable resource/natural resource*.

3 A *renewable resource/nonrenewable resource* is used more quickly than it can be replaced.

Key Concepts

4 Identify Which of the following is a renewable resource?

A oil

B sunlight

C gold

D natural gas

5 Describe How does reusing, reducing, and recycling conserve energy?

_____

_____

_____

6 Explain How can technology be used to conserve nonrenewable resources?

_____

_____

_____

_____

7 Compare What is the relationship between stewardship and conservation?

_____

_____

_____

_____

_____

_____

Critical Thinking

8 Contrast How might the management of nonrenewable resources be different from the management of renewable resources?

_____

_____

_____

_____

Use the photo below to answer the following questions.

9 Predict Could the resource in the picture become nonrenewable? Explain your answer.

_____

_____

_____

10 Apply How can individuals help to conserve the resource in the picture?

_____

_____

_____

_____

_____

© Houghton Mifflin Harcourt Publishing Company • Image Credits: (cr) ©Jeff Rotman/The Image Bank/Getty Images

My Notes

© Houghton Mifflin Harcourt Publishing Company

© Houghton Mifflin Harcourt Publishing Company

Unit 4 | Big Idea | Humans depend on natural resources for materials and for energy.

Lesson 1
ESSENTIAL QUESTION
How can Earth support life?

Explain how the unique properties of Earth allow life to exist.

Lesson 2
ESSENTIAL QUESTION
What are Earth's natural resources?

Understand the types and uses of Earth's natural resources.

Lesson 3
ESSENTIAL QUESTION
How do we use nonrenewable energy resources?

Describe how humans use energy resources and the role of nonrenewable energy resources in society.

Lesson 4
ESSENTIAL QUESTION
How do humans use renewable energy resources?

Describe how humans use energy resources and the role of renewable energy resources in society.

Lesson 5
ESSENTIAL QUESTION
Why should natural resources be managed?

Explain the consequences of society's use of natural resources and the importance of managing these resources wisely.

 Connect **ESSENTIAL QUESTIONS**
Lessons 2 and 5

1 Explain Why is it important to manage natural resources wisely?

_____

_____

_____

_____

Think Outside the Book

2 Synthesize Choose one of these activities to help synthesize what you have learned in this unit.

☐ Using what you learned in lessons 2, 3, and 4, create a poster presentation that compares and contrasts one renewable resource and one nonrenewable resource. Include a discussion of at least one drawback for each resource type.

☐ Using what you learned in lessons 2 and 3, write a short story about a fossil fuel that follows the fuel from its formation to its use by humans.

© Houghton Mifflin Harcourt Publishing Company • Image Credits: (tl) ©NASA/K. Horgan/Stone/Getty Images; (tr) ©ssuaphotos/Shutterstock; (cl) ©World Perspectives/Photographer's Choice/Getty Images; (bl) ©Chand Ehlers/Alamy; (br) ©Eco Images/Universal Images Group/Collection Mix:Subjects/Getty Images

Unit 4 Review

Name _____

Vocabulary

Check the box to show whether each statement is true or false.

T	F	
☐	☐	**1** The <u>ozone</u> layer helps insulate the Earth.
☐	☐	**2** A <u>material resource</u> is a renewable resource that is used to make objects.
☐	☐	**3** <u>Stewardship</u> is the application of various methods that use up natural resources.
☐	☐	**4** <u>Biomass</u> energy comes from organic matter such as plant material and manure.
☐	☐	**5** Rocks, water, air, minerals, forests, wildlife, and soil are all examples of a <u>natural resource</u>.

Key Concepts

Read each question below, and circle the best answer.

6 The chemical bonds in fuel are changed when the fuel is burned to move a car. What type of energy conversion is taking place in this example?

A kinetic energy to mechanical energy

B chemical energy to potential energy

C potential energy to kinetic energy

D mechanical energy to electrical energy

7 Sometimes, a renewable resource can be considered nonrenewable because it is used up faster than it can be replenished. Which of the following choices is an example of this?

A Coal supply getting smaller because it takes millions of years to form.

B Forests being cut down at a quicker rate than they can grow.

C Solar energy being used to provide electricity to a home.

D Water in streams replaced by rainfall from the atmosphere.

© Houghton Mifflin Harcourt Publishing Company

8 The diagram below shows the process of photosynthesis.

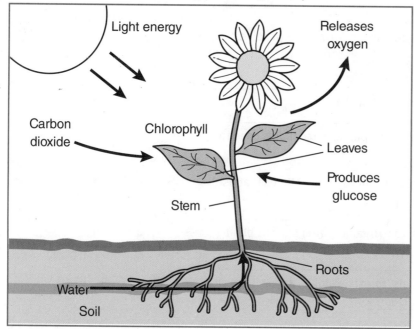

How is photosynthesis best summarized?

A The process by which oxygen enters a leaf and is converted into carbon dioxide.

B The process by which plants use the sun's energy to make chlorophyll.

C The process by which plants convert the sun's energy into energy stored as glucose.

D The process by which water enters through the roots and glucose is produced.

9 Which of the following is a disadvantage of managing resources?

A less of the natural resource is wasted

B reduction in pollution due to less manufacturing

C expense of recycling materials

D more resources extracted from Earth

10 What is a major reason solar energy is not used everywhere on a large scale?

A It is too difficult to purchase and install solar panels.

B Solar energy is not very effective at producing electricity.

C The manufacture of solar panels produces too much pollution.

D Solar panels are most efficient in places that receive lots of sunlight.

© Houghton Mifflin Harcourt Publishing Company

11 The chemicals released by burning petroleum in car engines contribute to what local and global effects?

A smog and global warming   **C** acid rain and fusion

B fog and radioactivity   **D** sulfur dioxide decrease and ozone buildup

12 What gas molecule found in Earth's atmosphere is made up of three oxygen atoms?

A ozone   **C** sulfur dioxide

B nitrogen   **D** carbon dioxide

13 Nuclear energy is best described as what type of energy resource?

A renewable   **C** renewable and inexhaustible

B nonrenewable   **D** nonrenewable because it is used up so rapidly

Critical Thinking

Answer the following questions in the space provided.

14 Below is an example of a technology used for alternative energy.

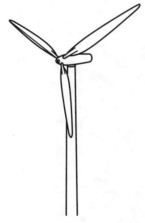

What type of energy does the equipment in the picture harness? _____

Is the type of energy harnessed by this equipment renewable or nonrenewable? Explain your answer. _____

_____

Name one advantage and one disadvantage of using this type of energy.

_____

_____

© Houghton Mifflin Harcourt Publishing Company

15 The unique properties of Earth make life possible. What are the five basic necessities that all living things need to survive on Earth?

_____

_____

Why is the distance from Earth to the sun important for life on Earth?

_____

_____

Why is the rotation of Earth important to conditions on Earth?

_____

_____

Connect ESSENTIAL QUESTIONS
Lessons 3 and 5

Answer the following question in the space provided.

16 Below is a graph of the production and use of petroleum in the United States in the past, present, and likely usage in the future.

U.S. Petroleum Usage for Transportation

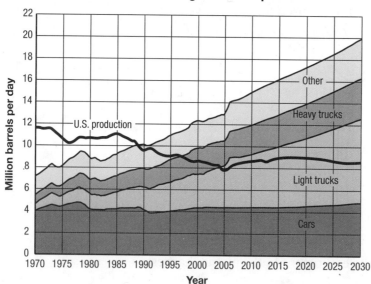

Summarize how current production and usage of petroleum compare.

_____

_____

Name two risks linked to offshore drilling and transporting petroleum.

_____

_____

© Houghton Mifflin Harcourt Publishing Company

Human Impact on the Environment

Big Idea

Humans and human population growth affect the environment.

6.ESS2.4, 6.ESS3.3, 6.LS2.1, 6.LS4.1, 6.PS3.4

Human actions, such as cutting down trees to build large housing developments, affect the surrounding ecosystem.

Factories cause pollution.

What do you think?

Human activities can affect Earth's air, water, and land resources in a variety of ways. What are some specific ways in which human activities affect the environment?

© Houghton Mifflin Harcourt Publishing Company • Image Credits: (bkgd) ©Cameron Davidson/Photographer's Choice RF/Getty Images; (br) ©David Hay Jones/Photo Researchers, Inc.

CITIZEN SCIENCE

Investigating Water Resources

Fresh water is an important natural resource. It is found underground and on Earth's surface. People need fresh water for many things, including drinking and household uses.

① Think about It

A What makes fresh surface water and groundwater such valuable resources?

_____

_____

_____

B How does human activity affect the availability of fresh water?

_____

_____

_____

Rain barrels collect rainwater for home use.

© Houghton Mifflin Harcourt Publishing Company • Image Credits: (bkgd) ©Stephen Wilkes/The Image Bank/Getty Images; (br) ©Wayne Hutchinson/Alamy

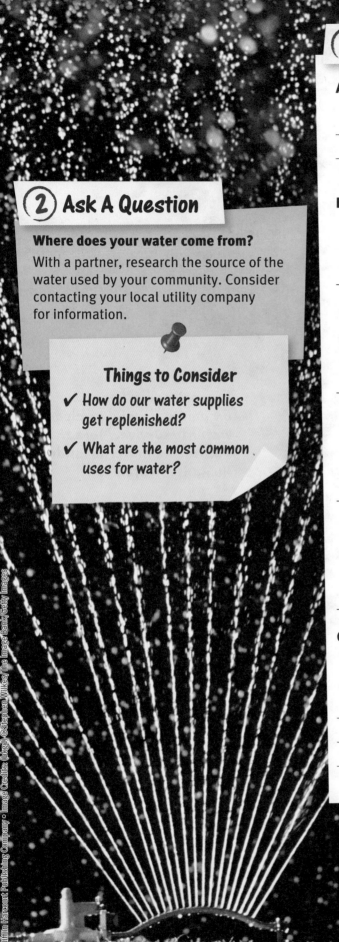

② Ask A Question

Where does your water come from?

With a partner, research the source of the water used by your community. Consider contacting your local utility company for information.

Things to Consider

✔ How do our water supplies get replenished?

✔ What are the most common uses for water?

③ Make A Plan

A Describe the environment that surrounds your local water source.

_____

_____

B Describe threats to your local water supply and how your water supply can be protected.

Threats to Water Supply	Ways to Protect Water Supply

C Choose one of the ideas for protecting the water supply that you listed above. Describe how this method of protection might be implemented by your community.

_____

_____

_____

Take It Home

Trace the water used in your home to its source. Use a map to determine the route by which the water you use must be transported from its source. See *ScienceSaurus*® for more information about the water cycle.

© Houghton Mifflin Harcourt Publishing Company • Image Credits: (bkgd) ©Stephen Wilkes/The Image Bank/Getty Images

Human Impact on Water

ESSENTIAL QUESTION

What impact can human activities have on water resources?

By the end of this lesson, you should be able to explain the impacts that humans can have on the quality and supply of fresh water.

6.ESS2.4, 6.ESS3.3, 6.LS2.1, 6.LS4.1, 6.PS3.4

Humans and other organisms depend on clean water to survive. More than half of the material inside humans is water.

© Houghton Mifflin Harcourt Publishing Company • Image Credits: ©Aurora Open/Justin Bailie/Getty Images

Lesson Labs

Quick Labs
- Ocean Pollution from Land
- Turbidity and Water Temperature

Field Lab
- Investigating Water Quality

Engage Your Brain

1 Analyze Write a list of the reasons humans need water. Next to this list, write a list of reasons fish need water. Are there similarities between your two lists?

2 Identify Circle the word that correctly completes the following sentences.
The man in this photo is testing *water*/*air* quality.
The flowing body of water next to the man is a *river*/*lake*.

Active Reading

3 Synthesize You can often define an unknown word if you know the meaning of its word parts. Use the word parts and the sentence below to make an educated guess about the meaning of the word *nonrenewable*.

Word part	Meaning
renew	restore, make like new
-able	able to be
non-	not

Example sentence
Some of Earth's <u>nonrenewable</u> resources include coal and oil.

nonrenewable:

_____

_____

_____

_____

_____

Vocabulary Terms
- water pollution
- point-source pollution
- nonpoint-source pollution
- thermal pollution
- eutrophication
- potable
- reservoir
- urbanization

4 Identify This list contains the key terms you'll learn in this lesson. As you read, circle the definition of each term.

© Houghton Mifflin Harcourt Publishing Company • Image Credits: (bkgd) ©Aurora Open/Justin Bailie/Getty Images; (tr) ©Terry Whittaker/Photo Researchers, Inc.

Close up of a
mayfly larva

Water, Water

Organisms need clean water for life
and good health. For example, young
mayflies live in water, humans drink
water, and brown pelicans eat fish
they catch in water.

Why is water important?

Earth is the only planet with large amounts of water. Water
shapes Earth's surface and affects Earth's weather and climates.
Most importantly, water is vital for life. Every living thing is
made mostly of water. Most life processes use water. Water is an
important natural resource. For humans and other organisms,
access to clean water is important for good health.

There is lots of water, so what's the problem?

About 97% of Earth's water is salty, which leaves only 3% as fresh
water. However, as you can see from the graph, over two-thirds
of Earth's fresh water is frozen as ice and snow. But a lot of the
liquid water seeps into the ground as groundwater. That leaves
much less than 1% of Earth's fresh liquid water on the surface.
Water is vital for people, so this small volume of fresh surface and
groundwater is a limited resource.

Areas with high densities of people, such as cities, need lots of
fresh water. Cities are getting bigger, and so the need for fresh
water is increasing. *Urbanization* (ER•buh•ny•zhay•shuhn) is
the growth of towns and cities that results from the movement of
people from rural areas into the urban areas. The greater demand
for fresh water in cities is threatening the availability of water for
many people. Fresh water is becoming a natural resource that
cannot be replaced at the same rate at which it is used.

Distribution of Earth's Fresh Water

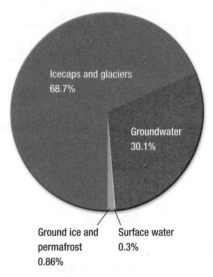

Icecaps and glaciers
68.7%

Groundwater
30.1%

Ground ice and
permafrost
0.86%

Surface water
0.3%

Visualize It!

5 Interpret What percentage of
fresh water on Earth is frozen?
What percentage of fresh water is
liquid?

_____

_____

© Houghton Mifflin Harcourt Publishing Company • Image Credits: (bkgd) ©Luigi Masella/Flickr/Getty Images; (l) ©blickwinkel/Alamy; (c) ©Biggie Productions/Taxi/Getty Images; (t) ©Richard Mittleman/Gon2Foto/Alamy

Everywhere...

Where do we get fresh water?

Fresh water may fall directly as precipitation, or may melt from ice and snow. Earth's fresh liquid water is found as surface water and groundwater. *Surface water* is any body of water above the ground. It includes liquid salt or fresh water, or solid water, like snow and ice. Water may seep below the surface to become *groundwater*. Groundwater is found under Earth's surface, in spaces in rocks or in soil, where it can be liquid or frozen.

Aquifers and Groundwater

Aquifers and ground ice are forms of groundwater. An *aquifer* is a body of rock or sediment that can store a lot of water, and that allows water to flow easily through it. Aquifers store water in spaces, called *pores,* between particles of rock or sediment. Wells are dug into aquifers to reach the water. In polar regions, water is often frozen in a layer of soil called *permafrost.*

Rivers, Streams, and Lakes

Rivers, streams, and most lakes are fresh surface waters. A stream or river may flow into a bowl-shaped area, which may fill up to form a lake. Many millions of people around the world depend on fresh water that is taken from rivers and fresh water lakes.

What are water quality and supply?

Water quality is a measure of how clean or polluted water is. Water quality is important because humans and other organisms depend on clean water to survive. It is vital for living things to not only have water, but also to have clean water. Dirty, contaminated water can make us sick or even kill us.

    Water supply is the availability of water. Water supply influences where and when farmers grow crops, and where people can build cities. *Water supply systems* carry water from groundwater or surface waters so people can use the water. The systems can be a network of underground pipes, or a bucket for scooping water from a well. A shortage of clean, fresh water reduces quality of life for people. Many people in developing countries do not have access to clean, fresh water.

© Houghton Mifflin Harcourt Publishing Company • Image Credits: ©Caroline Penn/Corbis; (b) ©Caroline Penn/Corbis

Active Reading

6 List What are the different sources of fresh water?

_____

_____

Think Outside the Book Inquiry

7 Observe Keep a water diary for a day. Record every time you use water at school, at home, or elsewhere. At the end of the day, review your records. How could you reduce your water usage?

Many people do not have a water supply to their homes. Instead, they have to go to a local stream, well, or pump to gather water for cooking, cleaning, and drinking.

Under Threat

What threatens fresh water quality?

When waste or other material is added to water so that it is harmful to organisms that use it or live in it, **water pollution** (WAW•ter puh•LOO•shuhn) occurs. It is useful to divide pollution sources into two types. **Point-source pollution** comes from one specific site. For example, a major chemical spill is point-source pollution. Usually this type of pollution can be controlled once its source is found. **Nonpoint-source pollution** comes from many small sources and is more difficult to control. Most nonpoint-source pollution reaches water supplies by runoff or by seeping into groundwater. The main sources of nonpoint-source pollution are city streets, roads and drains, farms, and mines.

 **Active Reading**

8 Identify As you read, underline the sources of water pollution.

Thermal Pollution

Any heating of natural water that results from human activity is called **thermal pollution**. For example, water that is used for cooling some power plants gets warmed up. When that water is returned to the river or lake it is at a higher temperature than the lake or river water. The warm water has less oxygen available for organisms that live in the water.

Chemical Pollution

Chemical pollution occurs when harmful chemicals are added to water supplies. Two major sources of chemical pollution are industry and agriculture. For example, refineries that process oil or metals and factories that make metal or plastic products or electronic items all produce toxic chemical waste. Chemicals used in agriculture include pesticides, herbicides, and fertilizers. These pollutants can reach water supplies by seeping into groundwater. Once in groundwater, the pollution can enter the water cycle and can be carried far from the pollution source. *Acid rain* is another form of chemical pollution. It forms when gases formed by burning fossil fuels mix with water in the air. Acid rain can harm both plants and animals. It can lower the pH of soil and water, and make them too acidic for life.

Biological Pollution

Many organisms naturally live in and around water, but they are not normally polluters. *Biological pollution* occurs when live or dead organisms are added to water supplies. Wastewater may contain disease-causing microbes from human or animal wastes. *Wastewater* is any water that has been used by people for such things as flushing toilets, showering, or washing dishes. Wastewater from feed lots and farms may also contain harmful microbes. These microbes can cause diseases such as dysentery, typhoid, or cholera.

Eutrophication

Fresh water often contains nutrients from decomposing organisms. An increase in the amount of nutrients in water is called **eutrophication** (yoo•TRAWF•ih•kay•shuhn). Eutrophication occurs naturally in water. However, *artificial eutrophication* occurs when human activity increases nutrient levels in water. Wastewater and fertilizer runoff that gets into waterways can add extra nutrients which upset the natural biology of the water. These extra nutrients cause the fast growth of algae over the water surface. An overgrowth of algae and aquatic plants can reduce oxygen levels and kill fish and other organisms in the water.

© Houghton Mifflin Harcourt Publishing Company

Visualize It!

Water can become polluted by human activities in many different ways.

Chemical Pollution
Sulfur in smoke and vehicle exhausts contributes to the acidification of rain, leading to acid rain. Acid rain can affect areas far from the point of pollution.

Biological pollution

Biological Pollution
Animal and human wastes can get washed into a water supply in runoff, or through leaking pipes.

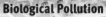

Thermal pollution

Eutrophication

Chemical pollution

9 Describe How is human activity impacting water quality in this image?

_____

_____

_____

_____

10 Apply Identify one point-source and one nonpoint-source of pollution in this image.

_____

_____

_____

_____

© Houghton Mifflin Harcourt Publishing Company • Image Credits: (tr) ©Tony Cortazzi/Alamy; (cl) ©Chris Howes/Wild Places Photography/Alamy; (cr) ©Dr. Jeremy Burgess/Photo Researchers, Inc.

How is water quality measured?

Before there were scientific methods of testing water, people could only look at water, taste it, and smell it to check its quality. Scientists can now test water with modern equipment, so the results are more reliable. Modern ways of testing water are especially important for finding small quantities of toxic chemicals or harmful organisms in water.

Water is a good solvent. So, water in nature usually contains dissolved solids, such as salt and other substances. Because most dissolved solids cannot be seen, it is important to measure them. Measurements of water quality include testing the levels of dissolved oxygen, pH, temperature, dissolved solids, and the number and types of microbes in the water. Quality standards depend on the intended use for the water. For example, drinking water needs to meet much stricter quality standards than environmental waters such as river or lake waters do.

Water Quality Measurement

Quality measurement	What is it?	How it relates to water quality
Dissolved solids	a measure of the amount of ions or microscopic suspended solids in water	Some dissolved solids could be harmful chemicals. Others such as calcium could cause scaling or build-up in water pipes.
pH	a measure of how acidic or alkaline water is	Aquatic organisms need a near neutral pH (approx. pH 7). Acid rain can drop the pH too low (acidic) for aquatic life to live.
Dissolved oxygen (DO)	the amount of oxygen gas that is dissolved in water	Aquatic organisms need oxygen. Animal waste and thermal pollution can decrease the amount of oxygen dissolved in water.
Turbidity	a measure of the cloudiness of water that is caused by suspended solids	High turbidity increases the chance that harmful microbes or chemicals are in the water.
Microbial load	the identification of harmful bacteria, viruses or protists in water	Microbes such as bacteria, viruses, and protists from human and animal wastes can cause diseases.

11 Predict Why might increased turbidity increase the chance of something harmful being in the water? _____

_____

© Houghton Mifflin Harcourt Publishing Company

How is water treated for human use?

Active Reading 12 **Identify** As you read, number the basic steps in the water treatment process.

Natural water may be unsafe for humans to drink. So, water that is to be used as drinking water is treated to remove harmful chemicals and organisms. Screens take out large debris. Then chemicals are added that make suspended particles stick together. These particles drop out of the water in a process called *flocculation*. Flocculation also removes harmful bacteria and other microbes. Chlorine is often added to kill microbes left in the water. In some cities, fluoride is added to water supplies to help prevent tooth decay. Finally, air is bubbled through the water. Water that is suitable to drink is called **potable** water. Once water is used, it becomes wastewater. It enters the sewage system where pipes carry it to a wastewater treatment plant. There the wastewater is cleaned and filtered before being released back into the environment.

Drinking water is often mixed in large basins to help remove chemicals and harmful organisms. Paddles stir the water in the basins.

Who monitors and protects our water quality?

Active Reading 13 **Identify** As you read, underline the government agency that is responsible for enforcing water quality rules.

If a public water supply became contaminated, many people could get very sick. As a result, public water supplies are closely monitored so that any problems can be fixed quickly. The Safe Drinking Water Act is the main federal law that ensures safe drinking water for people in the United States. The act sets strict limits on the amount of heavy metals or certain types of bacteria that can be in drinking water, among other things. The Environmental Protection Agency (EPA) has the job of enforcing this law. It is responsible for setting the standards drinking water must meet before the water can be pumped into public water systems. Water quality tests can be done by trained workers or trained volunteers.

Samples of water are routinely taken to make sure the water quality meets the standards required by law.

© Houghton Mifflin Harcourt Publishing Company • Image Credits: (t) ©Lawrence Migdale/Photo Researchers, Inc.; (b) ©Will & Deni McIntyre/Photo Researchers, Inc.

Supply and Demand

How does water get to the faucet?

In earlier times, humans had to live near natural sources of fresh water. Over time, engineers developed ways to transport and store large amounts of water. So, humans can now live in places where fresh water is supplied by water pipes and other infrastructure. The ability to bring fresh water safely from its source to a large population has led to the urbanization of cities.

Creating Water Supply Systems

Freshwater supply is often limited, so we have found ways to store and transport water far from its source to where it is used. Surface water is collected and pumped to places where people need it. Groundwater can be found by digging wells into aquifers. Water can be lifted from a well by hand in buckets. It can be pumped into pipes that supply homes, farms, factories and cities. Piped water supply systems can deliver water over great distances to where humans need it. Water supply and storage systems are expensive to build and maintain.

Visualize It!

A public water supply includes the water source, the treatment facilities, and the pipes and pumps that send it to homes, industries, businesses, and public facilities.

Water treatment and distribution

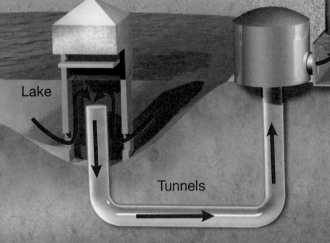

A Water can be moved far away from its source by pumping it through pipes to large urban areas.

Intake

Chemicals added

Lake

Mixing basins

Settling basins

Tunnels

Water treatment plant

B Water is treated to make it potable.

© Houghton Mifflin Harcourt Publishing Company • Image Credits: ©NASA; Image by Marit Jentoft-Nilsen, based on data from NOAA GOES, Blue Marble Imagery by NASA's Earth Observatory Team, ©artpartner-images/Photographer's Choice/Getty Images.

Changing the Flow of Water

Pumping and collecting groundwater and surface waters changes how water flows in natural systems. For example, a **reservoir** (REZ•uhr•vwohr) is a body of water that usually forms behind a dam. Dams stop river waters from flowing along their natural course. The water in a reservoir would naturally have flowed to the sea. Instead, the water can be diverted into a pipeline or into artificial channels called *canals* or *aqueducts*.

What threatens our water supply?

Active Reading **14 Identify** As you read, underline the things that are a threat to water supply.

As the human use of water has increased, the demand for fresh water has also increased. Demand is greater than supply in many areas of the world, including parts of the United States. The larger a population or a city gets, the greater the demand for fresh water. Increased demand for and use of water can cause water shortages. Droughts or leaking water pipes can also cause water shortages. Water is used to keep our bodies clean and healthy. It is also used to grow crops for food. Water shortages threaten these benefits.

15 Infer Why would a larger city have a larger demand for water?

_____

_____

_____

_____

_____

_____

C The infastructure shown here is used to supply clean water. Once water is used, it becomes wastewater. A different system, called a sewage system, carries wastewater away from urban areas to wastewater treatment plants.

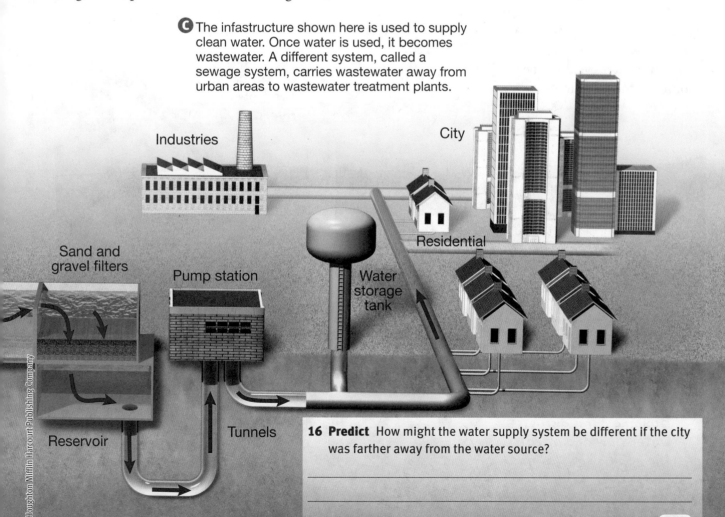

Industries

City

Sand and gravel filters

Pump station

Water storage tank

Residential

Reservoir

Tunnels

16 Predict How might the water supply system be different if the city was farther away from the water source?

_____

_____

© Houghton Mifflin Harcourt Publishing Company

How do efforts to supply water to humans affect the environment?

Growing urban populations place a greater demand on water supplies. Efforts to increase water supply can affect the environment. For example, building dams and irrigation canals changes the natural flow of water. The environment is physically changed by construction work. The local ecology changes too. Organisms that live in or depend on the water may lose their habitat and move away or die.

Aquifers are often used as freshwater sources for urban areas. When more water is taken from an aquifer than can be replaced by rain or snow, the water table can drop below the reach of existing wells. Rivers and streams may dry up and the soil that once held aquifer waters may collapse, or *subside*. In coastal areas, the overuse of groundwater can cause seawater to seep into the aquifer in a process called *saltwater intrusion*. In this way, water supplies can become contaminated with salt water.

Increasing population in an area can also affect water quality. The more people that use a water supply in one area, the greater the volume of wastewater that is produced in that area. Pollutants such as oil, pesticides, fertilizers, and heavy metals from city runoff, from industry, and from agriculture may seep into surface waters and groundwater. In this way, pollution could enter the water supply. This pollution could also enter the water cycle and be carried far from the initial source of the pollution.

Active Reading

17 Relate How can the increased demand on water affect water quality?

_____

_____

_____

_____

_____

_____

Digging irrigation canals changes the flow of rivers.

Building dams disrupts water flow and affects the ecology of the land and water.

Irrigating arid areas changes the ecology of those areas.

© Houghton Mifflin Harcourt Publishing Company • Image Credits: (l) ©Travel Ink/Gallo Images/Getty Images; (r) ©Derrick Francis Furlong/Alamy; (bc) ©Tony Roberts/Corbis

Death of a Sea

The Aral Sea in Central Asia was once the world's fourth-largest inland salty lake. But it has been shrinking since the 1960s. In the 1940s, the courses of the rivers that fed the lake were changed to irrigate the desert, so that crops such as cotton and rice could be grown. By 2004, the lake had shrunk to 25% of its original size. The freshwater flow into the lake was reduced and evaporation caused the lake to become so salty that most of the plants and animals in it died or left the lake.

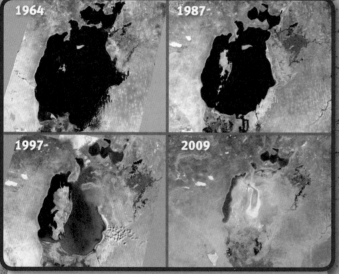

1964 1987 1997 2009

By 2007, the lake had shrunk to 10% of its original size and had split into three separate, smaller lakes.

Polluted Land

The Aral Sea is also heavily polluted by industrial wastes, pesticides, and fertilizer runoff. Salty dust that is blown from the dried seabed damages crops and pollutes drinking water. The salt- and dust-laden air cause serious public health problems in the Aral Sea region. One of the more bizarre reminders of how large the lake once was are the boats that lie abandoned on the exposed sea floor.

Extend

Inquiry

18 Identify What human activity has created the situation in the Aral Sea?

19 Apply Research the impact that of one of these two large water projects has had on people and on the environment: The Three Gorges Dam or the Columbia Basin Project.

20 Relate Research a current or past water project in the area where you live. What benefits will these projects have for people in the area? What risks might there be to the environment?

© Houghton Mifflin Harcourt Publishing Company • Image Credits: (bkgd) ©Gerd Ludwig/Corbis; (inset) ©NASA/Photo Researchers, Inc.

Visual Summary

To complete this summary, fill in the blanks with the correct word or phrase. Then use the key below to check your answers. You can use this page to review the main concepts of the lesson.

Human Impact on Water

Organisms need clean water for life and good health.

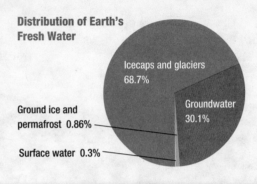

Distribution of Earth's Fresh Water

Icecaps and glaciers 68.7%

Groundwater 30.1%

Ground ice and permafrost 0.86%

Surface water 0.3%

21 Earth's fresh liquid water is found as surface water and _____

Water pollution can come from many different sources.

22 Runoff from farmland into a river is an example of _____ source pollution.

Federal laws set the standards for potable water quality. Water quality is constantly monitored.

23 Dissolved solids, pH, temperature, and dissolved oxygen are measures of _____.

Ensuring a constant supply of water for people can change the environment.

24 A _____ is a body of water that forms when a dam blocks a river.

Answers: 21 groundwater; 22 nonpoint; 23 water quality; 24 reservoir

25 Compare What is the difference between water quality and water supply?

© Houghton Mifflin Harcourt Publishing Company • Image Credits: (t) ©Richard Mittleman/Gon2Foto/Alamy; (tr) ©Dr. Jeremy Burgess/Photo Researchers, Inc.; (bl) ©Will & Deni McIntyre/Photo Researchers, Inc.; (br) ©Travel Ink/Gallo Images/Getty Images

Lesson Review

Vocabulary

Fill in the blank with the term that best completes the following sentences.

1 _____ water is a term used to describe water that is safe to drink.

2 The addition of nutrients to water by human activity is called artificial _____.

3 _____ pollution comes from many small sources.

Key Concepts

Complete the table below with the type of pollution described in each example.

Example	Type of pollution (chemical, thermal, or biological)
4 Identify A person empties an oil can into a storm drain.	
5 Identify A factory releases warm water into a local river.	
6 Identify Untreated sewage is washed into a lake during a rain storm.	

7 Describe Name two ways in which humans can affect the flow of fresh water.

_____

_____

_____

8 Explain Why does water quality need to be monitored?

_____

_____

Critical Thinking

Use this graph to answer the following questions.

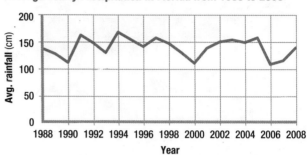

Average Yearly Precipitation in Florida from 1988 to 2008

Source: Florida State University Climate Center

9 Analyze Which year had the least precipitation?

_____

10 Infer What effect might many years of low precipitation have on water supply?

_____

_____

11 Explain Could a single person or animal be a cause of point-source pollution? Explain.

_____

_____

_____

_____

12 Apply In times of hot, dry, weather, some cities ban the use of garden sprinklers. Why do you think there is such a rule?

_____

_____

_____

_____

_____

_____

© Houghton Mifflin Harcourt Publishing Company

My Notes

© Houghton Mifflin Harcourt Publishing Company

© Houghton Mifflin Harcourt Publishing Company

Angel Montoya

CONSERVATION BIOLOGIST

In 1990, Angel Montoya was a student intern working at Laguna Atascosa National Wildlife Refuge in Texas. He became interested in the Aplomado falcon, a bird of prey that disappeared from the southwestern United States during the first half of the 20th century. Montoya decided to go looking for the raptors. He found a previously unknown population of Aplomados in Chihuahua, Mexico. His work helped to make it possible for the falcons to be reintroduced to an area near El Paso, Texas.

Restoration of the Aplomado falcon became Angel's lifework. He has monitored and researched the falcon since 1992. He helps release falcons that have been raised in captivity back into the wild and monitors falcons that have already been released. It isn't easy to keep tabs on a falcon, however. "Their first year they are pretty vulnerable, because they haven't had parents," Montoya says. "Just like juveniles, they're always getting into trouble. But I think they will do just fine."

Angel Montoya releases an Aplomado falcon back into the wild.

© Houghton Mifflin Harcourt Publishing Company • Image Credits: (bkgd) ©Rob Howard/Corbis; (b) ©The Peregine Fund/ Cal Sandfort; (tr) ©Ron Austing; Frank Lane Picture Agency/Corbis

JOB BOARD

Environmental Engineering Technician

What You'll Do: Work closely with environmental engineers and scientists to prevent or fix environmental damage. Take care of water and wastewater treatment systems, as well as equipment used for recycling. Test water and air quality and keep good records.

Where You Might Work: In a water treatment facility, or an environmental laboratory.

Education: an associate's degree in engineering technology.

Other Job Requirements: Good communication skills and the ability to work well with others.

Agronomist

What You'll Do: Study the best ways to grow crops and work with farmers to help them use their land better, and get better yields. Agronomists are scientists who study crops and soil.

Where You Might Work: On a farm, in an agricultural business, for the U.S. Department of Agriculture or state or local government agencies, or for seed companies. Agronomists may work both in fields and in laboratories.

Education: a four-year college degree in agronomy, agriculture, or soil conservation.

PEOPLE IN SCIENCE NEWS

YUMI Someya

Fueling the Family Business

Yumi Someya's family had worked in recycling for three generations, cleaning and recycling used cooking oil. In Japan, many people enjoy fried foods. They often throw out the used cooking oil. Yumi's family business collected used oil, cleaned it, and sold it for reuse.

When Yumi traveled to Nepal, she was caught in a landslide. She learned that deforestation was one cause of the landslide and began to think about environmental issues. When she returned home, she worked with her father to find new uses for the used cooking oil. They experimented with fertilizer and soap. Then, in 1992, they learned about biodiesel—fuel made from recycled soybean oil. They thought that used cooking oil might work to fuel cars, too. With a team of researchers, they created Vegetable Diesel Fuel (VDF).

Now, VDF fuels the company's oil-collecting trucks and some Tokyo buses. Yumi hopes to eventually recycle all of the cooking oil used in Japan.

© Houghton Mifflin Harcourt Publishing Company • Image Credits: (bkgd) ©Rob Howard/Corbis; (br) ©amana images inc./Alamy

Human Impact on Land

Human activities can carve up land features. A tunnel was cut into this mountain in Zion National Park, Utah, so that people may move around easily.

ESSENTIAL QUESTION

What impact can human activities have on land resources?

By the end of this lesson, you should be able to identify the impact that human activity has on Earth's land.

6.ESS3.3

© Houghton Mifflin Harcourt Publishing Company • Image Credits: ©Nature Animals/Alamy

Engage Your Brain

1 Predict Check T or F to show whether you think each statement is true or false.

T F
- ☐ ☐ Urban areas have more open land than rural areas do.
- ☐ ☐ Many building materials are made from land resources.
- ☐ ☐ Soil provides habitat for plants but not animals.
- ☐ ☐ Soil can erode when trees are removed from an area.

2 Illustrate Draw a picture of an object or material that is taken from the land and that is commercially important.

Active Reading

3 Synthesize You can often define an unknown word if you know the meaning of its word parts. Use the word parts to make an educated guess about the meaning of the words *land degradation* and *deforestation*.

Word part	Meaning
degrade	to damage something
deforest	to remove trees from an area
-ation	action or process

Vocabulary Terms

- urbanization
- land degradation
- desertification
- deforestation

4 Apply As you learn the definition of each vocabulary term in this lesson, create your own definition or sketch to help you remember the meaning of the term.

land degradation:

_____

_____

deforestation:

_____

_____

© Houghton Mifflin Harcourt Publishing Company • Image Credits: ©Nature Animals/Alamy

Land of Plenty

Why is land important?

It is hard to imagine human life without land. Land supplies a solid surface for buildings and roads. The soil in land provides nutrients for plants and hiding places for animals. Minerals below the land's surface can be used for construction materials. Fossil fuels underground can be burned to provide energy. Land and its resources affect every aspect of human life.

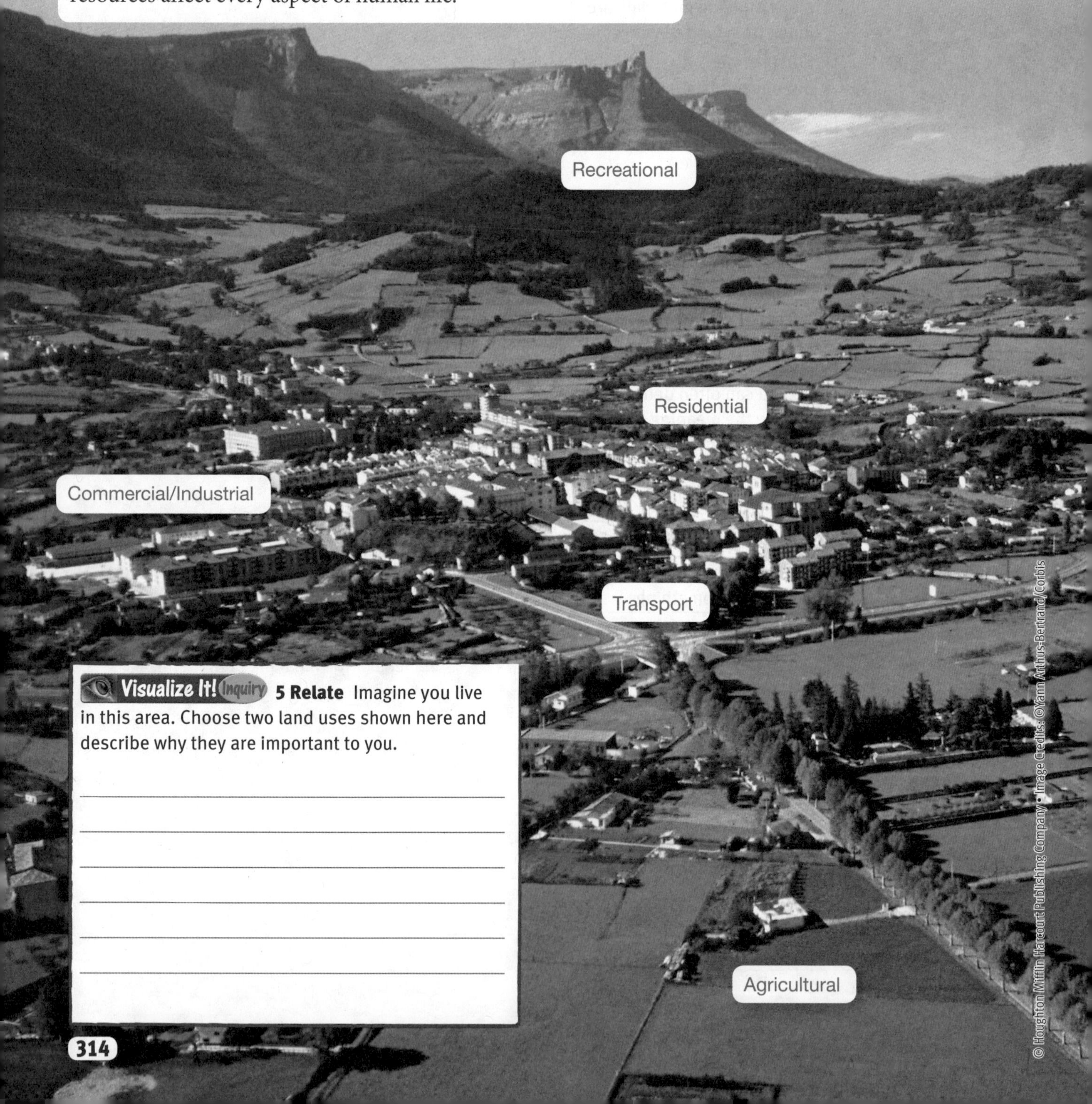

Recreational

Residential

Commercial/Industrial

Transport

Agricultural

Visualize It! **Inquiry** **5 Relate** Imagine you live in this area. Choose two land uses shown here and describe why they are important to you.

_____

_____

_____

_____

_____

© Houghton Mifflin Harcourt Publishing Company • Image Credits: ©Yann Arthus-Bertrand/Corbis

What are the different types of land use?

We live on land in urban or rural areas. Cities and towns are urban areas. Rural areas are open lands that may be used for farming. Humans use land in many ways. We use natural areas for *recreation*. We use roads that are built on land for *transport*. We grow crops and raise livestock on *agricultural* land. We live in *residential* areas. We build *commercial* businesses on land and extract resources such as metals and water from the land.

Recreational

Natural areas are places that humans have left alone or restored to a natural state. These wild places include forests, grasslands, and desert areas. People use natural areas for hiking, bird-watching, mountain-biking, hunting, and other fun or recreational activities.

Transport

A large network of roads and train tracks connect urban and rural areas all across the country. Roads in the U.S. highway system cover 4 million miles of land. Trucks carry goods on these highways and smaller vehicles carry passengers. Railroads carrying freight or passengers use over 120,000 miles of land for tracks. Roads and train tracks are often highly concentrated in urban areas.

Agricultural

Much of the open land in rural areas is used for agriculture. Crops such as corn, soybeans, and wheat are grown on large, open areas of land. Land is also needed to raise and feed cattle and other livestock. Agricultural land is open, but very different from the natural areas that it has replaced. Farmland generally contains only one or two types of plants, such as corn or cotton. Natural grasslands, forests, and other natural areas contain many species of plants and animals.

© Houghton Mifflin Harcourt Publishing Company • Image Credits: ©Yann Arthus-Bertrand/Corbis

Active Reading 6 **Identify** As you read, underline the ways rural areas differ from urban areas.

Residential

Where do you call home? People live in both rural and urban areas. Rural areas have large areas of open land and low densities of people. Urban areas have dense human populations and small areas of open land. This means that more people live in a square km of an urban area than live in a square km of a rural area. **Urbanization** is the growth of urban areas caused by people moving into cities. When cities increase in size, the population of rural areas near the city may decrease. When an area becomes urbanized, its natural land surface is replaced by buildings, parking lots, and roads. City parks, which contain natural surfaces, may also be built in urban areas.

Commercial and Industrial

As cities or towns expand, commercial businesses are built too, and replace rural or natural areas. Industrial businesses also use land resources. For example, paper companies and furniture manufacturers use wood from trees harvested on forest land. Cement companies, fertilizer manufacturers, and steel manufacturers use minerals that are mined from below the land's surface. Commercial and industrial development usually includes development of roads or railways. Transporting goods to market forms the basis of commerce.

Active Reading

7 **Identify** What effects does urbanization have on land?

_____
_____
_____
_____
_____
_____
_____

Why is soil important?

Soil is a mixture of mineral fragments, organic material, water, and air. Soil forms when rocks break down and dead organisms decay. There are many reasons why soil is important. Soil provides habitat for organisms such as plants, earthworms, fungi, and bacteria. Many plants get the water and nutrients they need from the soil. Because plants form the base of food webs, healthy soil is important for most land ecosystems. Healthy soil is also important for agricultural land, which supplies humans with food.

Active Reading

8 Identify As you read, underline the ways that soil is important to plants.

It Is a Habitat for Organisms

Earthworms, moles, badgers, and other burrowing animals live in soil. These animals also find food underground. *Decomposers* are organisms that break down dead animal and plant material, releasing the nutrients into the soil. Decomposers such as fungi and bacteria live in soil. Soil holds plant roots in place, providing support for the plant. In turn, plants are food for herbivores and are habitats for organisms such as birds and insects. Many animals on Earth depend on soil for shelter or food.

It Stores Water and Nutrients

Falling rain soaks into soil and is stored between soil particles. Different types of soil can store different amounts of water. Wetland soils, for example, store large amounts of water and reduce flooding. Soils are also part of the nutrient cycle. Plants take up nutrients and water stored in soil. Plants and animals that eat them die and are broken down by decomposers such as bacteria and earthworms. Nutrients are released back into the soil and the cycle starts again.

Visualize It!

Nutrients Cycle between Soil and Organisms

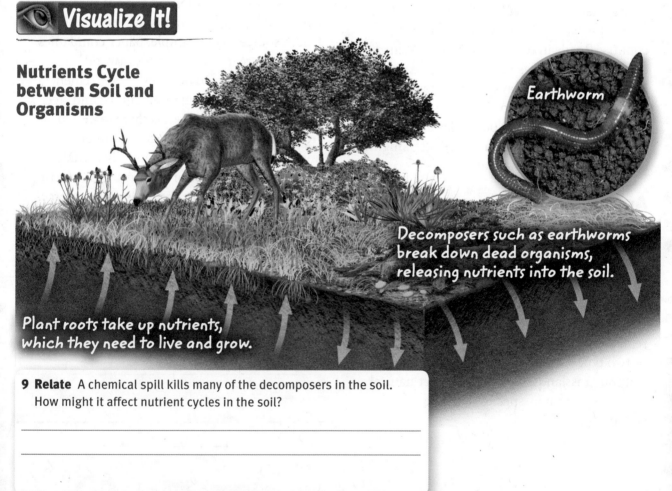

Earthworm

Decomposers such as earthworms break down dead organisms, releasing nutrients into the soil.

Plant roots take up nutrients, which they need to live and grow.

9 Relate A chemical spill kills many of the decomposers in the soil. How might it affect nutrient cycles in the soil?

_____

_____

© Houghton Mifflin Harcourt Publishing Company • Image Credits: ©Valerie Giles/Photo Reaserchers, Inc.

Why It Matters

Dust Bowl

In the 1930s, huge clouds of dusty soil rolled across the southern Great Plains of the United States. Areas that were once farmlands and homesteads were wiped out. What caused the soil to blow away?

Drought and Overuse

Farmers who settled in the southern Great Plains overplowed and overgrazed their land. When severe drought hit in 1931, topsoil dried out. Winds lifted the soil and carried it across the plains in huge storms that farmers called "black blizzards." The drought and dust storms continued for years.

Modern Day Dust Bowl

Today in northwest China another dust bowl is forming. Large areas of farmland were made there by clearing the natural vegetation and plowing the soil. Herds of sheep and cattle are overgrazing the land, and large dust storms are common.

Extend

Inquiry

10 Identify What type of land use by people contributed to the Dust Bowl? Does it remain a common use of land today?

11 Compare Research another area under threat from overuse that differs from the feature. What type of land use is causing the problem?

12 Illustrate Do one of the following to show how the Dust Bowl or the area you researched affected society: make a poster, write a play, write a song, or draw a cartoon strip. Present your findings to the class.

© Houghton Mifflin Harcourt Publishing Company • Image Credits: (bkgd) ©USDA; (cl) ©Science Source/Photo Researchers, Inc.; (b) ©Ryan Pyle/Corbis

Footprints

How can human activities affect land and soil?

Human activities can have positive and negative effects on land and soil. Some activities restore land to its natural state, or increase the amount of fertile soil on land. Other activities can degrade land. **Land degradation** is the process by which human activity and natural processes damage land to the point that it can no longer support the local ecosystem. Urbanization, deforestation, and poor farming practices can all lead to land degradation.

Think Outside the Book (Inquiry)

13 **Apply** With a classmate, discuss how you could help lessen the impact of urbanization on the land in the area where you live.

Active Reading

14 **Identify** As you read, underline the effects that urbanization can have on land.

Urban Sprawl

When urbanization occurs at the edge of a city or town, it is called *urban sprawl*. Urban sprawl replaces forests, fields, and grasslands with houses, roads, schools, and shopping areas. Urban sprawl decreases the amount of farmland that is available for growing crops. It decreases the amount of natural areas that surround cities. It increases the amount of asphalt and concrete that covers the land. Rainwater runs off hard surfaces and into storm drains instead of soaking into the ground and filling aquifers. Rainwater runoff from urban areas can increase the erosion of nearby soils.

Erosion

Erosion (ih•ROH•zhuhn) is the process by which wind, water, or gravity transports soil and sediment from one place to another. Some type of erosion occurs on most land. However, erosion can speed up when land is degraded. Roots of trees and plants act as anchors to the soil. When land is cleared for farming, the trees and plants are removed and the soil is no longer protected. This exposes soil to blowing wind and running water that can wash away the soil.

© Houghton Mifflin Harcourt Publishing Company • Image Credits: (bkgd) ©Dirk Ercken/iStock/ Getty Images Plus/Getty Images; (c) ©John Humble/Photographer's Choice/Getty Images

Nutrient Depletion and Land Pollution

Crops use soil nutrients to grow. If the same crops are planted year after year, the same soil nutrients get used up. Plants need the right balance of nutrients to grow. Farmers can plant a different crop each year to reduce nutrient loss. Pollution from industrial activities can damage land. Mining wastes, gas and petroleum leaks, and chemical wastes can kill organisms in the soil. U.S. government programs such as Superfund help to clean up polluted land.

Desertification

When too many livestock are kept in one area, they can overgraze the area. Overgrazing removes the plants and roots that hold topsoil together. Overgrazing and other poor farming methods can cause desertification. **Desertification** (dih•zer•tuh•fih•KAY•shuhn) is the process by which land becomes more desertlike and unable to support life. Without plants, soil becomes dusty and prone to wind erosion. Deforestation and urbanization can also lead to desertification.

Deforestation

The removal of trees and other vegetation from an area is called **deforestation**. Logging for wood can cause deforestation. Surface mining causes deforestation by removing vegetation and soil to get to the minerals below. Deforestation also occurs in rain forests, as shown in the photo, when farmers cut or burn down trees so they can grow crops. Urbanization can cause deforestation when forests are replaced with buildings. Deforestation leads to increased soil erosion.

👁 Visualize It!

15 Relate How has human activity affected the forest in this photo?

_____

_____

_____

_____

© Houghton Mifflin Harcourt Publishing Company • Image Credits: (bkgd) ©Gustavo Gilabert/Corbis SABA; (t) ©EPA; (c) ©Photoshot Holdings Ltd/Alamy

Visual Summary

To complete this summary, circle the correct word or phrase.
Then use the key below to check your answers. You can use this
page to review the main concepts of the lesson.

Humans use land in different ways.

16 Crops are grown on recreational/agricultural land.

Soil is important to all organisms, including humans.

17 Decomposers/plants that live in soil break down dead matter in the soil.

Human Impact on Land

Human activities can affect land and soil.

18 Poor farming practices and drought can lead to desertification/urbanization.

Answers: 16 agricultural; 17 decomposers; 18 desertification

19 Apply How could concentrating human populations in cities help to conserve agricultural and recreational lands?

© Houghton Mifflin Harcourt Publishing Company • Image Credits: (tl) ©Yann arthus-Bertrand/Corbis; (br) ©USDA

Lesson Review

Vocabulary

Draw a line to connect the following terms to their definitions.

1 urbanization

2 deforestation

3 land degradation

4 desertification

A the removal of trees and other vegetation from an area

B the process by which land becomes more desertlike

C the process by which human activity can damage land

D the formation and growth of cities

Key Concepts

5 Contrast How are natural areas different from rural areas?

_____

_____

_____

_____

6 Relate How might deforestation lead to desertification?

_____

_____

_____

_____

7 Relate Think of an animal that eats other animals. Why would soil be important to this animal?

_____

_____

_____

_____

Critical Thinking

Use this photo to answer the following questions.

8 Analyze What type of land degradation is occurring in this photo?

_____

9 Predict This type of soil damage can happen in urban areas too. Outline how urbanization could lead to this type of degradation.

_____

_____

_____

_____

_____

_____

_____

10 Apply What kinds of land uses are around your school? Write down each type of land use. Then describe how one of these land uses might affect natural systems.

_____

_____

_____

_____

_____

_____

_____

© Houghton Mifflin Harcourt Publishing Company • Image Credits: ©Science Source/Photo researchers, Inc.

My Notes

© Houghton Mifflin Harcourt Publishing Company

© Houghton Mifflin Harcourt Publishing Company

Protecting Earth's Water, Land, and Air

ESSENTIAL QUESTION

How can Earth's resources be used wisely?

By the end of this lesson, you should be able to summarize the value of conserving Earth's resources and the effect that wise stewardship has on land, water, and air resources.

6.ESS2.4, 6.ESS3.3

Picking up litter to clean streams or rivers is one way we can help preserve Earth's natural resources.

© Houghton Mifflin Harcourt Publishing Company • Image Credits: ©Tim Pannell/Corbis

Engage Your Brain

1 Predict Check T or F to show whether you think each statement is true or false.

T F

☐ ☐ Conservation is the overuse of natural resources.

☐ ☐ It is everybody's job to be a good steward of Earth's resources.

☐ ☐ Reforestation is the planting of trees to repair degraded lands.

☐ ☐ Alternative energy sources, like solar power, increase the amount of pollution released into the air.

2 Describe Have you ever done something to protect a natural resource? Draw a picture showing what you did. Include a caption.

Active Reading

3 Synthesize You can often guess the meaning of a word from its context, or how it is used in a sentence. Use the sentence below to guess the meaning of the word *stewardship*.

Example sentence

Stewardship of water resources will ensure that there is plenty of clean water for future generations.

Vocabulary Terms

• conservation   • stewardship

4 Apply As you learn the definition of each vocabulary term in this lesson, create your own definition or sketch to help remember the meaning of the term.

stewardship:

_____

_____

© Houghton Mifflin Harcourt Publishing Company • Image Credits: ©Tim Pannell/Corbis

Keeping It Clean

What are conservation and stewardship?

In the past, some people have used Earth's resources however they wanted, without thinking about the consequences. They thought it didn't matter if they cut down hundreds of thousands of trees or caught millions of fish. They also thought it didn't matter if they dumped trash into bodies of water. Now we know that it does matter how we use resources. Humans greatly affect the land, water, and air. If we wish to keep using our resources in the future, we need to conserve and care for them.

Active Reading

5 Identify As you read, underline the definitions of *conservation* and *stewardship*.

Conservation: Wise Use of Resources

Conservation (kahn•sur•VAY•shuhn) is the wise use of natural resources. By practicing conservation, we can help make sure that resources will still be around for future generations. It is up to everybody to conserve and protect resources. When we use energy or create waste, we can harm the environment. If we conserve whenever we can, we reduce the harm we do to the environment. We can use less energy by turning off lights, computers, and appliances. We can reuse shopping bags, as in the picture below. We can recycle whenever possible, instead of just throwing things away. By doing these things, we take fewer resources from Earth and put less pollution into the water, land, and air.

Visualize It!

6 Identify How are the people in the picture below practicing conservation?

_____

_____

_____

This old tire is being used as a planter instead of being thrown away.

© Houghton Mifflin Harcourt Publishing Company • Image Credits: (l) ©Ariel Skelley/Blend Images/Getty Images; (r) ©Gunter Marx/Alamy

Stewardship: Managing Resources

Stewardship (stoo•urd•SHIP) is the careful and responsible management of a resource. If we are not good stewards, we will use up a resource or pollute it. Stewardship of Earth's resources will ensure that the environment stays clean enough to help keep people and other living things healthy. Stewardship is everybody's job. Governments pass laws that protect water, land, and air. These laws determine how resources can be used and what materials can be released into the environment. Individuals can also act as stewards. For example, you can plant trees or help clean up a habitat in your community. Any action that helps to maintain or improve the environment is an act of stewardship.

7 Compare Fill in the Venn diagram to compare and contrast conservation and stewardship.

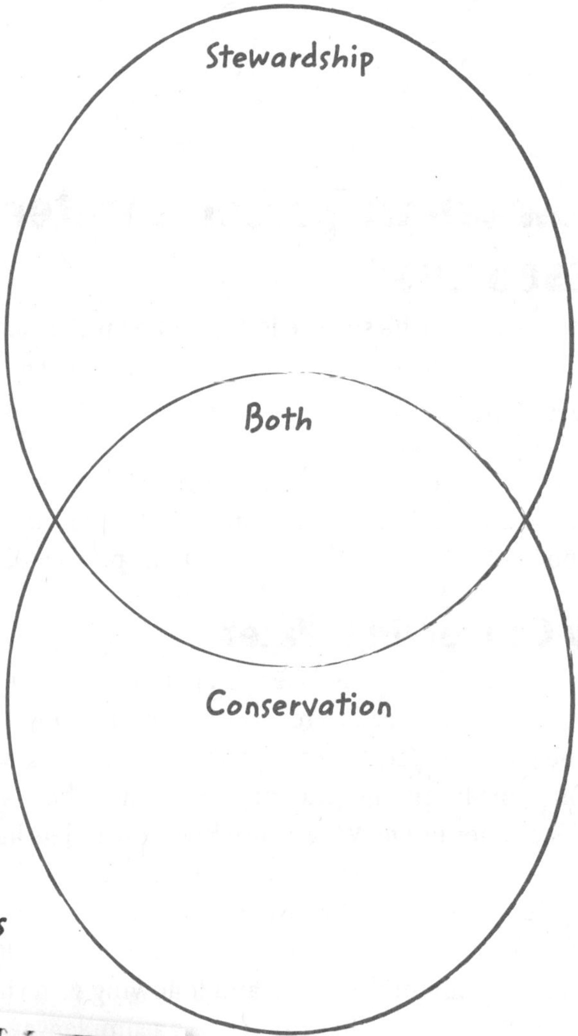

Stewardship

Both

Conservation

Turning empty lots into gardens improves the environment and provides people with healthy food.

Sea turtles are endangered. Scientists help sea turtles that have just hatched find their way to the sea.

🖝 **Visualize It!**

8 Identify How is the person in the picture to the right practicing stewardship?

_____

_____

_____

© Houghton Mifflin Harcourt Publishing Company • Image Credits: (l) ©Alistair Berg/DigitalVision Vectors/Getty Images; (r) ©Tyrone Turner/National Geographic/Getty Images

Water Wise!

How can we preserve water resources?

Most of the Earth's surface is covered by water, so you might think there is lots of water for humans to use. However, there is actually very little fresh water on Earth, so people should use freshwater resources very carefully. People should also be careful to avoid polluting water, because the quality of water is important to the health of both humans and ecosystems. Because water is so important to our health, we need to keep it clean!

By Conserving Water

If we want to make sure there is enough water for future generations, we need to reduce the amount of water we use. In some places, if people aren't careful about using water wisely, there soon won't be enough water for everyone. There are many ways to reduce water usage. We can use low-flow toilets and showerheads. We can take shorter showers. In agriculture and landscaping, we can reduce water use by installing efficient irrigation systems. We can also use plants that don't need much water. Only watering lawns the amount they need and following watering schedules saves water. The photo below shows a simple way to use less water—just turn off the tap while brushing your teeth!

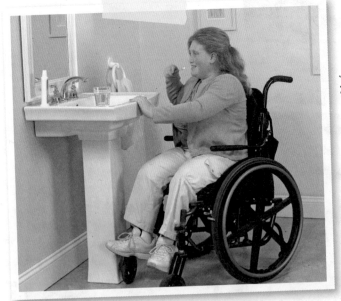

Do the Math

You Try It

9 Calculate How much fresh water is on Earth?

Solve

Each square on the grid equals 1%. Use the grid to fill in the percentage of each type of water found on Earth.

Earth's Water

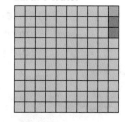

▢ Salt water _____

▢ Ice (fresh water) _____

▢ Fresh liquid water _____

10 Identify What are some ways you can reduce the amount of water you use?

- *Turn off the tap when brushing my teeth.*

- _____
  _____

- _____
  _____

- _____

© Houghton Mifflin Harcourt Publishing Company

With Water Stewardship

Humans and ecosystems need clean water. The diagram below shows how a community keeps its drinking water clean. The main way to protect drinking water is to keep pollution from entering streams, lakes, and other water sources. Laws like the Clean Water Act and Safe Drinking Water Act were passed to protect water sources. These laws indicate how clean drinking water must be and limit the types of chemicals that businesses and private citizens can release into water. These laws also help finance water treatment facilities. We can help protect water by not throwing chemicals in the trash or dumping them down the drain. We can also use nontoxic chemicals whenever possible. Reducing the amount of fertilizer we use on our gardens also reduces water pollution.

For healthy ecosystems and safe drinking water, communities need to protect water sources. The first step to protecting water sources is keeping them from becoming polluted.

Protecting Water Resources

Water testing makes sure water is safe for people to drink. It also helps us find out if there is a pollution problem that needs to be fixed.

Without clean water to drink, people can get sick. Clean water is also important for agriculture and natural ecosystems.

Water treatment plants remove pollution from wastewater before it is reused or put back into the environment.

Visualize It!

11 Apply What steps should a community take to manage its water resources?

_____

_____

_____

_____

© Houghton Mifflin Harcourt Publishing Company • Image Credits: (bkgd) ©Rich Reid/National Geographic/Getty Images; (c) ©Thinkstock/Corbis; (l) ©Flip Chalfant/The Image Bank/Getty Images

This Land Is Your Land

How can we preserve land resources?

People rely on land resources for recreation, agriculture, transportation, commerce, industry, and housing. If we manage land resources carefully, we can make sure that these resources will be around for generations and continue to provide resources for humans to use. We also need to make sure that there are habitats for wild animals. To do all these things, we must protect land resources from overuse and pollution. Sometimes we need to repair damage that is already done.

Through Preservation

Preservation of land resources is very important. *Preservation* means protecting land from being damaged or changed. Local, state, and national parks protect many natural areas. These parks help ensure that many species survive. Small parks can protect some species. Other species, such as predators, need larger areas. For example, wolves roam over hundreds of miles and would not be protected by small parks. By protecting areas big enough for large predators, we also protect habitats for many other species.

Active Reading

12 Identify As you read this page and the next, underline ways that we can protect land resources.

Yosemite National Park is one of the oldest national parks in the country. Like other national, state, and local parks, Yosemite was formed to preserve natural habitats.

Think Outside the Book

13 Apply Plant and animal species depend on land resources. Find out which endangered plant or animal species live in your area. Write a paragraph explaining how your community can help protect those species.

© Houghton Mifflin Harcourt Publishing Company • Image Credits: ©David Davis/Fotolia

Through Reforestation

People use the wood from trees for many things. We use it to make paper and to build houses. We also use wood to heat homes and cook food. In many places, huge areas of forest were cut down to use the wood and nothing was done to replant the forests. Now when we cut trees down, they are often replanted, as in the picture at right. We also plant trees in areas where forests disappeared many years ago in order to help bring the forests back. The process of planting trees to reestablish forestland is called *reforestation*. Reforestation is important, but we can't cut down all forests and replant them. It is important to keep some old forests intact for the animals that need them to survive.

Reforestation

Through Reclamation

In order to use some resources, such as coal, metal, and minerals, the resources first have to be dug out of the ground. In the process, the land is damaged. Sometimes, large areas of land are cleared and pits are dug to reach the resource. Land can also be damaged in other ways, including by development and agriculture. *Reclamation* is the process by which a damaged land area is returned to nearly the condition it was in before people used it. Land reclamation, shown in the lower right photo, is required for mines in many states once the mines are no longer in use. Many national and state laws, such as the Surface Mining and Reclamation Act and the Resource Conservation and Recovery Act, guide land reclamation.

A mine being reclaimed

Visualize It!

14 Compare What are the similarities between reforestation and reclamation?

_____

_____

_____

_____

© Houghton Mifflin Harcourt Publishing Company • Image Credits: (bkgd) ©David Davis/Fotolia; (tr) ©David R. Frazier/Photo Researchers, Inc.; (br) ©Photoshot Holdings Ltd/Alamy

One way to reduce urban sprawl is to locate homes and businesses close together.

Through Reducing Urban Sprawl

Urban sprawl is the outward spread of suburban areas around cities. As we build more houses and businesses across a wider area, there is less land for native plants and animals. Reducing urban sprawl helps to protect land resources. One way to reduce sprawl is to locate more people and businesses in a smaller area. A good way to do this is with vertical development—that means constructing taller buildings. Homes, businesses, and even recreational facilities can be placed within high-rise buildings. We also can reduce sprawl using mixed-use development. This development creates communities with businesses and houses very close to one another. Mixed-use communities are also better for the environment, because people can walk to work instead of driving.

Through Recycling

Recycling is one of the most important things we can do to preserve land resources. *Recycling* is the process of recovering valuable materials from waste or scrap. We can recycle many of the materials that we use. By recycling materials like metal, plastic, paper, and glass, we use fewer raw materials. Recycling aluminum cans reduces the amount of bauxite that is mined. We use bauxite in aluminum smelting. Everyone can help protect land resources by recycling. Lots of people throw away materials that can be recycled. Find out what items you can recycle!

Bauxite mine

15 Apply Aluminum is mined from the ground. Recycling aluminum cans decreases the need for mining bauxite. Paper can also be recycled. How does recycling paper preserve trees?

_____

_____

© Houghton Mifflin Harcourt Publishing Company • Image Credits: (t) ©Janis Kraulis/All Canada Photos/Getty Images; (bl) ©photka/Shutterstock; (br) ©Photoshot Holdings Ltd/Alamy

Through Using Soil Conservation Methods

Soil conservation protects soil from erosion or degradation by overuse or pollution. For example, farmers change the way they plow in order to conserve soil. Contour plowing creates ridges of soil across slopes. The small ridges keep water from eroding soils. In strip cropping, two types of crops are planted in rows next to each other to reduce erosion. Terracing is used on steep hills to prevent erosion. Areas of the hill are flattened to grow crops. This creates steps down the side of the hill. *Crop rotation* means that crops with different needs are planted in alternating seasons. This reduces the prevalence of plant diseases and makes sure there are nutrients for each crop. It also ensures that plants are growing in the soil almost year-round. In no-till farming, soils are not plowed between crop plantings. Stalks and cover crops keep water in the soils and reduce erosion by stopping soil from being blown away.

Active Reading

16 Identify As you read this page, underline five methods of soil conservation.

Visualize It!

Terracing involves building leveled areas, or steps, to grow crops on.

In contour plowing, crop rows are planted in curved lines along land's natural contours.

Strip cropping prevents erosion by creating natural dams that stop water from rushing over a field.

17 Analyze Which two soil conservation techniques would be best to use on gentle slopes?

☐ contour plowing

☐ crop terracing

☐ strip cropping

18 Analyze Which soil conservation technique would be best to use on very steep slopes?

☐ contour plowing

☐ crop terracing

☐ strip cropping

© Houghton Mifflin Harcourt Publishing Company • Image Credits: (cl) ©by marin.tomic/Flickr/Getty Images; (cr) ©NRCS/USDA; (bl) ©NRCS/USDA

Into Thin Air

19 Identify Underline the sentences that explain the relationship between burning fossil fuels and air pollution.

How can we reduce air pollution?

Polluted air can make people sick and harm organisms. Air pollution can cause the atmosphere to change in ways that are harmful to the environment and to people. There are many ways that we can reduce air pollution. We can use less energy. Also, we can develop new ways to get energy that produces less pollution. Everybody can help reduce air pollution in many different ways.

Through Energy Conservation

Energy conservation is one of the most important ways to reduce air pollution. Fossil fuels are currently the most commonly used energy resource. When they are burned, they release pollution into the air. If we use less energy, we burn fewer fossil fuels.

There are lots of ways to conserve energy. We can turn off lights when we don't need them. We can use energy-efficient lightbulbs and appliances. We can use air conditioners less in the summer and heaters less in the winter. We can unplug electronics when they are not in use. Instead of driving ourselves to places, we can use public transportation. We can also develop alternative energy sources that create less air pollution. Using wind, solar, and geothermal energy will help us burn less fossil fuel.

Using public transportation, riding a bike, sharing rides, and walking reduce the amount of air pollution produced by cars.

Energy can be produced with very little pollution. These solar panels help us use energy from the sun and replace the use of fossil fuels.

Many cities, such as Los Angeles, California, have air pollution problems.

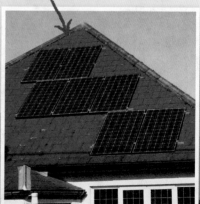

© Houghton Mifflin Harcourt Publishing Company • Image Credits: (bkgd) ©Chris Pritchard/Photodisc/Getty Images; (bl) ©Ekaterina Pokrovsky/Shutterstock; (br) ©Chris Cooper-Smith/Alamy

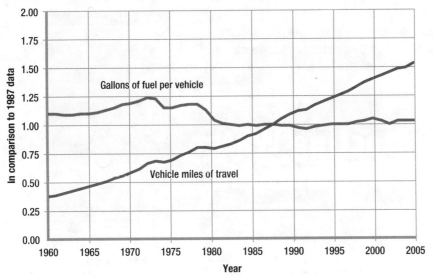

Vehicle Fuel Consumption and Miles Traveled, 1960–2005

In comparison to 1987 data (y-axis)

Gallons of fuel per vehicle

Vehicle miles of travel

Year (x-axis)

Source: U.S. Department of Transportation

© Houghton Mifflin Harcourt Publishing Company

Visualize It! Inquiry

20 Analyze How has vehicle fuel consumption in comparison to miles traveled changed since 1960? What is the likely cause for this change?

_____

_____

_____

_____

_____

_____

Through Technology

There are lots of ways to generate energy without creating much air pollution. By developing these alternative energy sources, we can reduce the amount of pollution created by burning fossil fuels. Wind turbines generate clean power. So do solar panels that use energy from the sun. We also can use power created by water flowing through rivers or moving with the tides. Geothermal energy from heat in Earth's crust can be used to generate electricity. Hybrid cars get energy from their brakes and store it in batteries. They burn less gas and release less pollution. Driving smaller cars that can go farther on a gallon of gas also reduces air pollution.

New technologies, such as this compact fluorescent lightbulb (CFL), help limit air pollution. CFL bulbs use less energy to make the same amount of light.

Through Laws

Governments in many countries work independently and together to reduce air pollution. They monitor air quality and set limits on what can be released into the air. In the United States, the Clean Air Act limits the amount of toxic chemicals and other pollutants that can be released into the atmosphere by factories and vehicles. It is up to the Environmental Protection Agency to make sure that these limits are enforced. Because air isn't contained by borders, some solutions must be international. The Kyoto Protocol is a worldwide effort to limit the release of greenhouse gases—pollution that can warm the atmosphere.

21 Summarize List three ways air pollution can be reduced.

- _____

  _____

- _____

  _____

  _____

- _____

  _____

Visual Summary

To complete this summary, fill in the blanks with the correct word or phrase. Then use the key below to check your answers. You can use this page to review the main concepts of the lesson.

Protecting Water, Land, and Air

Water resources are important to our health.

22 A community's water supply can be protected by:

- conserving water
- preventing pollution
- _____
- treating wastewater

Land resources are used to grow food and make products.

23 Land resources can be protected by:

- preservation
- reclamation and reforestation
- reducing urban sprawl
- _____
- soil conservation

Everybody needs clean air to breathe.

24 The main way to reduce air pollution is to:

_____

_____

_____

_____

_____

Answers: 22 testing water quality; 23 recycling; 24 reduce the amount of fossil fuels burned

25 **Relate** How can you personally act as a steward of water, land, and air resources?

© Houghton Mifflin Harcourt Publishing Company • Image Credits: (c) ©photka/Shutterstock; (t) ©Ekaterina Pokrovsky/Shutterstock

Lesson Review

Vocabulary

Fill in the blank with the term that best completes the following sentences.

1 _____ is the wise use of natural resources.

2 _____ is the careful and responsible management of a resource.

Key Concepts

3 Describe How can water pollution be prevented?

_____

_____

_____

_____

Fill in the table below.

Example	Type of land resource conservation
4 Identify A county creates a park to protect a forest.	
5 Identify A mining company puts soil back in the hole and plants grass seeds on top of it.	
6 Identify A logging company plants new trees after it has cut some down.	
7 Identify A plastic milk bottle is turned into planks for a boardwalk to the beach.	
8 Identify Instead of building lots of single houses, a city builds an apartment building with a grocery store.	

9 Determine How has technology helped decrease air pollution in recent years?

_____

_____

_____

_____

10 Explain Why is it important to protect Earth's water, land, and air resources?

_____

_____

_____

_____

Critical Thinking

11 Explain Land reclamation can be expensive. Why might recycling materials lead to spending less money on reclamation?

_____

_____

_____

Use the graph to answer the following question.

Average Water Usage of U.S. Household

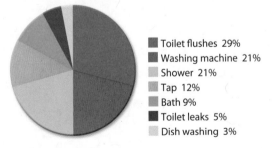

Toilet flushes 29%
Washing machine 21%
Shower 21%
Tap 12%
Bath 9%
Toilet leaks 5%
Dish washing 3%

Source: U.S. Environmental Protection Agency

12 Analyze The graph above shows water use in the average U.S. household. Using the graph, identify three effective ways a household could conserve water.

_____

_____

_____

_____

© Houghton Mifflin Harcourt Publishing Company

My Notes

© Houghton Mifflin Harcourt Publishing Company

© Houghton Mifflin Harcourt Publishing Company

Unit 5 **Big Idea** Humans and human population growth affect the environment.

Lesson 1

ESSENTIAL QUESTION

What impact can human activities have on water resources?

Explain the impact that humans can have on the quality and supply of fresh water.

Lesson 2

ESSENTIAL QUESTION

What impact can human activities have on land resources?

Identify the impact that human activity has on Earth's land.

Lesson 3

ESSENTIAL QUESTION

How can Earth's resources be used wisely?

Summarize the value of conserving Earth's resources and the effect that wise stewardship has on land, water, and air resources.

Connect ESSENTIAL QUESTIONS
Lessons 1 and 2

1 Explain How does an increasing human population affect land and water resources?

_____

_____

_____

_____

Think Outside the Book

2 Synthesize Choose one of these activities to help synthesize what you have learned in this unit.

☐ Using what you learned in Lessons 1 through 3, create an informational poster that explains what steps humans can take to protect Earth's water, land, and air.

☐ Using what you learned in Lessons 1 and 2, write a fable that explains how human activities can pollute Earth's resources. Provide a moral for your story that explains why pollution should be prevented.

© Houghton Mifflin Harcourt Publishing Company • Image Credits: (tl) ©Aurora Open/Justin Bailie/Getty Images; (tr) ©Tim Pannell/Corbis (bl) ©Nature Animals/Alamy; (br)

Unit 5 Review

Name _____

Vocabulary

Check the box to show whether each statement is true or false.

T	F	
☐	☐	**1** <u>Potable</u> water is suitable for drinking.
☐	☐	**2** <u>Conservation</u> is the wise use of natural resources.
☐	☐	**3** <u>Land degradation</u> is the process by which humans restore damaged land so that it can support the local ecosystem.
☐	☐	**4** <u>Stewardship</u> of Earth's resources helps make sure that the environment remains healthy.

Key Concepts

Read each question below, and circle the best answer.

5 Which of the following reduces erosion by planting different crops in rows next to each other?

A contour plowing   **C** strip cropping

B crop terracing   **D** crop rotation

6 Which of the following is true about the amount of water on Earth?

A There is an ever-increasing amount of water on Earth due to rain and snowfall.

B The amount of water on Earth is replaced much faster than it is being used up.

C There is a fixed amount of water on Earth that is continuously cycled.

D The water on Earth is more than enough for the growing population.

7 Which environmental problem is most closely related to the logging industry?

A eutrophication

B thermal pollution

C deforestation

D urbanization

© Houghton Mifflin Harcourt Publishing Company

8 Trees and other plants remove carbon dioxide from the air through respiration. Burning fossil fuels adds carbon dioxide to the air. The graph below shows how the amount of carbon dioxide in the atmosphere has changed since 1960.

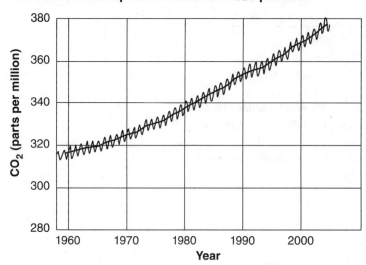

Amount of Atmospheric Carbon Dioxide per Year

Based on the information given in the graph, which of these practices has likely increased since 1960?

A reclamation

C burning of fossil fuels

B reforestation

D recycling

9 A manufacturing plant is built on the bank of the Mississippi River. Water is diverted into the plant for use in the making of a product and is then piped back out into the river. If the water that is released back into the river is contaminated, what is this form of pollution called?

A thermal pollution

B biological pollution

C point-source pollution

D nonpoint-source pollution

10 What is the water from an artificial reservoir most likely to be reserved for?

A for future use by homes and businesses

B for recreational purposes such as swimming

C to provide a habitat for fish

D to cool hot industrial equipment

© Houghton Mifflin Harcourt Publishing Company

11 The picture below shows a common human activity.

What are examples of the effects this kind of pollution may cause?

A acid rain, which may cause diseases such as asthma

B global warming, which may cause diseases such as skin cancer

C respiratory diseases such as emphysema

D artificial eutrophication, harming aquatic animals

12 Humans use land in many ways. How is an area described if it contains few people, has large areas of open space, and is a mix of natural land, farmland, and parks?

A rural area   **C** natural area

B urban area   **D** industrial area

Critical Thinking

Answer the following questions in the space provided.

13 How does air pollution affect Earth's natural resources?

_____

_____

Describe two ways air pollution can be reduced.

_____

_____

_____

© Houghton Mifflin Harcourt Publishing Company

14 The picture below is of a dam built on a river.

How does a dam affect the surrounding landscape behind and in front of the dam?

_____

_____

How does a dam affect the fish that live and breed in that river?

_____

Connect ESSENTIAL QUESTIONS

Lessons 1 and 2

Answer the following question in the space provided.

15 Urbanization has major effects on Earth's land and water. Natural vegetation is removed in order to make room for buildings, roads, and parking lots. How does removing vegetation affect the land?

_____

How do paved parking lots and roads with concrete or asphalt affect water flow on the land?

_____

What are three ways that urban populations can negatively affect water quality?

_____

_____

_____

How can urban populations affect a water supply?

_____

_____

© Houghton Mifflin Harcourt Publishing Company

Earth's Water

Waterfalls show the important role gravity plays in moving Earth's water.

Big Idea

Water moves through Earth's atmosphere, oceans, and land in a cycle and is essential for life on Earth.

6.ESS2.4, 6.ESS3.3, 6.PS3.4

What do you think?

Fresh water is found in ponds, lakes, streams, rivers, and underground in aquifers. Where does the water in your school come from?

Humans rely on water to stay healthy.

© Houghton Mifflin Harcourt Publishing Company • Image Credits: (bg) ©Ron Watts/Corbis; (inset) ©AE Pictures Inc./Digital Vision/Getty Images

Conserving Water

Fresh water evaporates into the air and then condenses to form clouds. It falls from the sky as precipitation and then flows over Earth's surface in streams and rivers. It seeps underground through soil and rocks. Fresh water makes up only a small fraction of Earth's water and is not evenly distributed.

Some watering methods lose a great deal of water to evaporation.

① Think About It

A Take a quick survey of your classmates. Ask them where the fresh water they use every day at home and at school comes from.

_____

_____

_____

B Ask your classmates to identify different uses of water at your school.

_____

_____

_____

© Houghton Mifflin Harcourt Publishing Company • Image Credits: (t) ©Ken Schulze/Alamy

② Ask a Question

How do you conserve water?

Water is an essential resource for everyone, but it is a limited resource. What are some ways that your school may be wasting water?

_____
_____
_____
_____
_____
_____
_____
_____
_____

Xeriscaping is a method of landscaping by using plants that require less water.

③ Make a Plan

A Make a list of five ways in which the school can conserve water.

_____
_____
_____
_____
_____

B In the space below, sketch out a design for a pamphlet or a poster that you can place in the hallways to promote water conservation at your school.

Take It Home

Take a pamphlet or a poster home. With an adult, talk about ways in which water can be conserved in and around your home. See *ScienceSaurus*® for more information about conservation.

© Houghton Mifflin Harcourt Publishing Company • Image credits: (b) ©Green Stock Media/Alamy

Water and Its Properties

ESSENTIAL QUESTION

What makes water so important?

By the end of this lesson, you should be able to describe water's structure, its properties, and its importance to Earth's systems.

Not all liquids form round droplets, but water does. Water's unique properties have to do with the way water molecules interact.

© Houghton Mifflin Harcourt Publishing Company • Image Credits: (bg) ZenShui/Odilon Dimier/PhotoAlto Agency RF Collections/Getty Images

Engage Your Brain

1 Predict Check T or F to show whether you think each statement is true or false.

T	F	
☐	☐	Most of the water on Earth is fresh water.
☐	☐	Water exists in three different states on Earth.
☐	☐	Water can dissolve many different substances, such as salt.
☐	☐	Flowing water can be used to generate electricity.

2 Identify The drawing below shows a water molecule. What do each of the three parts represent?

_____

_____

_____

Active Reading

3 Synthesize You can often define an unknown word if you know the meaning of its word parts. Use the word parts and sentence below to make an educated guess about the meaning of the word *cohesion*.

Word part	Meaning
co-	with, together
-hesion	sticking, joined

Example sentence
When water forms droplets, it is displaying the property of <u>cohesion</u>.

Vocabulary Terms

- polarity
- cohesion
- adhesion
- specific heat
- solvent

4 Apply As you learn the definition of each vocabulary term in this lesson, create your own definition or sketch to help you remember the meaning of the term.

Cohesion:

_____

_____

_____

_____

© Houghton Mifflin Harcourt Publishing Company • Image Credits: (bg) ZenShui/Odilon Dimier/PhotoAlto Agency RF Collections/Getty Images

Watered Down

What are some of water's roles on Earth?

Water shapes Earth's surface and influences Earth's weather. Water is also vital for life. Without water, your body could not regulate its temperature or convert food into a usable form of energy. Only about 3% of water on Earth is fresh water. Of this 3% of water that is drinkable, about 69% is frozen in glaciers and icecaps and is not readily available for our use. Therefore, it is important that we protect our water resources.

Influencing Weather

 **Active Reading** **6 Identify** As you read, underline four different forms of water that fall on Earth's surface.

Weather is related to water. Water constantly moves from Earth's surface to the atmosphere, where it may form clouds. Water falls back to Earth's surface again as rain, snow, hail, or sleet. Weather also depends on the amount of moisture in the air.

Shaping Earth's Surface

Over time, water can completely reshape a landscape. Water slowly wears away rock and carries away sediment and soil. Flowing rivers and pounding ocean waves are also examples of water shaping Earth's surface. Frozen water shapes Earth's surface, too. Glaciers, for example, scrape away rock and soil, depositing these materials elsewhere when the glacier melts.

Do the Math

You Try It

5 Graph About 3% of water on Earth is fresh water. The rest is salt water. Fill out the percentage grid to show the percentage of fresh water on Earth.

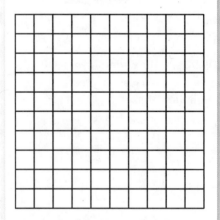

© Houghton Mifflin Harcourt Publishing Company • Image Credits: ©Scott Barrow/Corbis

Supporting Life

Every living thing is largely made up of water, and nearly all biological processes use water. All of an organism's cellular chemistry depends on water. Water regulates temperature and helps transport substances. Without water, animals and plants would dry up and die.

For humans, clean water is vital for good health. People must have clean water to drink in order to survive. Contaminated water sources are a major public health problem in many countries. Contaminated water is also harmful to plants, animals, and can affect crops that provide food for humans.

Supporting Human Activities

Clean drinking water is necessary for all humans. Many humans use water at home for bathing, cleaning, and watering lawns and gardens.

More fresh water is used in industry than is used in homes. Over 20% of the fresh water used by humans is used for industrial purposes—to manufacture goods, cool power stations, clean industrial products, extract minerals, and generate energy by using hydroelectric dams.

More water is used for agriculture than industry. Most water used for agriculture is used to irrigate crops. It is also used to care for farm animals.

Visualize It!

7 List List at least four roles of water in this scene.

_____

_____

_____

_____

_____

© Houghton Mifflin Harcourt Publishing Company

Molecular Attraction

What is the structure of a water molecule?

Matter is made up of tiny particles called *atoms*. Atoms can join with other atoms to make molecules. A water molecule is made up of two hydrogen atoms and one oxygen atom—in other words, H_2O. Each hydrogen atom is linked to the oxygen atom, forming a shape like a cartoon mouse's ears sticking out from its head.

What makes water a polar molecule?

In a water molecule, the hydrogen atoms have a small positive charge. The oxygen atom has a small negative charge. So the water molecule has a partial positive charge at one end (mouse ears) and a partial negative charge at the other (mouse chin). Anything that has a positive charge at one end and negative charge at the other end is said to have **polarity**. A water molecule is therefore a polar molecule. In liquid water, the negative end of one water molecule is attracted to the positive end of another water molecule. Each water molecule interacts with the surrounding water molecules.

👁 Visualize It!

8 Label Indicate the polarity of water by writing a + or − next to each atom that makes up the water molecule.

Because of polarity, the positive end of one water molecule interacts with the negative end of another molecule.

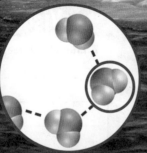

Water molecules have a positive end and a negative end.

© Houghton Mifflin Harcourt Publishing Company • Image Credits: (bg) ©Chris Cheadle/All Canada Photos/Corbis

What states of water occur on Earth?

Active Reading **9 Identify** As you read, underline the three states of water that occur on Earth.

Most of Earth's water is in liquid form. Earth is the only planet in our solar system with abundant liquid water. Gravity causes liquid water to flow downhill and to rest in low-lying areas. As a result, Earth has rivers, lakes, and oceans. Like other liquids, liquid water takes the shape of whatever contains it.

Liquid water can change into an invisible gas called water vapor, or it can freeze into solid ice or snow. Like liquid water, water vapor and ice also have the chemical formula H_2O. So liquid water, water vapor, and ice are simply varieties, or states, of water. Conditions on Earth allow water to exist in these three different states. The three states of water can change into one another. When water changes state, it either takes up or releases energy.

Water vapor is a gas, so most water vapor is found in Earth's atmosphere. Water vapor cannot be seen. Clouds form when water vapor in the atmosphere condenses into liquid water droplets. Like all gases, water vapor expands or contracts to fill available space.

Unlike other liquids, water expands when it freezes. Molecules in liquid water, therefore, are closer together than are the molecules of solid water. In other words, there is more open space between the water molecules in ice. Due to this fact, solid water, or ice, is less dense than liquid water. So ice floats on liquid water.

Visualize It!

10 Describe Using your own words in the spaces provided, identify the state of water, and describe the properties of each state of water.

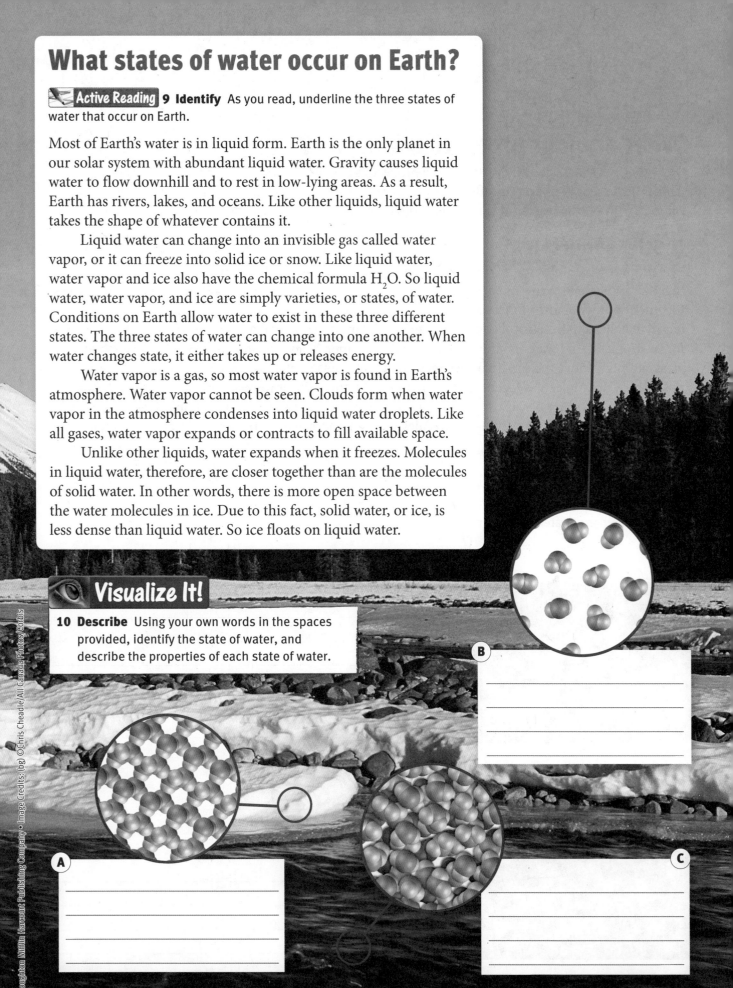

A

B

C

© Houghton Mifflin Harcourt Publishing Company • Image Credits: (bg) ©Chris Cheadle/All Canada Photos/Corbis

The Universal Solvent

What are four properties of water?

The polarity of water molecules affects the properties of water. This is because water's polarity affects how water molecules interact with one another and with other types of molecules.

It Sticks to Itself

The property that holds molecules of a substance together is **cohesion**. Water molecules stick together tightly because of their polarity, so water has high cohesion. Because of cohesion, water forms droplets. And water poured gently into a glass can fill it above the rim because cohesion holds the water molecules together. Some insects can walk on still water because their weight does not break the cohesion of the water molecules.

It Sticks to Other Substances

The property that holds molecules of different substances together is **adhesion**. Polar substances other than water can attract water molecules more strongly than water molecules attract each other. These substances are called "wettable" because water adheres, or sticks, to them so tightly. Paper towels, for example, are wettable. Water drops roll off unwettable, or "waterproof," surfaces, which are made of non-polar molecules.

Visualize It!

11 Label Identify each photo as representing either adhesion or cohesion. Then write captions explaining the properties of water shown by each photo.

A

B

© Houghton Mifflin Harcourt Publishing Company • Image Credits: (t) ©blickwinkel/Alamy; (b) ©Ocean/Corbis

These stalactites formed as water dripped down and left dissolved minerals behind.

It Can Absorb Large Amounts of Energy

The energy needed to heat a substance by a particular amount is called its **specific heat**. As water is warmed, its molecules are separated a little as the water expands. The attraction between polar water molecules means that separating them takes a great deal of energy, so the specific heat of water is very high. Because of its high specific heat, water can absorb more energy than many other substances can.

Warm water stores more energy than cold water does. And water vapor stores much more energy than liquid water does. The stored energy is released when warm water cools and when water vapor cools to form liquid. This ability of water to store and release heat is very important in weather and climate.

It Dissolves Many Things

A liquid that dissolves substances is called a **solvent**. Because of its polarity, water dissolves many substances. Therefore, water is often called the universal solvent. Salt, or NaCl, is a familiar substance that water dissolves.

Water as a solvent is very important to living things. Water transports vital dissolved substances through organisms. And most of the chemical reactions that take place inside organisms involve substances dissolved in water.

Only this one doesn't dissolve quickly in water.

12 Summarize What characteristic of water accounts for its properties of adhesion, cohesion, high specific heat, and nature as a solvent?

_____

Think Outside the Book Inquiry

13 Apply Water dissolves a substance until the water becomes saturated and can dissolve no more of the substance. Starting with 100 ml water, determine how much salt or sugar can be dissolved before the solution is saturated.

© Houghton Mifflin Harcourt Publishing Company • Image Credits: (bg) ©Alfredo Travaz/Getty Images; (c) ©HMH

Visual Summary

To complete this summary, fill in the blanks. Then use the key below to check your answers. You can use this page to review the main concepts of the lesson.

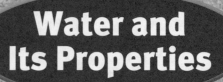

Water and Its Properties

Water plays many roles in Earth's systems.

14 Water has the following four major roles on Earth:

_____

_____

_____

_____

Water has high cohesion, high adhesion to polar substances, high specific heat, and is a good solvent.

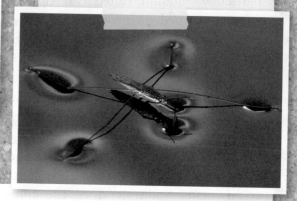

Water is a polar molecule. On Earth, water may be found as a liquid, a solid, and a gas.

15 Water is made up of two _____ atoms and one _____ atom.

16 Because water molecules have a negative end and a positive end, they have

_____

17 Water gets soaked up by a paper towel because of the property of

_____

18 Water is a commonly used _____ because it dissolves most substances.

Answers: 14 influencing weather, shaping Earth's surface, supporting life, use in human activities; 15 hydrogen, oxygen; 16 polarity; 17 adhesion; 18 solvent

19 Synthesize Which properties of water make it useful for washing and cleaning? Explain your answer.

© Houghton Mifflin Harcourt Publishing Company • Image Credits: (l) ©Scott Barrow/Corbis; (r) ©blickwinkel/Alamy

Lesson Review

Vocabulary

Fill in the blanks with the terms that best complete the following sentences.

1 Because a water molecule has a negative end and a positive end, it displays _____

2 Water's high _____ means that a large amount of energy is required to change the water's temperature.

3 When water molecules stick to the molecules of other substances, the molecules are displaying _____

Key Concepts

4 Summarize Why is water important to living things?

_____

_____

_____

_____

_____

5 Describe Draw a water molecule in the space below. Label the atoms that make up the molecule, as well as their partial charges.

[ ]

6 Explain Why does water have high cohesion?

_____

_____

_____

_____

_____

Critical Thinking

Use the graph to answer the following questions.

Household Water Use in the United States

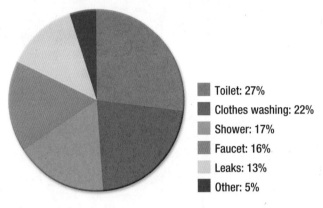

Toilet: 27%
Clothes washing: 22%
Shower: 17%
Faucet: 16%
Leaks: 13%
Other: 5%

Source: American Water Works Association Research Foundation, 1999

7 Identify In an average household, what is most water used for?

_____

8 Infer What do you think are the three biggest changes a household could make to reduce its use of water?

_____

_____

_____

_____

9 Explain Why do you think conserving fresh water might be important?

_____

_____

_____

10 Evaluate Which states of water can you find in your home? Explain.

_____

_____

_____

_____

_____

_____

© Houghton Mifflin Harcourt Publishing Company

My Notes

© Houghton Mifflin Harcourt Publishing Company

© Houghton Mifflin Harcourt Publishing Company

The Water Cycle

ESSENTIAL QUESTION

How does water change state and move around on Earth?

By the end of this lesson, you should be able to describe the water cycle and the different processes that are part of the water cycle on Earth.

6.ESS2.4, 6.PS3.4

Water from the ocean evaporates, forms clouds, then falls back into the ocean when it rains. Can you think of other ways water travels between Earth and Earth's atmosphere?

© Houghton Mifflin Harcourt Publishing Company • Image Credits: (bkgd) ©Ben Gunsberger/Workbook Stock/Getty Images

Lesson Labs

Quick Labs
- Modeling the Water Cycle
- Can You Make It Rain in a Jar?

Exploration Lab
- Changes in Water

Engage Your Brain

1 Predict Circle the word or phrase that best completes the following sentences.

The air inside a glass of ice would feel *warm/cold/room temperature*.

Ice would *melt/evaporate/remain frozen* if it were left outside on a hot day.

Water vapor will *condense on/evaporate from/ melt into* the glass of ice from the air.

The ice *absorbs energy from/maintains its energy/releases energy into* the surroundings when it melts.

2 Analyze Using the photo above, solve the word scramble to answer the question: What happens to ice as it warms up?

T I G A C N S E H E A S T T

_____

Active Reading

3 Synthesize You can often define an unknown word if you know the meaning of the word's origin. Use the meaning of the words' origins and the sentence below to make an educated guess about the meaning of *precipitation* and *evaporation*.

Latin word	Meaning
praecipitare	fall
evaporare	spread out in vapor or steam

Example sentence
Precipitation, in the form of rain, helps replace the water lost by evaporation from the lake.

precipitation:

_____

evaporation:

_____

Vocabulary Terms

- **water cycle**
- **evaporation**
- **transpiration**
- **sublimation**
- **condensation**
- **precipitation**

4 Apply As you learn the definition of each vocabulary term in this lesson, write out a sentence using that term to help you remember the meaning of the term.

© Houghton Mifflin Harcourt Publishing Company • Image Credits: (bkgd) ©Ben Gunsberger/Workbook Stock/Getty Images; (tr) ©Serge Krouglikoff/age fotostock

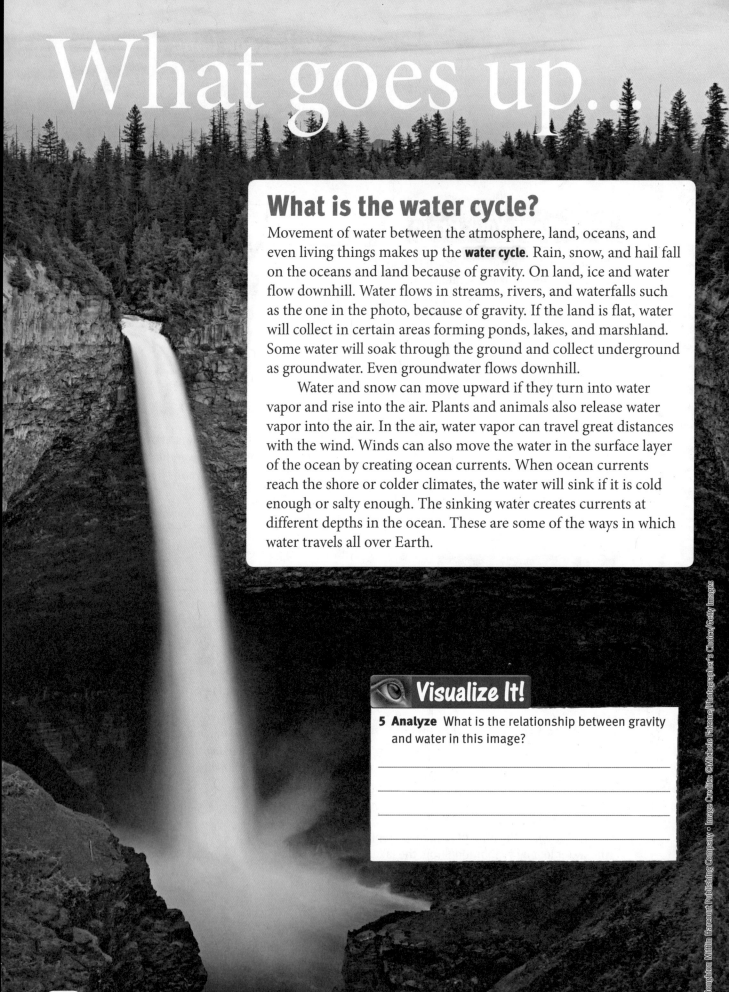

What goes up...

What is the water cycle?

Movement of water between the atmosphere, land, oceans, and even living things makes up the **water cycle**. Rain, snow, and hail fall on the oceans and land because of gravity. On land, ice and water flow downhill. Water flows in streams, rivers, and waterfalls such as the one in the photo, because of gravity. If the land is flat, water will collect in certain areas forming ponds, lakes, and marshland. Some water will soak through the ground and collect underground as groundwater. Even groundwater flows downhill.

Water and snow can move upward if they turn into water vapor and rise into the air. Plants and animals also release water vapor into the air. In the air, water vapor can travel great distances with the wind. Winds can also move the water in the surface layer of the ocean by creating ocean currents. When ocean currents reach the shore or colder climates, the water will sink if it is cold enough or salty enough. The sinking water creates currents at different depths in the ocean. These are some of the ways in which water travels all over Earth.

Visualize It!

5 Analyze What is the relationship between gravity and water in this image?

_____

_____

_____

_____

© Houghton Mifflin Harcourt Publishing Company • Image Credits: ©Michele Falzone/Photographer's Choice/Getty Images

How does water change state?

Water is found in three states on Earth: as liquid water, as solid water ice, and as gaseous water vapor. Water is visible as a liquid or a solid, but it is invisible as a gas in the air. Water can change from one state to another as energy is absorbed or released.

Water absorbs energy from its surroundings as it *melts* from solid to liquid. Water also absorbs energy when it *evaporates* from liquid to gas, or when it *sublimates* from solid to gas. Water releases energy into its surroundings when it *condenses* from gas to liquid. Water also releases energy when it *freezes* from liquid to solid, or *deposits* from gas to solid. No water is lost during these changes.

© Houghton Mifflin Harcourt Publishing Company • Image Credits: (t) ©Andrzej Tokarski/Alamy; (bl) ©Peter Lilja/The Image Bank/Getty Images; (br) ©Vincent MacNamara/Alamy

Active Reading

6 Identify As you read, underline each process in which energy is absorbed or released.

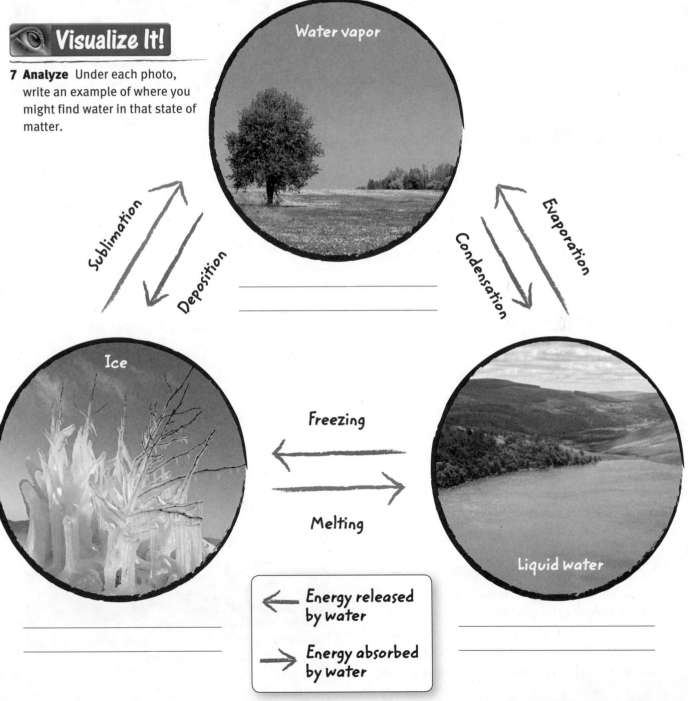

Visualize It!

7 Analyze Under each photo, write an example of where you might find water in that state of matter.

Water vapor

Sublimation

Deposition

Evaporation

Condensation

Ice

Freezing

Melting

Liquid water

← Energy released by water

→ Energy absorbed by water

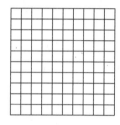

The evaporating water leaves behind a dry, cracked lake bed.

How does water reach the atmosphere?

Water reaches the atmosphere as water vapor in three ways: evaporation (i•VAP•uh•ray•shuhn), transpiration (tran•spuh•RAY•shuhn), and sublimation (suhb•luh•MAY•shuhn). It takes a lot of energy for liquid or solid water to turn into water vapor. The energy for these changes comes mostly from the sun, as solar energy.

◯ Evaporation

Evaporation occurs when liquid water changes into water vapor. About 90% of the water in the atmosphere comes from the evaporation of Earth's water. Some water evaporates from the water on land. However, most of the water vapor evaporates from Earth's oceans. This is because oceans cover most of Earth's surface. Therefore, oceans receive most of the solar energy that reaches Earth.

◯ Transpiration

Like many organisms, plants release water into the environment. Liquid water turns into water vapor inside the plant and moves into the atmosphere through stomata. Stomata are tiny holes that are found on some plant surfaces. This release of water vapor into the air by plants is called **transpiration**. About 10% of the water in the atmosphere comes from transpiration.

◯ Sublimation

When solid water changes directly to water vapor without first becoming a liquid, it is called **sublimation**. Sublimation can happen when dry air blows over ice or snow, where it is very cold and the pressure is low. A small amount of the water in the atmosphere comes from sublimation.

Do the Math **You Try It**

8 Graph Show the percentage of water vapor in the atmosphere that comes from evaporation by coloring the equivalent number of squares in the grid.

Water moves into the air.

A   B   C

Visualize It!

9 Identify Fill in the circles beside each red heading at left with the label of the arrow showing the matching process in this diagram.

© Houghton Mifflin Harcourt Publishing Company • Image Credits: (t) ©Photoshot Holdings Ltd/Alamy

What happens to water in the atmosphere?

Water reaches the atmosphere as water vapor. In the atmosphere, water vapor mixes with other gases. To leave the atmosphere, water vapor must change into liquid or solid water. Then the liquid or solid water can fall to Earth's surface.

◯ Condensation

Remember, **condensation** (kahn•den•SAY•shuhn) is the change of state from a gas to a liquid. If air that contains water vapor is cooled enough, condensation occurs. Some of the water vapor condenses on small particles, such as dust, forming little balls or tiny droplets of water. These water droplets float in the air as clouds, fog, or mist. At the ground level, water vapor may condense on cool surfaces as dew.

◯ Precipitation

In clouds, water droplets may collide and "stick" together to become larger. If a droplet becomes large enough, it falls to Earth's surface as precipitation (pri•sip•i•TAY•shuhn). **Precipitation** is any form of water that falls to Earth from clouds. Three common kinds of precipitation shown in the photos are rain, snow, and hail. Snow and hail form if the water droplets freeze. Most rain falls into the oceans because most water evaporates from ocean surfaces and oceans cover most of Earth's surface. But winds carry clouds from the ocean over land, increasing the amount of precipitation that falls on land.

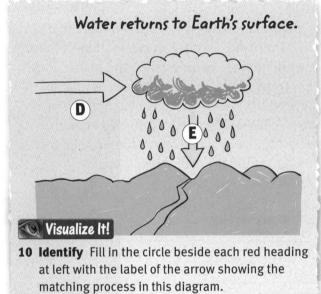

Water returns to Earth's surface.

D   E

👁 **Visualize It!**

10 Identify Fill in the circle beside each red heading at left with the label of the arrow showing the matching process in this diagram.

11 Summarize Fill in the boxes to describe how precipitation forms.

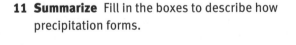

```
┌─────────────────────┐
│ _____   │ → Small droplet
│ _____   │
└─────────────────────┘
             ↓
        ┌─────────────────────┐
        │ _____   │ → Large droplet
        │ _____   │   falls to Earth.
        └─────────────────────┘
```

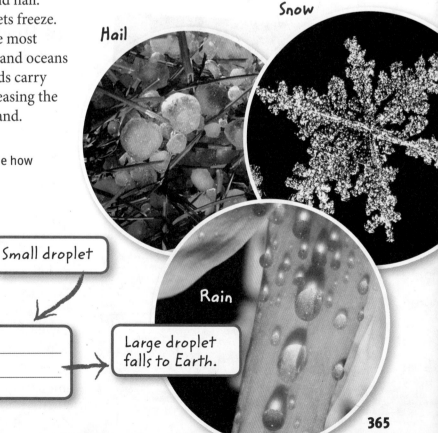

Hail

Snow

Rain

© Houghton Mifflin Harcourt Publishing Company • Image Credits: (cl) ©Jeff March/Alamy; (cr) ©Jim Zuckerman/Alamy; (b) ©Lambie Brothers/Alamy

How does water move on land and in the oceans?

After water falls to Earth, it flows and circulates all over Earth. On land, water flows downhill, both on the surface and underground. However, most of Earth's precipitation falls into the oceans. Ocean currents move water around the oceans.

Runoff and Infiltration

All of the water on land flows downhill because of gravity. Streams, rivers, and the water that flows over land are types of *runoff*. Runoff flows downhill toward oceans, lakes, and marshlands.

Some of the water on land seeps into the ground. This process is called *infiltration* (in•fil•TRAY•shuhn). Once undergound, the water is called *groundwater*. Groundwater also flows downhill through soil and rock.

 **Active Reading**

12 Compare How do runoff and groundwater differ?

_____

_____

_____

Visualize It!

13 Summarize Write a caption describing how water is moving in the diagram above.

_____

_____

Icebergs can be carried over long distances by ocean currents.

Ice Flow

Much of Earth's ice is stored in large ice caps in Antarctica and Greenland. Some ice is stored in glaciers at high altitudes all over Earth. Glaciers cover about 10% of Earth's surface. Glaciers can be called "rivers of ice" because gravity also causes glaciers to flow slowly downhill. Many glaciers never leave land. However, some glaciers flow to the ocean, where pieces may break off, as seen in the photo, and float far out to sea as icebergs.

Ocean Circulation

Winds move ocean water on the surface in great currents, sometimes for thousands of miles. At some shores, or if the water is very cold or salty, it will sink deep into the ocean. This movement helps create deep ocean currents. Both surface currents and deep ocean currents transport large amounts of water from ocean to ocean.

© Houghton Mifflin Harcourt Publishing Company • Image Credits: (bl) ©Marco Simoni/Robert Harding World Imagery/Getty Images

Water Works

What does the water cycle transport?

In the water cycle, each state of water has some energy in it. This energy is released into or absorbed from its surroundings as water changes state. The energy in each state of water is then transported as the water moves from place to place. Matter is also transported as water and the materials in the water move all over Earth. Therefore, the water cycle moves energy and matter through Earth's atmosphere, land, oceans, and living things.

Think Outside the Book

14 Apply With a classmate, discuss how the water cycle transfers energy.

Energy

Energy is transported in the water cycle through changes of state and by the movement of water from place to place. For example, water that evaporates from the ocean carries energy into the atmosphere. This movement of energy can generate hurricanes. Also, cold ocean currents can cool the air along a coastline by absorbing the energy from the air and leaving the air cooler. This energy is carried away quickly as the current continues on its path. Such processes affect the weather and climate of an area.

Matter

Earth's ocean currents move vast amounts of water all over the world. These currents also transport the solids in the water and the dissolved salts and gases. Rivers transfer water from land into the ocean. Rivers also carry large amounts of sand, mud, and gravel as shown below. Rivers form deltas and floodplains, where some of the materials from upstream collect in areas downstream. Rivers also carve valleys and canyons, and carry the excess materials downstream. Glaciers also grind away rock and carry the ground rock with them as they flow.

Visualize It!

15 Identify What do rivers, such as the ones in the photo, transport?

_____

_____

© Houghton Mifflin Harcourt Publishing Company • Image Credits: ©Yann Arthus-Bertrand/Corbis

Visualize It! The Water Cycle

Water is continuously changing state and moving from place to place in the water cycle. This diagram shows these processes and movements.

16 Identify Label each arrow to show which process the arrow represents.

17 Identify Shade in the arrows that indicate where water is changing state.

Condensation

_____

_____

Evaporation

_____

_____

_____

© Houghton Mifflin Harcourt Publishing Company

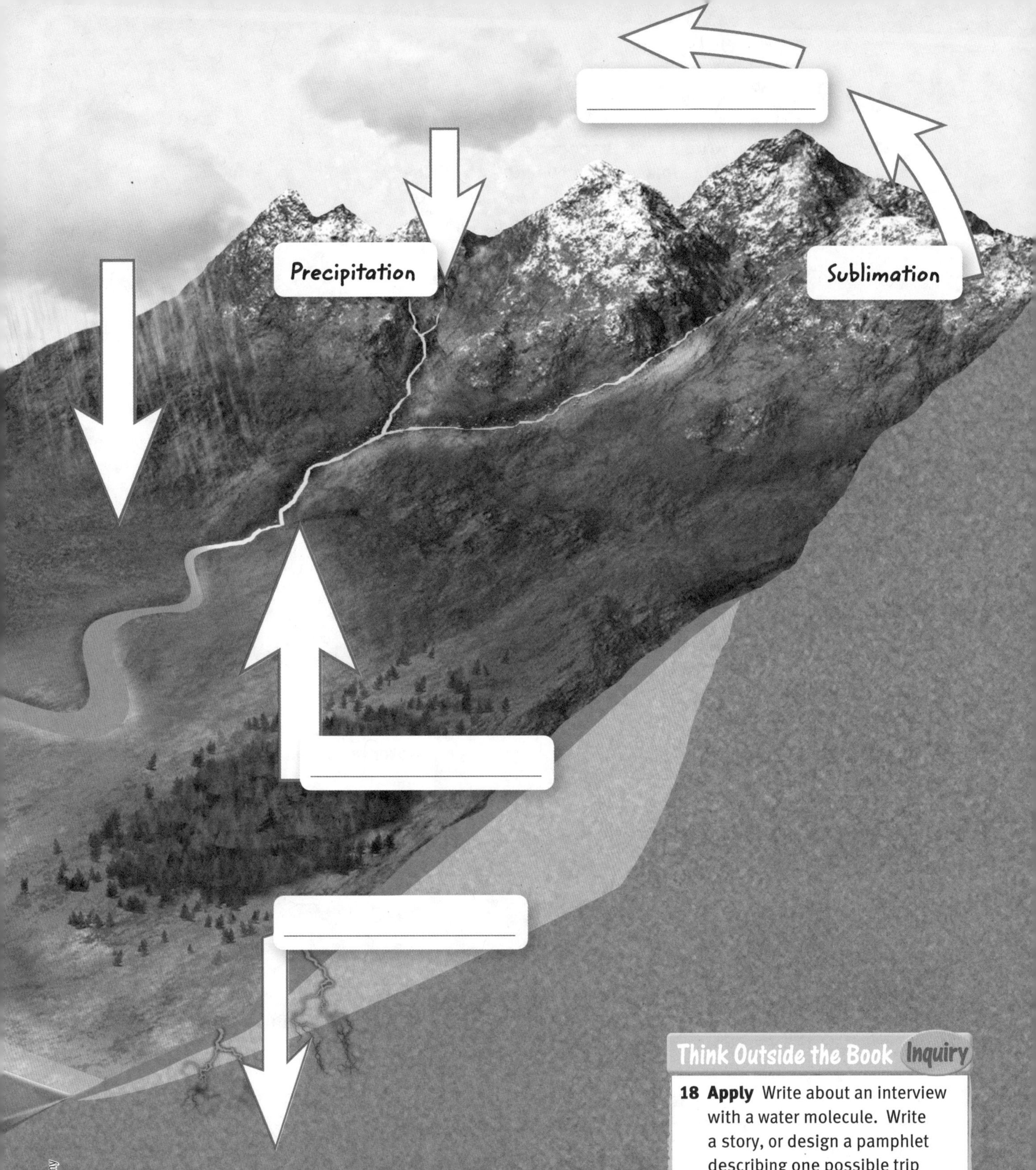

Precipitation

Sublimation

_____

_____

_____

© Houghton Mifflin Harcourt Publishing Company

Think Outside the Book Inquiry

18 Apply Write about an interview with a water molecule. Write a story, or design a pamphlet describing one possible trip that a water molecule could take through the water cycle. Share your project with classmates.

Visual Summary

To complete this summary, write a term that describes the process happening in each of the images. Then use the key below to check your answers. You can use this page to review the main concepts of the lesson.

Water moves in the atmosphere.

19 _____

The Water Cycle

Water moves into the atmosphere.

21 _____

Water moves on land and in oceans.

20 _____

Answers: 19 condensation or precipitation; 20 iceflow, runoff, infiltration, or ocean current; 21 evaporation, transpiration, or sublimation

22 Predict Describe what might happen to the water cycle if less solar energy reached Earth and how Earth's climate would be affected.

_____

© Houghton Mifflin Harcourt Publishing Company

Lesson Review

Vocabulary

Write the correct label A, B, C, or D under each term to indicate the definition of that term.

1 water cycle

_____

2 evaporation

_____

3 precipitation

_____

4 condensation

_____

A The change of state from a liquid to a gas

B The change of state from a gas to a liquid

C The movement of water between the atmosphere, land, oceans, and living things

D Any form of water that falls to Earth's surface from the clouds

Key Concepts

5 Identify List the three ways in which water reaches the atmosphere and tell which way accounts for most of the water in the atmosphere.

_____

_____

_____

6 Classify Which of the processes of the water cycle occur by releasing energy?

_____

_____

7 Identify What happens to water once it reaches Earth's surface?

_____

_____

_____

8 Summarize Describe how three common types of precipitation form.

_____

_____

_____

_____

_____

Critical Thinking

Use the image below to answer the following question.

9 Apply Describe the energy changes occurring in the process shown above.

_____

_____

10 Infer Why does the amount of water that flows in a river change during the year?

_____

_____

11 Predict During a storm, a tree fell over into a river. What might happen to this tree?

_____

_____

_____

12 Evaluate Warm ocean currents cool as they flow along a coastline, away from the equator. Explain what is transported and how.

_____

_____

_____

_____

_____

© Houghton Mifflin Harcourt Publishing Company

My Notes

© Houghton Mifflin Harcourt Publishing Company

© Houghton Mifflin Harcourt Publishing Company

S.T.E.M. Engineering & Technology

Engineering Design Process

Skills

Identify a need

Conduct research

✓ Brainstorm solutions

✓ Select a solution

✓ Design a solution

✓ Test and evaluate

✓ Redesign to improve

✓ Communicate results

Objectives

- Explain how humans and other organisms affect the water cycle.

- Design a filtration system to remove contaminants from water.

Altering the Water Cycle

Earth's water cycle would occur even if there were no life on Earth. But humans and other organisms influence the water cycle in many ways. For example, beavers build dams in rivers or streams using trees, sticks, and mud. Water pools behind the dam, forming a pond that the beaver uses as a habitat. This affects the water cycle by changing the natural movement of water.

Humans also build dams—much larger than the ones made by beavers. Manmade dams can turn rivers or streams into huge artificial lakes or reservoirs. Humans also affect the types of matter that are moved by the water cycle. Fertilizers and waste can seep into groundwater. Garbage and other pollution may also make their way into streams, rivers, and lakes as runoff.

1 Brainstorm List some other ways that human activity affects the water cycle. Divide your list into positive and negative impacts on the water cycle.

_____

_____

_____

_____

© Houghton Mifflin Harcourt Publishing Company • Image Credits: (bg) ©ChiaraPoggi/iStock/Getty Images; (t) ©NWLphs/iStock/Getty Images; (b) ©Jens MacDonald/Alamy; (br) ©dwiendecker/iStock/Getty Images

Constructing a Filtration System

Humans need water to survive. But as water moves through the water cycle, it can mix with other matter that is not so healthy. Most people get their drinking water from groundwater. Groundwater collects underground after seeping through layers of soil and rock. Because of this, it may contain chemicals, minerals, or microorganisms that are unhealthy for humans to consume.

Filtration is one way that humans can purify water to make it safer. A water filter is a mechanism designed to separate water from a mixture. It allows water to flow through it, but it traps other substances. Filters used to purify drinking water usually have more than one layer. Each layer is designed to trap certain types of matter, separating it from the water.

Water treatment plants use filtration and other methods to purify groundwater or surface water.

2 Infer What are some properties of an effective filtration system? How would this compare to a less effective filtration system?

_____

_____

_____

 You Try It! ⟶

Now it's your turn to design a water filtration system to remove contaminants from water.

© Houghton Mifflin Harcourt Publishing Company • Image Credits: (bg) ©Chiara Poggi/iStock/Getty Images; (b) ©Quechanwatthana/iStock/Getty Images

 # You Try It!

Now it's your turn to design a water filtration system to remove contaminants from water. Choose the materials you think will best filter the water.

Materials

✓ water mixed with soil and a small amount of vegetable oil

✓ plastic liter bottle, cut in half

✓ a beaker or other clear receptacle

✓ cotton balls

✓ pebbles

✓ napkins

✓ coffee filters

✓ rubber bands

✓ cloth

① Brainstorm Solutions

Which materials would you use to design a multi-layered filter? In what order would you place them? List three possibilities below and explain why they might work.

1. _____

   _____

2. _____

   _____

3. _____

   _____

② Select a Solution

From your list above, select a solution. Then create a diagram in the space below. Be sure to label your materials.

© Houghton Mifflin Harcourt Publishing Company

(3) Build a Prototype

Turn the top half of the liter bottle upside down. Place the materials for your filter (cotton balls, pebbles, etc.) inside the bottle. As you built your filter, were there any parts of your design that could not be assembled as you predicted? What parts did you have to revise as you were building your prototype?

_____

_____

_____

_____

(4) Test and Evaluate

Hold your bottle over the receptacle. Pour the dirty water through the filter and observe the results. Did your filter remove most of the materials from the water? How can you tell? (Caution: Do not taste or drink the water.)

_____

_____

_____

_____

_____

(5) Redesign to Improve

How could you adjust your filter to make it work better? Try using different materials or layering them in a different order. Test the filter again and describe your results.

_____

_____

_____

_____

(6) Communicate Results

Describe the best filter you created and why you decided to construct it that way. Why do you think it worked the best?

_____

_____

_____

_____

© Houghton Mifflin Harcourt Publishing Company • Image Credits:

Surface Water and Groundwater

ESSENTIAL QUESTION

How does fresh water flow on Earth?

By the end of this lesson, you should be able to explain the processes involved in the flow of water, both above and below the ground.

▬▬ 6.ESS2.4, 6.ESS3.3

Fresh water flows on Earth's surface, sometimes tumbling over waterfalls like these.

© Houghton Mifflin Harcourt Publishing Company • Image Credits: (bg) ©Digital Vision/Alamy

Lesson Labs

Quick Labs
• Modeling Groundwater
• Model a Stream

Exploration Lab
• Aquifers and Development

Engage Your Brain

1 Identify Read over the following vocabulary terms. In the spaces provided, place a + if you know the term well, a ~ if you have heard of the term but are not sure what it means, and a ? if you are unfamiliar with the term. Then write a sentence that includes one of the words you are most familiar with.

_____ tributary
_____ surface water
_____ aquifer

Sentence using known word:

_____
_____
_____

2 Describe Write your own caption for this photo.

_____
_____
_____
_____
_____

Active Reading

3 Apply Many scientific words, such as *channel*, also have everyday meanings. Use context clues to write your own definition for each meaning of the word *channel*.

Example sentence:
She didn't like the TV show, so she changed the <u>channel</u>.

channel:
_____
_____

Example sentence:
The <u>channel</u> of the river was broad and deep.

channel:
_____
_____

Vocabulary Terms

• surface water   • tributary
• groundwater   • watershed
• water table   • divide
• channel   • aquifer

4 Identify As you read, create a reference card for each vocabulary term. On one side of the card, write the term and its meaning. On the other side, draw an image that illustrates or makes a connection to the term. These cards can be used as bookmarks in the text so that you can refer to them while studying.

© Houghton Mifflin Harcourt Publishing Company • Image Credits: (bg) ©Digital Vision/Alamy; (t) ©Anders Ryman/Corbis

Getting Your Feet Wet

Where on Earth is fresh water found?

About 97% of Earth's water is salty, which leaves only 3% as fresh water. Most of that small amount of fresh water is frozen as ice and snow, so only about 1% of Earth's water is fresh liquid water. This fresh liquid water is found both on and below Earth's surface.

This tiny percentage of Earth's water must meet the large demand that all living things have for fresh, clean water. In addition to providing drinking water, fresh water is used for agriculture, industry, transportation, and recreation. It also provides a place to live for many plants and animals.

On Earth's Surface

Active Reading 5 **Identify** As you read, underline three examples of surface water.

Water above Earth's surface is called **surface water**. Surface water is found in streams, rivers, and lakes. It either comes from precipitation, such as rain, or from water that comes up from the ground to Earth's surface. Springs are an example of underground water coming up to the surface. Surface water flows from higher ground to lower ground. Water that flows across Earth's surface is called *runoff*. Eventually, runoff can enter bodies of water.

Beneath Earth's Surface

Active Reading 6 **Identify** As you read, underline how surface water becomes groundwater.

Not all runoff becomes surface water. Some runoff and surface water seep down into the ground. Water drains through the soil and filters down into underground rock, collecting in spaces between rock particles. The water found in the spaces between rock particles below Earth's surface is called **groundwater**.

Most drinking water in the United States comes from groundwater supplies. To use these supplies, people drill down to the water table to reach reservoirs of groundwater. The **water table** is the upper boundary, or surface, of groundwater.

© Houghton Mifflin Harcourt Publishing Company

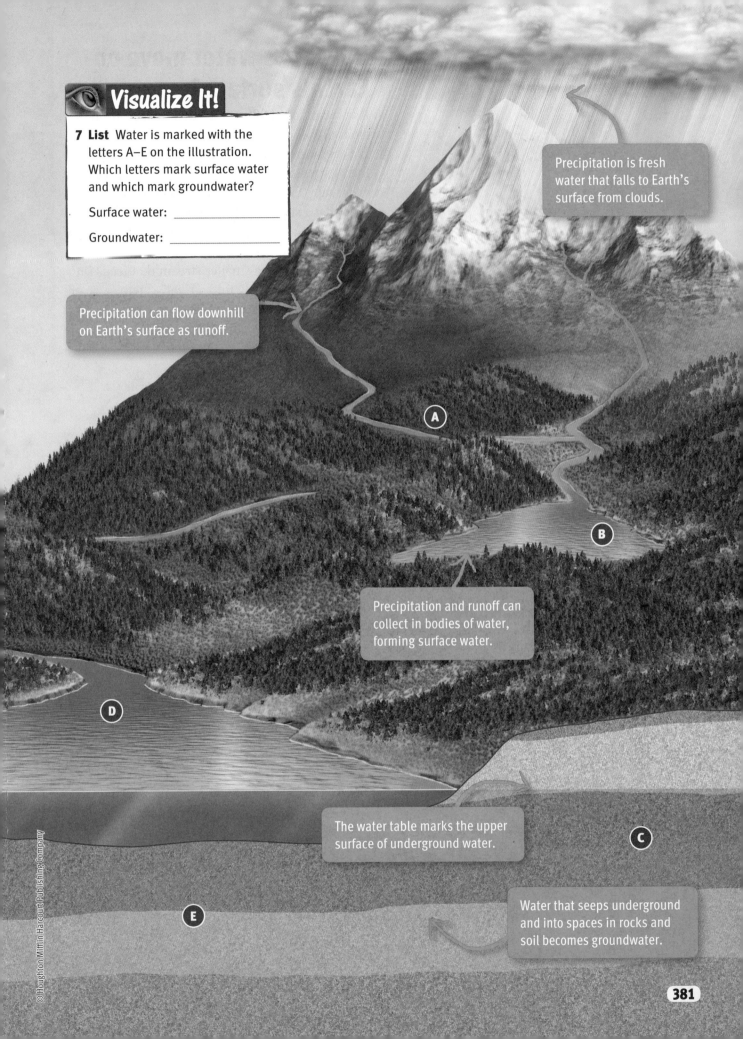

Visualize It!

7 List Water is marked with the letters A–E on the illustration. Which letters mark surface water and which mark groundwater?

Surface water: _____

Groundwater: _____

Precipitation is fresh water that falls to Earth's surface from clouds.

Precipitation can flow downhill on Earth's surface as runoff.

Precipitation and runoff can collect in bodies of water, forming surface water.

The water table marks the upper surface of underground water.

Water that seeps underground and into spaces in rocks and soil becomes groundwater.

© Houghton Mifflin Harcourt Publishing Company

Cry Me a River

How does water move on Earth's surface?

As precipitation falls on Earth's surface, it flows from higher to lower areas. The water that does not seep below the surface flows together and forms streams. The water erodes rocks and soil, eventually forming channels. A **channel** is the path that a stream follows. Over time, a channel gets wider and deeper, as the stream continues to erode rock and soil.

A **tributary** is a smaller stream that feeds into a river and eventually into a river system. A river system is a network of streams and rivers that drains an area of its runoff.

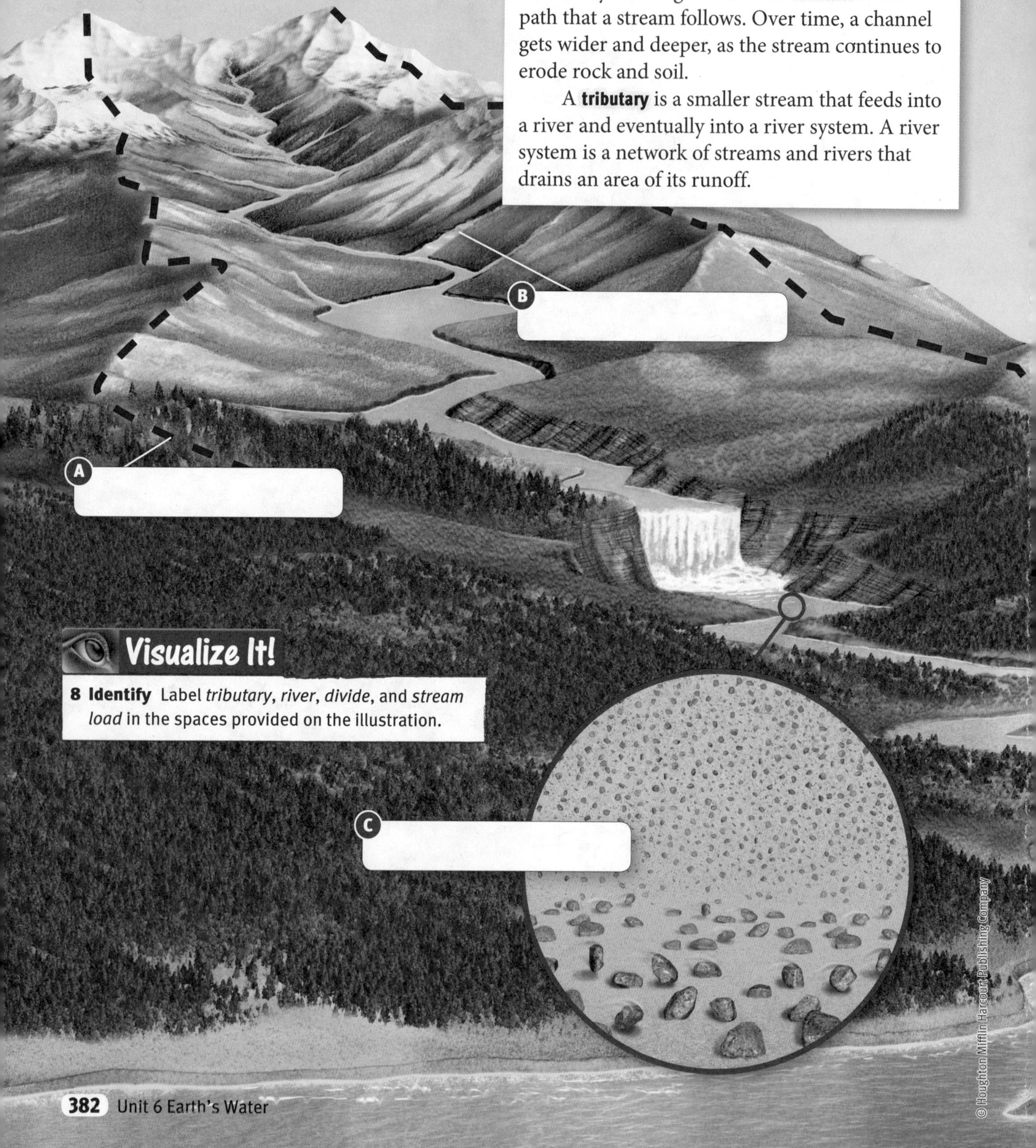

A

B

C

Visualize It!

8 Identify Label *tributary*, *river*, *divide*, and *stream load* in the spaces provided on the illustration.

© Houghton Mifflin Harcourt Publishing Company

Within Watersheds

A **watershed** is the area of land that is drained by a river system. Streams, rivers, flood plains, lakes, ponds, wetlands, and groundwater all contribute water to a watershed. Watersheds are separated from one another by a ridge or an area of higher ground called a **divide**. Precipitation that falls on one side of a divide enters one watershed while the precipitation that falls on the other side of a divide enters another watershed.

The largest watershed in the United States is the Mississippi River watershed. It has hundreds of tributaries. It extends from the Rocky Mountains, in the west, to the Appalachian Mountains, in the east, and down the length of the United States, from north to south.

Many factors affect the flow of water in a watershed. For example, plants slow runoff and reduce erosion. The porosity and permeability of rocks and sediment determine how much water can seep down into the ground. The steepness of land affects how fast water flows over a watershed.

Active Reading **9 State** Which land feature separates watersheds?

_____

In Rivers and Streams

Gradient is a measure of the change in elevation over a certain distance. In other words, gradient describes the steepness, or slope, of the land. The higher the gradient of a river or stream, the faster the water moves. The faster the water moves, the more energy it has to erode rock and soil.

A river's *flow* is the amount of water that moves through the river channel in a given amount of time. Flow increases during a major storm or when warm weather rapidly melts snow. An increase in flow causes an increase in a river's speed.

Materials carried by a stream are called *stream load*. Streams with a high flow carry a larger stream load. The size of the particles depends on water speed. Faster streams can carry larger particles. Streams eventually deposit their stream loads where the speed of the water decreases. This commonly happens as streams enter lakes and oceans.

Active Reading **10 Summarize** How would an increase in gradient affect the speed of water?

_____

_____

D

© Houghton Mifflin Harcourt Publishing Company

How does groundwater flow?

Although you can see some of Earth's fresh water in streams and lakes, you cannot see the large amount of water that flows underground as groundwater. Earth has much more fresh groundwater than fresh surface water.

It Trickles Down from Earth's Surface

Water from precipitation or streams may seep below the surface and become groundwater. Groundwater is either stored or it flows underground. It can enter back into streams and lakes, becoming surface water again. An **aquifer** is a body of rock or sediment that stores groundwater and allows it to flow.

Recall that the water table is the upper surface of underground water. The water table can rise or fall depending on the amount of water in the aquifer. In wet regions, the water table can be at or just beneath the soil's surface. In wetland areas, the water table is above the soil's surface.

It Fills Tiny Spaces Underground

An aquifer stores water in open spaces, or *pores,* between particles of rock or sediment. The storage space in an aquifer is measured by *porosity,* the percentage of the rock that is composed of pore space. The greater the pore space is, the higher the porosity is. A cup of gravel, for example, has higher porosity than a cup of sand does.

Permeability is a measure of how easily water can flow through an aquifer. High permeability means that many pores in the aquifer are connected, so water can flow easily. Aquifers with both high porosity and high permeability are useful as a water resource.

Visualize It!

11 Label Draw an arrow, ↑ (high) or ↓ (low), to indicate the porosity and permeability of each rock sample. One is already completed as an example.

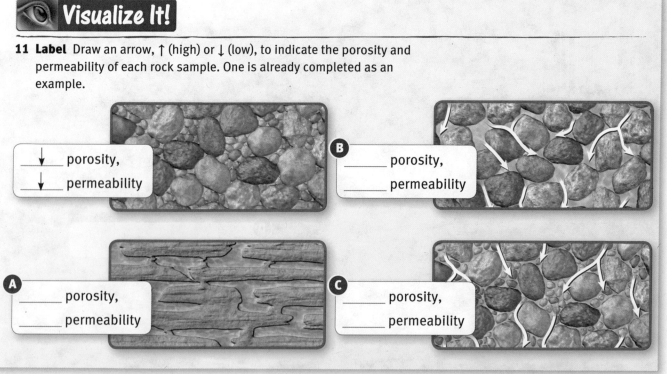

____↓____ porosity,
____↓____ permeability

B _____ porosity,
_____ permeability

A _____ porosity,
_____ permeability

C _____ porosity,
_____ permeability

© Houghton Mifflin Harcourt Publishing Company

It Is Recharged and Discharged

Surface water that trickles down into the ground can reach the water table and enter an aquifer. This process is called *recharge*, and occurs in an area called the *recharge zone*.

Where the water table meets the surface, water may pool to form a wetland or may flow out as a spring. The process by which groundwater becomes surface water is called *discharge* and happens in *discharge zones*. Discharge can feed rivers, streams, and lakes. Groundwater is also discharged where water is extracted from wells that are drilled down into the water table. Through discharge and recharge, the same water circulates between surface water and groundwater.

Think Outside the Book Inquiry

13 Debate During times of little or no rainfall, many communities have regulations limiting water use. Imagine that you live in a community with a depleted aquifer. As a class, develop a set of regulations that you think residents should follow. Start by brainstorming as many uses of water as you can. Then decide which uses should be regulated and to what extent.

Visualize It!

12 Label On the illustration below, write a caption for *discharge zone* and for *aquifer*.

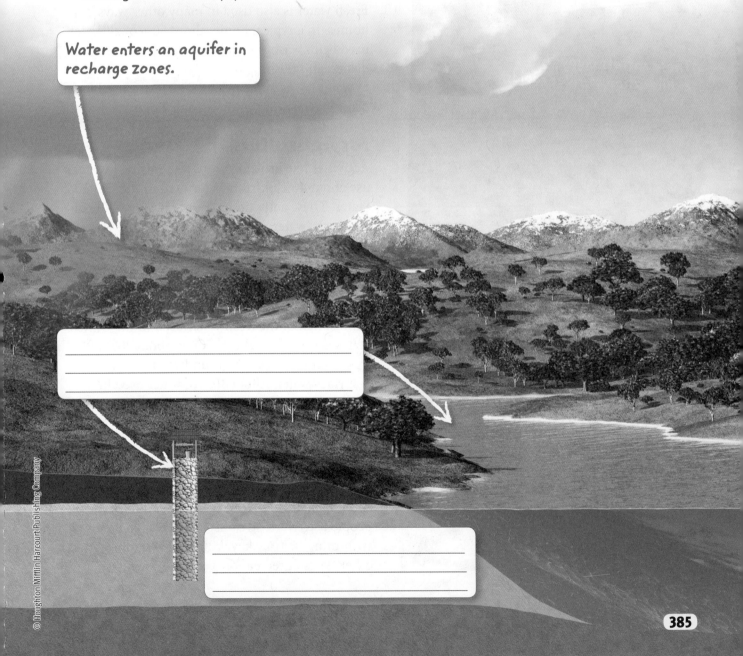

Water enters an aquifer in recharge zones.

© Houghton Mifflin Harcourt Publishing Company

Making a Splash

How do people use surface water and groundwater?

Active Reading

14 Identify As you read this page, underline how water is used in a typical home.

About 75% of all the fresh water used in the United States comes from surface water. The other 25% comes from groundwater. But surface water and groundwater are connected. In human terms, they are one resource. People use this freshwater resource in many different ways.

For Drinking and Use at Home

Groundwater is an important source of drinking water. Surface water is used for drinking, too. Fresh water is also used in many other ways in homes. In a typical home, about 50% of all water used is for washing clothes, bathing, washing dishes, and flushing toilets. About 33% is used to water lawns and gardens. The rest is used for drinking, cooking, and washing hands.

For Agriculture

Activities like growing crops and raising livestock use about 40% of fresh water used in the United States. These activities account for about 70% of all groundwater use. A little over half the water used in agriculture comes from surface water. A little less than half comes from groundwater.

For Industry

Almost half of the fresh water used in the United States is used for industry. Only about 20% of this water comes from groundwater. The rest is surface water. About 40% of water used in industry helps cool elements in power plants.

For Transportation and Recreation

Surface water is also used to transport products and people from place to place. In addition, people use rivers, streams, and lakes for swimming, sailing, kayaking, water skiing, and other types of recreation.

These rafters enjoy the exhilaration of river rapids.

© Houghton Mifflin Harcourt Publishing Company • Image Credits: ©Fuse/Getty Images

Troubled Waters

Each hour, about 15,114 babies are born around the world. The human population has skyrocketed over the last few hundred years. But the amount of fresh water on Earth has remained roughly the same. The limited supply of fresh water is an important resource that must be managed so that it can meet the demands of a growing population.

Scientists are developing technologies for obtaining clean, fresh water to meet global needs. Here, a boy uses a water purifier straw that filters disease-causing microbes and certain other contaminants from surface water. The straw is inexpensive and can filter 700 L of water before it needs to be replaced—that's about how much water the average person drinks in one year.

Like many places on Earth, Zimbabwe is experiencing severe water shortages. The country has been plagued by droughts since the 1980s. Scientists estimate that about 1 billion people around the world do not have an adequate supply of clean, fresh water.

© Houghton Mifflin Harcourt Publishing Company • Image Credits: (bg) © David Reed/Corbis; (r) ©HMH

Extend

Inquiry

15 Infer Most of Earth is covered by water. How can we be experiencing shortages of drinking water?

16 Research Find out which diseases are caused by microbes found in untreated surface water. How might the water purifier straw reduce the number of people getting these diseases?

17 Recommend Conserving water is one way to ensure adequate supplies of drinking water. Work with a group to develop a plan to reduce water use at school. Present your plan to the class. As a class, select the best aspects of each group's plan. Combine the best suggestions into a document to present to the school administration.

Visual Summary

To complete this summary, fill in the blank with the correct word or phrase. Then, use the key below to check your answers. You can use this page to review the main concepts of the lesson.

Surface Water and Groundwater

Fresh surface water is found in streams, rivers, and lakes.

18 Smaller streams, or _____, flow into the main river channel.

People use fresh water in homes, agriculture, and industry, for transportation, and for recreation.

20 Most industrial fresh water comes from rivers and other sources of _____

Groundwater is found in pore spaces in rocks and sediment below Earth's surface.

19 The surface area where water enters an aquifer is called the _____ zone.

Answers: 18 tributaries; 19 recharge; 20 surface water

21 Relate Describe how a raindrop could become surface water, then groundwater, and then end up back on Earth's surface again.

© Houghton Mifflin Harcourt Publishing Company • Image Credits: ©Fuse/Getty Images

Lesson Review

Vocabulary

In your own words, define the following terms.

1 surface water

_____

_____

2 watershed

_____

_____

3 groundwater

_____

_____

4 water table

_____

_____

5 aquifer

_____

_____

Key Concepts

6 Identify What three factors describe the movement of surface water in streams and rivers?

_____

_____

_____

7 Explain How does the gradient of a river affect its flow?

_____

_____

_____

8 Describe How quickly would groundwater flow through rock with high porosity and high permeability? Explain your answer.

_____

_____

_____

Critical Thinking

9 Conclude An area's rate of groundwater recharge exceeds its rate of groundwater discharge. What can you conclude about the area's groundwater supply?

_____

_____

_____

_____

Use this graph to answer the following questions.

Average Water-Level Changes in the High Plains Aquifer by State (1980–2013)

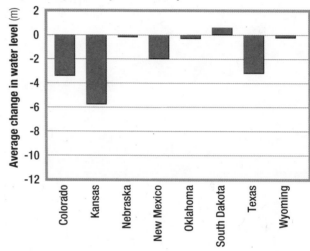

State *Source:* USGS, 2013

10 Analyze What has happened to the amount of water in the High Plains Aquifer over time?

_____

_____

11 Infer What might account for the changes described in question 10?

_____

_____

_____

_____

_____

© Houghton Mifflin Harcourt Publishing Company

My Notes

© Houghton Mifflin Harcourt Publishing Company

© Houghton Mifflin Harcourt Publishing Company

Unit 6 [Big Idea] Water moves through Earth's atmosphere, oceans, and land in a cycle and is essential for life on Earth.

Lesson 1
ESSENTIAL QUESTION
What makes water so important?

Describe water's structure, its properties, and its importance to Earth's systems.

Lesson 2
ESSENTIAL QUESTION
How does water change state and move around on Earth?

Describe the water cycle and the different processes that are part of the water cycle on Earth.

Lesson 3
ESSENTIAL QUESTION
How does fresh water flow on Earth?

Explain the processes involved in the flow of water, both above and below the ground.

Connect ESSENTIAL QUESTIONS
Lessons 2 and 3

1 Synthesize Explain why precipitation on Earth's surface is less common on land than it is over the oceans. Base your answer on the water cycle.

_____

_____

_____

_____

Think Outside the Book

2 Synthesize Choose one of these activities to help synthesize what you have learned in this unit.

☐ Using what you learned in lessons 1 and 2, make a poster to show how the stored energy in water is released to the environment during certain changes in state.

☐ Using what you learned in lessons 1, 2, and 3, make a flipbook to show how gravity affects the movement and flow of water.

© Houghton Mifflin Harcourt Publishing Company • Image Credits: (tl) ©ZenShui/Odilon Dimier/PhotoAlto Agency RF Collections/Getty Images; (tr) ©Ben Gunsberger/Workbook Stock/Getty Images; (b) ©Digital Vision/Alamy

Unit 6 Review

Name _____

Vocabulary

Fill in each blank with the term that best completes the following sentences.

1 Water is a _____ molecule because its hydrogen atoms have a small positive charge and its oxygen atom has a small negative charge.

2 Water is called the universal _____ because it dissolves a large number of substances.

3 The continuous movement of water between the atmosphere, the land, the oceans, and living things is called the _____.

4 Any form of water that falls to Earth's surface from the clouds is called _____.

5 A _____ is the area of land that is drained by a river system.

Key Concepts

Read each question below, and circle the best answer.

6 A glass of ice water is shown below before and after it reaches room temperature.

Which of the following correctly explains something that occurred in the time between these two images?

A The ice cubes expanded in volume as they melted into liquid water.

B As water vapor condensed on the glass, it absorbed energy.

C The water droplets outside the glass absorbed energy as they evaporated.

D Some liquid water inside the glass sublimated into water vapor in the air.

© Houghton Mifflin Harcourt Publishing Company

7 Which of these circle graphs most correctly shows the approximate proportions of fresh water and salt water on the surface of the earth?

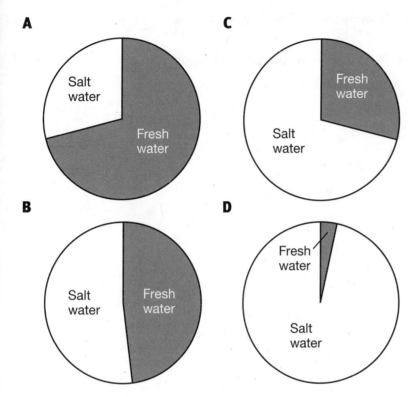

A

Salt water

Fresh water

C

Fresh water

Salt water

B

Salt water

Fresh water

D

Fresh water

Salt water

8 Which of the following is not a way that water reaches Earth's atmosphere?

A condensation

B evaporation

C sublimation

D transpiration

9 Which of the following correctly explains why icebergs float in the ocean?

A Ice is less dense than liquid water because water contracts when it freezes, filling in open space between molecules.

B Ice is less dense than liquid water because there is more open space between molecules in ice than in liquid water.

C Ice is more dense than liquid water because there is less open space between molecules in ice than in water.

D Water is a polar molecule, so the net positive electrical charges in the water repel the net positive electrical charges inside the iceberg.

© Houghton Mifflin Harcourt Publishing Company

10 A certain percentage of water that falls to Earth's surface as precipitation does not become surface water or groundwater and does not evaporate back into the atmosphere. Which of the following most likely explains what happens to this water?

A The water falls into the ocean, where it evaporates back into the atmosphere.

B The water is stored as snow and ice on Earth's surface.

C The water molecules are broken down into hydrogen and oxygen atoms.

D The water is absorbed and used by plants.

11 Which of the following is an incorrect statement about the flow of water through watersheds?

A A watershed can be fed by groundwater.

B The boundary separating two watersheds is called a divide.

C Plant life often alters the flow of water in a watershed by causing erosion.

D The gradient of the land can affect the flow of water through a watershed.

12 Which of the following is the name for all the materials carried by a stream other than the water itself?

A discharge   **C** gradient

B flow   **D** stream load

Critical Thinking

Answer the following questions in the space provided.

13 Give two examples of the importance of water to human activities, explaining how the water is used.

_____

_____

_____

_____

_____

_____

© Houghton Mifflin Harcourt Publishing Company

14 The diagram below shows the changes among the three states of water.

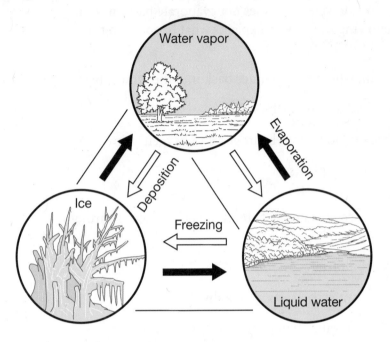

⇐ Energy absorbed / released by water

➡ Energy absorbed / released by water

Fill in each of the three blank lines with the correct term for the change of state shown by the arrows. In the key, circle the correct word to show whether water absorbs or releases energy in the changes of state shown by that type of arrow.

Connect **ESSENTIAL QUESTIONS**
Lessons 1, 2, and 3

Answer the following question in the space provided.

15 Describe what happens to a molecule of water as it moves through the water cycle along any path you choose. Be sure to mention the movement of the water molecule, any changes of state, and the absorption or release of energy.

_____

_____

_____

_____

_____

_____

_____

_____

_____

© Houghton Mifflin Harcourt Publishing Company

Circulation in Earth's Air and Oceans

Big Idea

Energy transfer causes Earth's air and oceans to circulate.

6.ESS2.1, 6.ESS2.2, 6.ESS2.3, 6.PS3.1, 6.PS3.4

Earth's atmosphere is a mixture of gases that interacts with solar energy.

Wind is the movement of air caused by differences in air pressure.

What do you think?

Like other parts of the Earth system, energy is transferred through Earth's atmosphere. What are the three processes by which energy is transferred through the atmosphere?

© Houghton Mifflin Harcourt Publishing Company • Image Credits: (bkgd) ©Scott Smith/Corbis; (br) ©DLILLC/Corbis

Circulation in Earth's Air and Oceans

Clearing the Air

In some areas, there are many vehicles on the roads every day. Some of the gases from vehicle exhausts react with sunlight and pollute the air. There are days when the air pollution is so high that it becomes a health hazard. Those days are especially difficult for people who have problems breathing. What can you do to reduce gas emissions?

① Think About It

A How do you get to school every day?

_____

_____

_____

B How many of the students in your class come to school by car?

_____

Gas emissions are high during rush-hour traffic.

© Houghton Mifflin Harcourt Publishing Company • Image Credits: ©Luis Castaneda Inc./The Image Bank/Getty Images

② Ask A Question

Keeping Earth's air clean is important for all living things. How can you reduce the number of vehicles students use to get to school one day each month?

With your teacher and classmates, brainstorm different ways in which you can reduce the number of vehicles students use to get to school.

Ride a bicycle to school.

Check off the points below as you use them to design your plan.

☐ how far a student lives from school

☐ the kinds of transportation students may have available to them

③ Make A Plan

A Write down different ways that you can reduce the number of vehicles that bring students to school.

_____
_____
_____
_____
_____
_____
_____

C In the space below, design a sign-up sheet that your classmates will use to choose how they will come to school on the designated day.

B Create a short presentation for your principal that outlines how the whole school could become involved in your vehicle-reduction plan. Write down the points of your presentation in the space below.

_____
_____
_____
_____
_____
_____
_____
_____
_____
_____

Take It Home

Give your presentation to an adult. Then, have the adult brainstorm ways to reduce their daily gas emissions.

© Houghton Mifflin Harcourt Publishing Company • Image Credits: (bkgd) ©Luis Castaneda Inc./The Image Bank/Getty Images

Energy Transfer

ESSENTIAL QUESTION

How does energy move through Earth's system?

By the end of this lesson, you should be able to summarize the three mechanisms by which energy is transferred through Earth's system.

6.ESS2.1, 6.ESS2.2, 6.ESS2.3, 6.PS3.1, 6.PS3.4

Ice absorbs energy from the sun. This can cause ice to melt—even when the temperature is below freezing.

© Houghton Mifflin Harcourt Publishing Company • Image Credits: ©yanikap/Shutterstock

🖐 Lesson Labs

Quick Labs
• The Sun's Angle and Temperature
• How Does Color Affect Temperature?
• Modeling Convection

S.T.E.M. Lab
• Heat from the Sun

🧠 Engage Your Brain

1 Describe Fill in the blank with the word or phrase that you think correctly completes the following sentences.

An example of something hot is
_____

An example of something cold is
_____

The sun provides us with
_____

A thermometer is used to measure
_____

2 Explain If you placed your hands around this mug of hot chocolate, what would happen to the temperature of your hands? Why do you think this would happen?

_____
_____
_____
_____
_____
_____

✏️ Active Reading

3 Apply Many scientific words, such as *heat*, are used to convey different meanings. Use context clues to write your own definition for each meaning of the word *heat*.

The student won the first <u>heat</u> of the race.

heat:
_____
_____

The man wondered if his rent included <u>heat</u>.

heat:
_____
_____

Energy in the form of <u>heat</u> was transferred from the hot pan to the cold counter.

heat:
_____
_____

Vocabulary Terms

• temperature   • radiation
• thermal energy   • convection
• thermal expansion   • conduction
• atmosphere   • heat

4 Identify This list contains the vocabulary terms you'll learn in this lesson. As you read, circle the definition of each term.

© Houghton Mifflin Harcourt Publishing Company • Image Credits: ©yanikap/Shutterstock

Hot and Cold

How are energy and temperature related?

All matter is made up of moving particles, such as atoms or molecules. When particles are in motion, they have kinetic energy. Because particles move at different speeds, each has a different amount of kinetic energy.

Temperature (TEMM•per•uh•choor) is a measure of the average kinetic energy of particles. The faster a particle moves, the more kinetic energy it has. As shown below, the more kinetic energy the particles of an object have, the higher the temperature of the object. Temperature does not depend on the number of particles. A teapot holds more tea than a cup. If the particles of tea in both containers have the same average kinetic energy, the tea in both containers is at the same temperature.

Thermal energy is the total kinetic energy of particles. A teapot full of tea at a high temperature has more thermal energy than a teapot full of tea at a lower temperature. Thermal energy also depends on the number of particles. The more particles there are in an object, the greater the object's thermal energy. The tea in a teapot and a cup may be at the same temperature, but the tea in the pot has more thermal energy because there is more of it.

Visualize It!

5 Analyze Which container holds particles with the higher average kinetic energy?

_____

_____

particle motion

particle motion

© Houghton Mifflin Harcourt Publishing Company

What is thermal expansion?

When the temperature of a substance increases, the substance's particles have more kinetic energy. Therefore, the particles move faster and move apart. As the space between the particles increases, the substance expands. The increase in volume that results from an increase in temperature is called **thermal expansion**. Most substances on Earth expand when they become warmer and contract when they become cooler. Water is an exception. Cold water expands as it gets colder and then freezes to form ice.

Thermal expansion causes a change in the density of a substance. *Density* is the mass per unit volume of a substance. When a substance expands, its mass stays the same but its volume increases. As a result, density decreases. Differences in density that are caused by thermal expansion can cause movement of matter. For example, air inside a hot-air balloon is warmed, as shown below. The air expands as its particles move faster and farther apart. As the air expands, it becomes less dense than the air outside the balloon. The less-dense air inside the balloon is forced upward by the colder, denser air outside the balloon. This same principle affects air movement in the atmosphere, water movement in the oceans, and rock movement in the geosphere.

7 Apply Why would an increase in the temperature of the oceans contribute to a rise in sea level?

_____

_____

_____

6 Predict What might happen to the hot-air balloon if the air inside it cooled down?

_____

_____

When the air in this balloon becomes hotter, it becomes less dense than the surrounding air. So, the balloon goes up, up, and away!

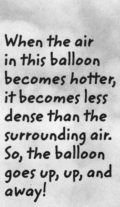

© Houghton Mifflin Harcourt Publishing Company • Image Credits: (r) ©Ron Crabtree/Photographer's Choice RF/Getty Images; (br) ©Photo by Andreas Rentz/Getty Images

Getting Warm

What is heat?

You might think of the word *heat* when you imagine something that feels hot. But heat also has to do with things that feel cold. In fact, heat is what causes objects to feel hot or cold. You may often use the word *heat* to mean different things. However, in this lesson, the word *heat* has only one meaning. **Heat** is the energy that is transferred between objects that are at different temperatures.

Energy Transferred Between Objects

When objects that have different temperatures come into contact, energy will be transferred between them until both objects reach the same temperature. The direction of this energy transfer is always from the object with the higher temperature to the object with the lower temperature. When you touch something cold, energy is transferred from your body to that object. When you touch something hot, like the pan shown below, energy is transferred from that object to your body.

Active Reading

8 Identify As you read, underline the direction of energy transfer between objects that are at different temperatures.

Visualize It!

9 Predict Draw an arrow to show the direction in which energy is transferred between the pan and the oven mitts.

This pan is being removed from the oven and is very hot.

© Houghton Mifflin Harcourt Publishing Company

What is Earth's atmosphere?

The mixture of gases that surrounds Earth is the **atmosphere**. This mixture is most often referred to as air. The atmosphere has many important functions. It protects you from the sun's damaging rays and also helps to maintain the right temperature range for life on Earth. For example, the temperature range on Earth allows us to have an abundant amount of liquid water. Many of the components of the atmosphere are essential for life, such as the oxygen you breathe.

Why can the temperatures of land, air, and water differ?

When the same amount of energy is being transferred, some materials will get warmer or cooler at a faster rate than other materials. Suppose you are walking along a beach on a sunny day. You may notice that the land feels warmer than the air and the water, even though they are all exposed to the same amount of energy from the sun. This is because the land warms up at a faster rate than the water and air do.

Specific Heat

The different rates at which materials become warmer or cooler are due to a property called *specific heat*. A substance that has a high specific heat requires a lot of energy to show an increase in temperature. A substance with a lower specific heat requires less energy to show the same increase in temperature. Water has a higher specific heat than land. So, water warms up more slowly than land does. Water also cools down more slowly than land does.

10 Predict Air has a lower specific heat than water. Once the sun goes down, will the air or the water cool off faster? Why?

_____

_____

_____

The temperatures of land, water, and air may differ—even when they are exposed to the same amount of energy from the sun.

© Houghton Mifflin Harcourt Publishing Company • Image Credits: ©Frank Vetere/Alamy

Heat

How is energy transferred by radiation?

On a summer day, you can feel warmth from the sun on your skin. But how did that energy reach you from the sun? The sun transfers energy to Earth by radiation. **Radiation** is the transfer of energy as electromagnetic (ee•LEK•troh•mag•NEH•tik) waves. Radiation can transfer energy between objects that are not in direct contact with each other. Many objects other than the sun also radiate energy as light and heat. These include a hot burner on a stove and a campfire, shown below.

Electromagnetic Waves

Energy from the sun is called *electromagnetic radiation*. This energy travels in waves. You are probably familiar with one form of radiation called *visible light*. You can see the visible light that comes from the sun. Electromagnetic radiation includes other forms of energy, which you cannot see. Most of the warmth that you feel from the sun is infrared radiation. This energy has a longer wavelength and lower energy than visible light. Higher-energy radiation includes x-rays and ultraviolet light.

👁 Visualize It!

11 Analyze Write a caption for the campfire photo on the right. Make sure the caption relates the image to radiation.

_____

_____

_____

Energy from this hot burner is being transferred by radiation.

© Houghton Mifflin Harcourt Publishing Company • Image Credits: (br) ©Creatas/age fotostock

Energy from the sun is transferred through space.

Where does radiation occur on Earth?

We live almost 150 million km from the sun. Yet almost all of the energy on Earth is transmitted from the sun by radiation. The sun is the major source of energy for processes at Earth's surface. Receiving that energy is absolutely vital for life on Earth. The electromagnetic waves from the sun also provide energy that drives the water cycle.

When solar radiation reaches Earth, some of the energy is reflected and scattered by Earth's atmosphere. But much of the energy passes through Earth's atmosphere and reaches Earth's surface. Some of the energy that Earth receives from the sun is absorbed by the atmosphere, geosphere, and hydrosphere. Then, the energy is changed into thermal energy. This thermal energy may be reradiated into the Earth system or into space. Much of the energy is transferred through Earth's systems by the two other ways—convection and conduction.

© Houghton Mifflin Harcourt Publishing Company

Think Outside the Book

13 Apply Research ultraviolet radiation from the sun and its role in causing sunburns.

12 Summarize Give two examples of what happens when energy from the sun reaches Earth.

_____

_____

_____

_____

How is energy transferred by convection?

Have you ever watched a pot of boiling water, such as the one below? If so, you have seen convection. **Convection** (kun•VECK•shuhn) is the transfer of energy due to the movement of matter. As water warms up at the bottom of the pot, some of the hot water rises. At the same time, cooler water from other parts of the pot sink and replace the rising water. This water is then warmed and the cycle continues.

Convection Currents

Convection involves the movement of matter due to differences in density. Convection occurs because most matter becomes less dense when it gets warmer. When most matter becomes warmer, it undergoes thermal expansion and a decrease in density. This less-dense matter is forced upward by the surrounding colder, denser matter that is sinking. As the hot matter rises, it cools and becomes more dense. This causes it to sink back down. This cycling of matter is called a *convection current*. Convection most often occurs in fluids, such as water and air. But convection can also happen in solids.

wax

energy sources

convection current

© Houghton Mifflin Harcourt Publishing Company

Visualize It! Inquiry

14 Apply How is convection related to the rise and fall of wax in lava lamps?

_____

_____

_____

_____

Where does convection occur on Earth?

If Earth's surface is warmer than the air, energy will be transferred from the ground to the air. As the air becomes warmer, it becomes less dense. This air is pushed upward and out of the way by cooler, denser air that is sinking. As the warm air rises, it cools and becomes denser and begins to sink back toward Earth's surface. This cycle moves energy through the atmosphere.

Convection currents also occur in the ocean because of differences in the density of ocean water. More dense water sinks to the ocean floor, and less dense water moves toward the surface. The density of ocean water is influenced by temperature and the amount of salt in the water. Cold water is denser than warmer water. Water that contains a lot of salt is more dense than less-salty water.

Energy produced deep inside Earth heats rock in the mantle. The heated rock becomes less dense and is pushed up toward Earth's surface by the cooler, denser surrounding rock. Once cooled near the surface, the rock sinks. These convection currents transfer energy from Earth's core toward Earth's surface. These currents also cause the movement of tectonic plates.

Active Reading 15 **Name** What are three of Earth's spheres in which energy is transferred by convection?

_____

_____

Visualize It!

16 **Apply** Draw the convection current that could occur in the body of water in this image.

Convection currents occur throughout the Earth system.

Ouch!

How is energy transferred by conduction?

Have you ever touched an ice cube and wondered why it feels cold? An ice cube has only a small amount of energy, compared to your hand. Energy is transferred to the ice cube from your hand through the process of conduction. **Conduction** (kun•DUHK•shuhn) is the transfer of energy from one object to another object through direct contact.

Direct Contact

Remember that the atoms or molecules in a substance are constantly moving. Even a solid block of ice has particles in constant motion. When objects at different temperatures touch, their particles interact. Conduction involves the faster-moving particles of the warmer object transferring energy to the slower-moving particles in the cooler object. The greater the difference in energy of the particles, the faster the transfer of energy by conduction occurs.

Active Reading **17 Apply** Name two examples of conduction that you experience every day.

_____
_____
_____

These desert sands would feel hot because of conduction.

© Houghton Mifflin Harcourt Publishing Company • Image Credits: (bkgd) ©Jean-Claude Winkler/Getty Images; (inset) ©afrendo Travel/Stockbyte/Getty Images

Where does conduction occur on Earth?

Energy can be transferred between the geosphere and the atmosphere by conduction. When cooler air molecules come into direct contact with the warm ground, energy is passed to the air by conduction. Conduction between the ground and the air happens only within a few centimeters of Earth's surface.

Conduction also happens between particles of air and particles of water. For example, if air transfers enough energy to liquid water, the water may evaporate. If water vapor transfers energy to the air, the kinetic energy of the water decreases. As a result, the water vapor may condense to form liquid water droplets.

Inside Earth, energy transfers between rock particles by conduction. However, rock is a poor conductor of heat, so this process happens very slowly.

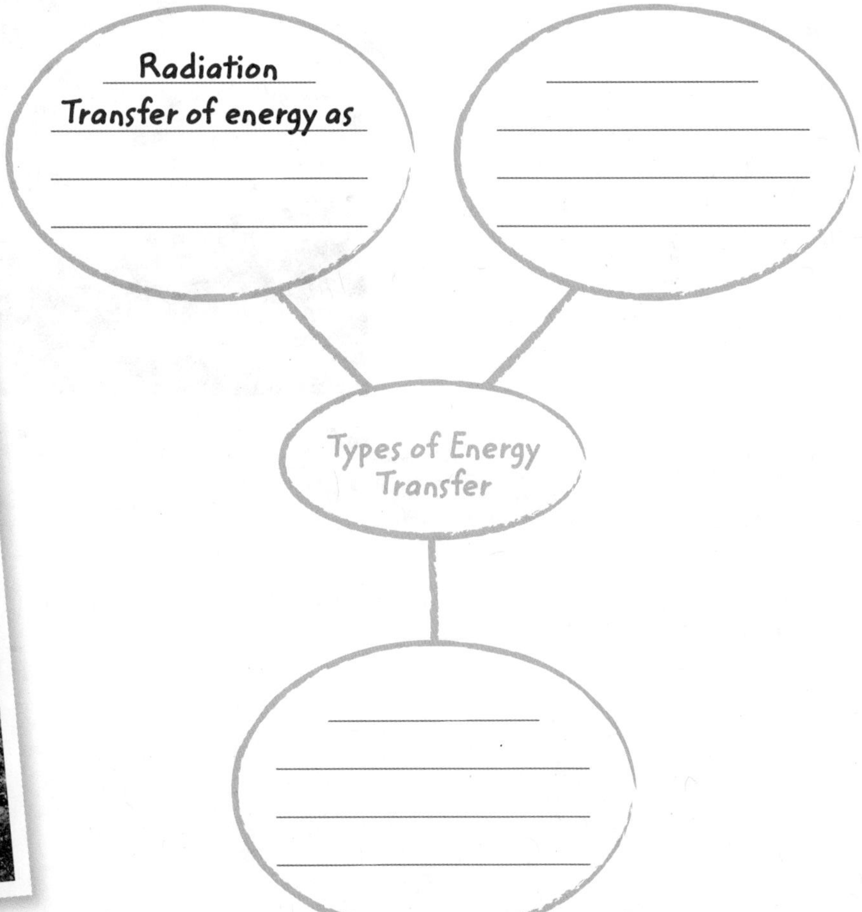

© Houghton Mifflin Harcourt Publishing Company • Image Credits: (bkgd) ©Jean-Claude Winkler/Getty Images; (inset) ©altrendo travel/Stockbyte/Getty Images

Visualize It!

18 Compare Does conduction also occur in a city like the one shown below? Explain.

_____

_____

_____

_____

_____

19 Summarize Complete the following spider map by describing the three types of energy transfer. One answer has been started for you.

Radiation
Transfer of energy as
_____
_____

_____
_____
_____

Types of Energy Transfer

_____
_____
_____
_____

Visual Summary

To complete this summary, fill in the blanks with the correct word or phrase. Then, use the key below to check your answers. You can use this page to review the main concepts of the lesson.

Energy Transfer

Heat is the energy that is transferred between objects that are at different temperatures.

20 The particles in a hot pan have _____ kinetic energy than the particles in a cool oven mitt.

Energy can be transferred in different ways.

21 The three ways that energy can be transferred are labeled in the image as

A: _____

B: _____

C: _____

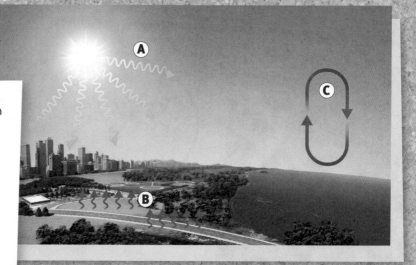

Answers: 20 more; 21 A: radiation, B: conduction, C: convection

22 Apply What type of energy transfer is responsible for making you feel cold when you are swimming in cool water? Explain your answer.

© Houghton Mifflin Harcourt Publishing Company

Lesson Review

Vocabulary

In your own words, define the following terms.

1 radiation

_____

_____

2 convection

_____

_____

3 conduction

_____

_____

Key Concepts

4 Compare What is the difference between temperature, thermal energy, and heat?

_____

_____

_____

_____

5 Describe What is happening to a substance undergoing thermal expansion?

_____

_____

_____

6 Explain What is the main source of energy for most processes at Earth's surface?

_____

7 Summarize What happens when two objects at different temperatures touch? Name one place where it occurs in Earth's system.

_____

_____

_____

8 Identify What is an example of convection in Earth's system?

_____

Critical Thinking

9 Apply Why can metal utensils get too hot to touch when you are cooking with them?

_____

_____

_____

10 Predict You are doing an experiment outside on a sunny day. You find the temperature of some sand is 28°C. You also find the temperature of some water is 25°C. Explain the difference in temperatures.

_____

_____

_____

_____

Use this image to answer the following questions.

11 Analyze Name one example of where energy transfer by radiation is occurring.

_____

12 Analyze Name one example of where energy transfer by conduction is occurring.

_____

13 Analyze Name one example of where energy transfer by convection is occurring.

_____

© Houghton Mifflin Harcourt Publishing Company

My Notes

© Houghton Mifflin Harcourt Publishing Company

© Houghton Mifflin Harcourt Publishing Company

Engineering Design Process

Skills
Identify a need
Conduct research
✓ Brainstorm solutions
✓ Select a solution
Design a prototype
✓ Build a prototype
✓ Test and evaluate
✓ Redesign to improve
✓ Communicate results

Objectives

- Explain how a need for clean energy has driven a technological solution.
- Describe two examples of wind-powered generators.
- Design a technological solution to a problem.
- Test and modify a prototype to achieve the desired result.

Building a Wind Turbine

During the Industrial Revolution, machines began to replace human and animal power for doing work. From agriculture and manufacturing to transportation, machines made work faster and easier. However, these machines needed fuel. Fossil fuels, such as coal, oil, and gasoline, powered the Industrial Revolution and are still used today. But burning fossil fuels produces waste products that harm the environment. In addition, fossil fuels will eventually run out. As a result, we need to better understand alternative, renewable sources of energy.

Brainstorming Solutions

There are many sources of energy besides fossil fuels. One of the most abundant renewable sources is wind. A wind turbine is a device that uses energy from the wind to turn an axle. The turning axle can be attached to other equipment to do jobs such as pumping water, cutting lumber, or generating electricity. To generate electricity, the axle spins magnets around a coiled wire. This causes electrons to flow in the wire. Flowing electrons produce an electric current. Electric current is used to power homes and businesses or electrical energy can be stored in a battery.

1 Brainstorm What are other possible sources of renewable energy that could be used to power a generator?

_____

_____

_____

_____

_____

_____

_____

© Houghton Mifflin Harcourt Publishing Company • Image Credits: ©Steve Cole/Getty Images

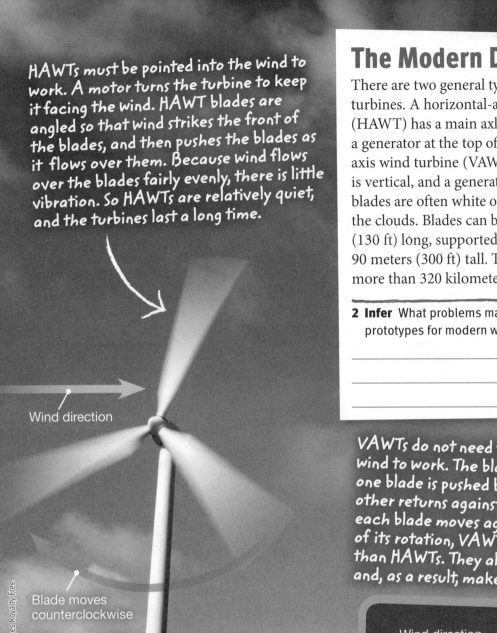

HAWTs must be pointed into the wind to work. A motor turns the turbine to keep it facing the wind. HAWT blades are angled so that wind strikes the front of the blades, and then pushes the blades as it flows over them. Because wind flows over the blades fairly evenly, there is little vibration. So HAWTs are relatively quiet, and the turbines last a long time.

Wind direction

Blade moves counterclockwise

© Houghton Mifflin Harcourt Publishing Company • Image Credits: (bg) ©Stockbyte/Alamy; (b) ©Getty Images Royalty Free

The Modern Design

There are two general types of modern wind turbines. A horizontal-axis wind turbine (HAWT) has a main axle that is horizontal, and a generator at the top of a tall tower. A vertical-axis wind turbine (VAWT) has a main axle that is vertical, and a generator at ground level. The blades are often white or light gray, to blend with the clouds. Blades can be more than 40 meters (130 ft) long, supported by towers more than 90 meters (300 ft) tall. The blade tips can travel more than 320 kilometers (200 mi) per hour!

2 Infer What problems may have been encountered as prototypes for modern wind turbines were tested?

_____

_____

_____

VAWTs do not need to be pointed into the wind to work. The blades are made so that one blade is pushed by the wind while the other returns against the wind. But because each blade moves against the wind for part of its rotation, VAWTs are less efficient than HAWTs. They also tend to vibrate more and, as a result, make more noise.

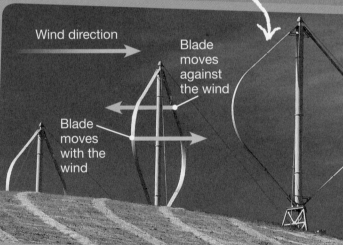

Wind direction

Blade moves against the wind

Blade moves with the wind

You Try It!

Now it's your turn to design a wind turbine that will generate electricity and light a small bulb.

 # You Try It!

Now it's your turn to design an efficient wind turbine that will generate enough electricity to light a small bulb.

Materials

✔ assorted wind turbine parts

✔ fan

✔ gears

✔ small bulb

✔ small motor

✔ socket

① Brainstorm solutions

Brainstorm ideas for a wind turbine that will turn an axle on a small motor. The blades must turn fast enough so that the motor generates enough electricity to light a small bulb. Fill in the table below with as many ideas as you can for each part of your wind turbine. Circle each idea you decide to try.

Type of axis	Shape of turbine	Attaching axis to motor	Control speed

② Select a solution

From the table above, choose the features for the turbine you will build. In the space below, draw a model of your wind turbine idea. Include all the parts and show how they will be connected.

© Houghton Mifflin Harcourt Publishing Company

(3) Build a prototype

Now build your wind turbine. As you built your turbine, were there some parts of your design that could not be assembled as you had predicted? What parts did you have to revise as you were building the prototype?

_____

_____

_____

_____

(4) Test and evaluate

Point a fan at your wind turbine and see what happens. Did the bulb light? If not, what parts of your turbine could you revise?

_____

_____

_____

_____

(5) Redesign to improve

Choose one part to revise. Modify your design and then test again. Repeat this process until your turbine lights up the light bulb.

_____

_____

_____

_____

(6) Communicate results

Which part of the turbine seemed to have the greatest effect on the brightness of the light bulb?

_____

_____

_____

_____

_____

© Houghton Mifflin Harcourt Publishing Company • Image Credits:

Wind in the Atmosphere

ESSENTIAL QUESTION

What is wind?

By the end of this lesson, you should be able to explain how energy provided by the sun causes atmospheric movement, called wind.

6.ESS2.2, 6.ESS2.3, 6.PS3.4

Although you cannot see wind, you can see how it affects things like these kites.

© Houghton Mifflin Harcourt Publishing Company • Image Credits: ©Martin Bennett/Alamy

Engage Your Brain

1 Predict Check T or F to show whether you think each statement is true or false.

T	F	
☐	☐	The atmosphere is often referred to as air.
☐	☐	Wind does not have direction.
☐	☐	During the day, there is often a wind blowing toward shore from the ocean or a large lake.
☐	☐	Cold air rises and warm air sinks.

2 Explain If you opened the valve on this bicycle tire, what would happen to the air inside of the tire? Why do you think that would happen?

_____

_____

_____

Active Reading

3 Synthesize You can often define an unknown phrase if you know the meaning of its word parts. Use the word parts below to make an educated guess about the meanings of the phrases *local wind* and *global wind*.

Word part	Meaning
wind	movement of air due to differences in air pressure
local	involving a particular area
global	involving the entire Earth

Vocabulary Terms

• wind
• Coriolis effect
• global wind
• jet stream
• local wind

4 Identify This list contains the vocabulary terms you'll learn in this lesson. As you read, circle the definition of each term.

local wind:

_____

_____

global wind:

_____

_____

© Houghton Mifflin Harcourt Publishing Company • Image Credits: (bkgd) ©Martin Bennett/Alamy; (t) ©Yo Oura/Photonica/Getty Images

Blow It Out!

What causes wind?

The next time you feel the wind blowing, you can thank the sun! The sun does not warm the whole surface of the Earth in a uniform manner. This uneven heating causes the air above Earth's surface to be at different temperatures. Cold air is more dense than warmer air is. Colder, denser air sinks. When denser air sinks, it places greater pressure on the surface of Earth than warmer, less-dense air does. This results in areas of higher air pressure. Air moves from areas of higher pressure toward areas of lower pressure. The movement of air caused by differences in air pressure is called **wind**. The greater the differences in air pressure, the faster the air moves.

Areas of High and Low Pressure

Cold, dense air at the poles creates areas of high pressure at the poles. Warm, less-dense air at the equator forms an area of lower pressure. This pressure gradient results in global movement of air. However, instead of moving in one circle between the equator and the poles, air moves in smaller circular patterns called *convection cells,* shown below. As air moves from the equator, it cools and becomes more dense. At about 30°N and 30°S latitudes, a high-pressure belt results from the sinking of air. Near the poles, cold air warms as it moves away from the poles. At around 60°N and 60°S latitudes, a low-pressure belt forms as the warmed air is pushed upward.

Visualize It!

5 Identify In the white oval area on the map, draw the convection cell that was left out. Use a pencil to indicate warm air and a pen to indicate cool air.

The warming and cooling of air produces pressure belts every 30° of latitude.

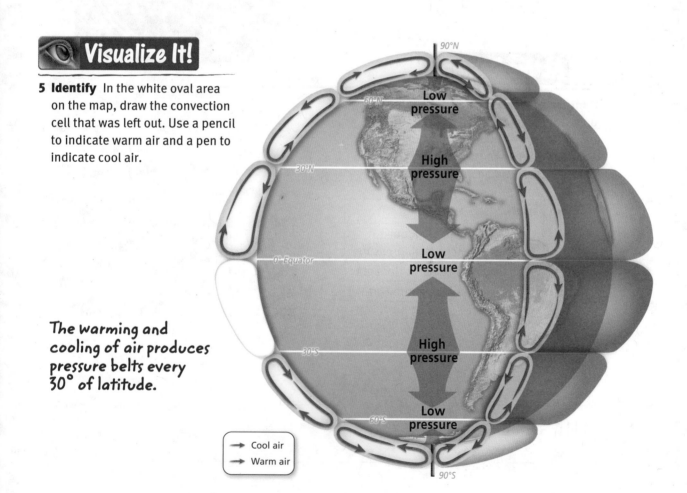

→ Cool air
→ Warm air

© Houghton Mifflin Harcourt Publishing Company • Image Credits: (t) ©Alejandro Ernesto/epa/Corbis

How does Earth's rotation affect wind?

Active Reading

6 Identify As you read, underline how air movement in the Northern Hemisphere is influenced by the Coriolis effect.

Pressure differences cause air to move between the equator and the poles. If Earth was not rotating, winds would blow in a straight line. However, winds are deflected, or curved, due to Earth's rotation, as shown below. The apparent curving of the path of a moving object from an otherwise straight path due to Earth's rotation is called the **Coriolis effect** (kawr•ee•OH•lis ih•FEKT). This effect is most noticeable over long distances.

Because each point on Earth makes one complete rotation every day, points closer to the equator must travel farther and, therefore, faster than points closer to the poles do. When air moves from the equator toward the North Pole, it maintains its initial speed and direction. If the air travels far enough north, it will have traveled farther east than a point on the ground beneath it. As a result, the air appears to follow a curved path toward the east. Air moving from the North Pole to the equator appears to curve to the west because the air moves east more slowly than a point on the ground beneath it does. Therefore, in the Northern Hemisphere, air moving to the north curves to the east and air moving to the south curves to the west.

Visualize It!

7 Label In the white ovals on the map, draw the direction and path of the winds that would occur at those locations on Earth.

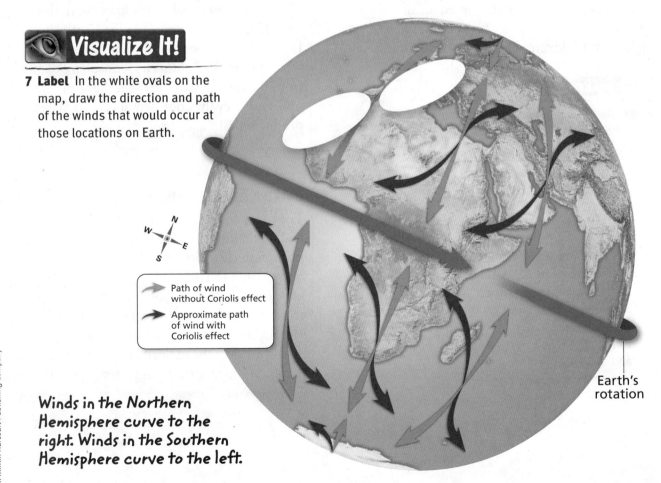

→ Path of wind without Coriolis effect

→ Approximate path of wind with Coriolis effect

Earth's rotation

Winds in the Northern Hemisphere curve to the right. Winds in the Southern Hemisphere curve to the left.

© Houghton Mifflin Harcourt Publishing Company

Blowin' Around

What are examples of global winds?

Recall that air travels in circular patterns called convection cells that cover approximately 30° of latitude. Pressure belts at every 30° of latitude and the Coriolis effect produce patterns of calm areas and wind systems. These wind systems occur at or near Earth's surface and are called **global winds**. As shown at the right, the major global wind systems are the *polar easterlies* (EE•ster•leez), the *westerlies* (WES•ter•leez), and the *trade winds*. Winds such as polar easterlies and westerlies are named for the direction from which they blow. Calm areas include the doldrums and the horse latitudes.

Active Reading

8 Explain If something is being carried by westerlies, what direction is it moving toward?

_____

_____

Think Outside the Book Inquiry

9 Model Winds are described according to their direction and speed. Research wind vanes and what they are used for. Design and build your own wind vane.

Trade Winds

The trade winds blow between 30° latitude and the equator in both hemispheres. The rotation of Earth causes the trade winds to curve to the west. Therefore, trade winds in the Northern Hemisphere come from the northeast, and trade winds in the Southern Hemisphere come from the southeast. These winds became known as the trade winds because sailors relied on them to sail from Europe to the Americas.

Westerlies

The westerlies blow between 30° and 60° latitudes in both hemispheres. The rotation of Earth causes these winds to curve to the east. Therefore, westerlies in the Northern Hemisphere come from the southwest, and westerlies in the Southern Hemisphere come from the northwest. The westerlies can carry moist air over the continental United States, producing rain and snow.

Polar Easterlies

The polar easterlies blow between the poles and 60° latitude in both hemispheres. The polar easterlies form as cold, sinking air moves from the poles toward 60°N and 60°S latitudes. The rotation of Earth causes these winds to curve to the west. In the Northern Hemisphere, polar easterlies can carry cold Arctic air over the majority of the United States, producing snow and freezing weather.

© Houghton Mifflin Harcourt Publishing Company

10 Identify Label the polar easterlies, the westerlies, and the trade winds in the white boxes on the map.

The major global wind systems

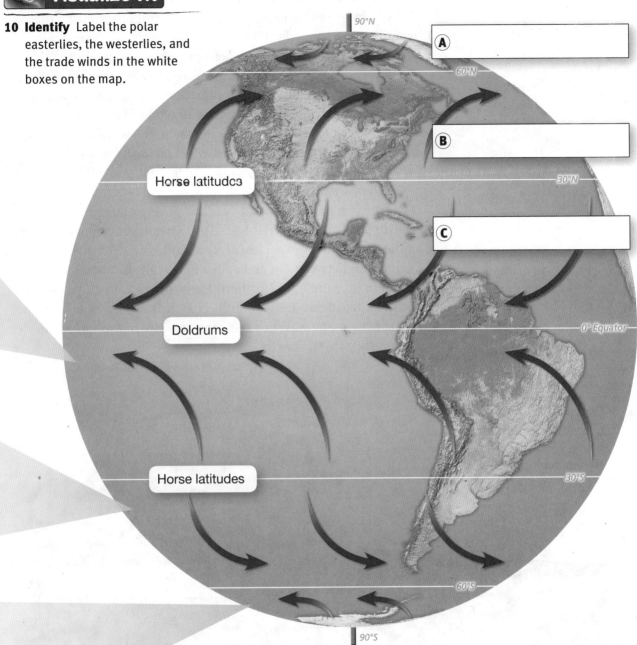

A

B

Horse latitudes

Doldrums

C

Horse latitudes

90°N

60°N

30°N

0° Equator

30°S

60°S

90°S

The Doldrums and Horse Latitudes

The trade winds of both hemispheres meet in a calm area around the equator called the *doldrums* (DOHL•druhmz). Very little wind blows in the doldrums because the warm, less-dense air results in an area of low pressure. The name doldrums means "dull" or "sluggish." At about 30° latitude in both hemispheres, air stops moving and sinks. This forms calm areas called the *horse latitudes*. This name was given to these areas when sailing ships carried horses from Europe to the Americas. When ships were stalled in these areas, horses were sometimes thrown overboard to save water.

© Houghton Mifflin Harcourt Publishing Company

The Jet Streams

A flight from Seattle to Boston can be 30 min faster than a flight from Boston to Seattle. Why? Pilots can take advantage of a jet stream. **Jet streams** are narrow belts of high-speed winds that blow from west to east, between 7 km and 16 km above Earth's surface. Airplanes traveling in the same direction as a jet stream go faster than those traveling in the opposite direction of a jet stream. When an airplane is traveling "with" a jet stream, the wind is helping the airplane move forward. However, when an airplane is traveling "against" the jet stream, the wind is making it more difficult for the plane to move forward.

The two main jet streams are the polar jet stream and the subtropical (suhb•TRAHP•i•kuhl) jet stream, shown below. Each of the hemispheres experiences these jet streams. Jet streams follow boundaries between hot and cold air and can shift north and south. In the winter, as Northern Hemisphere temperatures cool, the polar jet stream moves south. This shift brings cold Arctic air to the United States. When temperatures rise in the spring, this jet stream shifts to the north.

Active Reading

11 Identify As you read, underline the direction that the jet streams travel.

Visualize It!

12 Identify Label the polar jet stream and the subtropical jet stream in the Northern Hemisphere.

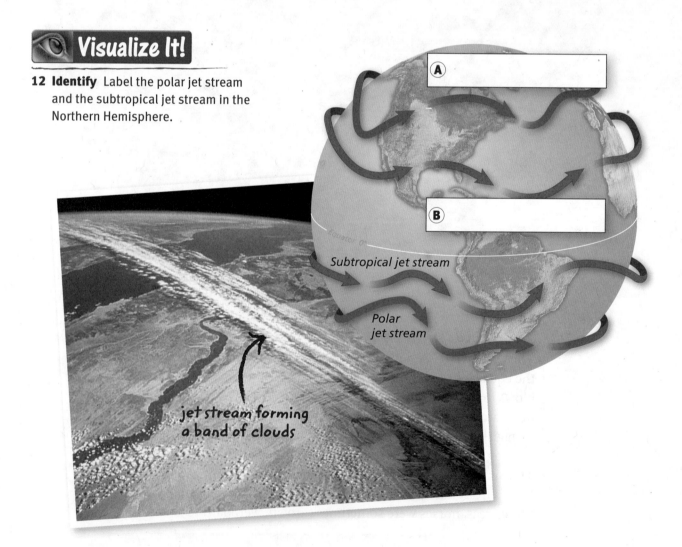

Subtropical jet stream

Polar jet stream

jet stream forming a band of clouds

© Houghton Mifflin Harcourt Publishing Company • Image Credits: (bl) ©NASA/Science Source/Photo Researchers, Inc.

Desert Trades

How does some of the Sahara end up in the Americas?
Global winds carry it.

Trade Wind Carriers
Trade winds can carry Saharan dust across the Atlantic Ocean to Florida and the Caribbean.

Africa

Florida Meets the Sahara
This hazy skyline in Miami is the result of a dust storm. Where did the dust come from? It all started in the Sahara.

The Sahara
The Sahara is the world's largest hot desert. Sand and dust storms that produce skies like this are very common in this desert.

Extend

Inquiry

13 Explain Look at a map and explain how trade winds carry dust from the Sahara to the Caribbean.

14 Relate Investigate the winds that blow in your community. Where do they usually come from? Identify the wind system that could be involved.

15 Apply Investigate how winds played a role in distributing radioactive waste that was released after an explosion at the Chernobyl Nuclear Power Plant in Ukraine. Present your findings as a map illustration or in a poster.

© Houghton Mifflin Harcourt Publishing Company • Image Credits: (bkgd) ©Andrew McConnell/Alamy; (l) ©Joe Raedle/Getty Images; (r) ©Orbital Imaging Corporation/Photo Researchers, Inc.

Feelin' Breezy

What are examples of local winds?

Local geographic features, such as a body of water or a mountain, can produce temperature and pressure differences that cause local winds. Unlike global winds, **local winds** are the movement of air over short distances. They can blow from any direction, depending on the features of the area.

Active Reading

16 Identify As you read, underline two examples of geographic features that contribute to the formation of local winds.

Sea and Land Breezes

Have you ever felt a cool breeze coming off the ocean or a lake? If so, you were experiencing a sea breeze. Large bodies of water take longer to warm up than land does. During the day, air above land becomes warmer than air above water. The colder, denser air over water flows toward the land and pushes the warm air on the land upward. While water takes longer to warm than land does, land cools faster than water does. At night, cooler air on land causes a higher-pressure zone over the land. So, a wind blows from the land toward the water. This type of local wind is called a land breeze.

Visualize It!

17 Analyze Label the areas of high pressure and low pressure.

sea breeze

B _____ pressure

A _____ pressure

land breeze

D _____ pressure

C _____ pressure

© Houghton Mifflin Harcourt Publishing Company • Image Credits: (t) ©Pascal Goetgheluck/Photo Researchers, Inc.

Valley and Mountain Breezes

Areas that have mountains and valleys experience local winds called mountain and valley breezes. During the day, the sun warms the air along the mountain slopes faster than the air in the valleys. This uneven heating results in areas of lower pressure near the mountain tops. This pressure difference causes a valley breeze, which flows from the valley up the slopes of the mountains. Many birds float on valley breezes to conserve energy. At nightfall, the air along the mountain slopes cools and moves down into the valley. This local wind is called a mountain breeze.

Visualize It!

18 Analyze Label the areas of high pressure and low pressure.

valley breeze

Ⓑ _____ pressure

Ⓐ _____ pressure

mountain breeze

Ⓓ _____ pressure

Ⓒ _____ pressure

© Houghton Mifflin Harcourt Publishing Company

Visual Summary

To complete this summary, circle the correct word or phrases. Then use the key below to check your answers. You can use this page to review the main concepts of the lesson.

Wind is the movement of air from areas of higher pressure to areas of lower pressure.

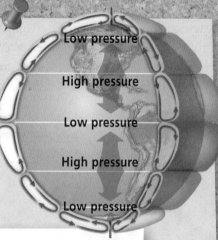

Low pressure

High pressure

Low pressure

High pressure

Low pressure

19 Cool air sinks, causing an area of high / low air pressure.

Global wind systems occur on Earth.

20 High-speed wind between 7 km and 16 km above Earth's surface is a jet stream / mountain breeze.

Wind in the Atmosphere

Geographic features can produce local winds.

21 During the day, an area of high / low air pressure forms over water and a sea / land breeze occurs.

Answers: 19 high; 20 jet stream; 21 high, sea

22 Explain Would there be winds if the air above Earth's surface was the same temperature everywhere? Explain your answer.

© Houghton Mifflin Harcourt Publishing Company • Image Credits: (tr) ©NASA/Science Source/Photo Researchers, Inc.

Lesson Review

Vocabulary

Fill in the blanks with the term that best completes the following sentences.

1 Another term for air movement caused by differences in air pressure is

_____

2 Pilots often take advantage of the _____ , which are high-speed winds between 7 km and 16 km above Earth's surface.

3 The apparent curving of winds due to Earth's rotation is the _____

Key Concepts

4 Explain How does the sun cause wind?

_____
_____
_____
_____

5 Predict If Earth did not rotate, what would happen to the global winds? Why?

_____
_____
_____

6 Explain How do convection cells in Earth's atmosphere cause high- and low-pressure belts?

_____
_____
_____
_____

7 Describe What factors contribute to global winds? Identify areas where winds are weak.

_____
_____
_____
_____

8 Identify Name a latitude where each of the following occurs: polar easterlies, westerlies, and trade winds.

_____
_____

Critical Thinking

9 Predict How would local winds be affected if water and land absorbed and released heat at the same rate? Explain your answer.

_____
_____
_____

10 Compare How is a land breeze similar to a sea breeze? How do they differ?

_____
_____
_____
_____

Use this image to answer the following questions.

11 Analyze What type of local wind would you experience if you were standing in the valley? Explain your answer.

_____
_____

12 Infer Would the local wind change if it was nighttime? Explain.

_____
_____
_____
_____

© Houghton Mifflin Harcourt Publishing Company

My Notes

© Houghton Mifflin Harcourt Publishing Company

© Houghton Mifflin Harcourt Publishing Company

Ocean Currents

ESSENTIAL QUESTION

How does water move in the ocean?

By the end of this lesson, you should be able to describe the movement of ocean water, explain what factors influence this movement, and explain why ocean circulation is important in Earth's system.

6.ESS2.1, 6.ESS2.2, 6.ESS2.3

This iceberg off the coast of Newfoundland broke off an Arctic ice sheet and drifted south on ocean surface currents.

© Houghton Mifflin Harcourt Publishing Company • Image Credits: ©Thomas Kitchin & Victoria Hurst/First Light/Getty Images

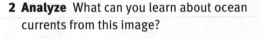

Lesson Labs

Quick Labs
- Modeling the Coriolis Effect
- The Formation of Deep Currents
- Can Messages Travel on Ocean Water?

 Engage Your Brain

1 Predict Check T or F to show whether you think each statement is true or false.

T	F	
☐	☐	Ocean currents are always cold.
☐	☐	Continents affect the directions of currents.
☐	☐	Currents only flow near the surface of the ocean.
☐	☐	Wind affects currents.
☐	☐	The sun affects currents near the surface of the ocean.

This image shows sea ice caught in ocean currents.

2 Analyze What can you learn about ocean currents from this image?

_____

_____

_____

_____

 Active Reading

3 Synthesize You can often define an unknown word if you know the meaning of its word parts. Use the word parts and sentence below to make an educated guess about the meaning of the word *upwelling*.

Word part	Meaning
up-	from beneath the ground or water
well	to rise

Example Sentence
In areas where <u>upwelling</u> occurs, plankton feed on nutrients from deep in the ocean.

upwelling:

_____

_____

Vocabulary Terms
- ocean current
- surface current
- Coriolis effect
- deep current
- convection current
- upwelling

4 Apply As you learn the definition of each vocabulary term in this lesson, create your own definition or sketch to help you remember the meaning of the term.

© Houghton Mifflin Harcourt Publishing Company • Image Credits: (bkg) ©Thomas Kitchin & Victoria Hurst/First Light/Getty Images; (t) ©NASA

Going with the Flow

What are ocean currents?

The oceans contain streamlike movements of water called **ocean currents**. Ocean currents that occur at or near the surface of the ocean, caused by wind, are called **surface currents**. Most surface currents reach depths of about 100 m, but some go deeper. Surface currents also reach lengths of several thousand kilometers and can stretch across oceans. An example of a surface current is the Gulf Stream. The Gulf Stream is one of the strongest surface currents on Earth. The Gulf Stream transports, or moves, more water each year than is transported by all the rivers in the world combined.

Infrared cameras on satellites provide images that show differences in temperature. Scientists add color to the images afterward to highlight the different temperatures, as shown below.

What affects surface currents?

Surface currents are affected by three factors: continental deflections, the Coriolis effect, and global winds. These factors keep surface currents flowing in distinct patterns around Earth.

Active Reading

5 Identify As you read, underline three factors that affect surface currents.

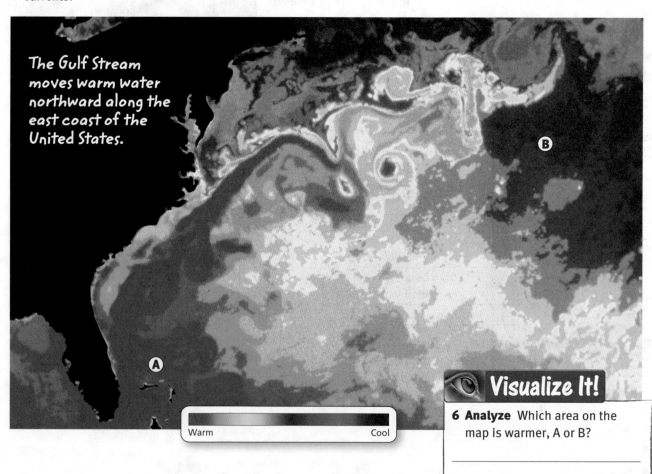

The Gulf Stream moves warm water northward along the east coast of the United States.

Ⓐ

Ⓑ

Warm   Cool

Visualize It!

6 Analyze Which area on the map is warmer, A or B?

_____

© Houghton Mifflin Harcourt Publishing Company • Image Credits: ©Raven/Photo Researchers, Inc.

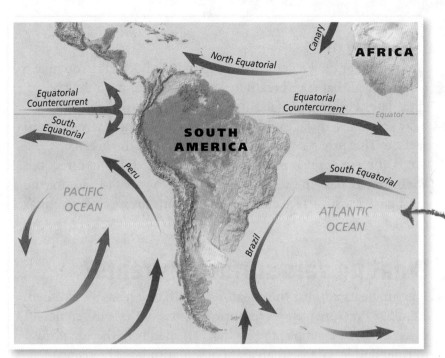

7 Identify Circle areas on the map where ocean currents have been deflected by a land mass.

Currents change direction when they meet continents.

Continental Deflections

If Earth's surface were covered only with water, surface currents would simply travel continually in one direction. However, water does not cover the entire surface of Earth. Continents rise above sea level over about one-third of Earth's surface. When surface currents meet continents, the currents are deflected and change direction. For example, the South Equatorial Current turns southward as it meets the coast of South America.

The Coriolis Effect

Earth's rotation causes all wind and ocean currents, except on the equator, to be deflected from the paths they would take if Earth did not rotate. The deflection of moving objects from a straight path due to Earth's rotation is called the **Coriolis effect** (kawr•ee•OH•lis ih•FEKT). Earth is spherical, so Earth's circumference at latitudes above and below the equator is shorter than the circumference at the equator. But the period of rotation is always 24 hours. Therefore, points on Earth near the equator travel faster than points closer to the poles.

The difference in speed of rotation causes the Coriolis effect. For example, wind and water traveling south from the North Pole actually go toward the southwest instead of straight south. Wind and water deflect to the right because the wind and water move east more slowly than Earth rotates beneath them. In the Northern Hemisphere, currents are deflected to the right. In the Southern Hemisphere, currents are deflected to the left.

The Coriolis effect is most noticeable for objects that travel over long distances, without any interruptions. Over short distances, the difference in Earth's rotational speed from one point to another point is not great enough to cause noticeable deflection.

In the Northern Hemisphere, currents are deflected to the right.

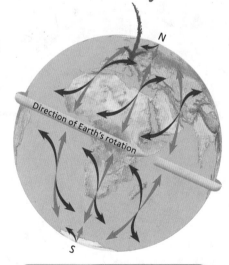

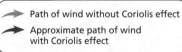

→ Path of wind without Coriolis effect
→ Approximate path of wind with Coriolis effect

© Houghton Mifflin Harcourt Publishing Company

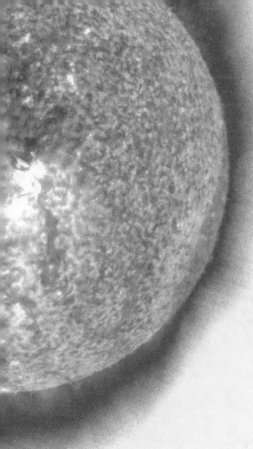

Global Winds

Have you ever blown gently on a cup of hot chocolate? You may have noticed that your breath makes ripples that push the hot chocolate across the surface of the liquid. Similarly, winds that blow across the surface of Earth's oceans push water across Earth's surface. This process causes surface currents in the ocean.

Different winds cause currents to flow in different directions. For example, near the equator, the winds blow east to west for the most part. Most surface currents in the same area follow a similar pattern.

What powers surface currents?

The sun heats air near the equator more than it heats air at other latitudes. Pressure differences form because of these differences in heating. For example, the air that is heated near the equator is warmer and less dense than air at other latitudes. The rising of warm air creates an area of low pressure near the equator. Pressure differences in the atmosphere cause the wind to form. So, the sun causes winds to form, and winds cause surface currents to form. Therefore, the major source of the energy that powers surface currents is the sun.

8 Analyze Fill in the cause-and-effect chart to show how the sun's energy powers surface ocean currents.

The sun heats the atmosphere.

© Houghton Mifflin Harcourt Publishing Company • Image Credits: ©NASA/Photo Researchers, Inc.

Global Surface Winds

- → Ocean surface wind

Global Surface Currents

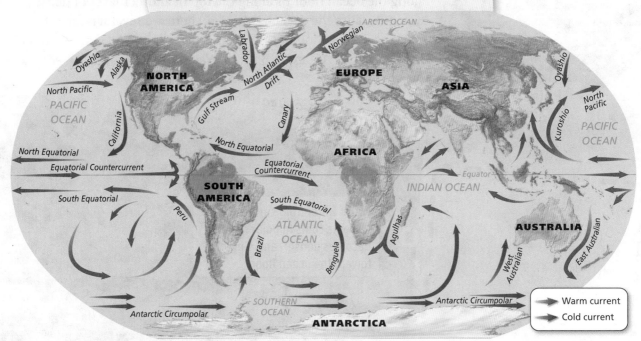

- → Warm current
- → Cold current

© Houghton Mifflin Harcourt Publishing Company

Visualize It!

9 Analyze Circle the same area on each map. Describe what you observe about these two areas.

_____

_____

_____

Current Events

How do deep currents form?

10 Identify As you read, underline the cause of deep currents.

Movements of ocean water far below the surface are called **deep currents**. Deep currents are caused by differences in water density. *Density* is the amount of matter in a given space or volume. The density of ocean water is affected by salinity (suh•LIN•ih•tee) and temperature. *Salinity* is a measure of the amount of dissolved salts or solids in a liquid. Water with high salinity is denser than water with low salinity. And cold water is denser than warm water. When water cools, it contracts and the water molecules move closer together. This contraction makes the water denser. When water warms, it expands and the water molecules move farther apart. The warm water is less dense, so it rises above the cold water.

When ocean water at the surface becomes denser than water below it, the denser water sinks. The water moves from the surface to the deep ocean, forming deep currents. Deep currents flow along the ocean floor or along the top of another layer of denser water. Because the ocean is so deep, there are several layers of water at any location in the ocean. The deepest and densest water in the ocean is Antarctic Bottom Water, near Antarctica.

Polar region

Convection current

B Warm water from surface currents cools in polar regions, becomes denser, and sinks toward the ocean floor.

C Deep currents carry colder, denser water in the deep ocean from polar regions to other parts of Earth.

Visualize It!

11 Illustrate Complete the drawing at part B on the diagram.

© Houghton Mifflin Harcourt Publishing Company • Image Credits: (inset) ©Andrew Watson/Fotolia

What are convection currents?

As you read about convection currents, refer to the illustration below. Surface currents and deep currents are linked in the ocean. Together they form convection currents. In the ocean, a **convection current** is a movement of water that results from density differences. Convection currents can be vertical, circular, or cyclical. Think of convection currents in the ocean as a conveyor belt. Surface currents make up the top part of the belt. Deep currents make up the bottom part of the belt. Water from a surface current may become a deep current in areas where water density increases. Deep current water then rises up to the surface in areas where the surface current is carrying low-density water away.

How do convection currents transfer energy?

Convection currents transfer energy. Water at the ocean's surface absorbs energy from the sun. Surface currents carry this energy to colder regions. The warm water loses energy to its surroundings and cools. As the water cools, it becomes denser and it sinks. The cold water travels along the ocean bottom. Then, the cold water rises to the surface as warm surface water moves away. The cold water absorbs energy from the sun, and the cycle continues.

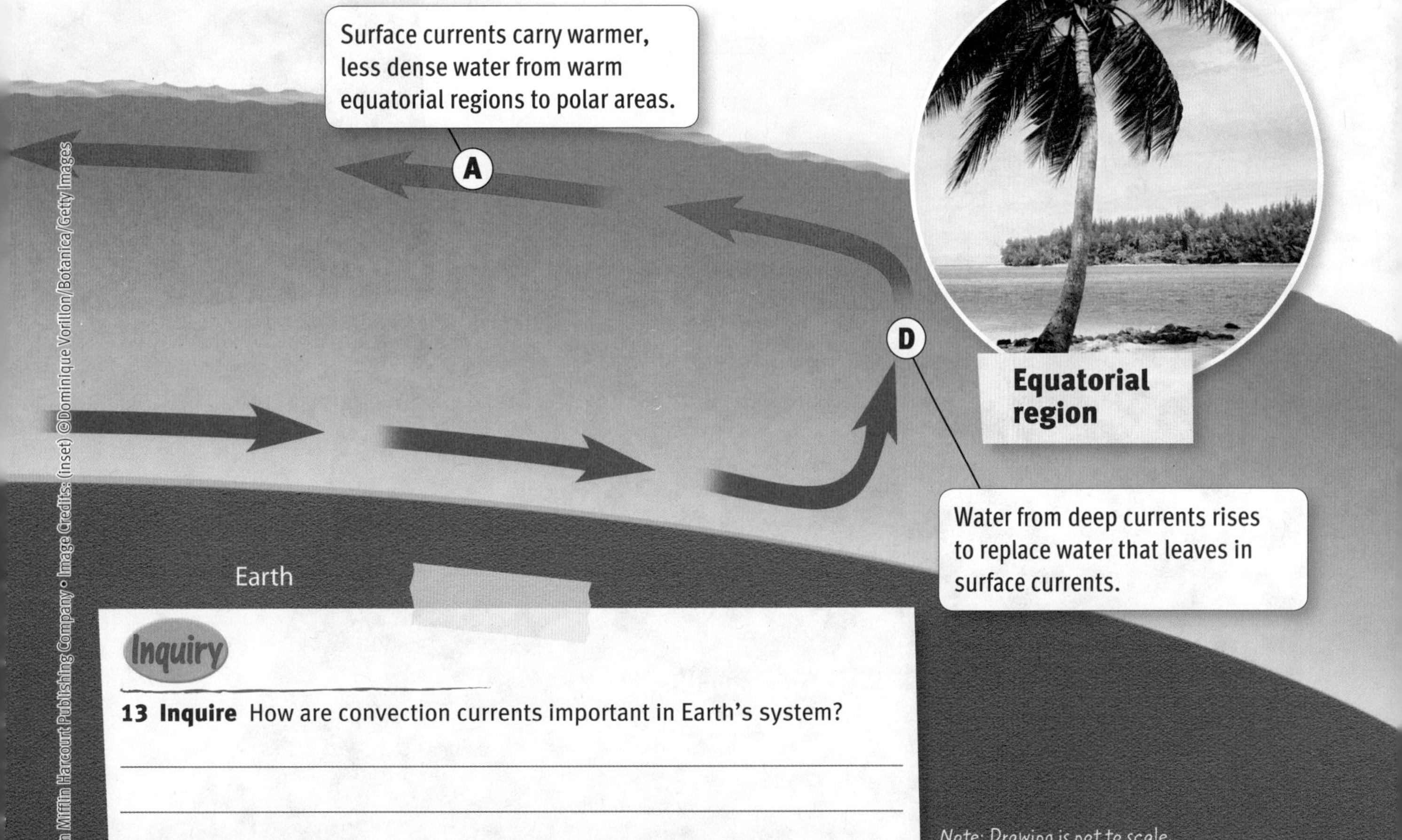

© Houghton Mifflin Harcourt Publishing Company • Image Credits: (inset) ©Dominique Vorillon/Botanica/Getty Images

Surface currents carry warmer, less dense water from warm equatorial regions to polar areas.

A

D

Equatorial region

Water from deep currents rises to replace water that leaves in surface currents.

Earth

Note: Drawing is not to scale.

Think Outside the Book Inquiry

12 Apply Write an interview with a water molecule following a convection current. Be sure to include questions and answers. Can you imagine the temperature changes the molecule would experience?

Inquiry

13 Inquire How are convection currents important in Earth's system?

_____

_____

_____

That's Swell!

Active Reading

14 Identify As you read, underline the steps that occur in upwelling.

What is upwelling?

At times, winds blow toward the equator along the northwest coast of South America and the west coast of North America. These winds cause surface currents to move away from the shore. The warm surface water is then replaced by cold, nutrient-rich water from the deep ocean in a process called **upwelling**. The deep water contains nutrients, such as iron and nitrate.

Upwelling is extremely important to ocean life. The nutrients that are brought to the surface of the ocean support the growth of phytoplankton (fy•toh•PLANGK•tuhn) and zooplankton. These tiny plants and animals are food for other organisms, such as fish and seabirds. Many fisheries are located in areas of upwelling because ocean animals thrive there. Some weather conditions can interrupt the process of upwelling. When upwelling is reduced, the richness of the ocean life at the surface is also reduced.

15 Predict What might happen to the fisheries if upwelling stopped?

_____

_____

_____

_____

_____

_____

The livelihood of these Peruvian fishermen depends on upwelling.

On the coast of California, upwelling sustains large kelp forests.

Wind

Warm surface water

During upwelling, cold, nutrient-rich water from the deep ocean rises to the surface.

© Houghton Mifflin Harcourt Publishing Company • Image Credits: (tl) ©Staffan Widstrand/Corbis; (tr) ©Bruce Hall/Alamy

Why It Matters

Hitching a Ride!

What do coconuts, plankton, and sea turtles have in common? They get free rides on ocean currents.

Sprouting Coconuts!

This sprouting coconut may be transported by ocean currents to a beach. This transport explains why coconut trees can grow in several areas.

World Travel

When baby sea turtles are hatched on a beach, they head for the ocean. They can then pick up ocean currents to travel. Some travel from Australia to South America on currents.

Fast Food

Diatoms are a kind of phytoplankton. They are tiny, one-celled plants that form the basis of the food chain. Diatoms ride surface currents throughout the world.

Extend

Inquiry

16 Identify List three organisms transported by ocean currents.

17 Research Investigate the Sargasso Sea. State why a lot of plastic collects in this sea. Find out whether any plastic collects on the shoreline nearest you.

18 Explain Describe how plastic and other debris can collect in the ocean by doing one of the following:
- make a poster
- write a song
- write a poem
- write a short story

© Houghton Mifflin Harcourt Publishing Company • Image Credits: (bkgd) ©Ethan Daniels/Alamy; (tr) ©Gerald Nowak/Getty Images; (bl) ©Ian Hinsch/Photo Researchers, Inc.

Traveling the World

What do ocean currents transport?

Ocean water circulates through all of Earth's ocean basins. The paths are like the main highway on which ocean water flows. If you could follow a water molecule on this path, you would find that the molecule takes more than 1,000 years to return to its starting point! Along with water, ocean currents also transport dissolved solids, dissolved gases, and energy around Earth.

Active Reading

19 Identify As you read, underline the description of how energy reaches the poles.

20 Describe Choose a location on the map. Using your finger, follow the route you would take if you could ride a current. Describe your route. Include the direction you go and the landmasses you pass.

_____

_____

_____

_____

_____

Antarctica is not shown on this map, but the currents at the bottom of the map circulate around Antarctica.

© Houghton Mifflin Harcourt Publishing Company

Ocean Currents Transport Energy

Global ocean circulation is very important in the transport of energy in the form of heat. Remember that ocean currents flow in huge convection currents that can be thousands of kilometers long. These convection currents carry about 40% of the energy that is transported around Earth's surface.

Near the equator, the ocean absorbs a large amount of solar energy. The ocean also absorbs energy from the atmosphere. Ocean currents carry this energy from the equator toward the poles. When the warm water travels to cooler areas, the energy is released back into the atmosphere. Therefore, ocean circulation has an important influence on Earth's climate.

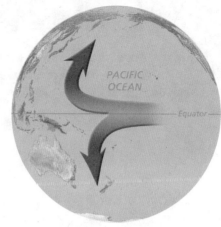

In the Pacific Ocean, surface currents transport energy from the tropics to latitudes above and below the equator.

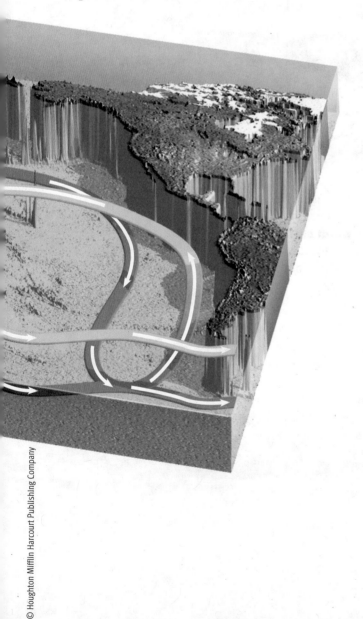

Ocean Currents Transport Matter

Besides water, ocean currents transport whatever is in the water. The most familiar dissolved solid in ocean water is sodium chloride, or table salt. Other dissolved solids are important to marine life. Ocean water contains many nutrients—such as nitrogen and phosphorus—that are important for plant and animal growth.

Ocean water also transports gases. Gases in the atmosphere are absorbed by ocean water at the ocean surface. As a result, the most abundant gases in the atmosphere—nitrogen, oxygen, argon, and carbon dioxide—are also abundant in the ocean. Dissolved oxygen and carbon dioxide are necessary for the survival of many marine organisms.

21 List Write three examples of matter besides water that are transported by ocean currents.

_____

_____

_____

_____

_____

© Houghton Mifflin Harcourt Publishing Company

Visual Summary

To complete this summary, draw an arrow to show each type of ocean current. Fill in the blanks with the correct word. Then use the key below to check your answers. You can use this page to review the main concepts of the lesson.

Surface currents are streamlike movements of water at or near the surface of the ocean.

22 The direction of a surface current is affected by

_____ ,

_____ ,

and _____

Deep currents are streamlike movements of ocean water located far below the surface.

23 Deep currents form where the

_____

of ocean water increases.

Ocean Currents

A convection current in the ocean is any movement of matter that results from differences in density.

24 A convection current in the ocean transports matter and

_____

Upwelling is the process in which warm surface water is replaced by cold water from the deep ocean.

25 The cold water from deep in the ocean contains

_____

Answers: 22 continental deflections, the Coriolis effect, global winds; 23 density; 24 energy; 25 nutrients

26 Describe State the two general patterns of global ocean circulation.

© Houghton Mifflin Harcourt Publishing Company

Lesson Review

Vocabulary

Fill in the blanks with the terms that best complete the following sentences.

1 _____ are streamlike movements of water in the ocean.

2 The _____ causes currents in open water to move in a curved path rather than a straight path.

3 _____ causes cold, nutrient-rich waters to move up to the ocean's surface.

Key Concepts

4 Explain List the steps that show how the sun provides the energy for surface ocean currents.

_____

_____

_____

_____

_____

5 Explain State how a deep current forms.

_____

_____

_____

_____

_____

6 Describe Explain how a convection current transports energy around the globe.

_____

_____

_____

_____

7 List Write the three factors that affect surface ocean currents.

_____

_____

_____

Critical Thinking

Use this diagram to answer the following questions.

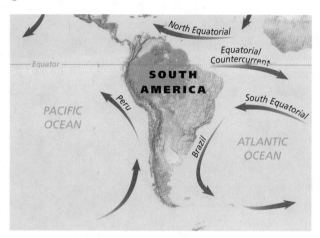

8 Apply Explain why the direction of the South Equatorial current changes.

_____

_____

_____

_____

9 Apply If South America were not there, explain how the direction of the South Equatorial current would be different.

_____

_____

_____

_____

_____

10 Apply Describe how surface currents would be affected if Earth did not rotate.

_____

_____

_____

_____

_____

_____

© Houghton Mifflin Harcourt Publishing Company

My Notes

© Houghton Mifflin Harcourt Publishing Company

© Houghton Mifflin Harcourt Publishing Company

Unit 7 [Big Idea] Energy transfer causes Earth's air and oceans to circulate.

Lesson 1

ESSENTIAL QUESTION
How does energy move through Earth's system?

Summarize the three mechanisms by which energy is transferred through Earth's system.

Lesson 2

ESSENTIAL QUESTION
What is wind?

Explain how energy provided by the sun causes atmospheric movement, called wind.

Lesson 3

ESSENTIAL QUESTION
How does water move in the ocean?

Describe the movement of ocean water, explain what factors influence this movement, and explain why ocean circulation is important in Earth's system.

Think Outside the Book

2 Synthesize Choose one of these activities to help synthesize what you have learned in this unit.

☐ Using what you learned in lessons 1 and 2, make a poster presentation explaining the role that radiation, conduction, and convection play in the transfer of energy in Earth's atmosphere.

☐ Using what you learned in lessons 2 and 3, make a poster presentation describing how wind currents and the temperature of ocean water are important to distributing energy as heat around Earth.

Connect ESSENTIAL QUESTIONS
Lessons 1 and 2

1 Synthesize Explain how the uneven warming of Earth causes air to move.

_____

_____

_____

_____

© Houghton Mifflin Harcourt Publishing Company • Image Credits: (tl) ©yanikap/Shutterstock; (tr) ©Frans Lanting/Corbis; (bl) ©Martin Bennett/Alamy

Unit 7 Review

Name _____

Vocabulary

Check the box to show whether each statement is true or false.

T	F	
☐	☐	**1** <u>Radiation</u> is a measure of the average kinetic energy of the particles in an object.
☐	☐	**2** <u>Thermal expansion</u> is the increase in volume that results from an increase in temperature.
☐	☐	**3** A <u>convection current</u> is any movement of matter that results from differences in density.
☐	☐	**4** <u>Upwelling</u> occurs when warm surface water is replaced by cold, nutrient-rich water from the deep ocean.
☐	☐	**5** The curving of the path of a moving object as a result of Earth's rotation is called the <u>Coriolis effect</u>.

Key Concepts

Read each question below, and circle the best answer.

6 The picture below shows all three methods of energy transfer.

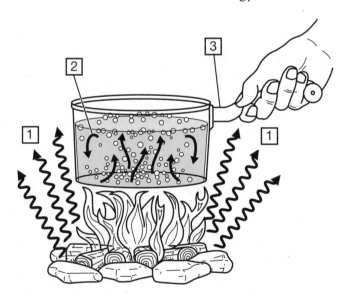

Which of these correctly identifies the three methods of energy transfer?

A 1: convection   2: radiation   3: conduction

B 1: radiation   2: conduction   3: convection

C 1: conduction   2: convection   3: radiation

D 1: radiation   2: convection   3: conduction

© Houghton Mifflin Harcourt Publishing Company

7 Which of these is not a way in which energy is transferred to Earth from the sun?

A conduction

C visible light

B infrared radiation

D x-rays

8 A plastic spoon that has a temperature of 78° F is placed into a bowl of soup that has a temperature of 84° F. Which of these correctly describes what will happen?

A Energy as heat moves from the spoon to the soup.

B Energy as heat does not move, because the spoon is plastic.

C Energy as heat moves from the soup to the spoon.

D Energy as heat does not move, because the temperature difference is too small.

9 Refer to the diagram of winds and currents below to answer the question.

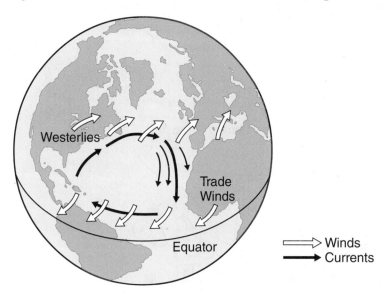

Which of the following best explains the curvature of the arrows for the westerlies and the trade winds?

A The ocean currents create winds flowing in a similar direction to the current.

B The Coriolis effect causes the winds to curve that way because the Earth rotates from left to right.

C The Coriolis effect causes the winds to curve that way because the Earth rotates from right to left.

D The sun is shining and warming the air from the right side of this diagram.

© Houghton Mifflin Harcourt Publishing Company

10 Which of the following correctly shows the chain of energy transfers that create surface currents on the ocean?

A solar energy → wind energy → surface currents

B wind energy → solar energy → surface currents

C tidal energy → wind energy → surface currents

D geothermal energy → wind energy → surface currents

11 Refer to the picture below to answer the question.

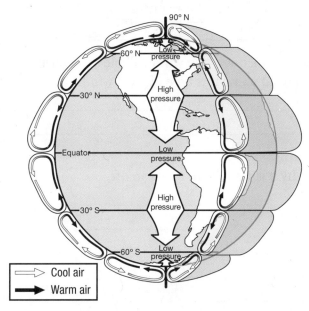

Which of the following is most responsible for the moving bands of air around Earth that are shown in the picture above?

A conduction   **C** Coriolis effect

B convection   **D** greenhouse effect

12 Which of the following describes the general pattern of winds near the equator?

A Winds are generally weak because the equator is a region where low and high air pressure atmospheric bands come together.

B Winds are generally strong because the equator is a region where low and high air pressure atmospheric bands come together.

C Winds are generally strong because the equator is a region of mostly high air pressure.

D Winds are generally weak because the equator is a region of mostly low air pressure.

© Houghton Mifflin Harcourt Publishing Company

Critical Thinking

Answer the following questions in the space provided.

13 The picture below shows a situation that causes local winds.

(B) Warm air

(A) Cool air

Draw an arrow on the picture to show which way the wind will blow. Describe why the wind blows in that direction and name this type of local wind.

_____

_____

14 Explain what an upwelling is and why it is important to ocean life.

_____

_____

_____

_____

_____

Connect **ESSENTIAL QUESTIONS**
Lessons 1 and 2

Answer the following question in the space provided.

15 Explain how Earth gets energy from the sun and what the atmosphere does with that energy to help life survive on Earth.

_____

_____

_____

_____

_____

© Houghton Mifflin Harcourt Publishing Company

Weather and Climate

Strong winds create huge
waves that crash on shore.

© Houghton Mifflin Harcourt Publishing Company • Image Credits: (bkgd) ©Burton McNeely/Stone/Getty Images; (br) ©Drake Fleege/Alamy

Big Idea

Air pressure, temperature, air movement, and humidity in the atmosphere affect both weather and climate.

6.ESS2.2, 6.ESS2.3, 6.ESS2.5, 6.ESS2.6, 6.ESS3.3, 6.PS3.4

What do you think?

The weather can change very quickly. In severe weather, people and pets can get hurt, and property can be damaged. Can you think of ways to keep people, pets, and property safe?

Warning flags are used to show how safe this beach is.

CITIZEN SCIENCE

Exit Strategy

When there is an emergency, knowing what to do helps keep people as safe as possible. So what's the plan?

① Think About It

A Do you know what to do if there were a weather emergency while you were in school?

_____

_____

B What kinds of information might you need to stay safe? List them below.

_____

_____

_____

_____

_____

Floods can happen very quickly during a bad storm.

THEO'S RESTAURANT

© Houghton Mifflin Harcourt Publishing Company • Image Credits: ©Joe Raedle/Getty Images

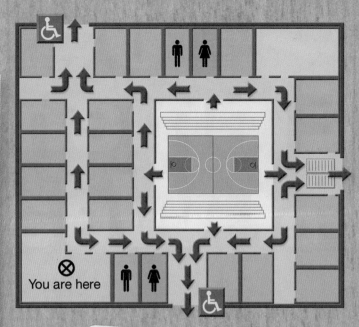

② Ask A Question

How well do you know your school's emergency evacuation plan? Obtain a copy of the school's emergency evacuation plan. Read through the plan and answer the following questions as a class.

A Is the emergency evacuation plan/map easy for students to understand?

_____

B How would you know which way to go?

_____

_____

C How often do you have practice drills?

_____

EMERGENCY EVACUATION ROUTE

③ Propose and Apply Improvements

A Using what you have learned about your school's emergency evacuation plan, list your ideas for improvements below.

_____
_____
_____
_____
_____

B Develop and give a short oral presentation to your principal about your proposal on ways to improve the school's emergency evacuation plan. Write the main points of your presentation below.

_____
_____
_____
_____
_____

C As a class, practice the newly improved emergency evacuation plan. Describe how well the improved emergency evacuation plan worked.

_____
_____
_____
_____
_____
_____
_____

Take It Home

With an adult, create an emergency evacuation plan for your family or evaluate your family's emergency evacuation plan and propose improvements. See *ScienceSaurus*® for more information about weather.

© Houghton Mifflin Harcourt Publishing Company • Image Credits:

Elements of Weather

ESSENTIAL QUESTION

What is weather and how can we describe different types of weather conditions?

By the end of this lesson, you should be able to describe elements of weather and explain how they are measured.

6.ESS2.5

Weather stations placed all around the world allow scientists to measure the elements, or separate parts, of weather.

A researcher checks an automatic weather station on Alexander Island, Antarctica.

© Houghton Mifflin Harcourt Publishing Company • Image Credits: (bkgd) ©British Antarctic Survey/Photo Researchers, Inc.

👋 Lesson Labs

Quick Labs
- Investigate the Measurement of Rainfall
- Classifying Features of Different Types of Clouds

Field Lab
- Comparing Different Ways to Estimate Wind Speed

Engage Your Brain

1 Predict Check T or F to show whether you think each statement is true or false.

T	F	
☐	☐	Weather can change every day.
☐	☐	Temperature is measured by using a barometer.
☐	☐	Air pressure increases as you move higher in the atmosphere.
☐	☐	Visibility is a measurement of how far we can see.

2 Describe Use at least three words that might describe the weather on a day when the sky looks like the picture above.

_____

_____

_____

_____

Active Reading

3 Distinguish The words *weather, whether,* and *wether* all sound alike but are spelled differently and mean entirely different things. You may have never heard of a wether—it is a neutered male sheep or ram.

Circle the correct use of the three words in the sentence below.

The farmer wondered *weather / whether / wether* the cold *weather / whether / wether* had affected his *weather / whether / wether*.

Vocabulary Terms

- weather
- humidity
- relative humidity
- dew point
- precipitation
- air pressure
- wind
- visibility

4 Apply As you learn the definition of each vocabulary term in this lesson, create your own definition or sketch to help you remember the meaning of the term.

© Houghton Mifflin Harcourt Publishing Company • Image Credits: (bkg) ©British Antarctic Survey/Photo Researchers, Inc.; (r) ©Laurance B. Aiuppy/Photographer's Choice/Getty Images

Wonder about Weather?

What is weather?

Weather is the condition of Earth's atmosphere at a certain time and place. Different observations give you clues to the weather. If you see plants moving from side to side, you might infer that it is windy. If you see a gray sky and wet, shiny streets, you might decide to wear a raincoat. People talk about weather by describing factors such as temperature, humidity, precipitation, air pressure, wind, and *visibility* (viz•uh•BIL•i•tee).

What is temperature and how is it measured?

Temperature is a measure of how hot or cold something is. An instrument that measures and displays temperature is called a *thermometer*. A common type of thermometer uses a liquid such as alcohol or mercury to display the temperature. The liquid is sealed in a glass tube. When the air gets warmer, the liquid expands and rises in the tube. Cooler air causes the liquid to contract and fill less of the tube. A scale, often in Celsius (°C) or Fahrenheit (°F), is marked on the glass tube.

Another type of thermometer is an electrical thermometer. As the temperature becomes higher, electric current flow increases through the thermometer. The strength of the current is then translated into temperature readings.

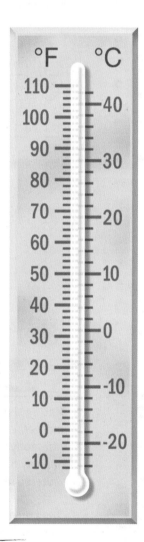

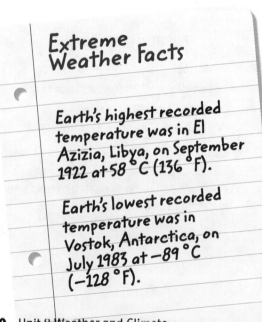

Extreme Weather Facts

Earth's highest recorded temperature was in El Azizia, Libya, on September 1922 at 58 °C (136 °F).

Earth's lowest recorded temperature was in Vostok, Antarctica, on July 1983 at −89 °C (−128 °F).

Visualize It!

5 Identify Color in the liquid in the thermometer above to show Earth's average temperature in 2009 (58 °F). Write the Celsius temperature that equals 58 °F on the line below.

© Houghton Mifflin Harcourt Publishing Company

What is humidity and how is it measured?

As water evaporates from oceans, lakes, and ponds, it becomes water vapor, or a gas that is in the air. The amount of water vapor in the air is called **humidity**. As more water evaporates and becomes water vapor, the humidity of the air increases.

Humidity is often described through relative humidity. **Relative humidity** is the amount of water vapor in the air compared to the amount of water vapor needed to reach saturation. As shown below, when air is saturated, the rates of evaporation and condensation are equal. Saturated air has a relative humidity of 100%. A psychrometer (sy•KRAHM•i•ter) is an instrument that is used to measure relative humidity.

Air can become saturated when evaporation adds water vapor to the air. Air can also become saturated when it cools to its dew point. The **dew point** is the temperature at which more condensation than evaporation occurs. When air temperature drops below the dew point, condensation forms. This can cause dew on surfaces cooler than the dew point. It also can form fog and clouds.

Active Reading

6 Identify Underline the name of the instrument used to measure relative humidity.

Visualize It!

7 Sketch In the space provided, draw what happens in air that is below the dew point.

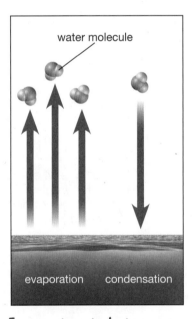

water molecule

evaporation   condensation

In unsaturated air, more water evaporates into the air than condenses back into the water.

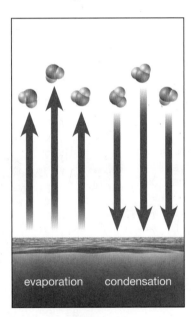

evaporation   condensation

In saturated air, the amount of water that evaporates equals the amount that condenses.

When air cools below its dew point, more water vapor condenses into water than evaporates.

8 Explain Why does dew form on grass overnight?

_____

_____

© Houghton Mifflin Harcourt Publishing Company • Image Credits: w(bkgd) ©Rick Lew/Stone/Getty Images

What is precipitation and how is it measured?

Water vapor in the air condenses not only on Earth's surfaces, but also on tiny particles in the air to form clouds. When this water from the air returns to Earth's surface, it falls as precipitation. **Precipitation** is any form of water that falls to Earth's surface from the clouds. The four main forms of precipitation are rain, snow, hail, and sleet.

Rain is the most common form of precipitation. Inside a cloud, the droplets formed by condensation collide and form larger droplets. They finally become heavy enough to fall as raindrops. Rain is measured with a rain gauge, as shown in the picture below. A funnel or wide opening at the top of the gauge allows rain to flow into a cylinder that is marked in centimeters.

Snow forms when air temperatures are so low that water vapor turns into a solid. When a lot of snow has fallen, it is measured with a ruler or meterstick. When balls or lumps of ice fall from clouds during thunderstorms it is called *hail*. Sleet forms when rain falls through a layer of freezing air, producing falling ice.

Visualize It! Inquiry

9 Synthesize What are two ways in which all types of precipitation are alike?

_____

_____

_____

Snow
Snow can fall as single ice crystals or ice crystals can join to form snowflakes.

Rain
Rain occurs when the water droplets in a cloud get so big they fall to Earth.

Sleet
Small ice pellets fall as sleet when rain falls through cold air.

Hail
Hailstones are layered lumps of ice that fall from clouds.

10 Measure How much rain has this rain gauge collected?

_____

© Houghton Mifflin Harcourt Publishing Company • Image Credits: (bl) ©Kent Knudson/PhotoLink/Photodisc/Getty Images; (bc) ©CamEl Creative/Workbook Stock/Getty Images; (br) ©Johner Images/Alamy

How has computer technology changed over time?

Modern, digital computer technology is less than 100 years old. Yet in that short amount of time, it has advanced rapidly. The earliest digital computers could perform only a limited number of tasks and were the size of an entire room. Over the decades, engineers continued to develop smaller, faster, and more powerful computers. Today's computers can process hundreds of millions of instructions per second!

Computer scientists and engineers think about what people want or need from computer technology. The most advanced hardware is not useful if people do not know how to use it. So computer scientists and engineers work to create software that is reliable, useful, and easy to use. Today's tablet computers, cell phones, and video game consoles can be used without any special training.

Advances in digital computer technology have helped make computers cheaper and easier to operate, which has allowed many more people to work and play with them.

1 Compare Are modern computers simpler or more complex than early computers? Explain.

_____

_____

© Houghton Mifflin Harcourt Publishing Company • (bl) ©zerocreatives/Westend61/Corbis; (r) ©Thomas Barwick/Taxi/Getty Images; (b) ©Marmaduke St. John/Alamy

What is air pressure and how is it measured?

Scientists use an instrument called a *barometer* (buh•RAHM•i•ter) to measure air pressure. **Air pressure** is the force of air molecules pushing on an area. The air pressure at any area on Earth depends on the weight of the air above that area. Although air is pressing down on us, we don't feel the weight because air pushes in all directions. So, the pressure of air pushing down is balanced by the pressure of air pushing up.

Air pressure and density are related; they both decrease with altitude. Notice in the picture that the molecules at sea level are closer together than the molecules at the mountain peak. Because the molecules are closer together, the pressure is greater. The air at sea level is denser than air at high altitude.

Air pressure and density are lower at a high altitude.

Air pressure and density are higher at sea level.

© Houghton Mifflin Harcourt Publishing Company • Image Credits: (tl) ©Phillipe Giraud/Sygma/Corbis; (bl) ©David Buffington/Photographer's Choice/Getty Images

Visualize It!

13 Identify Look at the photos below and write whether wind direction or wind speed is being measured.

Anemometer

An anemometer measures:

_____

Wind vane

A wind vane measures:

_____

What is wind and how is it measured?

Wind is air that moves horizontally, or parallel to the ground. Uneven heating of Earth's surface causes pressure differences from place to place. These pressure differences set air in motion. Over a short distance, wind moves directly from higher pressure toward lower pressure.

An anemometer (an•uh•MAHM•i•ter) is used to measure wind speed. It has three or four cups attached to a pole. The wind causes the cups to rotate, sending an electric current to a meter that displays the wind speed.

Wind direction is measured by using a wind vane or a windsock. A wind vane has an arrow with a large tail that is attached to a pole. The wind pushes harder on the arrow tail due to its larger surface area. This causes the wind vane to spin so that the arrow points into the wind. A windsock is a cone-shaped cloth bag open at both ends. The wind enters the wide end and the narrow end points in the opposite direction, showing the direction the wind is blowing.

What is visibility and how is it measured?

Visibility is a measure of the transparency of the atmosphere. Visibility is the way we describe how far we can see, and it is measured by using three or four known landmarks at different distances. Sometimes not all of the landmarks will be visible. Poor visibility can be the result of air pollution or fog.

Poor visibility can be dangerous for all types of travel, whether by air, water, or land. When visibility is very low, roads may be closed to traffic. In areas where low visibility is common, signs are often posted to warn travelers.

 **Active Reading**

14 Explain What are two factors that can affect visibility?

_____

_____

Fog forms as land cools overnight, causing water vapor in the air above the land to condense.

What are some ways to collect weather data?

Many forms of technology are used to gather weather data. The illustration below shows some ways weather information can be collected. Instruments within the atmosphere can make measurements of local weather conditions. Satellites can collect data from above the atmosphere.

 **Visualize It!** Inquiry

15 Infer What are the benefits of stationary weather collection? Moving weather collection?

_____

_____

_____

_____

Satellite

Airplane

Ground station

Stationary
Some forms of technology provide measurements from set locations.

Moving
Some forms of technology report changing measurements along their paths.

Weather buoy

Ship

© Houghton Mifflin Harcourt Publishing Company • Image Credits: (t) ©Grant V. Faint/Photodisc/Getty Images

Visual Summary

To complete this summary, fill in the blanks with the correct word or phrase. Then use the key below to check your answers. You can use this page to review the main concepts of the lesson.

Elements of Weather

Weather is a condition of the atmosphere at a certain time and place.

16 Weather is often expressed by describing _____, humidity, precipitation, air pressure, wind, and visibility.

Humidity describes the amount of water vapor in the air.

17 The amount of moisture in the air is commonly expressed as _____ humidity.

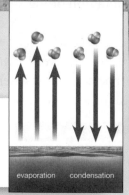

evaporation   condensation

Uneven heating of Earth's surface causes air pressure differences and wind.

18 Wind moves from areas of _____ pressure to areas of _____ pressure.

Visibility describes how far into the distance objects can be seen.

19 Visibility can be affected by air pollution and _____.

Precipitation occurs when the water that condenses as clouds falls back to Earth in solid or liquid form.

20 The main types of precipitation are hail, snow, _____, and rain.

Answers: 16 temperature; 17 relative; 18 higher, lower; 19 fog; 20 sleet

21 Synthesize What instruments would you take along if you were going on a 3-month field study to measure how the weather on a mountaintop changes over the course of a season?

© Houghton Mifflin Harcourt Publishing Company • Image Credits: (man on pier) ©Philippe Giraud/Sygma/Corbis; (person on bike) ©Grant V. Faint/Photodisc/Getty Images; (hand with ruler) ©CamEl Creative/Workbook Stock/Getty Images

Lesson Review

Vocabulary

In your own words, define the following terms.

1 weather _____

_____

2 humidity _____

_____

3 air pressure _____

_____

_____

4 visibility _____

_____

Key Concepts

Weather element	Instrument
5 Identify Measures temperature	
	6 Identify Is measured by using a barometer
7 Identify Measures relative humidity	
	8 Identify Is measured by using a rain gauge or meterstick
9 Identify Measures wind speed	

10 List What are four types of precipitation?

_____

_____

Critical Thinking

11 Apply Explain how wind is related to the uneven heating of Earth's surfaces by the sun.

_____

_____

_____

_____

12 Explain Why does air pressure decrease as altitude increases?

_____

_____

_____

13 Synthesize What is the relative humidity when the air temperature is at its dew point?

_____

_____

The weather data below was recorded from 1989–2009 by an Antarctic weather station similar to the station in the photo at the beginning of this lesson. Use these data to answer the questions that follow.

	Jan.	Apr.	July	Oct.
Mean max. temp. (°C)	2.1	−7.4	−9.9	−8.1
Mean min. temp. (°C)	−2.6	−14.6	−18.1	−15.1
Mean precip. (mm)	9.0	18.04	28.5	16.5

14 Identify Which month had the lowest mean minimum and maximum temperatures?

_____

15 Infer The precipitation that fell at this location was most likely in what form?

_____

_____

© Houghton Mifflin Harcourt Publishing Company

My Notes

© Houghton Mifflin Harcourt Publishing Company

© Houghton Mifflin Harcourt Publishing Company

Clouds and Cloud Formation

ESSENTIAL QUESTION

How do clouds form, and how are clouds classified?

By the end of this lesson, you should be able to describe the formation and classification of clouds.

6.ESS2.3

These altocumulus clouds cover the sky like a bluish-gray blanket. Clouds take various shapes and appear at different altitudes in the lower atmosphere. Scientists classify clouds by both their shape and the altitude at which they form.

© Houghton Mifflin Harcourt Publishing Company • Image Credits: (bg) ©Alan Struhikoff/Photo Researchers, Inc.

Engage Your Brain

1 Identify Read over the following vocabulary terms. In the spaces provided, place a + if you know the term well, a ~ if you have heard the term but are not sure what it means, and a ? if you are unfamiliar with the term. Then write a sentence that includes one of the words you are most familiar with.

_____ cloud
_____ dew point
_____ fog

Sentence using known word:

_____

_____

2 Compare Look at the photo below. How do these clouds compare to the clouds that you would see during a severe thunderstorm?

_____
_____
_____
_____
_____

Active Reading

3 Synthesize Many English words have their roots in other languages. Use the Latin words below to make an educated guess about the meaning of *cirrus cloud* and *cumulus cloud*.

Latin word	Meaning
cirrus	curl
cumulus	heap

Example sentence

<u>Cirrus clouds</u> are seen high in the sky.

cirrus cloud:

_____

_____

Example Sentence

<u>Cumulus clouds</u> change shape often.

cumulus cloud:

_____

_____

Vocabulary Terms

- cloud
- dew point
- stratus cloud
- cumulus cloud
- cirrus cloud
- fog

4 Apply As you learn the definition of each vocabulary term in this lesson, create your own definition or sketch to help you remember the meaning of the term.

© Houghton Mifflin Harcourt Publishing Company • Image Credits: (bg) ©Alan Strulnikoff/Photo Researchers, Inc.; (tl) ©Hubertus Kanus/Photo Researchers, Inc.

Head in the Clouds

Storm clouds appear dark gray. They are so full of water droplets that little light can pass through them.

What are clouds?

When you look into the sky, you see the amazing shapes that clouds take and how quickly those shapes change. But, have you ever asked yourself what clouds are made of or how they form? And did you know that there are different types of clouds?

A **cloud** is a collection of small water droplets or ice crystals that are suspended in the air. Clouds are visible because water droplets and ice crystals reflect light. Clouds are most often associated with precipitation. However, the reality is that most cloud types do not produce precipitation.

How do clouds affect climate?

The precipitation that falls from clouds has a significant effect on local climate. In particular, the pattern of precipitation of an area will determine the climate of that area. For instance, a desert is an area that receives less than 25 cm of precipitation a year. But, a tropical rainforest may average 250 cm of precipitation a year.

Clouds also affect temperatures on Earth. About 25% of the sun's energy that reaches Earth is reflected back into space by clouds. Low-altitude clouds, which are thick and reflect more sunlight, help to cool Earth. On the other hand, thin, high-altitude clouds absorb some of the energy that radiates from Earth. Part of this energy is reradiated back to Earth's surface. This warms Earth, because this energy is not directly lost to space.

Active Reading **5 Describe** What are two ways in which clouds affect Earth's climate?

_____

_____

_____

6 Apply Sketch a cloud, and write a caption that relates the drawing to the content on this page.

_____

_____

_____

_____

© Houghton Mifflin Harcourt Publishing Company • Image Credits: ©Mike Theiss/National Geographic/Getty Images

How do clouds form?

Clouds form when water vapor condenses, or changes from a gas to a liquid. For water vapor to condense, two things must happen. Air must be cooled to its dew point, and there must be a solid surface on which water molecules can condense.

Air Cools to the Dew Point

As warm air rises in Earth's atmosphere, it expands and cools. If air rises high enough into the atmosphere, it cools to its dew point. **Dew point** is the temperature at which the rate of condensation equals the rate of evaporation. *Evaporation* is the change of state from a liquid to a gas that usually occurs at the surface of a liquid. Evaporation takes place at the surface of an ocean, lake, stream, or other body of water. Water vapor in the air can condense and form water droplets or ice crystals when the temperature is at or below the dew point.

Water Droplets or Ice Crystals Form on Nuclei

Water molecules condense much more rapidly when there is a solid surface on which to condense. In clouds, tiny solid particles called *cloud condensation nuclei* are the surfaces on which water droplets condense. Examples of cloud condensation nuclei include dust, salt, soil, and smoke.

Clouds are most commonly made of very large numbers of very small water droplets. However, at high altitudes, where temperatures are very cold, clouds are composed of ice crystals.

D Cloud formation takes place.

C Condensation takes place on nuclei.

condensation nucleus
0.0002 millimeter diameter

cloud droplet
0.05 millimeter diameter

B
_____
_____

A Warm air rises, expands, and cools.

7 Conclude Complete the flow chart by filling in the missing information.

© Houghton Mifflin Harcourt Publishing Company

What is the role of solar energy in cloud formation?

The water cycle is the movement of water between the atmosphere, land, and ocean. Solar energy drives the water cycle and, therefore, provides the energy for cloud formation.

About 50 percent of the sun's incoming energy is absorbed by land, by water on the land's surface, and by surface waters in the oceans. This absorbed energy causes liquid water at the water's surface to become water vapor, a gas. This process is called evaporation. The water vapor rises into the atmosphere with air that has been warmed near Earth's surface.

Solar energy does not warm the surface of Earth evenly. Unequal heating of Earth's surface causes areas of high pressure and low pressure to form in the atmosphere. Air flows horizontally from areas of high pressure to areas of low pressure. This horizontal movement of air is called *wind*. Wind causes clouds to move around Earth's surface. However, for air to be cooled to its dew point so that clouds can form, the air is pushed up, or is lifted, into the atmosphere.

What processes cool air enough to form clouds?

Active Reading **8 Identify** As you read, underline the processes that can cool air enough to form clouds.

There are several ways in which air can be cooled to its dew point. These include frontal and orographic lifting (ohr•uh•GRAF•ik LIFT•ing). Frontal lifting can occur when a warm air mass rises over a cold air mass. Once the rising air cools to its dew point, condensation occurs and clouds form.

Frontal lifting can also occur when a mass of cold air slides under a mass of warm air, pushing the warm air upward. The rising air cools to the dew point. Clouds form that often develop into thunderstorms.

Orographic lifting occurs when an obstacle, such as a mountain range, forces a mass of air upward. Water vapor in the air cools to its dew point and condenses. The clouds that form release large amounts of precipitation as rain or snow as they rise up the mountain. The other side of the mountain receives little precipitation.

 **Visualize It!**

9 Compare The images below show two processes by which clouds form when an air mass is lifted. In what ways are these two processes similar? In what ways are these two processes different?

_____

_____

_____

Frontal Lifting

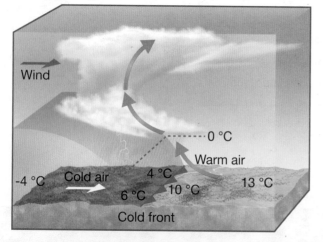

Orographic Lifting

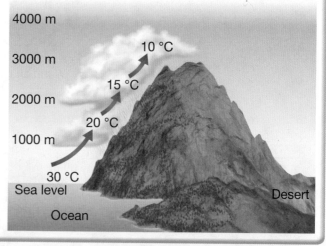

© Houghton Mifflin Harcourt Publishing Company

What are three cloud shapes?

You have probably noticed the different shapes that clouds take as they move through the sky. Some clouds are thick and puffy. Other clouds are thin and wispy. Scientists use shape as a way to classify clouds. The three classes of clouds based on shape are stratus (STRAT•uhs) clouds, cumulus (KYOOM•yuh•luhs) clouds, and cirrus (SIR•uhs) clouds.

Stratus Clouds

The lowest clouds in the atmosphere are stratus clouds. **Stratus clouds** are thin and flat, and their edges are not clearly defined. *Stratus* is a Latin word that means "layer." Stratus clouds often merge into one another and may look like a single layer that covers the entire sky. Stratus clouds are often gray. Light mist or drizzle may fall from these clouds. Fog is a type of stratus cloud that forms at or near the ground.

Cumulus Clouds

Cumulus is a Latin word that means "heap." **Cumulus clouds** are thick and puffy on top and generally flat on the bottom. These clouds have well-defined edges and can change shape rapidly. Some may tower high into the atmosphere, where the top of the cloud sometimes flattens.

Fair-weather cumulus clouds are bright and white. But cumulus clouds can become dark as more and more water droplets or ice crystals are added to the cloud. Cumulus clouds can produce severe weather. Thunder, lightning, and heavy precipitation are associated with cumulus clouds.

Cirrus Clouds

Cirrus is a Latin word that means "curl." **Cirrus clouds** look feathery, and their ends curl. Cirrus clouds are white.

Cirrus clouds form high in the atmosphere. At the altitudes where cirrus clouds form, there is little water vapor, and temperatures are very cold. As a result, cirrus clouds are made of ice crystals rather than liquid water droplets. They do not produce precipitation that reaches Earth's surface.

© Houghton Mifflin Harcourt Publishing Company • Image Credits: (t) ©Tom Mareschal/Alamy; (c) ©PictureNet/Corbis; (b) ©David R. Frazier/Photo Researchers, Inc.

Visualize It!

10 Identify Name the three different clouds based on shape.

A _____

B _____

C _____

I've Looked at Clouds

Active Reading

11 Identify As you read the text, underline the prefixes associated with each class of cloud. If a class has no prefix, underline that information too.

What are the types of clouds based on altitude?

Scientists classify clouds by altitude as well as shape. The four classes of clouds based on altitude are low clouds, middle clouds, high clouds, and clouds of vertical development. These four classes are made up of 10 cloud types. Prefixes are used to name the clouds that belong to some of these classes.

Low Clouds

Low clouds form between Earth's surface and 2,000 m altitude. Water droplets commonly make up these clouds. The three types of low clouds are stratus, stratocumulus, and nimbostratus. There is no special prefix used to name low clouds. However, *nimbus* means "rain," so *nimbo*stratus clouds are rain clouds.

Middle Clouds

Middle clouds form between 2,000 m and 6,000 m altitude. They are most commonly made up of water droplets, but may be made up of ice crystals. The prefix *alto-* is used to name middle clouds. The two types of middle clouds are altocumulus and altostratus.

High Clouds

High clouds form above 6,000 m altitude. At these high altitudes, air temperature is below freezing. Therefore, high clouds are made up of ice crystals. The prefix *cirro-* is used to name high clouds. Cirrus, cirrocumulus, and cirrostratus are the types of high clouds.

Clouds of Vertical Development

Clouds of vertical development can rise high into the atmosphere. Although the cloud base is at low altitude, cloud tops can reach higher than 12,000 m. Clouds of vertical development are commonly formed by the rapid lifting of moist, warm air, which can result in strong vertical growth. There is no special prefix used to name clouds of vertical development. The two types of clouds of vertical development are cumulus and cumulonimbus.

Cumulonimbus clouds have the greatest vertical development of any cloud type. Air currents within these clouds can move upward at as much as 20 m/s. Cumulonimbus clouds are linked to severe weather and can produce rain, hail, lightning, tornadoes, and dangerous, rapidly sinking columns of air that strike Earth.

Think Outside the Book **Inquiry**

12 Apply Research cumulonimbus clouds. When you complete your research, consider different materials that might be used to create a model of a cumulonimbus cloud. Then, use your materials to build a model that shows the structure of a cumulonimbus cloud.

© Houghton Mifflin Harcourt Publishing Company

from Both Sides Now

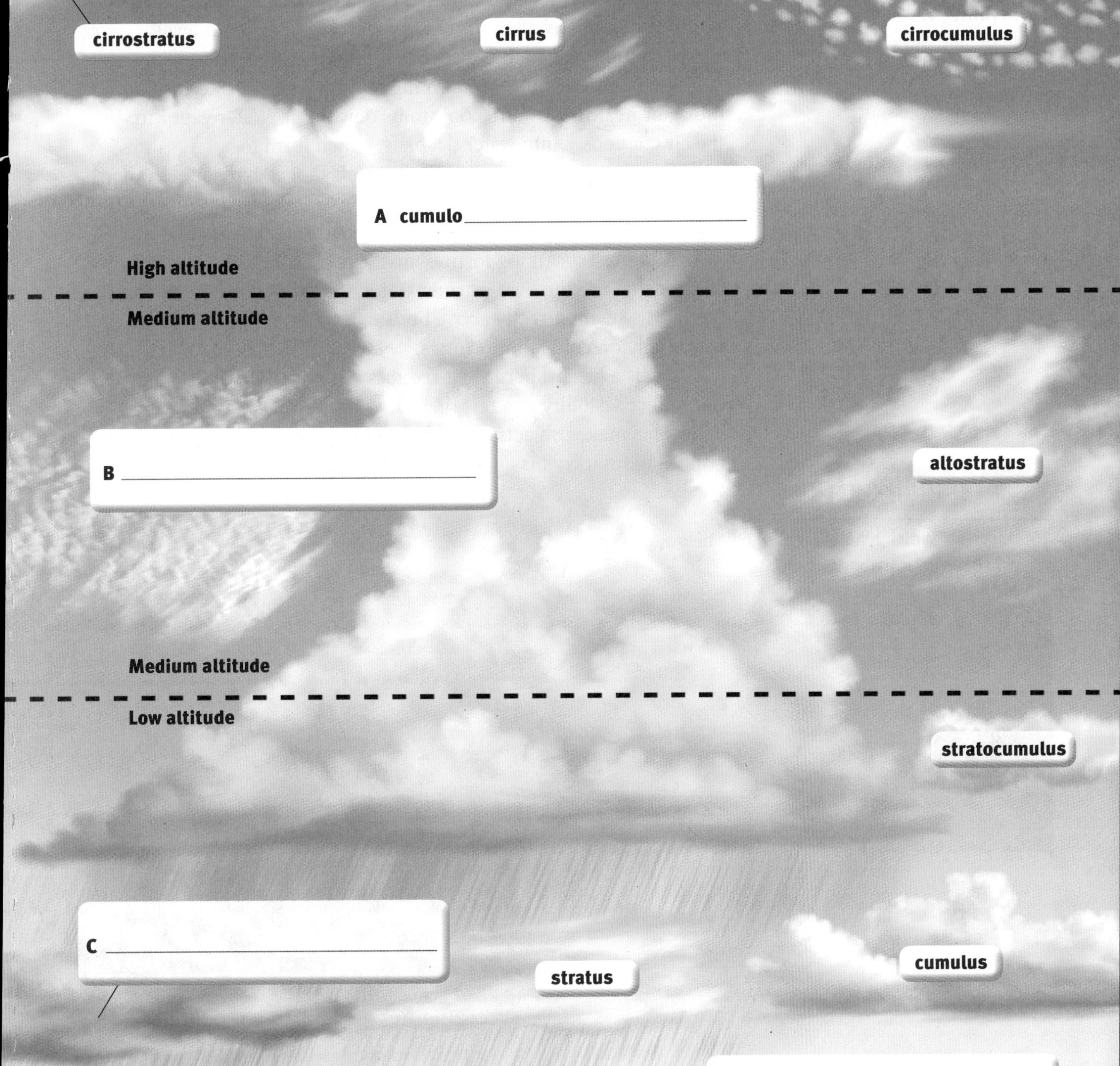

© Houghton Mifflin Harcourt Publishing Company

cirrostratus

cirrus

cirrocumulus

A cumulo_____

High altitude

Medium altitude

B _____

altostratus

Medium altitude

Low altitude

stratocumulus

C _____

stratus

cumulus

Visualize It!

13 Identify Meteorologists recognize 10 cloud types based on the altitude at which the clouds form. Using the illustration above, identify the names of the cloud types on the write-on lines provided.

Word Bank	
cirrocumulus	cirrostratus
stratus	cumulus
altostratus	cirrus
stratocumulus	cumulonimbus
altocumulus	nimbostratus

How does fog form?

Water vapor that condenses very near Earth's surface is called **fog**. Fog forms when moist air at or near Earth's surface cools to its dew point. Fog is simply a stratus cloud that forms at ground level.

Ground fog, which is also called *radiation fog*, generally forms in low-lying areas on clear, calm nights. As Earth's surface cools, moist air near the ground cools to its dew point. Water vapor in the air condenses into water droplets, which form fog.

Fog also forms when warm, moist air moves across cold water and is cooled to its dew point. This is how sea fog, or advection fog, forms. Unlike ground fog, sea fog occurs at all times of day.

Another type of fog forms when evaporation takes place into cold air that is lying over warmer water. Called *steam fog*, this fog appears as steam directly above bodies of water. It occurs most commonly on cold fall mornings.

Fog is a hazard because it reduces visibility. Very dense fog can reduce visibility to a few meters. Water droplets in fog scatter light. This makes objects difficult for people to see clearly. Without visible landmarks, it is also hard to judge distance and speed.

Active Reading

14 Identify As you read the text, underline ways in which fog forms.

Visualize It!

15 Describe Which type of fog is shown below, and why does it form above cold water?

_____

_____

_____

Ground fog forms at night when Earth's surface cools. Moist air near the ground cools to its dew point, which causes water vapor to condense.

© Houghton Mifflin Harcourt Publishing Company • Image Credits: (t) ©Ed Simpson/Photodisc/Getty Images; (b) ©Simon Bottomley/Photographer's Choice RF/Getty Images

Clouds on Other Worlds

Like Earth, other bodies in the solar system have clouds in their atmosphere. There are clouds on Venus and Mars. Jupiter and Saturn both have deep atmospheres with clouds arranged in bands that circle the planet. Even Saturn's moon Titan has clouds in a thick, planet-like atmosphere.

Venus is surrounded by thick clouds of sulfur dioxide that reflect much of the sunlight that falls on them back into space.

Clouds and dust can be seen in the Martian atmosphere. Mars is covered in a red iron oxide dust. Dust particles act as condensation nuclei that can cause clouds to have a pinkish color.

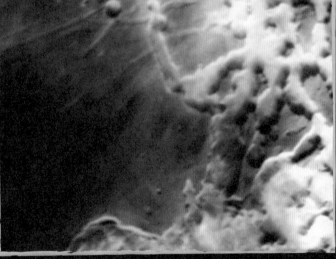

In 1976, *Viking Orbiter 1* took this photo of water-filled clouds that had formed over a large system of canyons just after the Martian sunrise.

© Houghton Mifflin Harcourt Publishing Company • Image Credits: (bg) ©Science & Society Picture Library/Contributor/SSPL/Getty Images; (bl) ©Science Source/Photo Researchers, Inc.; (br) ©Science & Society Picture Library/Contributor/SSPL/Getty Images

Extend

Inquiry

16 Infer Can clouds form on all bodies in the solar system?

17 Apply Research clouds on another body in the solar system. Describe properties of clouds there.

18 Design Create a poster presentation or a slide presentation that examines the way in which clouds on the solar system body that you chose to research differ from clouds on Earth.

Visual Summary

To complete this summary, circle the correct word. Then, use the key below to check your answers. You can use this page to review the main concepts of the lesson.

Clouds and Cloud Formation

Clouds form when rising air cools to the dew point and condensation occurs.

19 Warm air that is forced upward by a cold front is an example of frontal/orographic lifting.

Clouds can be classified by altitude.

20 Clouds that are made up entirely of ice crystals are middle/high clouds.

Clouds can be classified by shape.

21 Thin, wispy clouds that do not produce precipitation are cirrus/cumulus clouds.

Fog is a cloud that has formed very near Earth's surface.

22 Ground/Sea fog generally forms in low-lying areas, such as valleys.

Answers: 19 frontal; 20 high; 21 cirrus; 22 Ground

23 Synthesis How can clouds be used to help predict the weather?

© Houghton Mifflin Harcourt Publishing Company • Image Credits: (l) ©PictureNet/Corbis; (l) ©Alan Sir Jinikoff/Photo Researchers, Inc.

Lesson Review

Vocabulary

Fill in the blank with the term that best completes the following sentences.

1 A _____ cloud is thin, wispy, and made of ice crystals.

2 The temperature at which water vapor condenses is the _____

3 _____ is condensed water vapor that forms very close to Earth's surface.

Key Concepts

4 Compare What are two differences between stratus clouds and cirrus clouds?

_____

_____

_____

_____

5 List What are the four classes of clouds based on altitude?

_____

_____

_____

_____

6 Describe What are three ways in which clouds affect climate?

_____

_____

_____

_____

_____

7 Explain What part do tiny, solid particles in the atmosphere play in cloud formation?

_____

_____

_____

Critical Thinking

Use this diagram to answer the following questions.

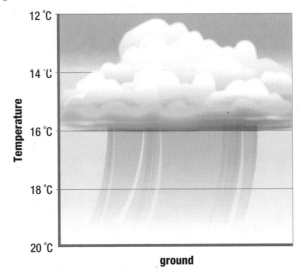

ground

8 Analyze What is the dew-point temperature at which cloud formation began?

_____

_____

9 Explain Why doesn't cloud formation take place until the dew-point temperature is reached?

_____

_____

_____

_____

10 Apply What kind of clouds would you expect to form at the leading edge of a cold front, where warm air is gradually being pushed above cold air?

_____

_____

_____

_____

© Houghton Mifflin Harcourt Publishing Company

My Notes

© Houghton Mifflin Harcourt Publishing Company

© Houghton Mifflin Harcourt Publishing Company

Evaluating Technological Systems

Skills
✔ Identify inputs
✔ Identify outputs
✔ Identify system processes
Evaluate system feedback
Apply system controls
✔ Communicate results

Objectives
• Analyze weather forecasting as a system.
• Identify the inputs and outputs of a forecasting system.
• Interpret weather data to generate a weather map.

Using Data in Systems

A system is a group of interacting parts that work together to do a job. Technological systems process inputs and generate outputs. An input is any matter, energy, or information that goes into a system. Outputs are matter, energy, or information that come out of the system. When you use a computer, the data set that is entered is the input. The computer delivers your output on the monitor or the printer.

Weather Data Go Into a System

What do you do if you have an outdoor activity planned tomorrow? You probably check the weather forecast to help you decide what to wear. Meteorologists are scientists who use data from different sources to find out what is happening in the atmosphere. Weather data are the input. The data set is processed by computers that perform complex calculations to generate weather models. Weather forecast systems combine 72 hours of data from weather stations, weather balloons, radar, aircraft, and weather satellites to show what is happening in Earth's atmosphere now and to predict what will happen in the future.

1 Explain How is a television weather forecast part of a technological system?

_____

_____

_____

The atmosphere is a system that can have dramatic outputs. Those outputs are inputs into a weather forecasting system.

© Houghton Mifflin Harcourt Publishing Company • Image Credits: ©Craig Aurness/Corbis

Forecast Data Come Out of the System

Weather maps are one type of output from a weather forecasting system. On a weather map you can find information about atmospheric pressure, and about the direction and temperature of moving air. The numbered lines on a weather map are called *isobars*. Isobars connect areas that have the same atmospheric pressure. Isobars center around areas of high and low pressure. An area of high pressure (H) indicates a place where cool, dense air is falling. An area of low pressure (L) indicates a place where warm, less dense air is rising. Pressure differences cause air to move. The leading edge of a cool air mass is called a *cold front*. The leading edge of a warm air mass is called a *warm front*. On a weather map, blue lines with triangles show cold fronts and red lines with half circles show warm fronts.

The direction of the triangles or half circles on a map shows which way a front is moving. Wind direction is described in terms of the direction from which the wind is blowing. A west wind is blowing from west to east.

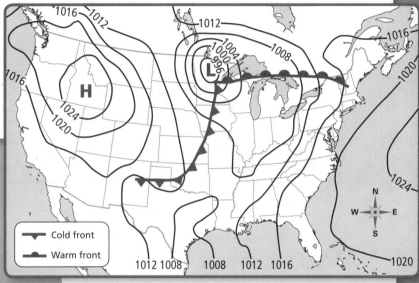

Anemometer (wind speed)

Wind vane (wind direction)

Barometer (air pressure) & Rain gauge (precipitation)

Thermometer (temperature) & Hygrometer (humidity)

2 Analysis How would you describe the wind direction behind the warm and cold fronts shown on the map?

_____

_____

_____

Weather instruments constantly measure conditions in the atmosphere and deliver data.

 You Try It! ⟶

Now it's your turn to use weather data to make a forecast.

© Houghton Mifflin Harcourt Publishing Company • Image Credits: ©reppans/Alamy

✋ You Try It!

Now it's your turn to become part of the weather forecasting system. The table and map on these pages show some weather data for several cities in the United States. You will use those data to analyze weather and make predictions.

(1) Identify Inputs

Which information in the table will you use to determine where the high and low pressure areas may be located?

_____

_____

City	Barometric pressure (mbar)	Wind direction	Temperature (°F)
Atlanta	1009	S	63
Chicago	1012	W	36
Cleveland	1006	S	35
Denver	1021	S	34
New York	990	S	58
Billings	1012	SW	28
Spokane	1009	SW	27
Los Angeles	1009	W	68
Dallas	1012	NW	50
Memphis	1012	NW	45
Orlando	1006	S	78
Raleigh	998	S	60

(2) Identify Outputs

What outputs from weather stations are included on a weather map?

_____

_____

(3) Identify System Processes

How will you process the information in the table and on the map to make predictions? Describe how you will use the inputs to develop an output.

_____

_____

_____

_____

© Houghton Mifflin Harcourt Publishing Company

4 Communicate Results

Use data from the table and the map to answer the questions below.

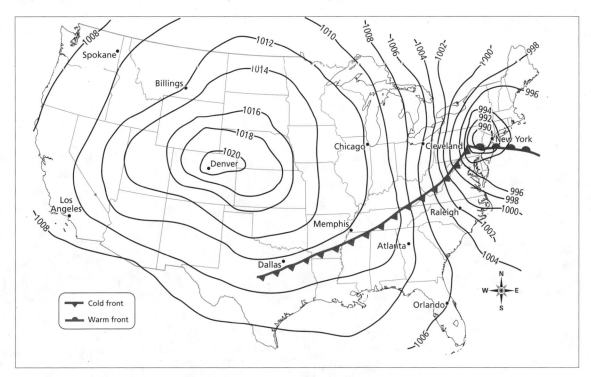

A According to the data in the table, where are the centers of the high and low pressure systems at this time? Mark them on the map using an H or an L.

B Add the temperature listed in the table for each city to the map.

C Imagine that you are a meteorologist in Atlanta and this is the current map. What temperature change would you predict over the next few hours, and why?

_____
_____
_____
_____

D What pressure change would you predict for Denver over the next few days, and why?

_____
_____
_____
_____

© Houghton Mifflin Harcourt Publishing Company

What Influences Weather?

ESSENTIAL QUESTION

How do the water cycle and other global patterns affect local weather?

By the end of this lesson, you should be able to explain how global patterns in Earth's system influence weather.

6.ESS2.2, 6.ESS2.3, 6.ESS2.6

The weather doesn't always turn out the way you want. But learning about the factors that affect weather can help you plan your next outing.

© Houghton Mifflin Harcourt Publishing Company • Image Credits: (bkgd) ©Bryan Bedder/Getty Images

Lesson Labs

Quick Labs
• Analyze Weather Patterns
• Coastal Climate Model

Exploration Lab
• Modeling El Niño

Engage Your Brain

1 Predict Check T or F to show whether you think each statement is true or false.

T   F

☐ ☐ The water cycle affects weather.

☐ ☐ Air can be warmed or cooled by the surface below it.

☐ ☐ Warm air sinks, cool air rises.

☐ ☐ Winds can bring different weather to a region.

2 Explain How can air temperatures along this coastline be affected by the large body of water that is nearby?

_____

_____

_____

Active Reading

3 Infer A military front is a contested armed frontier between opposing forces. A *weather front* occurs between two air masses, or bodies of air. What kind of weather do you think usually happens at a weather front?

_____

_____

_____

_____

_____

_____

Vocabulary Terms

• air mass
• front
• jet stream

4 Apply As you learn the definition of each vocabulary term in this lesson, create your own definition or sketch to help you remember the meaning of the term.

© Houghton Mifflin Harcourt Publishing Company • Image Credits: (bkgd) ©Bryan Beddar/Getty Images; (t) ©K-King Media Co. Ltd/Taxi/Getty Images

Water, Water

How does the water cycle affect weather?

Weather is the short-term state of the atmosphere, including temperature, humidity, precipitation, air pressure, wind, and visibility. These elements are affected by the energy received from the sun and the amount of water in the air. To understand what influences weather, then, you need to understand the water cycle.

The *water cycle* is the continuous movement of water between the atmosphere, the land, the oceans, and living things. In the water cycle, shown to the right, water is constantly being recycled between liquid, solid, and gaseous states. The water cycle involves the processes of evaporation, condensation, and precipitation.

Evaporation occurs when liquid water changes into water vapor, which is a gas. Condensation occurs when water vapor cools and changes from a gas to a liquid. A change in the amount of water vapor in the air affects humidity. Clouds and fog form through condensation of water vapor, so condensation also affects visibility. Precipitation occurs when rain, snow, sleet, or hail falls from the clouds onto Earth's surface.

Active Reading

5 List Name at least 5 elements of weather.

_____

_____

_____

Visualize It!

6 Summarize Describe how the water cycle influences weather by completing the sentences on the picture.

Ⓐ *Evaporation affects weather by* _____

_____

_____

© Houghton Mifflin Harcourt Publishing Company

Everywhere . . .

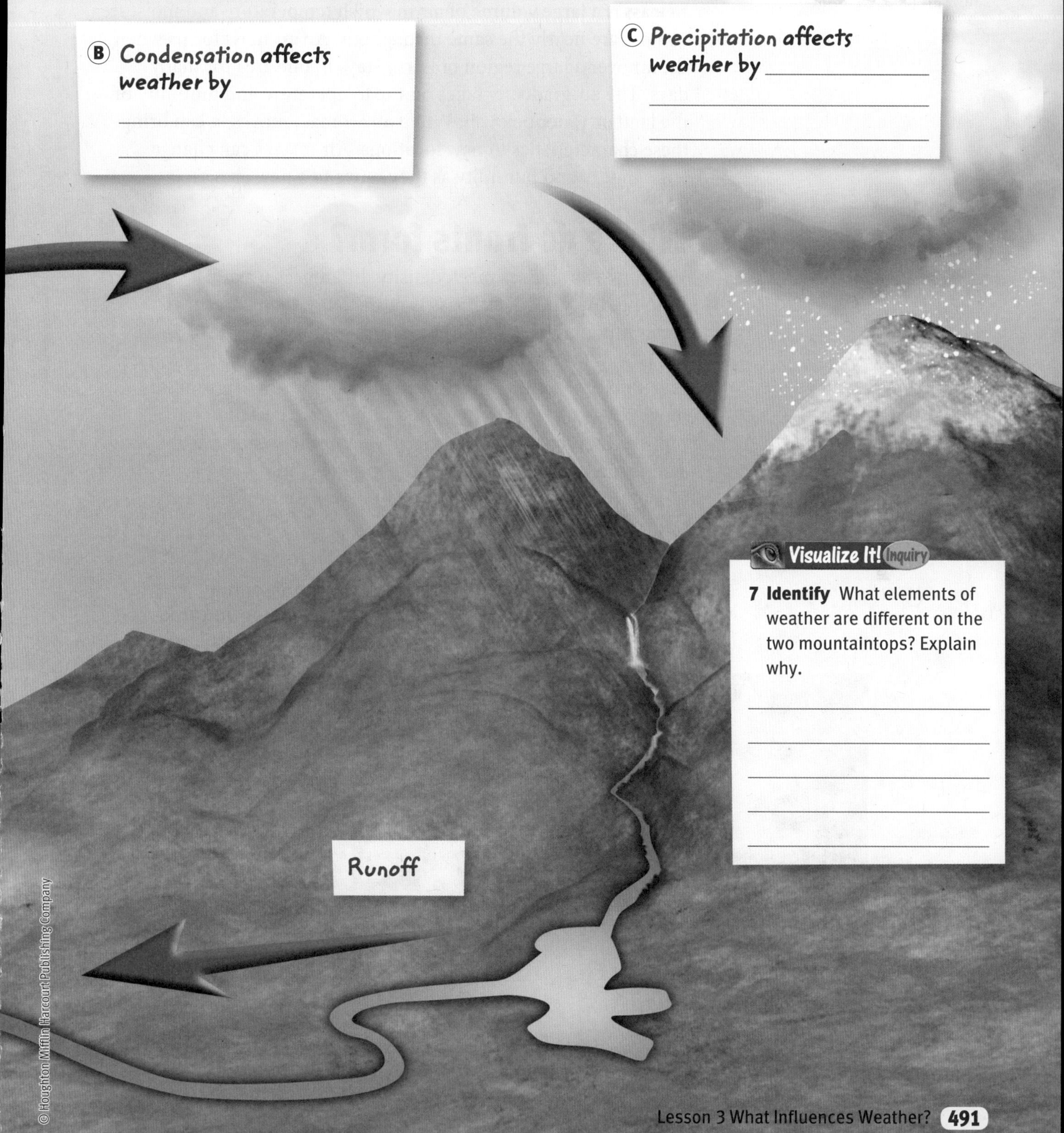

B Condensation affects
weather by _____
_____
_____

C Precipitation affects
weather by _____
_____
_____

Runoff

© Houghton Mifflin Harcourt Publishing Company

Visualize It! Inquiry

7 Identify What elements of
weather are different on the
two mountaintops? Explain
why.

_____
_____
_____
_____

Putting Up a **Front**

How do air masses affect weather?

You have probably experienced the effects of air masses—one day is hot and humid, and the next day is cool and pleasant. The weather changes when a new air mass moves into your area. An **air mass** is a large volume of air in which temperature and moisture content are nearly the same throughout. An air mass forms when the air over a large region of Earth stays in one area for many days. The air gradually takes on the temperature and humidity of the land or water below it. When an air mass moves, it can bring these characteristics to new locations. Air masses can change temperature and humidity as they move to a new area.

Where do fronts form?

When two air masses meet, density differences usually keep them from mixing. A cool air mass is more dense than a warm air mass. A boundary, called a **front**, forms between the air masses. For a front to form, one air mass must run into another air mass. The kind of front that forms depends on how these air masses move relative to each other, and on their relative temperature and moisture content. Fronts result in a change in weather as they pass. They usually affect weather in the middle latitudes of Earth. Fronts do not often occur near the equator because air masses there do not have big temperature differences.

Active Reading

8 Identify As you read, underline how air masses form.

The boundary between air masses, or front, cannot be seen, but is shown here to illustrate how air masses can take on the characteristics of the surface below them.

Air masses that form above water are moist.

Air masses that form above land are dry.

© Houghton Mifflin Harcourt Publishing Company

Cold Fronts Form Where Cold Air Moves under Warm Air

Warm air is less dense than cold air is. So, a cold air mass that is moving can quickly push up a warm air mass. If the warm air is moist, clouds will form. Storms that form along a cold front arc usually short-lived but can move quickly and bring heavy rain or snow. Cooler weather follows a cold front.

9 Apply If you hear that a cold front is headed for your area, what type of weather might you expect?

_____

_____

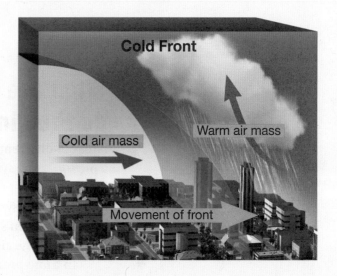

Cold Front

Cold air mass

Warm air mass

Movement of front

Warm Fronts Form Where Warm Air Moves over Cold Air

A warm front forms when a warm air mass follows a retreating cold air mass. The warm air rises over the cold air, and its moisture condenses into clouds. Warm fronts often bring drizzly rain and are followed by warm, clear weather.

10 Identify The rainy weather at the edge of a warm front is a result of

- ☐ the cold air mass that is leaving.

- ☐ the warm air rising over the cold air.

- ☐ the warm air mass following the front.

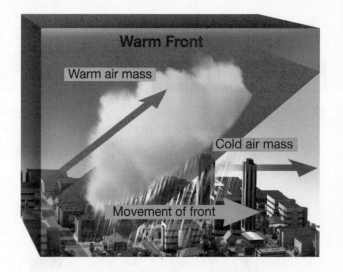

Warm Front

Warm air mass

Cold air mass

Movement of front

Stationary Fronts Form Where Cold and Warm Air Stop Moving

In a stationary front, there is not enough wind for either the cold air mass or the warm air mass to keep moving. So, the two air masses remain in one place. A stationary front can cause many days of unchanging weather, usually clear.

11 Infer When could a stationary front become a warm or cold front?

_____

_____

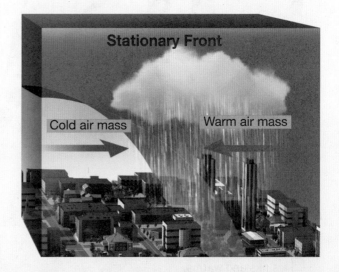

Stationary Front

Cold air mass

Warm air mass

© Houghton Mifflin Harcourt Publishing Company

Feeling the Pressure!

What are pressure systems, and how do they interact?

Areas of different air pressure cause changes in the weather. In a *high-pressure system*, air sinks slowly down. As the air nears the ground, it spreads out toward areas of lower pressure. Most high-pressure systems are large and change slowly. When a high-pressure system stays in one location for a long time, an air mass may form. The air mass can be warm or cold, humid or dry.

In a *low-pressure system*, air rises and so has a lower air pressure than the areas around it. As the air in the center of a low-pressure system rises, the air cools.

The diagram below shows how a high-pressure system can form a low-pressure system. Surface air, shown by the black arrows, moves out and away from high-pressure centers. Air above the surface sinks and warms. The green arrows show how air swirls from a high-pressure system into a low-pressure system. In a low-pressure system, the air rises and cools.

Visualize It!

12 Identify Choose the correct answer for each of the pressure systems shown below.

A high-pressure system can spiral into a low-pressure system, as illustrated by the green arrows below. In the Northern Hemisphere, air circles in the directions shown.

Ⓐ In a high-pressure system, air

☐ rises and cools.

☐ sinks and warms.

Ⓑ in a low-pressure system, air

☐ rises and cools.

☐ sinks and warms.

© Houghton Mifflin Harcourt Publishing Company

How do different pressure systems affect us?

When air pressure differences are small, air doesn't move very much. If the air remains in one place or moves slowly, the air takes on the temperature and humidity of the land or water beneath it. Each type of pressure system has it own unique weather pattern. By keeping track of high- and low-pressure systems, scientists can predict the weather.

High-Pressure Systems Produce Clear Weather

High-pressure systems are areas where air sinks and moves outward. The sinking air is denser than the surrounding air, and the pressure is higher. Cooler, denser air moves out of the center of these high-pressure areas toward areas of lower pressure. As the air sinks, it gets warmer and absorbs moisture. Water droplets evaporate, relative humidity decreases, and clouds often disappear. A high-pressure system generally brings clear skies and calm air or gentle breezes.

Low-Pressure Systems Produce Rainy Weather

Low-pressure systems have lower pressure than the surrounding areas. Air in a low-pressure system comes together, or converges, and rises. As the air in the center of a low-pressure system rises, it cools and forms clouds and rain. The rising air in a low-pressure system causes stormy weather.

A low-pressure system can develop wherever there is a center of low pressure. One place this often happens is along a boundary between a warm air mass and a cold air mass. Rain often occurs at these boundaries, or fronts.

Visualize It!

13 Match Label each picture as a result of a high- or low-pressure system. Then, draw a line from each photo to its matching air-pressure diagram.

Ⓐ

Ⓑ

Warm air rises

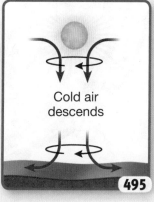
Cold air descends

© Houghton Mifflin Harcourt Publishing Company • Image Credits: (tl) ©Songquan Deng/Shutterstock; (bl) ©John A. Anderson/Shutterstock

Windy Weather

How do global wind patterns affect local weather?

Winds are caused by unequal heating of Earth's surface—which causes air pressure differences—and can occur on a global or on a local scale. On a local scale, air-pressure differences affect both wind speed and wind direction at a location. On a global level, there is an overall movement of surface air from the poles toward the equator. The heated air at the equator rises and forms a low-pressure belt. Cold air near the poles sinks and creates high-pressure centers. Because air moves from areas of high pressure to areas of low pressure, it moves from the poles to the equator. At high altitudes, the warmed air circles back toward the poles.

Temperature and pressure differences on Earth's surface also create regional wind belts. Winds in these belts curve to the east or the west as they blow, due to Earth's rotation. This curving of winds is called the *Coriolis effect* (kawr•ee•OH•lis eff•EKT). Winds would flow in straight lines if Earth did not rotate. Winds bring air masses of different temperatures and moisture content to a region.

Visualize It!

14 Apply Trade winds bring

☐ cool air to the warmer equatorial regions.

☐ warm air to the cooler, higher latitudes.

Belts of global winds circle Earth. The winds in these belts curve to the east or west. Between the global wind belts are calm areas.

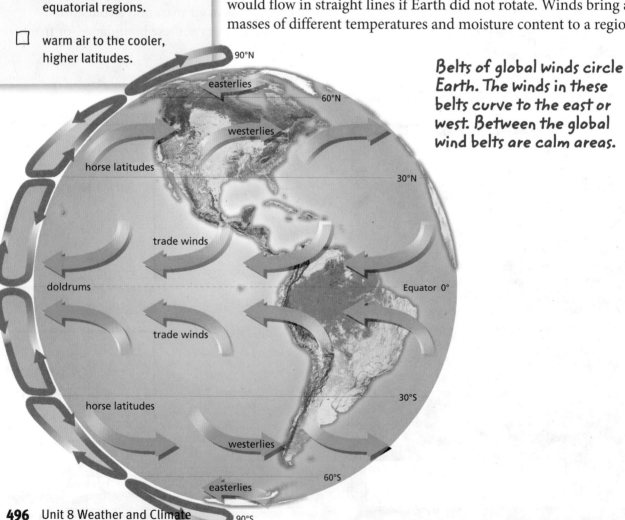

90°N
easterlies
60°N
westerlies
horse latitudes
30°N
trade winds
doldrums
Equator 0°
trade winds
horse latitudes
30°S
westerlies
60°S
easterlies
90°S

© Houghton Mifflin Harcourt Publishing Company

How do jet streams affect weather?

Long-distance winds that travel above global winds for thousands of kilometers are called **jet streams**. Air moves in jet streams with speeds that are at least 92 kilometers per hour and are often greater than 180 kilometers per hour. Like global and local winds, jet streams form because Earth's surface is heated unevenly. They flow in a wavy pattern from west to east.

Each hemisphere usually has two main jet streams, a polar jet stream and a subtropical jet stream. The polar jet streams flow closer to the poles in summer than in winter. Jet streams can affect temperatures. For example, a polar jet stream can pull cold air down from Canada into the United States and pull warm air up toward Canada. Jet streams also affect precipitation patterns. Strong storms tend to form along jet streams. Scientists must know where a jet stream is flowing to make accurate weather predictions.

Active Reading 15 **Identify** What are two ways jet streams affect weather?

_____

_____

_____

_____

In winter months, the polar jet stream flows across much of the United States.

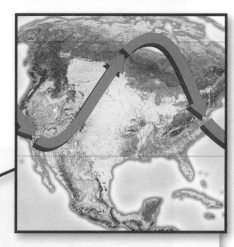

Polar jet stream

Subtropical jet streams

Polar jet stream

Visualize It!

16 **Infer** How does the polar jet stream influence the weather on the southern tip of South America?

_____

_____

_____

_____

© Houghton Mifflin Harcourt Publishing Company

Ocean Effects

How do ocean currents influence weather?

The same global winds that blow across the surface of Earth also push water across Earth's oceans, causing surface currents. Different winds cause currents to flow in different directions. The flow of surface currents moves energy as heat from one part of Earth to another. As the map below shows, both warm-water and cold-water currents flow from one ocean to another. Water near the equator carries energy from the sun to other parts of the ocean. The energy from the warm currents is transferred to colder water or to the atmosphere, changing local temperatures and humidity.

Oceans also have an effect on weather in the form of hurricanes and monsoons. Warm ocean water fuels hurricanes. Monsoons are winds that change direction with the seasons. During summer, the land becomes much warmer than the sea in some areas of the world. Moist wind flows inland, often bringing heavy rains.

Visualize It!

17 Summarize Describe how ocean currents help make temperatures at different places on Earth's surface more similar than they would be if there were no currents.

_____

_____

_____

_____

_____

Warm current
Cold current

Surface currents are caused by winds. They distribute energy across Earth's surface, changing local temperature and humidity.

© Houghton Mifflin Harcourt Publishing Company

Cool Ocean Currents Lower Coastal Air Temperatures

As currents flow, they warm or cool the atmosphere above, affecting local temperatures. The California current is a cold-water current that keeps the average summer high temperatures of coastal cities such as San Diego around 26 °C (78 °F). Cities that lie inland at the same latitude have warmer averages. The graph below shows average monthly temperatures for San Diego and El Centro, California.

Visualize It!

18 Explain Why are temperatures in San Diego, California, usually cooler than they are in El Centro, California?

_____

_____

_____

Average Monthly Temperatures

Source: weather.com

Warm Ocean Currents Raise Coastal Air Temperatures

In areas where warm ocean currents flow, coastal cities have warmer winter temperatures than inland cities at similar latitudes. For example, temperatures vary considerably from the coastal regions to the inland areas of Norway due to the warmth of the North Atlantic Current. Coastal cities such as Bergen have relatively mild winters. Inland cities such as Lillehammer have colder winters but temperatures similar to the coastal cities in summer.

Visualize It!

19 Identify Circle the city that is represented by each color in the graph.

■ Lillehammer/Bergen

■ Lillehammer/Bergen

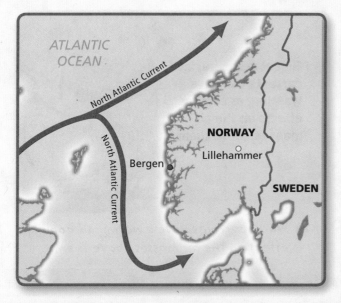

Average Monthly High Temperatures

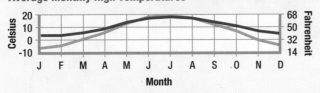

Source: worldweather.org

© Houghton Mifflin Harcourt Publishing Company

Visual Summary

To complete this summary, circle the correct word. Then, use the key below to check your answers. You can use this page to review the main concepts of the lesson.

Influences of Weather

Understanding the water cycle is key to understanding weather.

20 Weather is affected by the amount of oxygen / water in the air.

A front forms where two air masses meet.

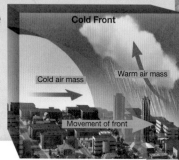

Cold Front

Cold air mass

Warm air mass

Movement of front

21 When a warm air mass and a cool air mass meet, the warm / cool air mass usually moves upward.

Low-pressure systems bring stormy weather, and high-pressure systems bring dry, clear weather.

Warm air rises

22 In a low-pressure system, air moves upward / downward.

Pressure differences from the uneven heating of Earth's surface cause predictable patterns of wind.

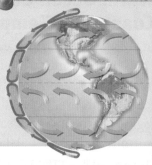

23 Global wind patterns occur as, due to temperature differences, air rises / sinks at the poles and rises / sinks at the equator.

Global ocean surface currents can have warming or cooling effects on the air masses above them.

24 Warm currents have a warming / cooling effect on the air masses above them.

Answers: 20 water; 21 warm; 22 upward; 23 sinks; rises; 24 warming

25 **Synthesize** How do air masses cause weather changes?

© Houghton Mifflin Harcourt Publishing Company

Lesson Review

Vocabulary

For each pair of terms, explain how the meanings of the terms differ.

1 *front* and *air mass*

_____

_____

_____

2 *high-pressure system* and *low-pressure system*

_____

_____

_____

3 *jet streams* and *global wind belts*

_____

_____

_____

Key Concepts

4 Apply If the weather becomes stormy for a short time and then becomes colder, which type of front has most likely passed?

_____

5 Describe Explain how an ocean current can affect the temperature and the amount of moisture of the air mass above the current and above nearby coastlines.

_____

_____

_____

_____

6 Synthesize How does the water cycle affect weather?

_____

_____

_____

_____

_____

Critical Thinking

Use the diagram below to answer the following question.

Cool air descends   Warm air rises

7 Interpret How does the movement of air affect the type of weather that forms from high-pressure and low-pressure systems?

_____

_____

_____

_____

_____

_____

8 Explain How does the polar jet stream affect temperature and precipitation in North America?

_____

_____

_____

_____

9 Describe Explain how changes in weather are caused by the interaction of air masses.

_____

_____

_____

_____

_____

© Houghton Mifflin Harcourt Publishing Company

My Notes

© Houghton Mifflin Harcourt Publishing Company

© Houghton Mifflin Harcourt Publishing Company

Severe Weather and Weather Safety

ESSENTIAL QUESTION

How can humans protect themselves from hazardous weather?

By the end of this lesson, you should be able to describe the major types of hazardous weather and the ways human beings can protect themselves from hazardous weather and from sun exposure.

6.ESS2.6, 6.PS3.4

Lightning is often the most dangerous part of a thunderstorm. Thunderstorms are one type of severe weather that can cause a lot of damage.

© Houghton Mifflin Harcourt Publishing Company • Image Credits: ©A. T. Willett/The Image Bank/Getty Images

Lesson Labs

Quick Labs
- Create your Own Lightning
- Sun Protection

Exploration Lab
- Preparing for Severe Weather

Engage Your Brain

1 Describe Fill in the blanks with the word or phrase that you think correctly completes the following sentences.

A _____ forms a funnel cloud and has high winds.

A flash or bolt of light across the sky during a storm is called _____

_____ is the sound that follows lightning during a storm.

One way to protect yourself from the sun's rays is to wear _____

2 Identify Name the weather event that is occurring in the photo. What conditions can occur when this event happens in an area?

_____

_____

_____

_____

Active Reading

3 Synthesize Use the sentence below to help you make an educated guess about what the term *storm surge* means. Write the meaning below.

Example sentence
Flooding causes tremendous damage to property and lives when a <u>storm surge</u> moves onto shore.

storm surge:

_____

_____

_____

_____

Vocabulary Terms
- thunderstorm
- lightning
- thunder
- hurricane
- storm surge
- tornado

4 Apply As you learn the definition of each vocabulary term in this lesson, create your own definition or sketch to help you remember the meaning of the term.

© Houghton Mifflin Harcourt Publishing Company • Image Credits: (bkgd) ©A. T. Willett/The Image Bank/Getty Images; (t) ©Terra Satellite/EOS/NASA

☑ Take Cover!

What do we know about thunderstorms?

SPLAAAAAT! BOOOOM! The loud, sharp noise of thunder might surprise you, and maybe even make you jump. The thunder may have been joined by lightning, wind, and rain. A **thunderstorm** is an intense local storm that forms strong winds, heavy rain, lightning, thunder, and sometimes hail. A thunderstorm is an example of severe weather. Severe weather is weather that can cause property damage and sometimes death.

Thunderstorms Form from Rising Air

Thunderstorms get their energy from humid air. When warm, humid air near the ground mixes with cooler air above, the warm air creates an updraft that can build a thunderstorm quickly. Cold downdrafts bring precipitation and eventually end the storm by preventing more warm air from rising.

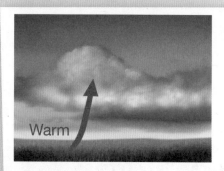

Step 1
In the first stage, warm air rises and forms a cumulus cloud. The water vapor releases energy when it condenses into cloud droplets. This energy increases the air motion. The cloud continues building up.

Step 2
Ice particles may form in the low temperatures near the top of the cloud. As the ice particles grow large, they begin to fall and pull cold air down with them. This strong downdraft brings heavy rain or hail.

Step 3
During the final stage, the downdraft can spread out and block more warm air from moving upward into the cloud. The storm slows down and ends.

 **Visualize It!**

5 Describe What role does warm air play in the formation of a thunderstorm?

_____

_____

_____

© Houghton Mifflin Harcourt Publishing Company

Lightning is a Discharge of Electrical Energy

If you have ever shuffled your feet on a carpet, you may have felt a small shock when you touched a doorknob. If so, you have experienced how lightning forms. **Lightning** is an electric discharge that happens between a positively charged area and a negatively charged area. While you walk around, electrical charges can collect on your body. When you touch someone or something else, the charges jump to that person or object in a spark of electricity. In a similar way, electrical charges build up near the tops and bottoms of clouds as pellets of ice move up and down through the clouds. Suddenly, a flash of lightning will spark from one place to another.

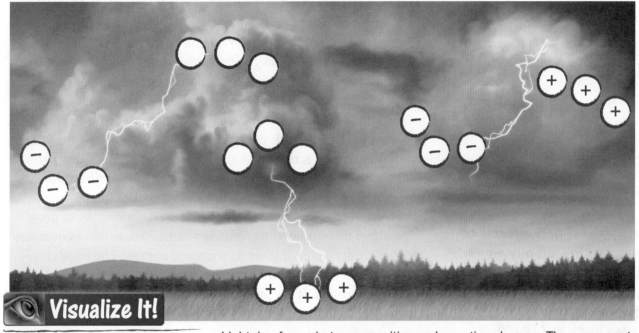

Visualize It!

6 Label Fill in the positive and negative charges in the appropriate spaces provided.

Lightning forms between positive and negative charges. The upper part of a cloud usually carries a positive electric charge. The lower part of the cloud carries mainly negative charges. Lightning is a big spark that jumps between parts of clouds, or between a cloud and Earth's surface.

Thunder Is a Result of Rapidly Expanding Air

Active Reading

7 Identify As you read, underline the explanation of what causes thunder during a storm.

When lightning strikes, the air along its path is heated to a high temperature. The superheated air quickly expands. The rapidly moving air causes the air to vibrate and release sound waves. The result is **thunder**, the sound created by the rapid expansion of air along a lightning strike.

You usually hear thunder a few seconds after you see a lightning strike, because light travels faster than sound. You can count the seconds between a lightning flash and the sound of thunder to figure out about how far away the lightning is. For every 3 seconds between lightning and its thunder, add about 1 km to the lightning strike's distance from you.

© Houghton Mifflin Harcourt Publishing Company

☑ Plan Ahead!

Active Reading

8 Identify As you read, underline the definition of *hurricane*.

What do we know about hurricanes?

A **hurricane** is a tropical low-pressure system with winds blowing at speeds of 119 km/h (74 mi/h) or more—strong enough to uproot trees. Hurricanes are called typhoons when they form over the western Pacific Ocean and cyclones when they form over the Indian Ocean.

Hurricanes Need Water to Form and Grow

A hurricane begins as a group of thunderstorms moving over tropical ocean waters. Thunderstorms form in areas of low pressure. Near the equator, warm ocean water provides the energy that can turn a low-pressure center into a violent storm. As water evaporates from the ocean, energy is transferred from the ocean water into the air. This energy makes warm air rise faster. Tall clouds and strong winds develop. As winds blow across the water from different directions into the low-pressure center, the paths bend into a spiral. The winds blow faster and faster around the low-pressure center, which becomes the center of the hurricane.

As long as a hurricane stays above warm water, it can grow bigger and more powerful. As soon as a hurricane moves over land or over cooler water, it loses its source of energy. The winds lose strength and the storm dies out. If a hurricane moves over land, the rough surface of the land reduces the winds even more.

Hurricanes in the Northern Hemisphere usually move westward with the trade winds. Near land, however, they will often move north or even back out to sea.

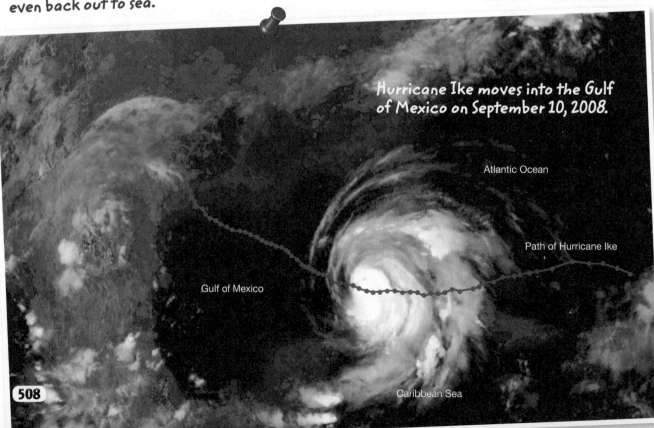

Hurricane Ike moves into the Gulf of Mexico on September 10, 2008.

Atlantic Ocean

Path of Hurricane Ike

Gulf of Mexico

Caribbean Sea

© Houghton Mifflin Harcourt Publishing Company • Image Credits: ©NOAA via Getty Images

Hurricanes Can Cause Extensive Damage

A hurricane can pound a coast with huge waves and sweep the land with strong winds and heavy rains. The storms cause damage and dangerous conditions in several ways. Hurricane winds can lift cars, uproot trees, and tear the roofs off buildings. Hurricanes may also produce tornadoes that can cause even more damage. Heavy rains from hurricanes may make rivers overflow their banks and flood nearby areas. When a hurricane moves into a coastal area, it also pushes a huge mass of ocean water known as a **storm surge**. In a storm surge, the sea level rises several meters, backing up rivers and flooding the shore. A storm surge can be the most destructive and deadliest part of a hurricane. Large waves add to the damage. A hurricane may affect an area for a few hours or a few days, but the damage may take weeks or even months to clean up.

Active Reading

9 Describe What are three of the dangers associated with hurricanes?

_____

_____

The storm surge and debris from Hurricane Ike cover a street on September 12, 2008, in Seabrook, Texas.

Think Outside the Book (Inquiry)

10 Apply With a classmate, discuss why hurricanes are more likely to make landfall in Florida than they are to hit California. You may need to refer to a map of ocean currents to find the answer.

© Houghton Mifflin Harcourt Publishing Company • Image Credits: AP Photo/Kim Christensen

☑ Secure Loose Objects!

What do we know about tornadoes?

A **tornado** is a destructive, rotating column of air that has very high wind speeds and that is sometimes visible as a funnel-shaped cloud. A tornado forms when a thunderstorm meets horizontal winds at a high altitude. These winds cause the warm air rising in the thunderstorm to spin. A storm cloud may form a thin funnel shape that has a very low pressure center. As the funnel reaches the ground, the higher-pressure air rushes into the low-pressure area. The result is high-speed winds, which cause the damage associated with tornadoes.

Clouds begin to rotate, signaling that a tornado may form.

The funnel cloud becomes visible as the tornado picks up dust from the ground or particles from the air.

The tornado moves along the ground before it dies out.

© Houghton Mifflin Harcourt Publishing Company • Image Credits: (t) ©Jim Edds/Photo Researchers, Inc.; (c) ©Digital Vision/Getty Images; (b) ©Reed Timmer/SPL/Photo Researchers, Inc.

Think Outside the Book

11 Illustrate Read the description of the weather conditions that cause tornadoes and draw a sketch of what those conditions might look like.

Most Tornadoes Happen in the Midwest

Tornadoes happen in many places, but they are most common in the United States in *Tornado Alley*. Tornado Alley reaches from Texas up through the midwestern United States, including Iowa, Kansas, Nebraska, and Ohio. Many tornadoes form in the spring and early summer, typically along a front between cool, dry air and warm, humid air.

Tornadoes Can Cause Extensive Damage

The danger of a tornado is mainly due to the high speed of its winds. Winds in a tornado's funnel may have speeds of more than 400 km/h. Most injuries and deaths caused by tornadoes happen when people are struck by objects blown by the winds or when they are trapped in buildings that collapse.

Active Reading

12 Identify As you read, underline what makes a tornado so destructive.

13 Summarize In the overlapping sections of the Venn diagram, list the characteristics that are shared by the different types of storms. In the outer sections, list the characteristics that are specific to each type of storm.

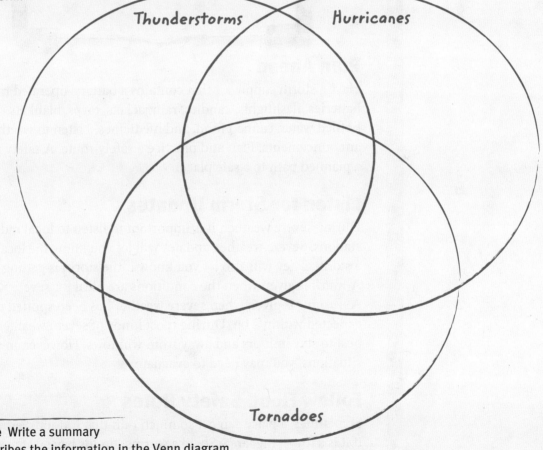

14 Conclude Write a summary that describes the information in the Venn diagram.

_____

_____

_____

_____

© Houghton Mifflin Harcourt Publishing Company

☑ Be Prepared!

What can people do to prepare for severe weather?

Severe weather is weather that can cause property damage, injury, and sometimes death. Hail, lightning, high winds, tornadoes, hurricanes, and floods are all part of severe weather. Hailstorms can damage crops and cars and can break windows. Lightning starts many forest fires and kills or injures hundreds of people and animals each year. Winds and tornadoes can uproot trees and destroy homes. Flooding is also a leading cause of weather-related deaths. Most destruction from hurricanes results from flooding due to storm surges.

Think Outside the Book · Inquiry

15 Apply Research severe weather in your area and come up with a plan for safety.

Plan Ahead

Have a storm supply kit that contains a battery-operated radio, batteries, flashlights, candles, rain jackets, tarps, blankets, bottled water, canned food, and medicines. Listen to weather announcements. Plan and practice a safety route. A safety route is a planned path to a safe place.

Listen for Storm Updates

During severe weather, it is important to listen to local radio or TV stations. Severe weather updates will let you know the location of a storm. They will also let you know if the storm is getting worse. A *watch* is given when the conditions are ideal for severe weather. A *warning* is given when severe weather has been spotted or is expected within 24 h. During most kinds of severe weather, it is best to stay indoors and away from windows. However, in some situations, you may need to evacuate.

Follow Flood Safety Rules

Sometimes, a place can get so much rain that it floods, especially if it is a low-lying area. So, like storms, floods have watches and warnings. However, little advance notice can usually be given that a flood is coming. A flash flood is a flood that rises and falls very quickly. The best thing to do during a flood is to find a high place to stay until it is over. You should always stay out of floodwaters. Even shallow water can be dangerous because it can move fast.

© Houghton Mifflin Harcourt Publishing Company • Image Credits: ©IMAGEMORE Co. Ltd./Alamy

What can people do to stay safe during thunderstorms?

Stay alert when thunderstorms are predicted or when dark, tall clouds are visible. If you are outside and hear thunder, seek shelter immediately and stay there for 30 min after the thunder ends. Heavy rains can cause sudden, or flash, flooding, and hailstones can damage property and harm living things.

Lightning is one of the most dangerous parts of a thunderstorm. Because lightning is attracted to tall objects, it is important to stay away from trees if you are outside. If you are in an open area, stay close to the ground so that you are not the tallest object in the area. If you can, get into a car. Stay away from ponds, lakes, or other bodies of water. If lightning hits water while you are swimming or wading in it, you could be hurt or killed. If you are indoors during a thunderstorm, avoid using electrical appliances, running water, and phone lines.

How can people stay safe during a tornado?

Tornadoes are too fast and unpredictable for you to attempt to outrun, even if you are in a car. If you see or hear a tornado, go to a place without windows, such as basement, a storm cellar, or a closet or hallway. Stay away from areas that are likely to have flying objects or other dangers. If you are outside, lie in a ditch or low-lying area. Protect your head and neck by covering them with your arms and hands.

How can people stay safe during a hurricane?

If your family lives where hurricanes may strike, have a plan to leave the area, and gather emergency supplies. If a hurricane is approaching your area, listen to weather reports for storm updates. Secure loose objects outside, and cover windows with storm shutters or boards. During a storm, stay indoors and away from windows. If ordered to evacuate the area, do so immediately. After a storm, be aware of downed power lines, hanging branches, and flooded areas.

16 Apply What would you do in each of these scenarios?

Scenario	What would you do?
You are swimming at an outdoor pool when you hear thunder in the distance.	
You and your family are watching TV when you hear a tornado warning that says a tornado has been spotted in the area.	
You are listening to the radio when the announcer says that a hurricane is headed your way and may make landfall in 3 days.	

© Houghton Mifflin Harcourt Publishing Company • Image Credits: ©Bert Kohlgraf/Flickr/Getty Images

☑ Use Sun Sense!

How can people protect their skin from the sun?

Active Reading

17 Identify As you read, underline when the sun's ray's are strongest during the day.

Human skin contains melanin, which is the body's natural protection against ultraviolet (UV) radiation from the sun. The skin produces more melanin when it is exposed to the sun, but UV rays will still cause sunburn when you spend too much time outside. It is particularly important to protect your skin when the sun's rays are strongest, usually between 10 A.M and 4 P.M.

Know the Sun's Hazards

It's easy to notice the effects of a sunburn. Sunburn usually appears within a few hours after sun exposure. It causes red, painful skin that feels hot to the touch. Prolonged exposure to the sun will lead to sunburn in even the darkest-skinned people. Sunburn can lead to skin cancer and premature aging of the skin. The best way to prevent sunburn is to protect your skin from the sun, even on cloudy days. UV rays pass right through clouds and can give you a false feeling of protection from the sun.

Wear Sunscreen and Protective Clothing

Even if you tan easily, you should still use sunscreen. For most people, a sun protection factor (SPF) of 30 or more will prevent burning for about 1.5 h. Babies and people who have pale skin should use an SPF of 45 or more. In addition, you can protect your skin and eyes in different ways. Seek the shade, and wear hats, sunglasses, and perhaps even UV light-protective clothing.

Have fun in the sun! Just be sure to protect your skin from harmful rays.

© Houghton Mifflin Harcourt Publishing Company • Image Credits: (bkgd) ©Imagebroker/Alamy; (l) ©Vision/Krasnig/Digital Vision/Getty Images

How can people protect themselves from summer heat?

Heat exhaustion is a condition in which the body has been exposed to high temperatures for an extended period of time. Symptoms include cold, moist skin, normal or near-normal body temperature, headache, nausea, and extreme fatigue. *Heat stroke* is a condition in which the body loses its ability to cool itself by sweating because the victim has become dehydrated.

Limit Outdoor Activities

When outdoor temperatures are high, be cautious about exercising outdoors for long periods of time. Pay attention to how your body is feeling, and go inside or to a shady spot if you are starting to feel light-headed or too warm.

Drink Water

Heat exhaustion and heat stroke can best be prevented by drinking 6 to 8 oz of water at least 10 times a day when you are active in warm weather. If you are feeling overheated, dizzy, nauseous, or are sweating heavily, drink something cool (not cold). Drink about half a glass of cool water every 15 min until you feel like your normal self.

Drinking water is one of the best things you can do to keep yourself healthy in hot weather.

Visualize It!

18 Describe List all the ways the people in the photo of the beach may have protected themselves from overexposure to the sun.

_____

_____

_____

_____

_____

_____

_____

_____

Know the Signs of Heat Stroke

Active Reading **19 Identify** Underline signs of heat stroke in the paragraph below.

Heat stroke is life threatening, so it is important to know the signs and treatment for it. Symptoms of heat stroke include hot, dry skin; higher than normal body temperature; rapid pulse; rapid, shallow breathing; disorientation; and possible loss of consciousness.

What to Do In Case of Heat Stroke

☐ Seek emergency help immediately.

☐ If there are no emergency facilities nearby, move the person to a cool place.

☐ Cool the person's body by immersing it in a cool (not cold) bath or using wet towels.

☐ Do not give the person food or water if he or she is vomiting.

☐ Place ice packs under the person's armpits.

© Houghton Mifflin Harcourt Publishing Company • Image Credits: (bkgd) ©Imagebroker/Alamy; (l) ©Visual Ideas/Nora Pelaez/Blend Images/Getty Images; (r) ©Andy Crawford/Dorling Kindersley/Getty Images

Visual Summary

To complete this summary, circle the correct word or phrase. Then use the key below to check your answers. You can use this page to review the main concepts of the lesson.

Severe Weather

Thunderstorms are intense weather systems that produce strong winds, heavy rain, lightning, and thunder.

20 One of the most dangerous parts of a thunderstorm is lightning / thunder.

A hurricane is a large, rotating tropical weather system with strong winds that can cause severe property damage.

21 An important step to plan for a hurricane is to buy raingear / stock a supply kit.

Tornadoes are rotating columns of air that touch the ground and can cause severe damage.

22 The damage from a tornado is mostly caused by associated thunderstorms / high-speed winds.

It is important to plan ahead and listen for weather updates in the event of severe weather.

23 One of the biggest dangers of storms that produce heavy rains or storm surges is flooding / low temperatures.

Prolonged exposure to the sun can cause sunburn, skin cancer, and heat-related health effects.

24 One of the best ways to avoid heat-related illnesses while in the sun is to stay active / drink water.

Answers: 20 lightning; 21 stock a supply kit; 22 high-speed winds; 23 flooding; 24 drink water

---

25 **Synthesize** What are three ways in which severe weather can be dangerous?

© Houghton Mifflin Harcourt Publishing Company • Image Credits: (l) ©Reed Timmer/SPL/Photo Researchers, Inc.; (tr) ©Bert Kohlgraf/Flickr/Getty Images; (cr) ©NOAA via Getty Images

Lesson Review

Vocabulary

Draw a line that matches the term with the correct definition.

1 hurricane

2 tornado

3 severe weather

4 thunderstorm

5 storm surge

A a huge mass of ocean water that floods the shore

B a storm with lightning and thunder

C a violently rotating column of air stretching to the ground

D weather that can potentially destroy property or cause loss of life

E a tropical low-pressure system with winds of 119 km/h or more

Key Concepts

6 Thunder is caused by _____

7 An electrical discharge between parts of clouds or a cloud and the ground is called _____

8 The sun's ultraviolet rays can cause skin damage including sunburn and even skin _____

9 **Explain** How can a person prepare for hazardous weather well in advance?

_____

_____

_____

10 **Describe** What can people do to stay safe before and during a storm with high winds and heavy rains?

_____

_____

_____

_____

Critical Thinking

Use the map below to answer the following question.

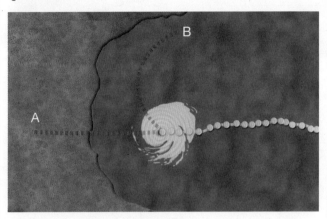

11 **Interpret** Would a hurricane be more likely to remain a hurricane if it reached point A or point B? Explain your answer.

_____

_____

_____

12 **Explain** Why do hurricanes form in tropical latitudes?

_____

_____

_____

13 **Describe** What two weather conditions are needed for tornadoes to form?

_____

_____

14 **Explain** Why is hail sometimes dangerous?

_____

_____

_____

15 **Summarize** What can you do to avoid overexposure to the sun's rays?

_____

_____

© Houghton Mifflin Harcourt Publishing Company

My Notes

© Houghton Mifflin Harcourt Publishing Company

© Houghton Mifflin Harcourt Publishing Company

Weather Maps and Weather Prediction

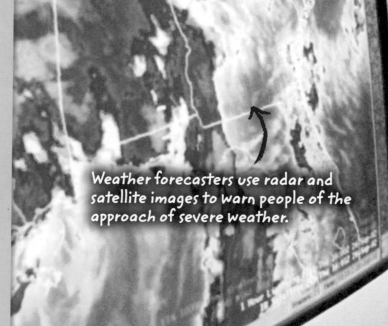

Weather forecasters use radar and satellite images to warn people of the approach of severe weather.

ESSENTIAL QUESTION

What tools do we use to predict weather?

By the end of this lesson, you should understand how meteorologists forecast the weather using weather maps and other data.

6.ESS2.5

© Houghton Mifflin Harcourt Publishing Company • Image Credits: (bg) ©Erik S. Lesser/Stringer/Getty Images News/Getty Images

Engage Your Brain

1 Describe Fill in the blank with the word or phrase that you think correctly completes the following sentences.

The job of a _____ is to analyze scientific data to predict future weather conditions.

The location, movement, and intensity of precipitation can be found by using

_____

The elements of weather that are measured and analyzed to make accurate forecasts include

_____

2 Assess What industry is represented in the photo below? What other industries rely on accurate weather forecasts?

_____

_____

Active Reading

3 Synthesize You can often define an unknown word if you know the meaning of its word parts. Use the word parts and sentence below to make an educated guess about the meaning of the word *meteorology*.

Word part	Meaning
meteoron	phenomenon in the sky
-ology	the study of, science of

Example sentence
Studying <u>meteorology</u> helps you to understand weather events.

meteorology:

_____

_____

Vocabulary Terms

• weather forecasting
• meteorology
• station model

4 Identify This list contains the vocabulary terms you'll learn in this lesson. As you read, circle the definition of each term.

© Houghton Mifflin Harcourt Publishing Company • Image Credits: (bg) ©Erik S. Lesser/Stringer/Getty Images News/Getty Images; (tr) ©David Vaughan/Photo Researchers, Inc.

Cloudy with a chance of ...

What is weather forecasting?

Looking at the weather outdoors in the morning helps you to decide what clothes to wear that day. Different observations give clues to the current weather. The leaves in the trees may be moving if it is windy. If the sky is gray and the streets are shiny, it may be raining.

Checking the weather forecast also helps determine how the weather might change. **Weather forecasting** is the analysis of scientific data to predict future weather conditions.

What elements of weather are forecast?

Weather forecasters study the elements of weather to make detailed predictions. The study of weather and Earth's atmosphere is called **meteorology** [mee•tee•uh•RAHL•uh•jee]. Scientists who study meteorology are called *meteorologists*.

Eight elements of weather are observed around the clock. These elements are air temperature, humidity, wind direction, wind speed, clouds, precipitation, atmospheric pressure, and visibility. Using these eight elements to make accurate weather forecasts helps people stay safe and comfortable. To make the best predictions, meteorologists need accurate data.

5 Infer Forest firefighters need accurate and detailed weather forecasts. What weather elements would these firefighters be most interested in? Explain.

_____
_____
_____
_____
_____
_____

6 Apply Identify three elements of weather that appear in this beach scene.

A _____

B _____

C _____

© Houghton Mifflin Harcourt Publishing Company

The Hurricane Hunters

Flying in stormy weather can be an uncomfortable and frightening experience. Yet, some pilots are trained to fly into the most intense storms. The Hurricane Hunters of the National Oceanic and Atmospheric Administration (NOAA) fly right into the eye of tropical storms and hurricanes to collect valuable data. Weather forecasters use the data to predict a storm's path and intensity.

Hurricane Hunter Planes

The weather-sensing equipment aboard NOAA's WP-3D Orion is quite advanced. The planes are equipped with radar in the nose, in the tail, and on the underside of the fuselage. Radiometers on the wings measure wind speed once every second. These and other data are sent immediately to the airplane's computer system.

UNITED STATES DEPT. OF COMM

Wind gust probe

Weather radar for 360-degree view

Sensors are released from the plane's belly.

Falling Dropsonde

A lightweight instrument package called a *dropsonde* [DRAHP•sahnd] is launched from the aircraft. As the dropsonde descends through the storm, it collects data twice every second. Data about temperature, humidity, wind speed, and air pressure are sent back to the plane.

Extend

Inquiry

7 Explain How do airplanes help weather forecasters make predictions about the movement and intensity of storms?

8 Research Find out about another technology that is used to gather weather data by sea or by air.

9 Assess Explain how this technology is used in an oral report, poster presentation, or slide show.

© Houghton Mifflin Harcourt Publishing Company • Image Credits: (bg) ©NOAA; (c) ©NOAA/AOC

What's Going on *up There?*

How are weather data collected?

To predict the weather, meteorologists must look at data that come from different sources. Meteorologists use many kinds of advanced technologies to gather this data. These technologies are found at ground stations and in balloons, aircraft, and satellites.

By Ground Stations

Land-based ground stations, also called *automated surface stations*, collect weather data from the lower atmosphere 24 hours a day. A variety of weather-sensing instruments are found at these ground stations. These instruments measure pressure, temperature, humidity, precipitation, wind speed, visibility, and cloud cover. Many ground stations are located near airports and transmit computer-generated voice observations to aircraft regularly.

By Radar

Weather radar is useful for finding the location, movement, and intensity of storms. Radar works by bouncing radio waves off precipitation. The stronger the signal that is returned to the radar, the heavier the precipitation is. Also, the longer it takes for the signal to return to the radar, the farther away the precipitation is.

Doppler radar, a type of weather radar, can detect precipitation and air motion within a storm. This technology is important for detecting and tracking severe storms and tornadoes.

Satellites, balloons, and aircraft can provide wide views of Earth's weather systems.

Visualize It!

10 Apply Which town is experiencing the most severe weather?

_____

_____

11 Apply In which town is it raining lightly?

_____

_____

Colors represent the intensity of precipitation.

Radar Map of a Strong Storm

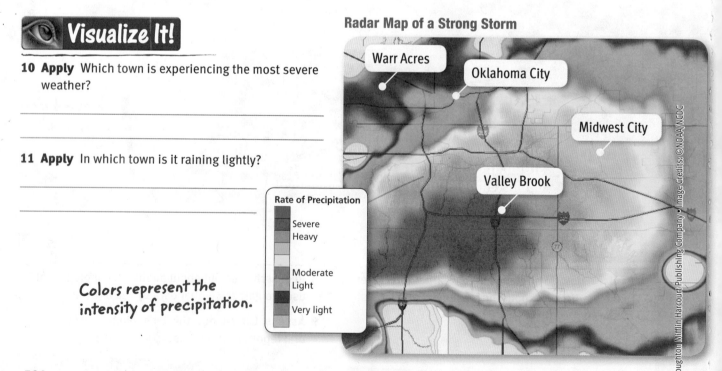

Warr Acres

Oklahoma City

Midwest City

Valley Brook

Rate of Precipitation

Severe
Heavy

Moderate
Light

Very light

© Houghton Mifflin Harcourt Publishing Company • Image Credits: ©NOAA/NCDC

By Balloons and Aircraft

Weather-sensing instruments carried by aircraft and balloons measure weather conditions in the middle to upper atmosphere. Aircraft can carry a variety of weather-sensing instruments and collect data in places far from ground stations, such as over oceans.

Weather balloons are released twice daily from stations around the world. These balloons collect weather information at different altitudes. Weather balloons carry a small instrument package called a radiosonde [RAY•dee•oh•sahnd]. Radiosondes measure atmospheric pressure, air temperature, and humidity up to about 32 km. They also measure wind speed and direction. Radiosondes send data by radio signal to ground stations.

Balloons such this one can gather weather data from high up in the atmosphere.

By Satellites

Orbiting weather satellites at high altitudes provide data on water vapor, cloud-top temperatures, and the movement of weather systems. Geostationary satellites and polar-orbiting satellites monitor Earth's weather. Geostationary weather satellites monitor Earth from a fixed position thousands of kilometers above Earth. Polar-orbiting satellites circle Earth and provide global information from hundreds of kilometers above Earth's surface. Cameras on satellites take images at regular intervals to track weather conditions on Earth. Digital images are sent back to ground stations. These images can be animated to show changes in weather over time.

Active Reading 12 **Compare** What is the difference between geostationary and polar-orbiting satellites?

_____

_____

Think Outside the Book Inquiry

13 **Describe** Research ways that weather predictions were made before the use of aircraft, balloons, and satellites.

© Houghton Mifflin Harcourt Publishing Company • Image Credits: (l) ©StockTreck/Photodisc/Getty Images; (r) ©David Parker/Photo Researchers, Inc.

What kinds of symbols and maps are used to analyze the weather?

In the United States, meteorologists with the National Weather Service (NWS) collect and analyze weather data. The NWS prepares weather maps and station models to make weather data easy to use and understand.

Station Models

A **station model** is a set of meteorological symbols that represent the weather at a particular observing station. Station models are often shown on weather maps. Placing many station models on a map makes it possible to see large weather patterns, such as fronts.

A station model is a small circle that is surrounded by a set of symbols and numbers that represent current weather data at a specific location. Key weather elements shown on a station model are temperature, wind speed and direction, cloud cover, air pressure, and dew point. Note that the pointer, or wind barb, for wind direction points *into* the wind.

14 Identify What are the key weather elements shown by a station model?

_____

_____

_____

_____

_____

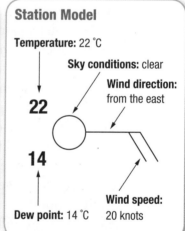

Visualize It!

15 Observe Where are the temperature and dew point recorded on a station model?

_____

Wind Speed		Cloud Coverage	
◎	calm	○ clear	
\	5 knots	◑	1/10
⟍	10 knots	◔	1/4
⟍	15 knots	◐	1/2
⟍	20 knots	◕	3/4
⟍	30 knots	◑	9/10
◤	50 knots	●	completely overcast
		⊗	sky obscured

Station Model

Temperature: 22 °C

Sky conditions: clear

Wind direction: from the east

Wind speed: 20 knots

Dew point: 14 °C

22

14

16 Apply Draw a station model below to represent the following conditions: air temperature 8 °C; dew point 6 °C; sky 1/2 overcast; wind 15 knots from the south.

© Houghton Mifflin Harcourt Publishing Company • Image Credits: ©Steve Mason/Photodisc/Getty Images

Surface Weather Maps

Meteorologists commonly use surface weather maps to show forecasts on television. A surface weather map displays air pressure and the locations of fronts. Precipitation may also be shown.

Air pressure is shown by using isobars. Isobars are lines that connect points of equal air pressure and are marked in units called *millibars*. Isobars form closed loops. The center of these loops is marked with either a capital H (high) or L (low). A capital H represents a center of high pressure, and a capital L represents a center of low pressure.

Fronts are also shown on surface weather maps. Blue lines with blue triangles are cold fronts. Red lines with red half circles are warm fronts. Stationary fronts alternate between blue and red.

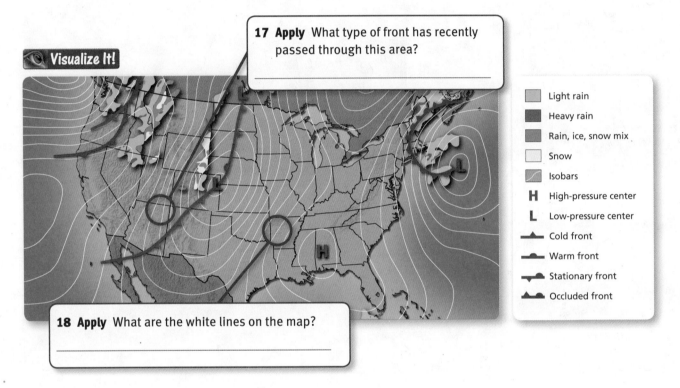

Visualize It!

17 Apply What type of front has recently passed through this area?
_____

18 Apply What are the white lines on the map?
_____

Legend:
- Light rain
- Heavy rain
- Rain, ice, snow mix
- Snow
- Isobars
- H High-pressure center
- L Low-pressure center
- Cold front
- Warm front
- Stationary front
- Occluded front

Upper-Air Charts

Another type of weather map used to analyze weather is the upper-air chart. Upper-air charts are based on data collected by instruments carried into the atmosphere by weather balloons.

Upper-air charts show wind and air pressure at middle and upper levels of Earth's atmosphere. Information from upper air charts indicates if and where weather systems will form, and if these systems will move, remain stationary, or fall apart. In addition, these charts are used to determine the position of jet streams. Airlines and airplane pilots use upper-air charts to determine flight paths and possible areas of turbulence.

© Houghton Mifflin Harcourt Publishing Company

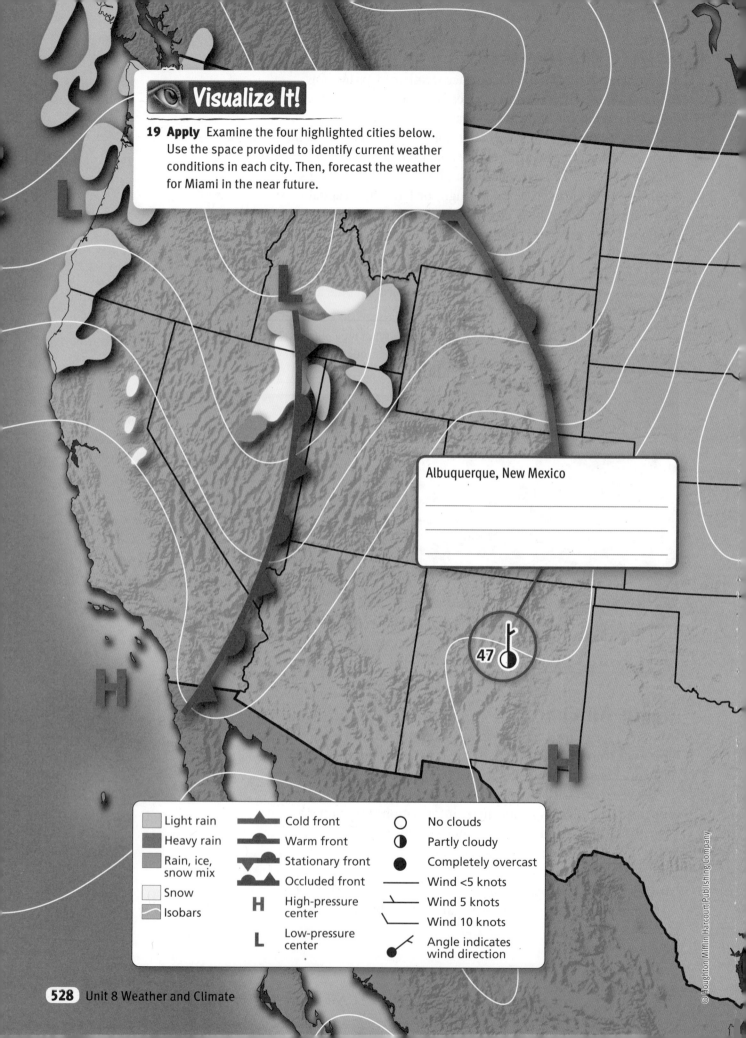

Visualize It!

19 Apply Examine the four highlighted cities below. Use the space provided to identify current weather conditions in each city. Then, forecast the weather for Miami in the near future.

Albuquerque, New Mexico

_____

_____

_____

47

▨ Light rain	◣▬ Cold front	◯ No clouds
▨ Heavy rain	◗▬ Warm front	◗ Partly cloudy
▨ Rain, ice, snow mix	◣◗▬ Stationary front	● Completely overcast
▨ Snow	◗◣ Occluded front	— Wind <5 knots
◠ Isobars	**H** High-pressure center	⌐ Wind 5 knots
	L Low-pressure center	⌐ Wind 10 knots
		⟋● Angle indicates wind direction

© Houghton Mifflin Harcourt Publishing Company

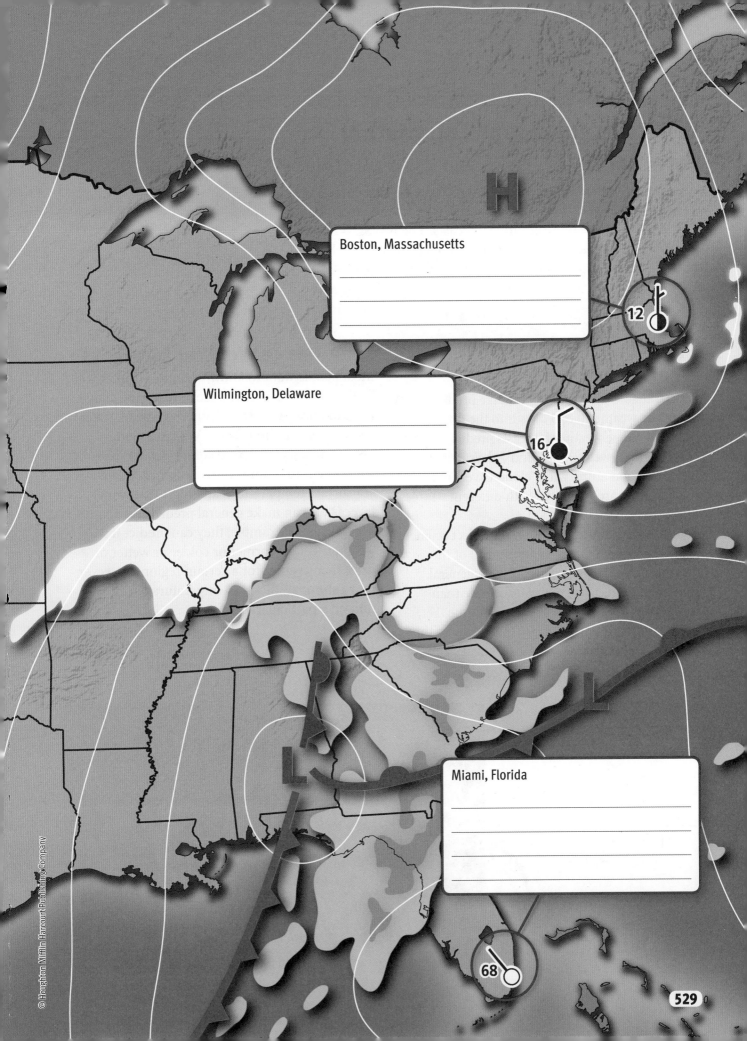

Boston, Massachusetts

_____

_____

_____

12

Wilmington, Delaware

_____

_____

_____

16

Miami, Florida

_____

_____

_____

_____

68

H

L

L

© Houghton Mifflin Harcourt Publishing Company

What are some types of weather forecasts?

As supercomputers have become faster in recent years, forecasts have also improved. Increasing amounts of weather data can be combined to create more accurate forecasts. The NWS, NOAA, and local meteorologists use computer models to develop short-range, medium-range, and long-range forecasts. These forecasts are made available to the public by radio, television, newspaper, and the Internet.

Short-Range and Medium-Range Weather Forecasts

Short-range weather forecasts make predictions about the weather 0 to 3 days into the future. Medium-range weather forecasts predict weather conditions between 3 days and 7 days into the future. Temperature, wind, cloud cover, and precipitation are predicted with different degrees of accuracy.

Weather forecasting is an imperfect science. Many variables affect weather, and all of these variables are changing constantly. In general, short-term forecasts are more accurate than forecasts made for longer periods of time. Yet, given the continuous changes that occur in the atmosphere, even short-range forecasts cannot always be accurate.

Long-Range Weather Forecasts

Most people want to know what the weather will be like in the near future. However, some people need to know what the weather will be like over a longer time period. The NWS issues long-range forecasts for periods of time that range from weeks to months into the future. Using sea surface temperatures and high-level winds, forecasters can make general predictions about the future. For example, they can predict if the weather will be warmer or colder or wetter or drier than average for a certain region. However, they cannot predict the temperature or if it will rain on a particular day.

20 Infer Why is it important for the farmer to know the long-range forecast?

_____

_____

_____

Some meteorologists prepare specialized forecasts for farmers.

© Houghton Mifflin Harcourt Publishing Company • Image Credits: ©Harald Sund/Brand X Pictures/Getty Images

Hazardous Weather Forecasts

An important job of meteorologists is to warn the public about severe weather. This information is shown as a weather "crawl" at the bottom of a television screen. The NWS issues three types of hazardous weather forecasts: weather advisories, weather watches, and weather warnings.

A weather advisory is issued when the expected weather conditions will not be a serious hazard but may cause inconvenience if caution is not used. When severe weather conditions are possible over a large geographic area, a weather watch is issued. People should prepare and have a plan of action in place in case a storm threatens. A weather warning is issued when weather conditions that pose a threat to life and property are happening or are about to happen. People who live in the path of the storm need to take immediate action.

Active Reading **21 Compare** What is the difference between a weather watch and a weather warning?

_____
_____
_____
_____
_____
_____
_____
_____

The National Weather Service issues weather advisories, weather watches, and weather warnings to inform the public about hazardous weather.

Visualize It!

22 Compose Write a caption for the photo based on a hazardous weather forecast.

_____

© Houghton Mifflin Harcourt Publishing Company • Image Credits: (bg) ©Ian Cumming/Axiom Photographic Agency/Getty Images; (br) ©Jim McDonald/Corbis

Visual Summary

To complete this summary, check the box that indicates true or false. Then use the key below to check your answers. You can use this page to review the main concepts of the lesson.

Weather Maps and Weather Prediction

Weather forecasting is the analysis of scientific data to predict likely future weather conditions.

T F

23 ☐ ☐ In order to forecast the weather, meteorologists gather weather data for five important weather elements.

Different kinds of weather data can be shown together on station models and weather maps.

T F

24 ☐ ☐ Two types of weather maps that meteorologists use to show the weather are surface weather maps and upper-air charts.

Weather data come from many sources on land and in the air.

T F

25 ☐ ☐ Weather balloons and aircraft allow for surface weather observations.

Meteorologists use computer models to make short-range, medium-range, and long-range weather forecasts.

T F

26 ☐ ☐ Three types of hazardous weather forecasts are weather advisories, weather watches, and weather warnings.

Answers: 23 F; 24 T; 25 F; 26 T

27 Synthesis Describe the technologies used to gather data, prepare a forecast, and broadcast a forecast for a town in the path of a hurricane.

© Houghton Mifflin Harcourt Publishing Company • Image Credits: ©David Parker/Photo Researchers, Inc.

Lesson Review

Vocabulary

Fill in the blank with the term that best completes the following sentences.

1 A _____ is a group of meteorological symbols that represents the weather at a particular observing station.

2 _____ is the analysis of scientific data to predict likely future weather conditions.

3 The scientific study of Earth's atmosphere and weather is called _____

Key Concepts

4 List What are the eight elements of weather that are observed for making weather forecasts?

_____
_____
_____
_____

5 Identify What kinds of data do surface weather maps provide?

_____
_____
_____

6 Summarize Describe each of the three types of hazardous weather forecasts.

_____
_____
_____
_____
_____
_____
_____
_____
_____

Critical Thinking

Use the diagram to answer the following questions.

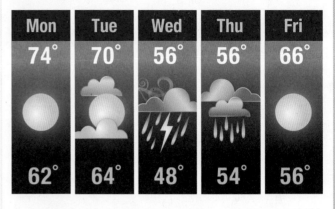

Mon	Tue	Wed	Thu	Fri
74°	70°	56°	56°	66°
62°	64°	48°	54°	56°

7 Analyze On what day will there likely be severe weather?

_____

8 Infer Between which two days will a cold front arrive? Explain.

_____
_____
_____

9 Diagram Draw a station model based on the Thursday forecast, if winds are 15 knots from the northwest.

10 Assess Why do you think weather observations are made frequently at airports around the world?

_____
_____
_____
_____
_____

© Houghton Mifflin Harcourt Publishing Company

My Notes

© Houghton Mifflin Harcourt Publishing Company

© Houghton Mifflin Harcourt Publishing Company

J. Marshall Shepherd

METEOROLOGIST AND CLIMATOLOGIST

J. Marshall Shepherd

Dr. Marshall Shepherd, who works at the University of Georgia, has been interested in weather since he made his own weather-collecting instruments for a school science project. Although the instruments he uses today, like computers and satellites, are much larger and much more powerful than the ones he made in school, they give him some of the same information.

In his work, Dr. Shepherd tries to understand weather events, such as hurricanes and thunderstorms, and relate them to current weather and climate change. He once led a team that used space-based radar to measure rainfall over urban areas. The measurements confirmed that the areas downwind of major cities experience more rainfall in summer than other areas in the same region. He explained that the excess heat retained by buildings and roads changes the way the air circulates, and this causes rain clouds to form.

While the most familiar field of meteorology is weather forecasting, research meteorology is also used in air pollution control, weather control, agricultural planning, climate change studies, and even criminal and civil investigations.

Social Studies Connection

An almanac is a type of calendar that contains various types of information, including weather forecasts and astronomical data, for every day of the year. Many people used almanacs before meteorologists started to forecast the weather. Use an almanac from the library or the Internet to find out what the weather was on the day that you were born.

© Houghton Mifflin Harcourt Publishing Company • Image Credits: (bkgd) ©Mike Theiss/National Geographic/Getty Images

JOB BOARD

Atmospheric Scientist

What You'll Do: Collect and analyze data on Earth's air pressure, humidity, and winds to make short-range and long-range weather forecasts. Work around the clock during weather emergencies like hurricanes and tornadoes.

Where You Might Work: Weather data collecting stations, radio and television stations, or private consulting firms.

Education: A bachelor's degree in meteorology, or in a closely related field with courses in meteorology, is required. A master's degree is necessary for some jobs.

Airplane Pilot

What You'll Do: Fly airplanes containing passengers or cargo, or for crop dusting, search and rescue, or fire-fighting. Before flights, check the plane's control equipment and weather conditions. Plan a safe route. Pilots communicate with air traffic control during flight to ensure a safe flight and fill out paperwork after the flight.

Where You Might Work: Flying planes for airlines, the military, radio and tv stations, freight companies, flight schools, farms, national parks, or other businesses that use airplanes.

Education: Most pilots will complete a four-year college degree before entering a pilot program. Before pilots become certified and take to the skies, they need a pilot license and many hours of flight time and training.

Snow Plow Operator

What You'll Do: In areas that receive snowfall, prepare the roads by spreading a mixture of sand and salt on the roads when snow is forecast. After a snowfall, drive snow plows to clear snow from roads and walkways.

Where You Might Work: For public organizations or private companies in cities and towns that receive snowfall.

Education: In most states, there is no special license needed, other than a driver's license.

© Houghton Mifflin Harcourt Publishing Company • Image Credits: (bkgd) ©Mike Theiss/National Geographic/Getty Images; (tr) ©Steve Bloom/Taxi

Climate

ESSENTIAL QUESTION

How is climate affected by energy from the sun and variations on Earth's surface?

By the end of this lesson, you should be able to describe the main factors that affect climate and explain how scientists classify climates.

🢒 6.ESS2.3, 6.ESS2.5, 6.ESS3.3, 6.PS3.4

Earth has a wide variety of climates, including polar climates like the one shown here. What kind of climate do you live in?

© Houghton Mifflin Harcourt Publishing Company • Image Credits: (bkgd) ©Arctic-Images/Iconica/Getty Images

Lesson Labs

Quick Labs
- Determining Climate
- Factors That Affect Climate
- The Angles of the Sun's Rays

Field Lab
- How Land Features Affect Climate

Engage Your Brain

1 Predict Check T or F to show whether you think each statement is true or false.

T	F	
☐	☐	Locations in Florida and Oregon receive the same amount of sunlight on any given day.
☐	☐	Temperature is an important part of determining the climate of an area.
☐	☐	The climate on even the tallest mountains near the equator is too warm for glaciers to form.
☐	☐	Winds can move rain clouds from one location to another.

2 Infer Volcanic eruptions can send huge clouds of gas and dust into the air. These dust particles can block sunlight. How might the eruption of a large volcano affect weather for years to come?

_____

_____

_____

_____

_____

_____

Active Reading

3 Synthesize You can often define an unknown word if you know the meaning of its word parts. Use the word parts and sentence below to make an educated guess about the meaning of the word *topography*.

Word part	Meaning
topos-	place
-graphy	writing

Example sentence
The <u>topography</u> of the area is varied, because there are hills, valleys, and flat plains all within a few square miles.

topography:

_____

_____

Vocabulary Terms

- weather
- climate
- latitude
- topography
- elevation
- surface currents

4 Apply As you learn the definition of each vocabulary term in this lesson, create your own definition or sketch to help you remember the meaning of the term.

© Houghton Mifflin Harcourt Publishing Company • Image Credits: (bkgd) ©Arctic-Images/Iconica/Getty Images; (tr) ©Prof. Stewart lowther/Photo Researchers, Inc.

How's the **Climate?**

What determines climate?

Weather conditions change from day to day. **Weather** is the condition of Earth's atmosphere at a particular time and place. **Climate**, on the other hand, describes the weather conditions in an area over a long period of time. For the most part, climate is determined by temperature and precipitation (pree•SIP•uh•tay•shuhn). But what factors affect the temperature and precipitation rates of an area? Those factors include latitude, wind patterns, elevation, locations of mountains and large bodies of water, and nearness to ocean currents.

Temperature

Temperature patterns are an important feature of climate. Although the average temperature of an area over a period of time is useful information, using only average temperatures to describe climate can be misleading. Areas that have similar average temperatures may have very different temperature ranges.

A temperature range includes all of the temperatures in an area, from the coldest temperature extreme to the warmest temperature extreme. Organisms that thrive in a region are those that can survive the temperature extremes in that region. Temperature ranges provide more information about an area and are unique to the area. Therefore, temperature ranges are a better indicator of climate than are temperature averages.

Active Reading

5 Identify As you read, underline two elements of weather that are important in determining climate.

Visualize It!

6 Infer How might the two different climates shown below affect the daily lives of the people who live there?

_____

_____

_____

_____

_____

Desert region

Polar region

© Houghton Mifflin Harcourt Publishing Company • Image Credits: (l) ©Wayne R Bilenduke/Photographer's Choice/Getty Images; (r) ©Mitchell Kanashkevich/The Image Bank/Getty Images

Precipitation

Precipitation, such as rain, snow, or hail, is also an important part of climate. As with temperature, the average yearly precipitation alone is not the best way to describe a climate. Two places that have the same average yearly precipitation may receive that precipitation in different patterns during the year. For example, one location may receive small amounts of precipitation throughout the year. This pattern would support plant life all year long. Another location may receive all of its precipitation in a few months of the year. These months may be the only time in which plants can grow. So, the pattern of precipitation in a region can determine the types of plants that grow there and the length of the growing season. Therefore, the pattern of precipitation is a better indicator of the local climate than the average precipitation alone.

Think Outside the Book Inquiry

8 Apply With a classmate, discuss what condition, other than precipitation, is likely related to better plant growth in the temperate area shown directly below than in the desert on the bottom right.

Visualize It!

7 Interpret Match the climates represented in the bar graph below to the photos by writing *A*, *B*, or *C* in the blank circles.

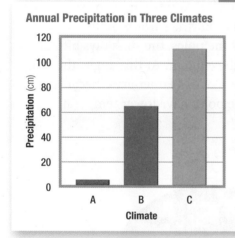

Annual Precipitation in Three Climates

There are enough resources in the area for plants to thickly cover the ground.

Some plants that grow in deserts have long roots to reach the water deep underground.

Conditions in a tropical forest allow lots of plants to grow quickly and closely together.

© Houghton Mifflin Harcourt Publishing Company • Image Credits: (t) ©Scott Kemper/Alamy; (b) ©Danita Delimont/Alamy; (c) ©Douglas Peebles Photography/Alamy

Here Comes the Sun!

How is the sun's energy related to Earth's climate?

The climate of an area is directly related to the amount of energy from the sun, or *solar energy*, that the area receives. This amount depends on the latitude (LAHT•ih•tood) of the area. **Latitude** is the angular distance in degrees north and south from the equator. Different latitudes receive different amounts of solar energy. The available solar energy powers the water cycle and winds, which affect the temperature, precipitation, and other factors that determine the local climate.

Latitude Affects the Amount of Solar Energy an Area Receives and that Area's Climate

Latitude helps determine the temperature of an area, because latitude affects the amount of solar energy an area receives. The figure below shows how the amount of solar energy reaching Earth's surface varies with latitude. Notice that the sun's rays travel in lines parallel to one another. Near the equator, the sun's rays hit Earth directly, at almost a 90° angle. At this angle, the solar energy is concentrated in a small area of Earth's surface. As a result, that area has high temperatures. At the poles, the sun's rays hit Earth at a lesser angle than they do at the equator. At this angle, the same amount of solar energy is spread over a larger area. Because the energy is less concentrated, the poles have lower temperatures than areas near the equator do.

Active Reading

9 Identify As you read, underline how solar energy affects the climate of an area.

Visualize It!

10 Analyze What is the difference between the sun's rays that strike at the equator and the sun's rays that strike at the poles?

_____

_____

_____

_____

The amount of solar energy an area receives depends on latitude.

Drawing is not to scale.

© Houghton Mifflin Harcourt Publishing Company

The Sun Powers the Water Cycle

It is easy to see how the water cycle affects weather and climate. For example, when it rains or snows, you see precipitation. In the water cycle, energy from the sun warms the surface of the ocean or other body of water. Some of the liquid water evaporates, becoming invisible water vapor, a gas. When cooled, some of the vapor condenses, turning into droplets of liquid water and forming clouds. Some water droplets collide, becoming larger. Once large enough, they fall to Earth's surface as precipitation.

Visualize It!

11 Apply Using the figure below, explain how the water cycle affects the climate of an area.

_____

_____

_____

_____

_____

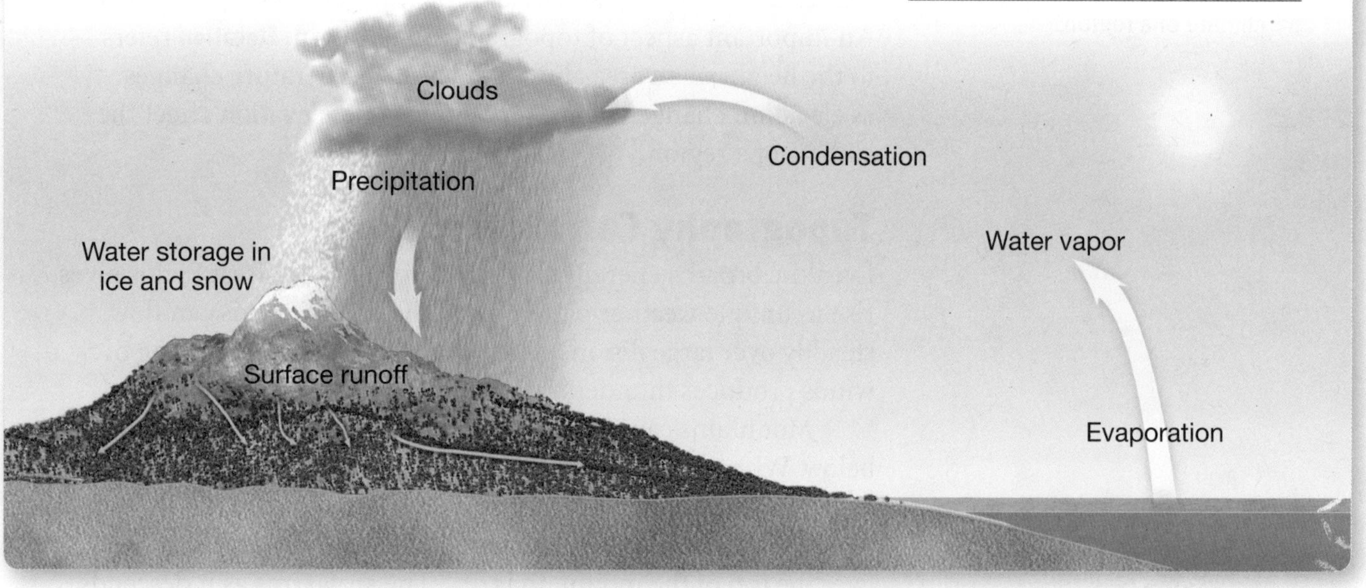

Clouds

Condensation

Precipitation

Water vapor

Water storage in ice and snow

Surface runoff

Evaporation

The Sun Powers Wind

The sun warms Earth's surface unevenly, creating areas of different air pressure. As air moves from areas of higher pressure to areas of lower pressure, it is felt as wind, as shown below. Global and local wind patterns transfer energy around Earth's surface, affecting global and local temperatures. Winds also carry water vapor from place to place. If the air cools enough, the water vapor will condense and fall as precipitation. The speed, direction, temperature, and moisture content of winds affect the climate and weather of the areas they move through.

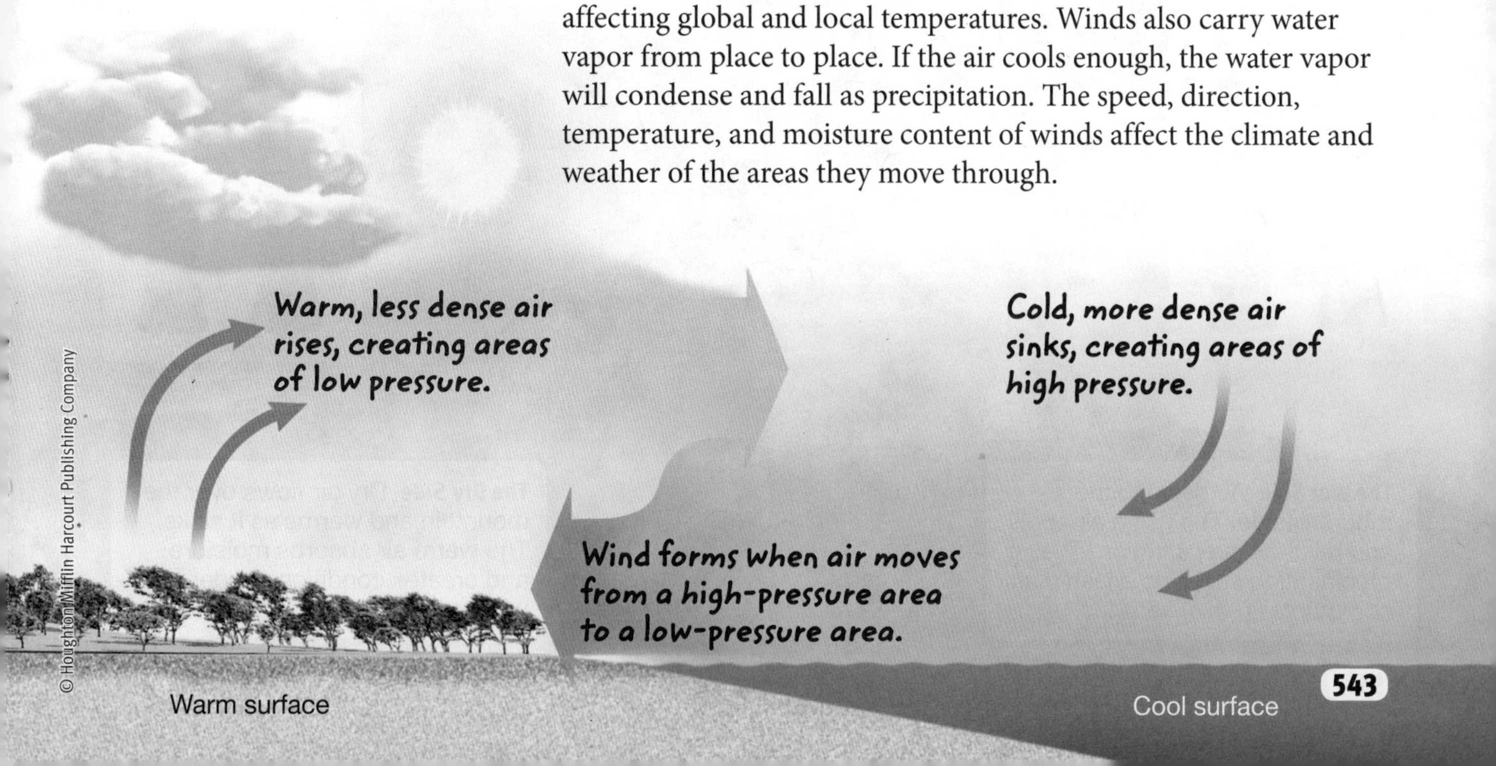

Warm, less dense air rises, creating areas of low pressure.

Cold, more dense air sinks, creating areas of high pressure.

Wind forms when air moves from a high-pressure area to a low-pressure area.

© Houghton Mifflin Harcourt Publishing Company

Warm surface

Cool surface

543

Latitude Isn't Everything

How do Earth's features affect climate?

On land, winds have to flow around or over features on Earth's surface, such as mountains. The surface features of an area combine to form its **topography** (tuh•POG•ruh•fee). Topography influences the wind patterns and the transfer of energy in an area. An important aspect of topography is elevation. **Elevation** refers to the height of an area above sea level. Temperature changes as elevation changes. Thus, topography and elevation affect the climate of a region.

Topography Can Affect Winds

Even the broad, generally flat topography of the Great Plains gives rise to unique weather patterns. On the plains, winds can flow steadily over large distances before they merge. This mixing of winds produces thunderstorms and even tornadoes.

Mountains can also affect the climate of an area, as shown below. When moist air hits a mountain, it is forced to rise up the side of the mountain. The rising air cools and often releases rain, which supports plants on the mountainside. The air that moves over the top of the mountain is dry. The air warms as it descends, creating a dry climate, which supports desert formation. Such areas are said to be in a *rain shadow,* because the air has already released all of its water by the time that it reaches this side of the mountain.

Active Reading

12 Identify As you read, underline how topography affects the climate of a region.

Visualize It!

13 Apply Circle the rain gauge in each set that corresponds to how much rain each side of the mountain is likely to receive.

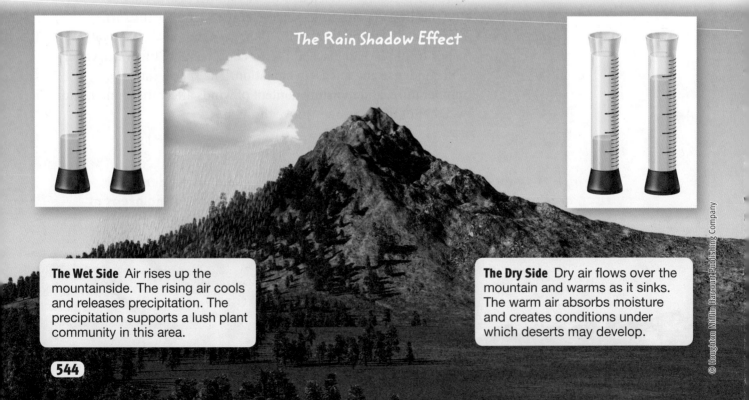

The Rain Shadow Effect

The Wet Side Air rises up the mountainside. The rising air cools and releases precipitation. The precipitation supports a lush plant community in this area.

The Dry Side Dry air flows over the mountain and warms as it sinks. The warm air absorbs moisture and creates conditions under which deserts may develop.

© Houghton Mifflin Harcourt Publishing Company

Elevation Influences Temperature

Elevation has a very strong effect on the temperature of an area. If you rode a cable car up a mountain, the temperature would decrease by about 6.5 °C (11.7 °F) for every kilometer you rose in elevation. Why does it get colder as you move higher up? Because the lower atmosphere is mainly warmed by Earth's surface that is directly below it. The warmed air lifts to higher elevations, where it expands and cools. Even close to the equator, temperatures at high elevations can be very cold. For example, Mount Kilimanjaro in Tanzania is close to the equator, but it is still cold enough at the peak to support a permanent glacier. The example below shows how one mountain can have several types of climates.

 **Visualize It!**

14 Apply Circle the thermometer that shows the most likely temperature for each photo at different elevations.

 Effects of Elevation

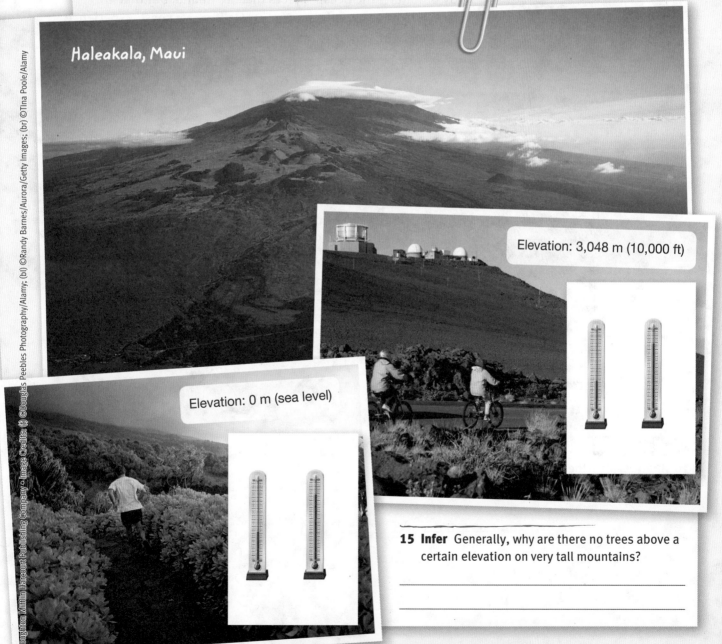

Haleakala, Maui

Elevation: 3,048 m (10,000 ft)

Elevation: 0 m (sea level)

15 Infer Generally, why are there no trees above a certain elevation on very tall mountains?

_____

_____

© Houghton Mifflin Harcourt Publishing Company • Image Credits: (t) ©Douglas Peebles Photography/Alamy; (bl) ©Randy Barnes/Aurora/Getty Images; (br) ©Tina Poole/Alamy

Waterfront Property

How do large bodies of water affect climate?

Large bodies of water, such as the ocean, can influence an area's climate. Water absorbs and releases energy as heat more slowly than land does. So, water helps moderate the temperature of nearby land. Sudden or extreme temperature changes rarely take place on land near large bodies of water. The state of Michigan, which is nearly surrounded by the Great Lakes, has more moderate temperatures than places far from large bodies of water at the same latitude. California's coastal climate is also influenced by a large body of water—the ocean. Places that are inland, but that are at the same latitude as a given place on California's coast, experience wider ranges of temperature.

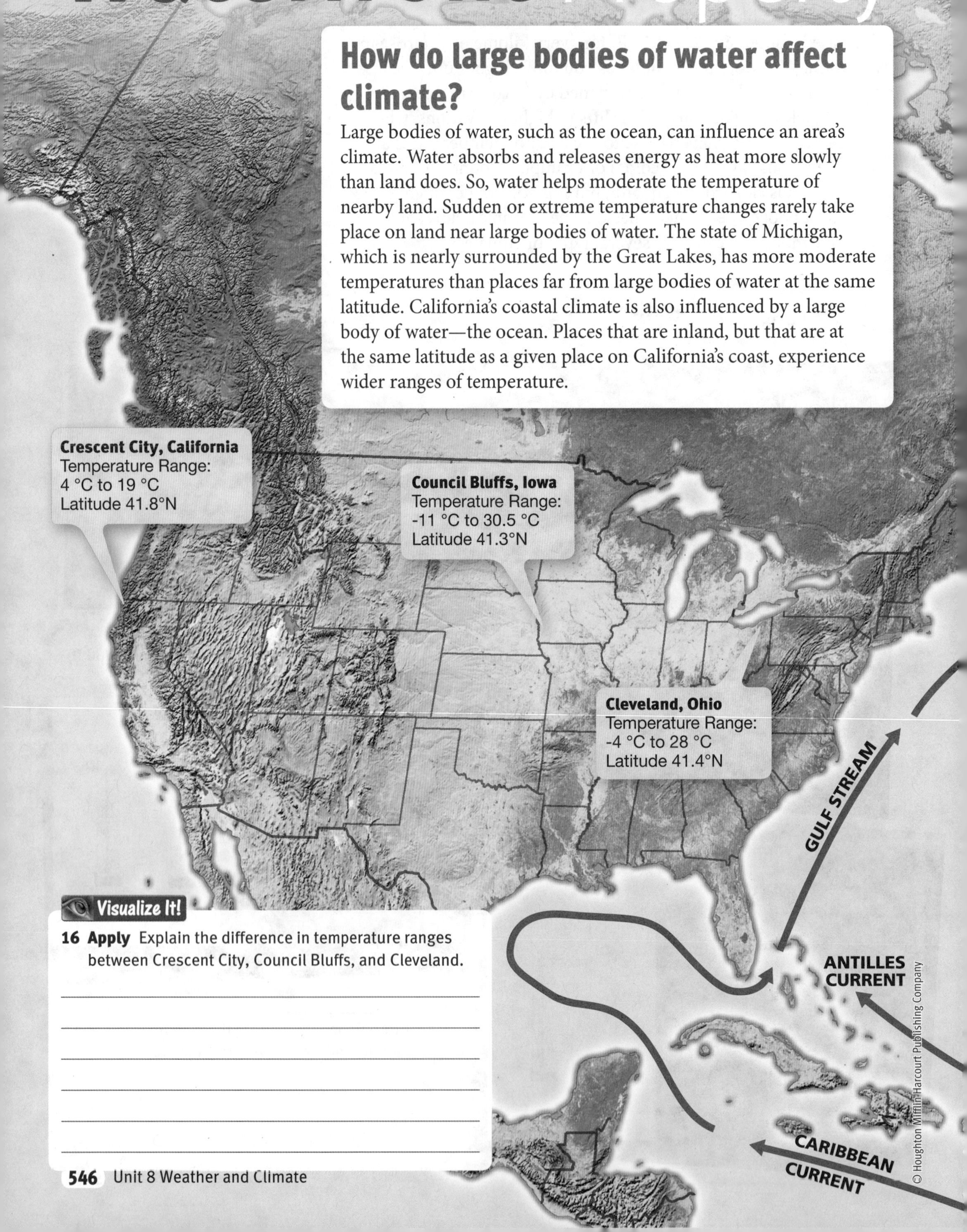

Crescent City, California
Temperature Range:
4 °C to 19 °C
Latitude 41.8°N

Council Bluffs, Iowa
Temperature Range:
-11 °C to 30.5 °C
Latitude 41.3°N

Cleveland, Ohio
Temperature Range:
-4 °C to 28 °C
Latitude 41.4°N

GULF STREAM

ANTILLES CURRENT

CARIBBEAN CURRENT

Visualize It!

16 Apply Explain the difference in temperature ranges between Crescent City, Council Bluffs, and Cleveland.

_____

_____

_____

_____

_____

_____

_____

© Houghton Mifflin Harcourt Publishing Company

How do ocean currents affect climate?

An *ocean current* is the movement of water in a certain direction. There are many different currents in the oceans. Ocean currents move water and distribute energy and nutrients around the globe. The currents on the surface of the ocean are called **surface currents.** Surface currents are driven by winds and carry warm water away from the equator and carry cool water away from the poles.

Cold currents cool the air in coastal areas, while warm currents warm the air in coastal areas. Thus, currents moderate global temperatures. For example, the Gulf Stream is a surface current that moves warm water from the Gulf of Mexico northeastward, toward Great Britain and Europe. The British climate is mild because of the warm Gulf Stream waters. Polar bears do not wander the streets of Great Britain, as they might in Natashquan, Canada, which is at a similar latitude.

NORWAY CURRENT

Natashquan, Canada
Temperature Range:
-18 °C to 14 °C
Latitude: 50.2°N

LABRADOR CURRENT

London, England
Temperature Range:
2 °C to 22 °C
Latitude 51.5°N

NORTH ATLANTIC CURRENT

GULF STREAM

ATLANTIC OCEAN

17 Summarize How do currents distribute heat around the globe?

_____

_____

_____

👁 **Visualize It!**

18 Infer How do you think that the Canary current affects the temperature in the Canary Islands?

_____

_____

_____

CANARY CURRENT

Canary Islands, Spain
Temperature Range:
12 °C to 26 °C
Latitude 28°N

NORTH EQUATORIAL CURRENT

© Houghton Mifflin Harcourt Publishing Company

Zoning Out

What are the three major climate zones?

Earth has three major types of climate zones: tropical, temperate, and polar. These zones are shown below. Each zone has a distinct temperature range that relates to its latitude. Each of these zones has several types of climates. These different climates result from differences in topography, winds, ocean currents, and geography.

Active Reading

19 Identify Underline the factor that determines the temperature ranges in each zone.

Temperate

Temperate climates have an average temperature below 18 °C (64 °F) in the coldest month and an average temperature above 10 °C (50 °F) in the warmest month. There are five temperate zone subclimates: marine west coast climates, steppe climates, humid continental climate, humid subtropical climate, and Mediterranean climate. The temperate zone is characterized by lower temperatures than the tropical zone. It is located between the tropical zone and the polar zone.

Visualize It!

20 Label What climate zone is this?

_____

Polar

The polar zone, at latitudes of 66.5° and higher, is the coldest climate zone. Temperatures rarely rise above 10 °C (50 °F) in the warmest month. The climates of the polar regions are referred to as the *polar climates*. There are three types of polar zone subclimates: subarctic climates, tundra climates, and polar ice cap climates.

ARCTIC OCEAN

NORTH AMERICA

ATLANTIC OCEAN

23.5°N

0°–Equator

PACIFIC OCEAN

SOUTH AMERICA

23.5°S

66.5°S

SOUTH[

© Houghton Mifflin Harcourt Publishing Company

21 Summarize Fill in the table for either the factor that affects climate or the effect on climate the given factor has.

Factor	Effect on climate
Latitude	
	Cooler temperatures as you travel up a tall mountain
Winds	
	Moderates weather so that highs and lows are less extreme
Surface ocean currents	
	Impacts wind patterns and the transfer of energy in an area

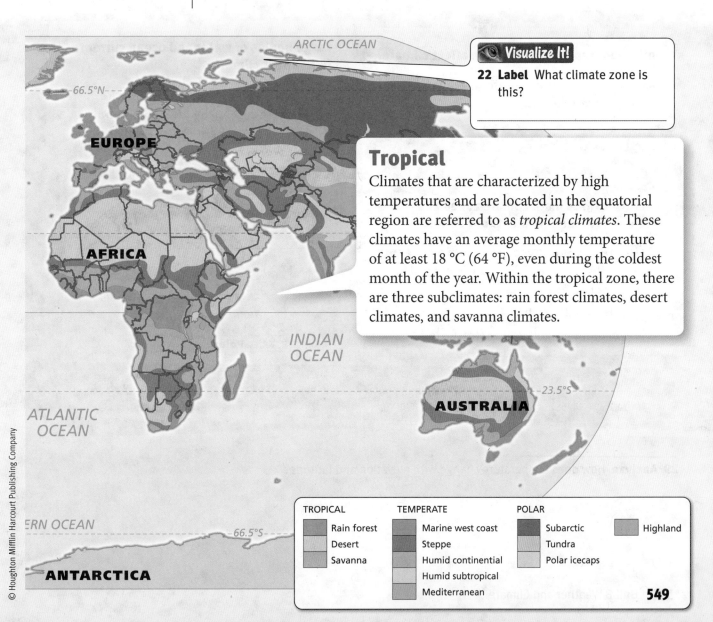

ARCTIC OCEAN

66.5°N

EUROPE

AFRICA

INDIAN OCEAN

AUSTRALIA

23.5°S

ATLANTIC OCEAN

ERN OCEAN

66.5°S

ANTARCTICA

© Houghton Mifflin Harcourt Publishing Company

Visualize It!

22 Label What climate zone is this?

_____

Tropical

Climates that are characterized by high temperatures and are located in the equatorial region are referred to as *tropical climates*. These climates have an average monthly temperature of at least 18 °C (64 °F), even during the coldest month of the year. Within the tropical zone, there are three subclimates: rain forest climates, desert climates, and savanna climates.

TROPICAL	TEMPERATE	POLAR	
Rain forest	Marine west coast	Subarctic	Highland
Desert	Steppe	Tundra	
Savanna	Humid continental	Polar icecaps	
	Humid subtropical		
	Mediterranean		

Visual Summary

To complete this summary, circle the correct word or phrase. Then, use the key below to check your answers. You can use this page to review the main concepts of the lesson.

Climate

Temperature and precipitation are used to describe climate.

23 Climate is the characteristic weather conditions in a place over a short/long period.

Both topography and elevation affect climate.

25 Temperatures decrease as elevation increases/decreases.

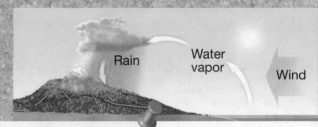

Winds transfer energy and moisture to new places.

24 Winds can affect the amount of precipitation in/elevation of an area.

Large bodies of water and ocean currents both affect climate.

26 Large bodies of water affect the climate of nearby land when cool waters absorb energy as heat from the warm air/cold land.

There are three main climate zones and many subclimates within those zones.

27 The three main types of climate zones are polar, temperate, and equatorial/tropical.

28 The three main climate zones are determined by elevation/latitude.

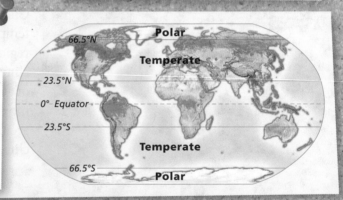

Answers: 23 long; 24 precipitation; 25 increases; 26 warm air; 27 tropical; 28 latitude

29 **Analyze** How does temperature change with elevation and latitude?

© Houghton Mifflin Harcourt Publishing Company • Image Credits: (tl) ©Danita Delimont/Alamy

Lesson Review

Vocabulary

In your own words, define the following terms.

1 topography

_____

_____

2 climate

_____

_____

Key Concepts

Fill in the table below.

Factor	Effect on Climate
3 Identify Latitude	
4 Identify Elevation	
5 Identify Large bodies of water	
6 Identify Wind	

7 Explain What provides Great Britain with a moderate climate? How?

_____

_____

_____

8 Identify What are two characteristics used to describe the climate of an area?

_____

Critical Thinking

Use the image below to answer the following question.

9 Explain Location A receives nearly 200 cm of rain each year, while Location B receives only 30 cm. Explain why Location A gets so much more rain. Use the words *rain shadow* and *precipitation* in your answer.

_____

_____

_____

_____

_____

_____

_____

10 Analyze What climate zone are you in if the temperatures are always very warm? Where is this zone located on Earth?

_____

11 Analyze How does the sun's energy affect the climate of an area?

_____

_____

_____

_____

_____

© Houghton Mifflin Harcourt Publishing Company

My Notes

© Houghton Mifflin Harcourt Publishing Company

© Houghton Mifflin Harcourt Publishing Company

Unit 8 ⟨Big Idea⟩ Air pressure, temperature, air movement, and humidity in the atmosphere affect both weather and climate.

Lesson 1
ESSENTIAL QUESTION
What is weather and how can we describe types of weather conditions?

Describe elements of weather and explain how they are measured.

Lesson 2
ESSENTIAL QUESTION
How do clouds form, and how are clouds classified?

Describe the formation and classification of clouds.

Lesson 3
ESSENTIAL QUESTION
How do the water cycle and other global patterns affect local weather?

Explain how global patterns in Earth's system influence weather.

Lesson 4
ESSENTIAL QUESTION
How can humans protect themselves from hazardous weather?

Describe the major types of hazardous weather and the ways human beings can protect themselves from hazardous weather and from sun exposure.

Lesson 5
ESSENTIAL QUESTION
What tools do we use to predict weather?

Understand how meteorologists forecast the weather using weather maps and other data.

Lesson 6
ESSENTIAL QUESTION
How is climate affected by energy from the sun and variations on Earth's surface?

Describe the main factors that affect climate and explain how scientists classify climates.

Connect ESSENTIAL QUESTIONS
Lessons 3 and 5

1 Synthesize Explain how a change in air pressure can signal a change in weather.

_____

_____

Think Outside the Book

2 Synthesize Choose one of these activities to help synthesize what you have learned in this unit.

☐ Using what you learned in lessons 1, 2, 3, and 4, present a poster about water vapor and the formation of severe weather.

☐ Using what you learned in lessons 5 and 6, explain in a short essay how weather predictions might change based on an area's topography, elevation, or proximity to a large body of water.

© Houghton Mifflin Harcourt Publishing Company • Image Credits: (tl) ©British Antarctic Survey/Photo Researchers, Inc.; (tcl) ©Alan Sirulnikoff/Photo Researchers, Inc.; (bcl) ©Bryan Bedder/Getty Images; (bl) ©Warren Faidley/Corbis; (tr) ©Erik S. Lesser/Stringer/Getty Images News/Getty Images; (cr) ©Arctic-Images/Iconica/Getty Images

Unit 8 Review

Name _____

Vocabulary

Fill in each blank with the term that best completes the following sentences.

1 _____ is the ratio of the amount of water vapor in the air to the amount of water vapor needed to reach saturation at a given temperature.

2 White, thin clouds with a feathery appearance are called _____.

3 A(n) _____ is a violently rotating column of air stretching from a cloud to the ground.

4 _____ is the characteristic weather conditions in an area over a long period of time.

5 _____ influences the wind patterns and transfer of energy in an area.

Key Concepts

Read each question below, and circle the best answer.

6 The graph shows the temperatures recorded at school one day.

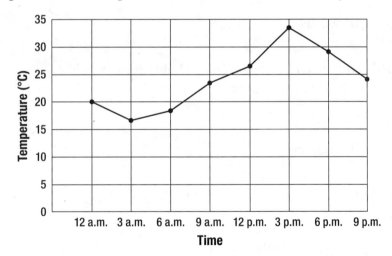

What can these temperature data tell us?

A The highest temperature of the day occurred at 6 p.m.

B The amount of water vapor in the air changed that day.

C The amount of energy as heat in the air changed during that day.

D The climate changed between 3 a.m. and 3 p.m.

© Houghton Mifflin Harcourt Publishing Company

7 Which of these types of weather data is measured using a barometer?

A air pressure

C relative humidity

B precipitation

D wind speed

8 The picture below shows the four parts of the water cycle labeled A, B, C, and D.

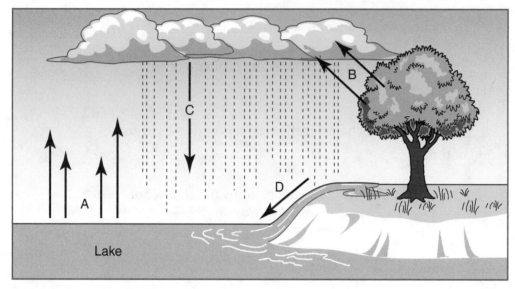

If rain (C) is falling as part of a thunderstorm, which type of clouds are shown?

A altostratus clouds

C cumulonimbus clouds

B cirrus clouds

D stratus clouds

9 If it rained all day but stopped and then cooled down considerably at night, what weather phenomenon would you likely see that night?

A fog

C sleet

B hail

D thunder

10 What results when air surrounding a bolt of lightning experiences a rapid increase in temperature and pressure?

A A tornado forms.

C Thunder sounds.

B Hail forms.

D Rain condenses.

© Houghton Mifflin Harcourt Publishing Company

11 Refer to the regions A, B, C, and D shown on the U.S. map below.

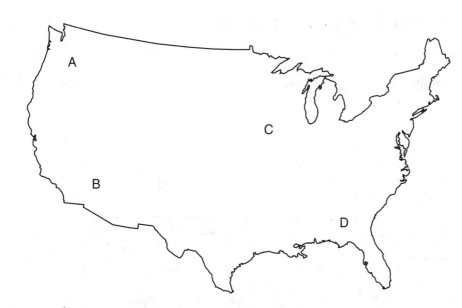

In which of these directions is the jet stream most likely to flow?

A from D to C   **C** from C to A

B from A to C   **D** from C to B

12 Which of the following should you do to escape a flood?

A Seek a high, safe point above the floodwaters and wait for assistance.

B Walk carefully into the floodwaters to get to safety.

C Swim through the floodwaters until you find a safer place.

D Use a lifejacket or flotation device to help you wade through the floodwaters.

13 What are the two main factors that determine climate?

A temperature and wind

B temperature and precipitation

C air pressure and humidity

D wind and precipitation

© Houghton Mifflin Harcourt Publishing Company

14 What do the curved concentric lines on weather forecast maps show?

    A The lines show the direction in which the wind will blow.

    B The lines show where rain will fall.

    C The lines connect points of equal temperature.

    D The lines connect points of equal air pressure.

15 The picture below shows an exaggerated side view of an ocean on the left and a mountain range on the right. The arrows indicate the movement of air and moisture from the ocean.

Which region is most likely to have a dry, desert-like climate?

    A region R   **C** region T

    B region S   **D** region W

16 Which of these factors would most likely contribute to a region having a cold climate?

    A latitude near the equator

    B high elevation

    C near a coastline

    D proximity to a warm ocean current

© Houghton Mifflin Harcourt Publishing Company

17 The table below shows the average daily temperature in a particular area.

Average Daily Temperature (°C)											
Jan	Feb	Mar	Apr	May	Jun	Jul	Aug	Sep	Oct	Nov	Dec
1	−5	−14	−17	−19	−20	−23	−21	-16	−13	−6	0

Based on this data, identify the climate zone in which the area is located.

A temperate

B polar

C equatorial

D tropical

Critical Thinking

Answer the following questions in the space provided.

18 Explain generally what makes a cloud form.

_____

_____

Describe one specific situation in which a cloud can form.

_____

_____

19 Explain two ways in which forecasters collect weather data.

_____

_____

© Houghton Mifflin Harcourt Publishing Company

20 The map below shows the three different climate zones on Earth.

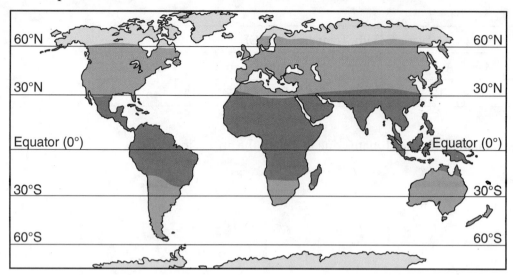

Label each climate zone on the map. Then describe the temperature and precipitation typical of each zone.

_____

_____

_____

Explain how latitude affects the climate of each zone.

_____

_____

_____

Connect ESSENTIAL QUESTIONS
Lessons 1, 2, 3, 4, and 6

Answer the following question in the space provided.

21 Even if you do not live on a coast, the movement of water in the oceans and water vapor in the atmosphere over the oceans does affect your weather. Using what you learned in lessons 1, 2, 3, 4, and 6, describe how the water cycle and the global movement of water through ocean currents and winds affect the climate of your local region.

_____

_____

_____

_____

_____

© Houghton Mifflin Harcourt Publishing Company

⟨Technology⟩ and ⟨Coding⟩

This breathtaking image of Earth was taken from the International Space Station, an international laboratory orbiting Earth. The operation of the International Space Station is controlled by 52 computers and millions of lines of computer code. Its many high-tech features include solar panels that power the laboratory and a human-like robotic astronaut.

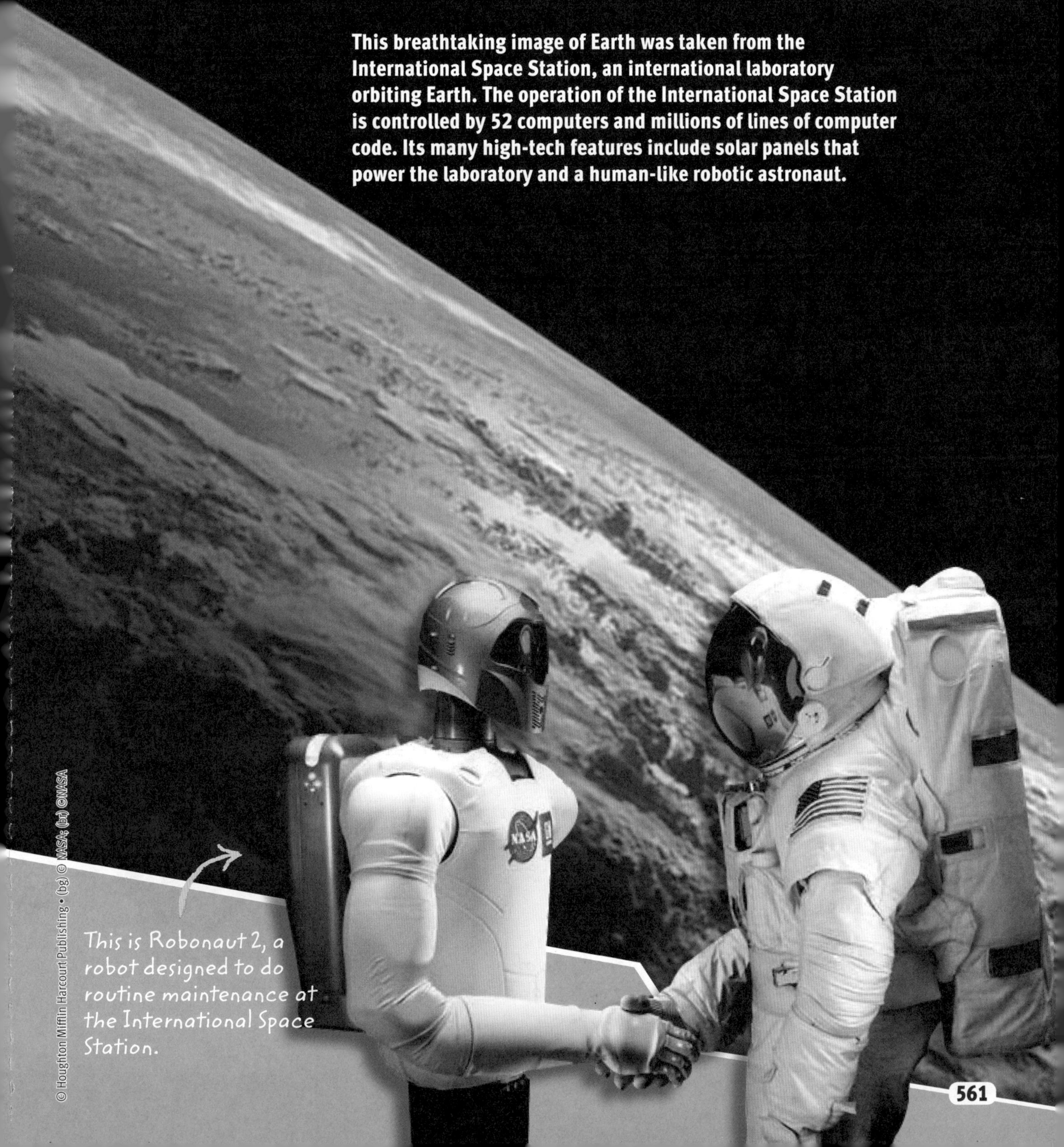

This is Robonaut 2, a robot designed to do routine maintenance at the International Space Station.

© Houghton Mifflin Harcourt Publishing • (bg) © NASA; (br) © NASA

Data Driven

What is computer science?

If you like computer technology and learning about how computers work, computer science might be for you. *Computer science* is the study of computer technology and how data is processed, stored, and accessed by computers. Computer science is an important part of many other areas, including science, math, engineering, robotics, medicine, game design, and 3D animation.

Computer technology is often described in terms of *hardware*, which are the physical components, and *software,* which are the programs or instructions that a computer runs. Computer scientists must understand how hardware and software work together. Computer scientists may develop new kinds of useful computer software. Or they may work with engineers to improve existing computer hardware.

The first electronic computer, the computer ENIAC (Electronic Numerical Integrator And Computer), was developed at the University of Pennsylvania in 1946.

The integrated circuit (IC), first developed in the 1950s, was instrumental in the development of small computer components.

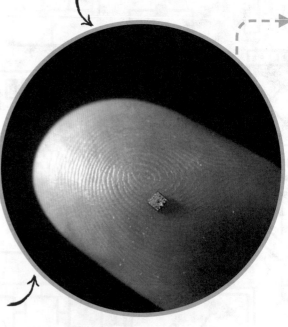

The development of the IC made it possible to reduce the overall size of computers and their components and to increase their processing speed.

© Houghton Mifflin Harcourt Publishing Company • (bl) ©Apic/Hulton Archive/Getty Images; (br) ©NELSON MORRIS/Photo Researchers, Inc.

How has computer technology changed over time?

Modern, digital computer technology is less than 100 years old. Yet in that short amount of time, it has advanced rapidly. The earliest digital computers could perform only a limited number of tasks and were the size of an entire room. Over the decades, engineers continued to develop smaller, faster, and more powerful computers. Today's computers can process hundreds of millions of instructions per second!

Computer scientists and engineers think about what people want or need from computer technology. The most advanced hardware is not useful if people do not know how to use it. So computer scientists and engineers work to create software that is reliable, useful, and easy to use. Today's tablet computers, cell phones, and video game consoles can be used without any special training.

Advances in digital computer technology have help make computers cheaper and easier to operate, which has allowed many more people to work and play with them.

1 Compare Are modern computers simpler or more complex than early computers? Explain.

_____

_____

© Houghton Mifflin Harcourt Publishing Company • (bl) ©zerocreatives/Westend61/Corbis; (cr) ©Thomas Barwick/Taxi/Getty Images; (br) ©Marmaduke St John/Alamy

Computer Logic

What do computer scientists do?

Many people enjoy developing computer technology for fun. Learning how to create mobile phone games or Internet-enabled gadgets can be rewarding hobbies. For some people, that hobby may one day become a career in computer science. Working in computer science is a bit like solving a puzzle. Applying knowledge of how computers work to solve real-world problems requires collaboration, creativity, and logical, step-by-step thinking.

This is a kayak folded up.

They collaborate across many disciplines

Computers are valuable tools in math and science because they can perform complex calculations very quickly. Computers are useful to many other fields, too. For example, animators use computer technology to create realistic lighting effects in 3D animated films. Mechanics use computers to diagnose problems in car systems. For every field that relies on special software or computer technology, there is an opportunity for computer scientists and engineers to collaborate and develop solutions for those computing needs. Computer scientists must be able to define and understand the problems presented to them and to communicate and work with experts in other fields to develop the solutions.

Computational origami is a computer program used to model the ways in which different materials, including paper, can be folded. It combines computer science and the art of paper folding to create new technologies, such as this kayak.

© Houghton Mifflin Harcourt Publishing Company • (t) ©Rex Features/AP Images (bg) ©Rex Features/AP Images

Tracking software helps biologists study animal behavior.

satellite

satellite data receiving center

satellite data processing center

transmitter

They help solve real-world problems

Some computer scientists carry out theoretical research. Others apply computer science concepts to develop software. Theoretical computer science and practical software development help solve real-world problems. For example, biologists need ways to safely and accurately track endangered animals. Computer science theories on artificial intelligence and pattern recognition have been applied to advanced animal-tracking technologies, such as satellite transmitters and aerial cameras. New kinds of image processing software now allow biologists to analyze the collected data in different ways.

They use logical, step-by-step thinking

Computers perform tasks given to them, and they do this very well. But in order to get the results they expect, computer scientists and programmers must write very accurate instructions. Computer science and programming requires logical thinking, deductive reasoning, and a good understanding of cause-and-effect relationships. When designing software, computer scientists must consider every possible user action and how the computer should respond to each action.

2 Explain How is computer science helping this scientist do her research?

_____

_____

_____

_____

Transmitters can be attached to animals to help track their movements.

© Houghton Mifflin Harcourt Publishing Company • (br) ©NPS/ZUMA Press, Inc./NewsCom

Up to <Code>

How is computer software created?

Imagine that you are using a computer at the library to learn more about the history of electronic music. You use the library's database application to start searching for Internet resources. You also do a search to look for audio recordings. Finally, you open a word processor to take notes on the computer. Perhaps without realizing it, you've used many different pieces of software. Have you ever wondered how computer software is created?

Computer software is designed to address a need

Computer software can help us to learn more about our world. It can be useful to business. Or it can simply entertain us. Whatever its purpose, computer software should fulfill some human want or need. The first steps in creating software are precisely defining the **need** or want **being addressed** and planning how the software will work.

Computer software source code is written in a programming language

The instructions that tell a computer how to run video games, word processors, and other kinds of software are not written in a human language. They are written in a special programming language, or *code*. Javascript, C++, and Python are examples of programming languages. Programming languages—like human languages—must follow certain rules in order to be understood by the computer. A series of instructions written in a programming language is called *source code*.

Identifying what need a computer program addresses is one of the first development steps.

© Houghton Mifflin Harcourt Publishing Company

Source code is revised

Sometimes, programmers make mistakes in their code. Many programming environments have a feature that alerts the programmer to certain errors, such as spelling mistakes in commands, missing portions of code, or logical errors in the sequence of instructions. However, many mistakes go undetected, too. Some errors may cause the program to function incorrectly or not at all. When this happens, the programmer must identify the error, correct it, and test the software again.

Computer software is user tested, and revised

Once the software is created, it must be tested thoroughly to make sure it does not fail or behave in unexpected ways. It must also be tested to ensure that it meets users' needs. The creators of a piece of software might observe how people use it. Or they might ask users to provide feedback on certain features and test the software again.

3 Identify This source code contains an error. Infer where the error is located. What does this code "tell" the computer to do? Write your answers below.

_____

_____

_____

```
13
14   # Scores are not tied, so check
15   # which player wins the round
16 ▾ if player1_score > player2_score:
17       print ("Player 1 wins!")
18 ▾ else:
19       prnt ("Player 2 wins!")
20

! Syntax error, line 19
```

Test running a program is important for finding and fixing errors in the code.

© Houghton Mifflin Harcourt Publishing Company

Play it Safe

How should I work with computers?

It is easy to lose track of time when you're sitting in front of a computer or game console. It's also easy to forget that things you say or do online can be seen and shared by many different people. Here are some tips for using computers safely and responsibly.

✓ Maintain good posture

Time can pass by quickly when you are working on a computer or another device. Balance computer time with other activities, including plenty of physical activity. When you are sitting at a computer, sit upright with your shoulders relaxed. Your eyes should be level with the top of the monitor and your feet should be flat on the ground.

✓ Observe electrical safety

Building your own electronics projects can be fun, but it's important to have an understanding of circuits and electrical safety first. Otherwise, you could damage your components or hurt yourself. The potential for an electrical shock is real when you open up a computer, work with frayed cords or, use ungrounded plugs or attempt to replace parts without understanding how to do so safely. Ask an adult for help before starting any projects. Also, avoid using a connected computer during thunderstorms.

head and neck in a straight, neutral position

shoulders are relaxed

wrists are straight

feet are flat on the ground

Good posture will help you avoid the aches and injuries related to sitting in front of a computer for a long time.

© Houghton Mifflin Harcourt Publishing Company

✓ Handle and maintain computers properly

Be cautious when handling and transporting electronic devices. Dropping them or spilling liquids on them could cause serious damage. Keep computers away from dirt, dust, liquids, and moisture. Never use wet cleaning products unless they are specifically designed for use on electronics. Microfiber cloths can be used to clear smudges from device screens. Spilled liquids can cause circuits to short out and hardware to corrode. If a liquid spills on a device, unplug it and switch it off immediately, remove the battery and wipe up as much of the liquid inside the device as possible. Don't switch the device back on until it is completely dry.

✓ Do not post private information online

Talk to your family about rules for Internet use. Do not use the Internet to share private information such as photographs, your phone number, or your address. Do not respond to requests for personal details from people you do not know.

✓ Treat yourself and others with respect

It is important to treat others with respect when on the Internet. Don't send or post messages online that you wouldn't say to someone in person. Unfortunately, not everyone acts respectfully while online. Some people may say hurtful things to you or send you unwanted messages. Do not reply to unwanted messages. Alert a trusted adult to any forms of contact, such as messages or photos, that make you feel uncomfortable.

4 Apply Fill in the chart below with a suitable response to each scenario.

SCENARIO	YOUR RESPONSE
You receive a text message from an online store asking for your home address.	
You've been lying down in front of a laptop, and you notice that your neck is feeling a little sore.	
You need to take a laptop computer with you on your walk to school.	
You want to try assembling a robotics kit with a friend.	
Someone posts unfriendly comments directed at you.	

© Houghton Mifflin Harcourt Publishing Company

Career in Computing:
Game Programmer

What do video game programmers do?

Creating your own universe with its own set of rules is fun. Just ask a programmer who works on video games!

What skills are needed in game programming?

A programmer should know how to write code, but there are other important skills a programmer needs as well. An understanding of physics and math is important for calculating how objects move and interact in a game. Game programmers usually work on a team with other people, such as artists, designers, writers, and musicians. They must be able to communicate effectively, and ideally, the programmer should understand the other team members' roles.

How can I get started with game development?

You don't need a big budget or years of experience to try it out. There are books, videos, and websites that can help you get started. When you're first experimenting with game development, start small. Try making a very simple game like Tic-Tac-Toe. Once you've mastered that, you can try something more complex.

---

5 Brainstorm Why would working on a team be important to the game development process?

_____

_____

_____

© Houghton Mifflin Harcourt Publishing Company • (t) ©OJO Images/Getty Images; (b) ©Maté/Shutterstock

Resources

© Houghton Mifflin Harcourt Publishing Company

Glossary

<table>
<tr><th colspan="4">Pronunciation Key</th></tr>
<tr><th>Sound</th><th>Symbol</th><th>Example</th><th>Respelling</th></tr>
<tr><td>ă</td><td>a</td><td>pat</td><td>PAT</td></tr>
<tr><td>ā</td><td>ay</td><td>pay</td><td>PAY</td></tr>
<tr><td>âr</td><td>air</td><td>care</td><td>KAIR</td></tr>
<tr><td>ä</td><td>ah</td><td>father</td><td>FAH•ther</td></tr>
<tr><td>är</td><td>ar</td><td>argue</td><td>AR•gyoo</td></tr>
<tr><td>ch</td><td>ch</td><td>chase</td><td>CHAYS</td></tr>
<tr><td>ĕ</td><td>e</td><td>pet</td><td>PET</td></tr>
<tr><td>ĕ (at end of a syllable)</td><td>eh</td><td>settee
lessee</td><td>seh•TEE
leh•SEE</td></tr>
<tr><td>ĕr</td><td>ehr</td><td>merry</td><td>MEHR•ee</td></tr>
<tr><td>ē</td><td>ee</td><td>beach</td><td>BEECH</td></tr>
<tr><td>g</td><td>g</td><td>gas</td><td>GAS</td></tr>
<tr><td>ĭ</td><td>i</td><td>pit</td><td>PIT</td></tr>
<tr><td>ĭ (at end of a syllable)</td><td>ih</td><td>guitar</td><td>gih•TAR</td></tr>
<tr><td>ī</td><td>y eye (only for a complete syllable)</td><td>pie
island</td><td>PY
EYE•luhnd</td></tr>
<tr><td>îr</td><td>ir</td><td>hear</td><td>HIR</td></tr>
<tr><td>j</td><td>j</td><td>germ</td><td>JERM</td></tr>
<tr><td>k</td><td>k</td><td>kick</td><td>KIK</td></tr>
<tr><td>ng</td><td>ng</td><td>thing</td><td>THING</td></tr>
<tr><td>ngk</td><td>ngk</td><td>bank</td><td>BANGK</td></tr>
</table>

<table>
<tr><th>Sound</th><th>Symbol</th><th>Example</th><th>Respelling</th></tr>
<tr><td>ŏ</td><td>ah</td><td>bottle</td><td>BAHT'l</td></tr>
<tr><td>ō</td><td>oh</td><td>toe</td><td>TOH</td></tr>
<tr><td>ô</td><td>aw</td><td>caught</td><td>KAWT</td></tr>
<tr><td>ôr</td><td>ohr</td><td>roar</td><td>ROHR</td></tr>
<tr><td>oi</td><td>oy</td><td>noisy</td><td>NOYZ•ee</td></tr>
<tr><td>o͝o</td><td>u</td><td>book</td><td>BUK</td></tr>
<tr><td>o͞o</td><td>oo</td><td>boot</td><td>BOOT</td></tr>
<tr><td>ou</td><td>ow</td><td>pound</td><td>POWND</td></tr>
<tr><td>s</td><td>s</td><td>center</td><td>SEN•ter</td></tr>
<tr><td>sh</td><td>sh</td><td>cache</td><td>CASH</td></tr>
<tr><td>ŭ</td><td>uh</td><td>flood</td><td>FLUHD</td></tr>
<tr><td>ûr</td><td>er</td><td>bird</td><td>BERD</td></tr>
<tr><td>z</td><td>z</td><td>xylophone</td><td>ZY•luh•fohn</td></tr>
<tr><td>z</td><td>z</td><td>bags</td><td>BAGZ</td></tr>
<tr><td>zh</td><td>zh</td><td>decision</td><td>dih•SIZH•uhn</td></tr>
<tr><td>ə</td><td>uh</td><td>around
broken
focus</td><td>uh•ROWND
BROH•kuhn
FOH•kuhs</td></tr>
<tr><td>ər</td><td>er</td><td>winner</td><td>WIN•er</td></tr>
<tr><td>th</td><td>th</td><td>thin
they</td><td>THIN
THAY</td></tr>
<tr><td>w</td><td>w</td><td>one</td><td>WUHN</td></tr>
<tr><td>wh</td><td>hw</td><td>whether</td><td>HWETH•er</td></tr>
</table>

© Houghton Mifflin Harcourt Publishing Company

abiotic factor (ay·by·AHT·ik FAK·ter) an environmental factor that is not associated with the activities of living organisms (75)
factor abiótico un factor ambiental que no está asociado con las actividades de los seres vivos

adhesion (ad·HEE·zhuhn) the attractive force between two bodies of different substances that are in contact with each other (354)
adhesión la fuerza de atracción entre dos cuerpos de diferentes sustancias que están en contacto

air mass (AIR MAS) a large body of air throughout which temperature and moisture content are similar (492)
masa de aire un gran volumen de aire, cuya temperatura y cuyo contenido de humedad son similares en toda su extensión

air pressure (AIR PRESH·er) the measure of the force with which air molecules push on a surface (464)
presión del aire la medida de la fuerza con la que las moléculas del aire empujan contra una superficie

aquifer (AH·kwuh·fer) a body of rock or sediment that stores groundwater and allows the flow of groundwater (384)
acuífero un cuerpo rocoso o sedimento que almacena agua subterránea y permite que fluya

atmosphere (AT·muh·sfir) a mixture of gases that surrounds a planet, moon, or other celestial body (218, 405)
atmósfera una mezcla de gases que rodea un planeta, una luna, u otras cuerpos celestes

biodiversity (by·oh·dih·VER·sih·tee) the number and variety of organisms in a given area during a specific period of time (176, 189)
biodiversidad el número y la variedad de organismos que se encuentran en un área determinada durante un período específico de tiempo

biomass (BY·oh·mas) plant material, manure, or any other organic matter that is used as an energy source (264)
biomasa materia vegetal, estiércol o cualquier otra materia orgánica que se usa como fuente de energía

biome (BY·ohm) a large region characterized by a specific type of climate and certain types of plant and animal communities (78, 142)
bioma una región extensa caracterizada por un tipo de clima específico y ciertos tipos de comunidades de plantas y animales

biotic factor (by·AHT·ik FAK·ter) an environmental factor that is associated with or results from the activities of living organisms (74)
factor biótico un factor ambiental que está asociado con las actividades de los seres vivos o que resulta de ellas

calorie (KAL·uh·ree) the amount of energy needed to raise the temperature of 1 g of water 1 °C; the Calorie used to indicate the energy content of food is a kilocalorie (35)
caloría la cantidad de energía que se requiere para aumentar la temperatura de 1 g de agua en 1 °C; la Caloría que se usa para indicar el contenido energético de los alimentos es la kilocaloría

carnivore (KAR·nuh·vohr) an organism that eats animals (91)
carnívoro un organismo que se alimenta de animales

carrying capacity (KAIR·ee·ing kuh·PAS·ih·tee) the largest population that an environment can support at any given time (108)
capacidad de carga la población más grande que un ambiente puede sostener en cualquier momento dado

channel (CHAN·uhl) the path that a stream follows (382)
canal el camino que sigue un arroyo

cirrus cloud (SIR·uhs KLOWD) a feathery cloud that is composed of ice crystals and that has the highest altitude of any cloud in the sky (475)
nube cirro una nube liviana formada por cristales de hielo, la cual tiene la mayor altitud de todas las nubes en el cielo

climate (KLY·mit) the weather conditions in an area over a long period of time (540)
clima las condiciones del tiempo en un área durante un largo período de tiempo

cloud (KLOWD) a collection of small water droplets or ice crystals suspended in the air, which forms when the air is cooled and condensation occurs (472)
nube un conjunto de pequeñas gotitas de agua o cristales de hielo suspendidos en el aire, que se forma cuando el aire se enfría y ocurre condensación

cohesion (koh·HEE·zhuhn) the force that holds molecules of a single material together (354)
cohesión la fuerza que mantiene unidas a las moléculas de un solo material

commensalism (kuh·MEN·suh·liz·uhm) a relationship between two organisms in which one organism benefits and the other is unaffected (122)
comensalismo una relación entre dos organismos en la que uno se beneficia y el otro no es afectado

community (kuh·MYOO·nih·tee) all of the populations of species that live in the same habitat and interact with each other (77)
comunidad todas las poblaciones de especies que viven en el mismo hábitat e interactúan entre sí

competition (kahm·pih·TISH·uhn) ecological relationship in which two or more organisms depend on the same limited resource (112, 124)
competencia la relación ecológica en la que dos o más organismos dependen del mismo recurso limitado

condensation (kahn·den·SAY·shuhn) the change of state from a gas to a liquid (365)
condensación el cambio de estado de gas a líquido

© Houghton Mifflin Harcourt Publishing Company

conduction (kuhn·DUHK·shuhn) the transfer of energy as heat through a material (37, 410)
conducción la transferencia de energía en forma de calor a través de un material

conductor (kuhn·DUK·ter) a material that transfers energy easily (37)
conductor un material a través del cual se transfiere energía

coniferous tree (kuh·NIF·er·uhs TREE) cone-bearing trees that usually keep their leaves or needles during all the seasons of the year (145)
árbol conifero los árboles que producen conos o piñas y que generalmente conservan sus hojas o agujas durante todas las estaciones del año

conservation (kahn·ser·VAY·shuhn) the wise use of and preservation of natural resources (195, 278, 326)
conservación el uso inteligente y la preservación de los recursos naturales

consumer (kuhn·SOO·mer) an organism that eats other organisms or organic matter (91)
consumidor un organismo que se alimenta de otros organismos o de materia orgánica

convection (kuhn·VEK·shuhn) the movement of matter due to differences in density; the transfer of energy due to the movement of matter (38, 408)
convección el movimiento de la materia debido a diferencias en la densidad; la transferencia de energía debido al movimiento de la materia

convection current (kuhn·VEK·shuhn KER·uhnt) any movement of matter that results from differences in density; may be vertical, circular, or cyclical (441)
corriente de convección cualquier movimiento de la materia que se produce como resultado de diferencias en la densidad; puede ser vertical, circular o cíclico

cooperation (koh·ahp·uh·RAY·shuhn) an interaction between two or more living things in which they are said to work together (113)
cooperación la interacción entre dos o más organismos vivos en la cualse dice que trabajan juntos

Coriolis effect (kohr·ee·OH·lis ih·FEKT) the curving of the path of a moving object from an otherwise straight path due to Earth's rotation (423, 437)
efecto de Coriolis la desviación de la trayectoria recta que experimentan los objetos en movimiento debido a la rotación de la Tierra

cumulus cloud (KYOOM·yuh·luhs KLOWD) a low-level, billowy cloud that commonly has a top that resembles cotton balls and a dark bottom (475)
nube cúmulo una nube esponjada ubicada en un nivel bajo, cuya parte superior normalmente parece una bola de algodón y es obscura en la parte inferior

deciduous tree (dih·SIJ·oo·uhs TREE) trees that lose their leaves at the end of the growing season (148)
árbol caducifolio los árboles que pierden sus hojas al final de una estación de crecimiento

decomposer (dee·kuhm·POH·zer) an organism that gets energy by breaking down the remains of dead organisms or animal wastes and consuming or absorbing the nutrients (90)
descomponedor un organismo que, para obtener energía, desintegra los restos de organismos muertos o los desechos de animales y consume o absorbe los nutrientes

deep current (DEEP KER·uhnt) a streamlike movement of ocean water far below the surface (440)
corriente profunda un movimiento del agua del océano que es similar a una corriente y ocurre debajo de la superficie

deforestation (dee·fohr·ih·STAY·shuhn) the removal of trees and other vegetation from an area (319)
deforestación la remoción de árboles y demás vegetación de un área

degrees (dih·GREEZ) the units of a temperature scale (32)
grado la unidad de una escala de temperatura

desert (DEZ·ert) a region characterized by a very dry climate and extreme temperatures (146)
desierto una región que se caracteriza por tener un clima muy seco y temperaturas extremas

desertification (dih·zer·tuh·fih·KAY·shuhn) the process by which human activities or climatic changes make arid or semiarid areas more desertlike (319)
desertificación el proceso por medio del cual las actividades humanas o los cambios climáticos hacen que un área árida o semiárida se vuelva más parecida a un desierto

dew point (DOO POYNT) at constant pressure and water vapor content, the temperature at which the rate of condensation equals the rate of evaporation (461, 473)
punto de rocío a presión y contenido de vapor de agua constantes, la temperatura a la que la tasa de condensación es igual a la tasa de evaporación

divide (dih·VYD) the boundary between drainage areas that have streams that flow in opposite directions (383)
división el límite entre áreas de drenaje que tienen corrientes que fluyen en direcciones opuestas

ecology (ee·KAHL·uh·jee) the study of the interactions of living organisms with one another and with their environment (74)
ecología el estudio de las interacciones de los seres vivos entre sí mismos y entre sí mismos y su ambiente

ecosystem (EE·koh·sis·tuhm) a community of organisms and their abiotic, or nonliving, environment (77)
ecosistema una comunidad de organismos y su ambiente abiótico o no vivo

elevation (el·uh·VAY·shuhn) the height of an object above sea level (544)
elevación la altura de un objeto sobre el nivel del mar

energy (EN·er·jee) the ability to cause change (6)
energía la capacidad de producir un cambio

© Houghton Mifflin Harcourt Publishing Company

energy pyramid (EN·er·jee PIR·uh·mid) a triangular diagram that shows an ecosystem's loss of energy, which results as energy passes through the ecosystem's food chain; each row in the pyramid represents a trophic (feeding) level in an ecosystem, and the area of a row represents the energy stored in that trophic level (98)
pirámide de energía un diagrama con forma de triángulo que muestra la pérdida de energía que ocurre en un ecosistema a medida que la energía pasa a través de la cadena alimenticia del ecosistema; cada hilera de la pirámide representa un nivel trófico (de alimentación) en el ecosistema, y el área de la hilera representa la energía almacenada en ese nivel trófico

energy resource (EN·er·jee REE·sohrs) a natural resource that humans use to generate energy (230, 244, 258)
recurso energético un recurso natural que utilizan los humanos para generar energía

energy transformation (EN·er·jee trans·fohr·MAY·shuhn) the process of energy changing from one form into another (12)
transformación de energía el proceso de cambio de un tipo de energía a otro

estuary (ES·choo·ehr·ee) an area where fresh water mixes with salt water from the ocean (160)
estuario un área donde el agua dulce de los ríos se mezcla con el agua salada del océano

eutrophication (yoo·trohf·ih·KAY·shuhn) an increase in the amount of nutrients, such as nitrates, in a marine or aquatic ecosystem (172, 192, 298)
eutrofización un aumento en la cantidad de nutrientes, tales como nitratos, en un ecosistema marino o acuático

evaporation (ee vap uh RAY shuhn) the change of state from a liquid to a gas that usually occurs at the surface of a liquid over a wide range of temperatures (364)
evaporación el cambio de estado de líquido a gaseoso que ocurre generalmente en la superficie de un líquido en un amplio rango de temperaturas

fission (FISH·uhn) the process by which a nucleus splits into two or more fragments and releases neutrons and energy (249)
fisión el proceso por medio del cual un núcleo se divide en dos o más fragmentos y libera neutrones y energía

fog (FAWG) a cloud that forms near the ground and results in a reduction in visibility (478)
niebla una nube que se forma cerca del suelo y causa una reducción de la visibilidad

food chain (FOOD CHAYN) the pathway of energy transfer through various stages as a result of the feeding patterns of a series of organisms (93)
cadena alimenticia la vía de transferencia de energía través de varias etapas, que ocurre como resultado de los patrones de alimentación de una serie de organismos

food web (FOOD WEB) a diagram that shows the feeding relationships between organisms in an ecosystem (94)
red alimenticia un diagrama que muestra las relaciones de alimentación entre los organismos de un ecosistema

fossil fuel (FAHS·uhl FYOO·uhl) a nonrenewable energy resource formed from the remains of organisms that lived long ago; examples include oil, coal, and natural gas (54, 227, 244)
combustible fósil un recurso energético no renovable formado a partir de los restos de organismos que vivieron hace mucho tiempo; algunos ejemplos incluyen el petróleo, el carbón y el gas natural

front (FRUHNT) the boundary between air masses of different densities and usually different temperatures (492)
frente el límite entre masas de aire de diferentes densidades y, normalmente, diferentes temperaturas

geothermal energy (jee·oh·THER·muhl EN·er·jee) the energy produced by heat within Earth (265)
energía geotérmica la energía producida por el calor del interior de la Tierra

global wind (GLOH·buhl WIND) the movement of air over Earth's surface in patterns that are worldwide (424)
viento global el movimiento del aire sobre la superficie terrestre según patrones globales

grassland (GRAS·land) a region that is dominated by grasses, that has few woody shrubs and trees, that has fertile soils, and that receives moderate amounts of seasonal rainfall (147)
pradera una región en la que predomina la hierba, tiene algunos arbustos leñosos y árboles, y suelos fértiles, y recibe cantidades moderadas de precipitaciones estacionales

groundwater (GROWND·waw·ter) the water that is beneath Earth's surface (380)
agua subterránea el agua que está debajo de la superficie de la Tierra

habitat (HAB·ih·tat) the place where an organism usually lives (80)
hábitat el lugar donde generalmente vive un organismo

heat (HEET) the energy transferred between objects that are at different temperatures (34, 404)
calor la transferencia de energía entre objetos que están a temperaturas diferentes

herbivore (HER·buh·vohr) an organism that eats only plants (91)
herbívoro un organismo que sólo come plantas

humidity (hyoo·MID·ih·tee) the amount of water vapor in the air (461)
humedad la cantidad de vapor de agua que hay en el aire

© Houghton Mifflin Harcourt Publishing Company

hurricane (HER·ih·kayn) a severe storm that develops over tropical oceans and whose strong winds of more than 119 km/h spiral in toward the intensely low-pressure storm center (508)

huracán una tormenta severa que se desarrolla sobre océanos tropicales, con vientos fuertes que soplan a más de 119 km/h y que se mueven en espiral hacia el centro de presión extremadamente baja de la tormenta

hydroelectric energy (hy·droh·ee·LEK·trik EN·er·jee) electrical energy produced by the flow of water (261)

energía hidroeléctrica energía eléctrica producida por el flujo del agua

insulator (IN·suh·lay·ter) a material that reduces or prevents the transfer of energy (37)

aislante un material que reduce o evita la transferencia de energía

jet stream (JET STREEM) a narrow band of strong winds that blow in the upper troposphere (426, 497)

corriente en chorro un cinturón delgado de vientos fuertes que soplan en la parte superior de la troposfera

kinetic energy (kih·NET·ik EN·er·jee) the energy of an object that is due to the object's motion (6)

energía cinética la energía de un objeto debido al movimiento del objeto

land degradation (LAND deg·ruh·DAY·shuhn) the process by which human activity and natural processes damage land to the point that it can no longer support the local ecosystem (318)

degradación del suelo el proceso por el cual la actividad humana y los procesos naturales dañan el suelo de modo que el ecosistema local no puede subsistir

latitude (LAT·ih·tood) the distance north or south from the equator; expressed in degrees (542)

latitud la distancia hacia el norte o hacia el sur del ecuador; se expresa en grados

law of conservation of energy (LAW UHV kahn·suhr·VAY·shuhn UHV EN·er·jee) the law that states that energy cannot be created or destroyed but can be changed from one form to another (13)

ley de la conservación de la energía la ley que establece que la energía ni se crea ni se destruye, sólo se transforma de una forma a otra

lightning (LYT·ning) an electric discharge that takes place between two oppositely charged surfaces, such as between a cloud and the ground, between two clouds, or between two parts of the same cloud (507)

relámpago una descarga eléctrica que ocurre entre dos superficies que tienen carga opuesta, como por ejemplo, entre una nube y el suelo, entre dos nubes o entres dos partes de la misma nube

limiting factor (LIM·ih·ting FAK·ter) an environmental factor that prevents an organism or population from reaching its full potential of size or activity (110)

factor limitante un factor ambiental que impide que un organismo o población alcance su máximo potencial de distribución o de actividad

local wind (LOH·kuhl WIND) the movement of air over short distances; occurs in specific areas as a result of certain geographical features (428)

viento local el movimiento del aire a través de distancias cortas; se produce en áreas específicas como resultado de ciertas características geográficas

material resource (muh·TIR·ee·uhl REE·sohrs) a natural resource that humans use to make objects or to consume as food and drink (228)

recurso material un recurso natural que utilizan los seres humanos para fabricar objetos o para consumir como alimento o bebida

mechanical energy (mih·KAN·ih·kuhl EN·er·jee) the sum of an object's kinetic energy and potential energy due to gravity or elastic deformation; does not include chemical energy or nuclear energy (24)

energía mecánica la suma de las energías cinética y potencial de un objeto debido a la gravedad o a la deformación elástica; no incluye la energía química ni nuclear

meteorology (mee·tee·uh·RAHL·uh·jee) the scientific study of Earth's atmosphere, especially in relation to weather and climate (522)

meteorología el estudio científico de la atmósfera de la Tierra, sobre todo en lo que se relaciona al tiempo y al clima

mutualism (MYOO·choo·uh·liz·uhm) a relationship between two species in which both species benefit (122)

mutualismo una relación entre dos especies en la que ambas se benefician

natural resource (NACH·uh·ruhl REE·sohrs) any natural material that is used by humans, such as water, petroleum, minerals, forests, and animals (226, 276)

recurso natural cualquier material natural que es utilizado por los seres humanos, como agua, petróleo, minerales, bosques, y animales

© Houghton Mifflin Harcourt Publishing Company

niche (NICH) the role of a species in its community, including use of its habitat and its relationships with other species (80)
nicho el papel que juega una especie en su comunidad, incluidos el uso de su hábitat y su relación con otras especies

nonpoint-source pollution
(nahn·POYNT SOHRS puh·LOO·shuhn) pollution that comes from many sources rather than from a single specific site; an example is pollution that reaches a body of water from streets and storm sewers (298)
contaminación no puntual contaminación que proviene de muchas fuentes, en lugar de provenir de un solo sitio específico; un ejemplo es la contaminación que llega a una masa de agua a partir de las calles y los drenajes

nonrenewable resource (nahn·rih·NOO·uh·buhl REE·sohrs) a resource that forms at a rate that is much slower than the rate at which the resource is consumed (53, 227, 276)
recurso no renovable un recurso que se forma a una tasa que es mucho más lenta que la tasa a la que se consume

nuclear energy (NOO·klee·er EN·er·jee) the energy released by a fission or fusion reaction; the binding energy of the atomic nucleus (244)
energía nuclear la energía liberada por una reacción de fisión o fusión; la energía de enlace del núcleo atómico

ocean current (OH·shuhn KER·uhnt) a movement of ocean water that follows a regular pattern (436)
corriente oceánica un movimiento del agua del océano que sigue un patrón regular

omnivore (AHM·nuh·vohr) an organism that eats both plants and animals (91)
omnívoro un organismo que come tanto plantas como animales

ozone (OH·zohn) a gas molecule that is made up of three oxygen atoms (219)
ozono una molécula de gas que está formada por tres átomos de oxígeno

parasitism (PAIR·uh·sih·tiz·uhm) a relationship between two species in which one species, the parasite, benefits from the other species, the host, which is harmed (123)
parasitismo una relación entre dos especies en la que una, el parásito, se beneficia de la otra, el huésped, que resulta perjudicada

photosynthesis (foh·toh·SIN·thih·sis) the process by which plants, algae, and some bacteria use sunlight, carbon dioxide, and water to make food (214)
fotosíntesis el proceso por medio del cual las plantas, las algas, y algunas bacterias utilizan la luz solar, el dióxido de carbono, y el agua para producir alimento

pioneer species (py·uh·NIR SPEE·sheez) a species that colonizes an uninhabited area and that starts a process of succession (174)
especie pionera una especie que coloniza un área deshabitada y empieza un proceso de sucesión

point-source pollution (POYNT SOHRS puh·LOO·shuhn) pollution that comes from a specific site (298)
contaminación puntual contaminación que proviene de un lugar específico

polarity (poh·LAIR·ih·tee) a property of a system in which two points have opposite characteristics, such as charges or magnetic poles (352)
polaridad la propiedad de un sistema en la que dos puntos tienen características opuestas, tales como las cargas o polos magnéticos

population (pahp·yuh·LAY·shuhn) a group of organisms of the same species that live in a specific geographical area (76)
población un grupo de organismos de la misma especie que viven en un área geográfica específica

potable (POH·tuh·buhl) suitable for drinking (301)
potable que puede beberse

potential energy (puh·TEN·shuhl EN·er·jee) the energy that an object has because of the position, condition, or chemical composition of the object (7)
energía potencial la energía que tiene un objeto debido a su posición, condición o composición química

precipitation (prih·sip·ih·TAY·shuhn) any form of water that falls to Earth's surface from the clouds (365, 462)
precipitación cualquier forma de agua que cae de las nubes a la superficie de la Tierra

predator (PRED·uh·ter) an organism that kills and eats all or part of another organism (120)
depredador un organismo que mata y se alimenta de otro organismo o de parte de él

prey (PRAY) an organism that is killed and eaten by another organism (120)
presa un organismo al que otro organismo mata para alimentarse de él

producer (pruh·DOO·ser) an organism that can make its own food by using energy from its surroundings (90)
productor un organismo que puede elaborar sus propios alimentos utilizando la energía de su entorno

radiation (ray·dee·AY·shuhn) the transfer of energy as electromagnetic waves (38, 406)
radiación la transferencia de energía en forma de ondas electromagnéticas

relative humidity (REL·uh·tiv hyoo·MID·ih·tee) the ratio of the amount of water vapor in the air to the amount of water vapor needed to reach saturation at a given temperature (461)
humedad relativa la proporción de la cantidad de vapor de agua que hay en el aire respecto a la cantidad de vapor de agua que se necesita para alcanzar la saturación a una temperatura dada

© Houghton Mifflin Harcourt Publishing Company

renewable resource (rih·NOO·uh·buhl REE·sohrs) a natural resource that can be replaced at the same rate at which the resource is consumed (53, 227, 276)

recurso renovable un recurso natural que puede reemplazarse a la misma tasa a la que se consume

reservoir (REZ·er·vwar) an artificial body of water that usually forms behind a dam (303)

represa una masa artificial de agua que normalmente se forma detrás de una presa

solar energy (SOH·ler EN·er·jee) the energy received by Earth from the sun in the form of radiation (262)

energía solar la energía que la Tierra recibe del Sol en forma de radiación

solvent (SAHL·vuhnt) in a solution, the substance in which the solute dissolves (355)

solvente en una solución, la sustancia en la que se disuelve el soluto

species (SPEE·sheez) a group of organisms that are closely related and can mate to produce fertile offspring (76)

especie un grupo de organismos que tienen un parentesco cercano y que pueden aparearse para producir descendencia fértil

specific heat (spih·SIF·ik HEET) the quantity of heat required to raise a unit mass of homogeneous material 1 K or 1 °C in a specified way, given constant pressure and volume (355)

calor específico la cantidad de calor que se requiere para aumentar una unidad de masa de un material homogéneo 1 K ó 1 °C de una manera especificada, dados un volumen y una presión constantes

station model (STAY·shuhn MAHD·l) a pattern of meteorological symbols that represents the weather at a particular observing station and that is recorded on a weather map (526)

estación modelo el modelo de símbolos meteorológicos que representan el tiempo en una estación de observación determinada y que se registra en un mapa meteorológico

stewardship (STOO·erd·ship) the careful and responsible management of a resource (194, 278, 327)

gestión ambiental responsable el manejo cuidadoso y responsable de un recurso

storm surge (STOHRM SERJ) a local rise in sea level near the shore that is caused by strong winds from a storm, such as those from a hurricane (509)

marea de tempestad un levantamiento local del nivel del mar cerca de la costa, el cual es resultado de los fuertes vientos de una tormenta, como por ejemplo, los vientos de un huracán

stratus cloud (STRAY·tuhs KLOWD) a gray cloud that has a flat, uniform base and that commonly forms at very low altitudes (475)

nube estrato una nube gris que tiene una base plana y uniforme y que comúnmente se forma a altitudes muy bajas

sublimation (suhb·luh·MAY·shuhn) the change of state from a solid directly to a gas (364)

sublimación cambio de estado por el cual un sólido se convierte directamente en un gas

succession (suhk·SESH·uhn) the replacement of one type of community by another at a single location over a period of time (174)

sucesión el reemplazo de un tipo de comunidad por otro en un mismo lugar a lo largo de un período de tiempo

surface current (SER·fuhs KER·uhnt) a horizontal movement of ocean water that is caused by wind and that occurs at or near the ocean's surface (436, 547)

corriente superficial un movimiento horizontal del agua del océano que es producido por el viento y que ocurre en la superficie del océano o cerca de ella

surface water (SER·fuhs WAW·ter) all the bodies of fresh water, salt water, ice, and snow that are found above the ground (380)

agua superficial todas las masas de agua dulce, agua salada, hielo y nieve que se encuentran arriba del suelo

symbiosis (sim·by·OH·sis) a relationship in which two different organisms live in close association with each other (122)

simbiosis una relación en la que dos organismos diferentes viven estrechamente asociados uno con el otro

taiga (TY·guh) a region of evergreen, coniferous forest below the arctic and subarctic tundra regions (145)

taiga una región de bosques siempreverdes de coníferas, ubicado debajo de las regiones árticas y subárticas de tundra

temperature (TEM·per·uh·chur) a measure of how hot (or cold) something is; specifically, a measure of the average kinetic energy of the particles in an object (32, 402)

temperatura una medida de qué tan caliente (o frío) está algo; específicamente, una medida de la energía cinética promedio de las partículas de un objeto

thermal energy (THER·muhl EN·er·jee) the kinetic energy of a substance's atoms (32, 402)

energía térmica la energía cinética de los átomos de una sustancia

thermal expansion (THER·muhl ek·SPAN·shuhn) an increase in the size of a substance in response to an increase in the temperature of the substance (403)

expansión térmica un aumento en el tamaño de una sustancia en respuesta a un aumento en la temperatura de la sustancia

© Houghton Mifflin Harcourt Publishing Company

thermal pollution (THER·muhl puh·LOO·shuhn) a temperature increase in a body of water that is caused by human activity and that has a harmful effect on water quality and on the ability of that body of water to support life (298)
contaminación térmica un aumento en la temperatura de una masa de agua, producido por las actividades humanas y que tiene un efecto dañino en la calidad del agua y en la capacidad de esa masa de agua para permitir que se desarrolle la vida

thunder (THUHN·der) the sound caused by the rapid expansion of air along an electrical strike (507)
trueno el sonido producido por la expansión rápida del aire a lo largo de una descarga eléctrica

thunderstorm (THUHN·der·stohrm) a usually brief, heavy storm that consists of rain, strong winds, lightning, and thunder (506)
tormenta eléctrica una tormenta fuerte y normalmente breve que consiste en lluvia, vientos fuertes, relámpagos y truenos

topography (tuh·PAHG·ruh·fee) the size and shape of the land surface features of a region, including its relief (544)
topografía el tamaño y la forma de las características de una superficie de terreno, incluyendo su relieve

tornado (tohr·NAY·doh) a destructive, rotating column of air that has very high wind speeds and that may be visible as a funnel-shaped cloud (510)
tornado una columna destructiva de aire en rotación cuyos vientos se mueven a velocidades muy altas y que puede verse como una nube con forma de embudo

transpiration (tran·spuh·RAY·shuhn) the process by which plants release water vapor into the air through stomata; also the release of water vapor into the air by other organisms (364)
transpiración el proceso por medio del cual las plantas liberan vapor de agua al aire por medio de los estomas; también, la liberación de vapor de agua al aire por otros organismos

tributary (TRIB·yuh·tehr·ee) a stream that flows into a lake or into a larger stream (382)
afluente un arroyo que fluye a un lago o a otro arroyo más grande

tundra (TUHN·druh) a region found at far northern and far southern latitudes characterized by low-lying plants, a lack of trees, and long winters with very low temperatures (145)
tundra una región que se encuentra en latitudes muy al norte o muy al sur y que se caracteriza por las plantas bajas, la ausencia de árboles, y los inviernos prolongados con temperaturas muy bajas

ultraviolet radiation (uhl·truh·VY·uh·lit ray·dee·AY·shuhn) electromagnetic wave frequencies immediately above the visible range (219)
radiación ultravioleta longitudes de onda electromagnéticas inmediatamente adyacentes al color violeta en el espectro visible

upwelling (UHP·well·ing) the movement of deep, cold, and nutrient-rich water to the surface (442)
surgencia el movimiento de las aguas profundas, frías y ricas en nutrientes hacia la superficie

urbanization (er·buh·nih·ZAY·shuhn) an increase in the proportion of a population living in urban areas rather than in rural areas (189, 315)
urbanización un aumento de la proporción de población en las áreas urbanas en lugar de en las áreas rurales

visibility (viz·uh·BIL·ih·tee) the distance at which a given standard object can be seen and identified with the unaided eye (465)
visibilidad la distancia a la que un objeto dado es perceptible e identificable para el ojo humano

water cycle (WAW·ter SY·kuhl) the continuous movement of water between the atmosphere, the land, the oceans, and living things (362)
ciclo del agua el movimiento continuo del agua entre la atmósfera, la tierra, los océanos y los seres vivos

water pollution (WAW·ter puh·LOO·shuhn) waste matter or other material that is introduced into water and that is harmful to organisms that live in, drink, or are exposed to the water (298)
contaminación del agua material de desecho u otro material que se introduce en el agua y que daña a los organismos que viven en el agua, la beben o están expuestos a ella

water table (WAW·ter TAY·buhl) the upper surface of underground water; the upper boundary of the zone of saturation (380)
capa freática el nivel más alto del agua subterránea; el límite superior de la zona de saturación

watershed (WAW·ter·shed) the area of land that is drained by a river system (383)
cuenca hidrográfica el área del terreno que es drenada por un sistema de ríos

weather (WETH·er) the short-term state of the atmosphere, including temperature, humidity, precipitation, wind, and visibility (460, 540)
tiempo el estado de la atmósfera a corto plazo que incluye la temperatura, la humedad, la precipitación, el viento y la visibilidad

© Houghton Mifflin Harcourt Publishing Company

weather forecasting (WETH·er FOHR·kast·ing) the process of predicting atmospheric conditions by collecting and analyzing atmospheric data (522)

pronóstico del tiempo el proceso de predecir las condiciones atmosféricas reuniendo y analizando datos atmosféricos

wetland (WET·land) an area of land that is periodically underwater or whose soil contains a great deal of moisture (158)

pantano un área de tierra que está periódicamente bajo el agua o cuyo suelo contiene una gran cantidad de humedad

wind (WIND) the movement of air caused by differences in air pressure (422, 464)

viento el movimiento de aire producido por diferencias en la presión barométrica

wind energy (WIND EN·er·jee) the use of the force of moving air to drive an electric generator (260)

energía eólica el uso de la fuerza del aire en movimiento para hacer funcionar un generador eléctrico

© Houghton Mifflin Harcourt Publishing Company

Index

Page numbers for definitions are printed in **boldface** type.
Page numbers for illustrations, maps, and charts are printed in *italics*.

© Houghton Mifflin Harcourt Publishing Company

D

dam, 192, 374
death, 107
deciduous tree, **148**
decomposer, **90**, *90*
    energy transfer and, *92, 93*
    in soil, 316
deep current, 366, **440–441**
deep ocean ecosystem, 163
deforestation, *189*, 276, **319**, *319*
    population size and, *108*
    reforestation and, 331
density
    of air, 422, 464, 492–493
    of ocean water, 409, 440–441
    thermal expansion and, 403
    of water, 353
deposition
    by rivers and streams, 383
    of water, 363
desert, **146**, *146*, *177*
    characteristics, 78
    community, 79
    ecosystem, *74–75*
    mature, *177*
desert climate, 549
desert dust storm, 427, *427*
desertification, **319**, *319*
dew point, **461**, **473**
diatom, *443*, *443*
diesel fuel, 245
direction
    kinetic energy and, 21
disease, population growth and, *110*,
    111, *111*
discharge, 385
discharge zone, 385
dissolved oxygen (DO), 300
dissolved solids, 300
divide (watershed), **383**
doldrums, 424, 425, *425*
Doppler radar, 524
Do the Math!, 21, 23, 25, 244, 328,
    350, 364
drinking water, 329, *329*, 380, 386
dropsonde, 523
drought, 317, *317*
    carrying capacity and, 109
Dust Bowl, 317, *317*

E

eagle, *120*
Earth, life on, 214–219
    atmosphere, 218–219, *218–219*
    as energy source, 258, 260–261,
        265
    extreme conditions on, 217, *217*
    formation, 216, *216*
    impact on climate, 544–545
    location of water on, 380, *381*,
        382–383
    liquid water on, 216, *216*

rotation, 215, *215*
    shaping of, 350, 367
    temperature, 215, *215*
earthworm, 316, *316*
echolocation, 125
ecologist, 86
ecology, **74**
ecosystem, 70, **77**, *76*, *77*. *See also*
        environment
    abiotic factor and, 75, 80, 110,
        142–143, 156
    aquatic, 156–163
    biodiversity and, *176*
    biome and, 78, 144, *144*
    biotic factor and, 75, 80, 110
    catastrophic natural events and,
        172–173
    change in, 172–175
    community in, 79
    desert, 74, *74–75*
    estuary, 160–161, *160–161*
    eutrophication, **172**, *172*
    freshwater, 157, *157*
    habitat and, 80
    human impact on, 188–195
    mature, 176–177, *176–177*
    ocean, 162, *162*, 163, *163*
    organization of, 76–77, *76–77*
    protecting, 194–195
    rivers and streams, 159, *159*
    succession, *174*
    wetlands, 70, 158, *158*
elastic potential energy, 22
electrical energy, 9
    generated by alternative energy
        source, 56–57, 270–273
    lightning and, 507
electricity production, 232, *232*
    from fossil fuel, 245, 270
    from geothermal energy, 265, *265*,
        270–273
    from moving water, 261, *261*,
        270–273
    from nuclear fuel, *249*
    from solar energy, 263, *263*,
        270–273
    from wind energy, 260, *260*, 270–
        273
electromagnetic energy, 9
electromagnetic wave, 9, 406
    radiation, **38**
elevation, **544**
elk, *145*
emergent layer (tropical rain forest),
    149
emigration, 106
emperor penguin, 113
energy, **6**
    alternative source of, 56–58,
        270–273
    change of form and, 12–13
    chemical, 10, 12
    clean, 233, *233*
    conservation of, 13
    conversion and transfer of, 92–93,
        92–93, 230–232, *232*

electrical, 9
electromagnetic, 9
heat and, 10, 34, 35, 37–39
in food chain, 90, 92–93
in food web, 94–95, *94–95*
kinetic, **6**, 8, 12, **20–21**, 32, 230,
    232, 402–403
mechanical, **8**, 13, **24–25**
nonrenewable source of, 53, 270
nuclear power and, 56, *56*
particle motion and, 9
potential, 7, 8, 10, **22–23**, 230, 232
renewable source of, 53, 270
solar, 9, 10, *10*, 11, 38, 53, 56, *56*
sound, 8, 12, 13
sources of, 52–53, 56–58
sun as source of, 90, 214–215
temperature and, 34–35, *34–35*,
    402–403, 404, 406
thermal, 10, 12, 13, **32**, 35, **402**, 407
transmitted by conduction, 410–411
transmitted by convection, 408–409
transmitted by ocean currents, 441,
    441, 445
transmitted by water cycle, 367
uses of, 52
from water and wind, 416–417
energy pyramid, **96**, *96*, 97, *97*
energy resource, **230**, 244, **258**
    conserving, 334
    Earth as, 258, 260–261, 265
    evaluating, 210–211
    sun as, 90, 214–215, 258,
        262–263
energy transformation, **12**
Engage Your Brain, 5, 17, 19, 31, 51,
    73, 89, 105, 119, 141, 155, 171,
    187, 213, 225, 243, 257, 275,
    295, 313, 325, 349, 361, 379,
    401, 421, 435, 459, 471, 489,
    505, 521, 539
Engineering and Technology. *See
    also* STEM (Science, Technology,
    Engineering, and Mathematics)
    Alternate Thinking: Different Forms
        of Energy, 270–273
    Analyzing the Life Cycle of a Paper
        Cup, 238–241
    Building a Wind Turbine, 416–419
    Constructing a Filtration System,
        374–377
    Combating an Invasive Species,
        200–203
    Design an Ecosystem, 182–185
    Engineering Design Process, 46–49
    Using Data in Systems, 484–487
environment. *See also* ecosystem
    carrying capacity, 108–109
    changes in, 107
    habitat and, 80
    interconnectedness of living things,
        70–71, 74–75, 76–77, 98, 112–
        113, 120–123
    niche and, 80
    organization in, 76–77
    resource availability, 108–109

© Houghton Mifflin Harcourt Publishing Company

© Houghton Mifflin Harcourt Publishing Company

as source of geothermal energy, 265, *265*
guano, 127, *127*
gull, *95*
Gulf Stream, 436, *436*, 547

H

habitat, **80**, *81*
  destruction, *188–192*, 189–192
  soil as, 316
hail, 365, *365*, 462
hairdresser, 87
hawk, *93*
HAWT (horizontal-axis wind turbine), 418, *418*
heat, **34**, **404**. *See also* temperature
  change of state and, 36
  conduction, **37**, 46–49
  convection, **38**, 46–49
  energy and, 34, 37–39
  geothermal, 258, 265
  measuring, 35
  production, 262, 264, 265
  radiation, **38**–39, 46–49
  specific heat, **355**, 405
  thermal energy and, 10, 35
heat exhaustion, 515
heat stroke, 515
hedgehog, *91*
helium, 218
  solar energy and, 10
herbicide, 201, *201*
herbivore, **91**
heron, 77, *77*
  in estuary, *160*
herpetology, 86
herring, *95*
high-pressure system, 422, 494–495
horizontal-axis wind turbine (HAWT), 418, *418*
horse latitudes, 424, 425, *425*
host, 123, *123*
human activity. *See also* environmental issue.
  need for water, 351, 386–387
human impact on environment, 188.
  See also environmental issue
humid continental climate, 548
humidity, **461**, *461*
hurricane, 172, 498, *508*, **508**–509, 513
  forecasting, 523
  Ike, damage caused by, *509*
  safety, 512–513
hybrid car, 335
hydrocarbon, 245
hydroelectric dam, *261*
hydroelectric energy, 57, *57*, **261**, 335
hydrogen, 218
  nuclear energy and, 10
hydrogen fuel cell, 232, *233*
hydrothermal vent community, 163, *163*

I

ice, 353, 363
iceberg, 366
ice cap, 366
ice flow, 366
immigration, 106
individual, 76, *76*, *107*
industrial water use, 351, 386
industry, 298
  land use, 315, 319
inexhaustible resource, 227
infiltration, 366
infrared light, 38
infrared radiation, 219, *219*, *406*
insulator, **37**
interaction of living things, *127*
  commensalism as, 122
  competition as, 81, *81*, 112, *112*, 126
  cooperation as, 113, *113*
  in ecosystem, 70–71, 76–77
  in food web, 98, *98*
  mutualism as, 122
  parasitism as, 123
  predators and prey, 120–121
  symbiosis as, 122
intertidal zone, 162
introduced species, 86, 99, *99*, 193, *193*
invasive exotic species, 193, 200–203
inventor, 311
iron, 229
iron ore, 227
isobar, 485, *485*, 527

J

jet streams, **426**, **497**, *497*
joule (J), 8, 21, 32, 35

K

kelp forest, 162, *162*
kerosene, 245
killer whale, 94, *95*
  cooperation among, 113
kinetic energy, **6**, 20–21, 230, 232, 402–403
  calculating, 21
  energy transformation and, 12
  in mechanical energy, 8
  motion, 20
  and potential energy, 7
  thermal energy and, 32
kinetic theory of matter, 36
Komodo dragon, *91*
Krysko, Kenneth, 86, *86*
kudzu, 99, *99*
Kyoto Protocol, 335

L

lake, 157, *157*, 297, 380–383, *381–382*. *See also* surface water
land
  preservation, 330
  reclamation, 331, *331*
  reforestation, 331, *331*
land biome, *142*, 145–149
  desert, **146**, *146*
  taiga, 78, **145**, *145*
  temperate deciduous forest, 148, *148*
  temperate grassland, 147, *147*
  temperate rain forest, 148, *148*
  tropical grassland, 147, *147*
  tropical rain forest, 149, *149*
  tundra, 78, 79, **145**, *145*
land breeze, 428, *428*
land degradation, **318**
  deforestation, 319, *319*
  desertification, 319, *319*
  erosion, 318, *318*
  human activities and, 318–319
  nutrient depletion and, 319
  pollution, 319
  preservation and, 330
  reclamation and, 331
  recycling and, 332
  reforestation and, 331
  soil conservation and, 333
  urbanization, 296, **315**, 318–319, 332
  use, *314–315*, 315
landfill, 188, *188*, 280
latitude, **542**
law of conservation of energy, 13
leather, 229
Lesson Review, 15, 27, 41, 61, 83, 101, 115, 129, 151, 165, 179, 197, 221, 235, 253, 267, 283, 307, 321, 337, 357, 371, 389, 413, 431, 447, 467, 481, 501, 517, 533, 551
lichen, *122*, 174
light, in aquatic ecosystem, 156, 162, 163
light, visible, 406
light bulb, compact fluorescent, 279, *279*, 335, *335*
light energy, 90. *See also* sun
lightning, **507**
  ecosystem change and, 172
lignite, 247
limiting factor, **110**
lion, *120*, 121, *121*, 147
liquid
  convection and, 38
liquid water, 353, 355, 363
living space, population size and, 110
lizard, *93*
local winds, **428**–429
low-pressure system, 494–495
Lyme disease, 123

© Houghton Mifflin Harcourt Publishing Company

© Houghton Mifflin Harcourt Publishing Company

park naturalist, 87
particle motion
    electrical energy and, 9
    thermal energy and, 10
peat, 247
peat pellet, *264*
pelican, *296*
People in Science
    Krysko, Kenneth, 86, 86
    McCrory, Phil, 87
    Montoya, Angel, 310, *310*
    Shepherd, J. Marshall, 536, *536*
    Someya, Yumi, 311
permafrost, 145, 297
permeability, aquifer, 384
permeable rock, 246
petroleum, 54
    formation, 246, *246*
    as natural resource, 245, *245*
    as nonrenewable resource, *53*
    use, 248
pH, 300
photosynthesis, **214**
    producers and, 90, *90*
photovoltaic cell, 263, *263*
phytoplankton, 94, 442
pioneer species, **174**
plankton, 163
plant, 316
    biodiversity, 176–177, *176–177*
    in biomes, 78, 142, 143
    competition and, 112
    in deciduous forest, 148
    in desert, 146
    in estuary, 160, *160*
    in freshwater ecosystem, 157–159,
      157–159
    in garden, 138–139, *138–139*
    in grassland, 147
    as natural resource, 226, 228, 229
    need for atmosphere, 218
    need for healthy soil, 316
    in ocean ecosystem, 162, *162*, 163,
      163
    as producer, 90
    in rain forest, 148, 149
    in taiga and tundra, 145
    in water cycle, 364
    in wetland, 158
plastic, 229
    foam, 37
plastic bag, as pollution, 190, *190*
plowing, contour, 333, *333*
point-source pollution, 190, **298**
poison dart frog, 214, *214*
polar bear hair, *37*
polar climate, 548
polar easterlies, 424
polarity, **352**
polar jet stream, 426, 497
polar-orbiting satellite, 525
polar zone, 548
pollution, 188, 277–278
    air, 192, **334–335**
    biological, 298, *299*
    chemical, 298, *299*
    estuary, 161

from fossil fuel, 192, 251, 334
freshwater, 192, *192*
land, 319
ocean, 190–191, *190–191*
radioactive, 250
types of, 298, *299*
water, 298–299, *299*, 304–305,
    304–305, 329, *329*
wetland, 158
pond, 77, 157, *157*
    eutrophication, 172, *172*, 192, *192*
population, **76**, *76*, *107*
    habitat and niche, 80
population crash, 109
population dynamic, 106–112, *107*
    abiotic limitation, 110
    biotic limitation, 110
    birth, 107
    carrying capacity, **108**
    competition, **112**
    cooperation, **113**
    death, 107
    disease, 111, *111*
    emigration, 106
    environmental change, 109
    immigration, 106
    limiting factor, **110**
pore (aquifer), 297
porosity, aquifer, 384
position
    gravitational potential energy
      and, 22
    mechanical energy and, 24
potable water, **301**
potential energy, **7**, 22–23, 230, 232
    in chemical energy, 10
    in mechanical energy, 8
power plant, 232, *232*
    geothermal, 265, *265*
    hydroelectric, 261, *261*
    nuclear, *249*, 250
    solar, 263
prairie dog, *80, 147*
precipitation, **365**, **462**. *See also* storm
    acid, 192, 237, *237*, 298
    air pressure system and, 495
    in biome, 78, *78*, 142
    climate and, 541
    in deciduous forest, 148
    in desert, 146
    in grassland, 147
    measuring, 462
    in taiga, 145
    in temperate rain forest, 148
    in tropical rain forest, 149
    in tundra, 145
    in water cycle, 365, *369*
    weather and, 490–491, *490–491*
predator, *95, 95*, **120**–121, 330
    carrying capacity and, 109
    in food web, *95*
    interaction with prey, 120–121,
      120–121
    in tropical grassland, 147
preservation, land, 330
prey, **120**–121
primary consumer, 93, *96, 97*

primary succession, 174, *174*
producer, **90**, *90*
    energy transfer and, 93, 96–97
    in food web, 95
propane, 245
properties, of water, 354–355
psychrometer, 461
public transportation, 334
puffin, 94, *94*
python, 86, *86*

© Houghton Mifflin Harcourt Publishing Company

© Houghton Mifflin Harcourt Publishing Company

© Houghton Mifflin Harcourt Publishing Company

© Houghton Mifflin Harcourt Publishing Company